# Global Strategic Management

## Second Edition

### Jędrzej George Frynas
Professor of CSR and Strategic Management, Middlesex University Business School

### Kamel Mellahi
Professor of Strategic Management, Warwick Business School, University of Warwick

OXFORD
UNIVERSITY PRESS

# OXFORD
## UNIVERSITY PRESS

Great Clarendon Street, Oxford OX2 6DP

Oxford University Press is a department of the University of Oxford.
It furthers the University's objective of excellence in research, scholarship,
and education by publishing worldwide in

Oxford New York

Auckland Cape Town Dar es Salaam Hong Kong Karachi
Kuala Lumpur Madrid Melbourne Mexico City Nairobi
New Delhi Shanghai Taipei Toronto

With offices in

Argentina Austria Brazil Chile Czech Republic France Greece
Guatemala Hungary Italy Japan Poland Portugal Singapore
South Korea Switzerland Thailand Turkey Ukraine Vietnam

Oxford is a registered trade mark of Oxford University Press
in the UK and in certain other countries

Published in the United States
by Oxford University Press Inc., New York

British Library Cataloguing in Publication Data

Data available

Library of Congress Cataloguing in Publication Data

Library of Congress Control Number: 2011920658

Typeset by TNQ Books and Journals Pvt. Ltd.
Printed in Italy
on acid-free paper by
L.E.G.O. S.p.A.—Lavis TN

ISBN 978-0-19-954393-9

10 9 8 7 6 5 4 3 2 1

# Preface

Some time ago, we realized that strategic management books no longer reflected the world we live in. Globalization had arrived on the doorstep of many industries and books on global competition were mushrooming. But strategic management textbooks did not reflect that change. Most of them started including case studies of multinational companies and sometimes mentioned international competition, but they continued to use the same old frameworks and provided the same prescriptions as before.

We felt that a new type of textbook was needed, which combined the tools of strategic management with insights from international business studies. We were encouraged by our enthusiastic Oxford University Press editor and colleagues who thought that this was a book waiting to be written.

We also found that existing textbooks concentrated mainly on large US companies, which did not reflect the new global markets, where US, European, Asian, or Latin American companies vie for success. So, we put a lot of emphasis in our book on case studies of firms from emerging economies such as India and Brazil, alongside US and European firms, and we also tried to keep in mind the needs of small- and medium-sized firms, which only recently started internationalizing. We hope that, in the age of globalization, this book feels much more inclusive than previous books.

We have written the book in a user-friendly style and designed it so that it can be used by students who did not previously study strategic management. In this second edition, we have introduced new material to make this book even more useful to students. We have included a new chapter on innovation and knowledge management (Chapter 11), and a new chapter on Corporate Social Responsibility (CSR) and innovation (Chapter 12), in order to demonstrate how innovation can be the key ingredient of a successful multinational firm in the 21st century. At the same time, we have removed the chapter on global strategic control—this issue is now discussed throughout the book. There are new case studies, reflecting the changing global marketplace: a closing case study on global retailing (Chapter 1); a new opening case study on super luxury cars (Chapter 3); a new closing case study on the Spanish fashion retailer, Zara, (Chapter 4); a new closing case study on the Chinese multinational firm, the Haier Group, (Chapter 5); a new opening case study on the Italian auto company, Fiat, (Chapter 6); a new opening case study on Dell in China (Chapter 7); a new closing case study on Nestlé in China (Chapter 7); a new opening case study on Procter & Gamble (Chapter 9); a new opening case study on Shanghai Volkswagen (Chapter 10); and a new closing case study on LG (Chapter 10). There is much more additional material throughout the book.

The book is organized in five parts. Part I, the Introduction, provides a big-picture approach and introduces the field of global strategic management. Part II, Global strategic analysis, deals with the external macro environment, the industry environment, and the internal business environment within which multinational firms operate. Part III, Global strategic development, covers the internationalization process, international strategic alliances, and subsidiary and headquarter level strategies. Part IV, Global strategic implementation, focuses on structures and designs of multinational firms, and global management of change. Part V, Global strategic innovation, discusses strategic innovation and knowledge management.

Jędrzej George Frynas was the lead author on Chapters 1, 2, 3, 4, 5, 6, and 12. Kamel Mellahi was the lead author on Chapters 7, 8, 9, and 10. However, the book is a product of a collaborative effort between the authors, who contributed to each others' chapters. Chapters 9 and 10 are revised and updated versions of original chapters authored by Paul Finlay. Anjali Bakhru has written Chapter 11 as a guest author and we are grateful for her excellent contribution.

*Jędrzej George Frynas*
*Kamel Mellahi*
*2010*

# Acknowledgements

We would like to take this opportunity to thank all of those individuals whose insight, time, and hard work have contributed to this book. First and foremost, we want to thank our editors, Alex Lazarus-Priestley and Claire Brewer, whose professionalism, unflagging patience (especially when things were not going very well), and superb support for the project made the second edition possible. We also want to thank our copy-editor Roza I.M. El-Eini and production editor Philippa Hendry. The manuscript was reviewed by a number of global strategic management professors. We appreciate the time and effort that those reviewers put into the reading of the chapters as well as their many useful suggestions for improvement.

## Publisher's Acknowledgement

We are grateful to the following for permission to reproduce copyright material:

Exhibit 1.5, The world's 100 largest non-financial multinational firms, ranked by foreign assets (US$ millions and number of employees), 2008, from the United Nations Conference on Trade and Development (UNCTAD) (2008) website at http://www.unctad.org, reprinted with permission of the United Nations Conference on Trade and Development.

Exhibit 1.6, Transnationality index for host economies, 2005, from the United Nations Conference on Trade and Development (UNCTAD) (2008), World Investment Report 2008 (New York and Geneva: United Nations), 12, reprinted with permission of the United Nations Conference on Trade and Development.

Exhibit 2.6, The Diamond Model, from M. E. Porter (1990), The Competitive Advantage of Nations (Basingstoke: Macmillan), reprinted with permission of MacMillan (world rights excl. United States and Canada) and reprinted with permission of The Free Press, a Division of Simon & Schuster, Inc. (United States and Canada rights).

Exhibit 3.1, Strategic groups in the global car industry, adapted from R. M. Grant (2005), Contemporary Strategy Analysis, 5th edn (Malden, MA: Blackwell), 125, reprinted with permission of John Wiley & Sons.

Exhibit 3.2, The Five Forces Model, from M. E. Porter (1979), 'How competitive forces shape strategy', Harvard Business Review, 57(2): 137–45, reprinted with permission of Harvard Business School Publishing; Copyright © 1979 by the Harvard Business School Publishing Corporation; all rights reserved.

Exhibit 3.5, The International Product Life Cycle (IPLC), from L. T. Wells, Jr. (1968), 'A product life cycle for international trade?' Journal of Marketing 32 (July): 1–6, reprinted with permission of Journal of Marketing, published by the American Marketing Association.

Exhibit 4.2, VRIO framework, from J. B. Barney (1997), Gaining and Sustaining Competitive Advantage (Reading, MA: Addison-Wesley), 173, reprinted with permission of Prentice Hall.

Exhibit 4.3, Link between subsidiary resource and competitive advantage, adapted from J. Birkinshaw, N. Hood, and S. Jonsson, (1998), 'Building firm-specific advantages in multinational corporations: the role of subsidiary initiative', Strategic Management Journal 19(3): 225, reprinted with permission of John Wiley & Sons.

Exhibit 4.4, The product value of South African peaches, from D. Kaplan and R. Kaplinsky (1999), 'Trade and industrial policy on an uneven playing field: the case of the deciduous fruit canning industry in South Africa', World Development 27(10): 1787–801, reprinted with permission of Elsevier.

Exhibit 4.5, The Value Chain, reprinted with permission of The Free Press, a Division of Simon & Schuster, Inc., from Competitive Advantage: Creating and Sustaining Superior Performance by Michael E. Porter. Copyright © 1985, 1998 by Michael E. Porter. All rights reserved.

Exhibit 4.8, The changing distribution of value added in three industries, from R. M. Kaplinsky (2000), 'Globalisation and unequalisation: what can be learned from value chain analysis?' Journal of Development Studies 37(2): 133. reprinted with permission of Taylor and Francis.

Exhibit 4.9, Value-added chain of comparative advantage, from B. Kogut (1985), 'Designing global strategies: comparative and competitive value-added chains', Sloan Management Review (Summer): 19, reprinted with permission of MIT Sloan Management Review, © 2010 by Massachusetts Institute of Technology. All rights reserved. Distributed by Tribune Media Services.

Exhibit 4.10, The intelligence onion, from C. M. O'Guin and T. Ogilvie (2001), 'The science, not art, of business intelligence', Competitive Intelligence Review 12(4): 21, reprinted with permission of John Wiley & Sons.

Exhibit 4.11, Xerox ten-step benchmarking process, from A. Cox and I. Thompson (1998), 'On the appropriateness of benchmarking', Journal of General Management 23(3): 4, reprinted with permission of Braybrooke Press.

Exhibit 6.1, Alliances between non-competing firms, adapted from P. Dussauge and B. Garrette (1999), Cooperative Strategy: Competing Successfully through Strategic Alliances (Chichester: Wiley), 51, reprinted with permission of John Wiley & Sons. Exhibit 6.2, Alliances between competitors, from P. Dussauge and B. Garrette (1999), Cooperative Strategy: Competing Successfully through Strategic Alliances (Chichester: Wiley), 58, reprinted with permission of John Wiley & Sons.

Exhibit 6.4, Partner selection criteria used by Korean and US executives (in order of importance), from T. M. Dacin, M. A. Hitt, and E. Levitas (1997), 'Selecting partners for successful international alliances: examination of US and Korean firms', Journal of World Business 32(1): 11, reprinted with permission of Elsevier.

Exhibit 6.6, Model of control in international joint ventures, adapted from J. Child and Y. Yan (1999), 'Investment and control in international joint ventures: the case of China', Journal of World Business 34(1): 7, reprinted with permission of Elsevier.

Exhibit 6.8, Phases in the evolution of trust in strategic alliances, from J. Child, D. Faulkner, and S. Tallman (2005), Cooperative Strategy: Managing Alliances, Networks and Joint Ventures (Oxford: Oxford University Press), 61, reprinted with permission of Oxford University Press.

Exhibit 8.2, Johnson & Johnson Credo, reprinted with permission of Johnson & Johnson. Exhibit 8.9, A Global Market Portfolio Matrix, from D. G. Harrell and O. R. Kiefer (1993), 'Multinational market portfolios in global strategy development', International Marketing Review 10(1): 60–72, reprinted with permission of Emerald Group Publishing Limited.

Exhibit 9.2, The Stopford and Wells Model of multinationals structures, from J. M. Stopford and L. T. Wells, Jr. (1972), Managing the Multinational Enterprise: Organization of the Firm and

Ownership of the Subsidiaries (New York: Basic Books), reprinted with permission of Basic Books.

Exhibit 10.3, The requirements of a change agent, adapted from D. Buchanan and D. Boddy (1992), The Expertise of the Change Agent: Public Performance and Backstage Activity (New York: Prentice Hall), 92–3, reprinted with permission of Prentice Hall.

Exhibit 10.4, The coping cycle, from C. A. Carnall (1990), Managing Change in Organisations (Harlow: Prentice Hall), reprinted with permission of Prentice Hall.

Exhibit 10.5, Styles of change management, reprinted with permission of Sage Publications Ltd.

Exhibit 11.6, The knowledge spiral or SECI Process, adapted from I. Nonaka and H. Takeuchi (1995), The Knowledge-Creating Company (Oxford: Oxford University Press), 62, 71, reprinted with permission of Oxford University Press.

Exhibit 12.1, Different views of Corporate Social Responsibility (CSR), from R. Holme and P. Watts (2000), Corporate Social Responsibility: Making Good Business Sense (Geneva: World Business Council for Sustainable Development, January): 8–9, reprinted with permission of World Business Council for Sustainable Development.

Exhibit 12.3, Stakeholders of Shell International, adapted from Platform website at http://www.carbonweb.org/, reproduced with permission of Platform.

Exhibit 12.4, Example of cross-impact analysis, from U. Steger (2003), Corporate Diplomacy—The Strategy for a Volatile, Fragmented Business Environment (Chichester: Wiley), reprinted with permission of John Wiley & Sons.

Exhibit 12.5, Levels of social innovation, from A. Henriques (2005), 'Good decision—bad business', International Journal of Management and Decision Making 6(3/4): 277, reprinted with permission of Inderscience Enterprises Ltd.

Exhibit 12.7, Complementary contributions to partnerships, adapted from M. Blowfield and A. Murray (2008), Corporate Responsibility—A Critical Introduction (Oxford: Oxford University Press), 262, reprinted with permission of Oxford University Press.

Exhibit 12.8, Principles for managing non-traditional partnerships, adapted from M. Blowfield and A. Murray (2008), Corporate Responsibility—A Critical Introduction (Oxford: Oxford University Press), 269, reprinted with permission of Oxford University Press.

Every effort has been made to trace and contact copyright holders but this has not been possible in every case. If notified, the publisher will undertake to rectify any errors or omissions at the earliest opportunity.

# Contents

# Introduction to global strategic management

## Learning outcomes

After reading this chapter, you should be able to:

➤ Understand the characteristics of the strategic management process.

➤ List and describe the key phases of global strategy.

➤ Understand the differences between international strategy and global strategy.

➤ Examine the national-, sector-, and firm-level drivers for global strategy.

➤ Formulate a strategy for a multinational firm.

## Opening case study IKEA

Established in the 1940s in a small village in Sweden by Ingvar Kamprad, IKEA has become one of the world's leading retailers of home furnishings. In 2009, it was ranked 28th out of the world's top 100 brands by Interbrand, topping other known brands such as Sony and Amazon.com. In 2009, IKEA had more than 301 stores (including thirty four franchised stores not owned by IKEA) and 123,000 co-workers in thirty seven countries, with annual sales of more than €21.5 billion.

IKEA's strategy is based on selling standardized, Swedish designed, self-assembly furniture products at low price. The IKEA business idea is: 'We shall offer a wide range of well-designed, functional home furnishing products at prices so low that as many people as possible will be able to afford them.' IKEA targets price-conscious young couples and families who are willing and able to transport and assemble furniture kits.

By the early 1960s, the Swedish market was saturated and IKEA decided to expand its business formula outside Sweden. IKEA's CEO, Anders Dehlvin, noted: 'Sweden is a very small country. It's pretty logical: in a country like this, if you have a very strong and successful business, you're bound to go international at some point. The reason is simple—you cannot grow any more.'

IKEA opened its first store outside Sweden in 1963 in Norway. In 1969, it opened its second international store, in Denmark. It moved outside the Scandinavian countries when it opened its store in Switzerland in 1973, and then entered a new country every couple of years. Under IKEA's global strategy, suppliers are usually located in low-cost nations, with close proximity to raw materials and reliable access to distribution channels. IKEA has over 2,500 suppliers scattered in over sixty countries. IKEA works closely with its suppliers by helping them to reduce costs, and sharing technical advice and managerial know-how with them. In return, IKEA has exclusive contracts with its suppliers. These suppliers produce highly standardized products intended for the global market.

IKEA's internationalization strategy in Scandinavian countries and the rest of Europe has not paid significant attention to local tastes and preferences in the different European countries. Only necessary changes were allowed, to keep costs under control. IKEA's business formula is based on low cost and affordability. Adaptation to each country's local requirement would lead to higher cost of production and subsequently put pressure on the company to increase its prices. IKEA applied its initial vision—to sell a basic product range that is 'typically Swedish' wherever it ventures. To emphasize its Swedish roots, it often uses a Swedish theme in its advertising campaign, and has a Swedish blue and gold colour scheme for its stores. The firm reaps huge economies of scale from the size of each store, and the big production runs made possible by selling the same products all over the world. IKEA's low responsiveness to local needs strategy seems to work. In 1997, its international sales represented around 89 per cent of its total sales. IKEA sales in Germany (42.5 per cent) were much higher than its sales in Sweden (11 per cent).

IKEA's strategy of not paying attention to local market peculiarities has worked well in Europe. The company has been able to sell its standardized products across Europe, and as a result was able to build considerable economies of scale into its operations and maintain a price advantage over its competitors. The first challenge came when IKEA entered the Japanese market in 1974 through a joint venture. IKEA faced several problems in the Japanese market. The root of most of these problems was the company's lack of attention to local needs and wants. For example, Swedish three-seater sofas were too big for small Japanese apartments. The Japanese were used to higher levels of customer service and they were not used to the idea of assembling their own furniture. Even IKEA's Japanese joint-venture partners were not convinced that IKEA's business model could work in Japan. Finally, IKEA decided to exit the Japanese market in 1986.

Another major challenge came when IKEA entered the US market in 1985. Although between 1985 and 1996, IKEA opened twenty-six stores in North America, these stores were not as successful as their counterparts in Europe. Similar to Japan, IKEA paid too little attention to local needs and wants. US customers preferred large furniture kits and household items. For example, Swedish beds were five inches narrower than those US customers were used to, IKEA's kitchen cupboards were too narrow for the large dinner plates typically used in the US, IKEA's glasses were too small for US customers who typically add ice to their drink and hence require large glasses—it is said that US customers bought flower vases thinking they were drinking glasses—and bedroom chests of drawers were too shallow for US consumers, who tend to store sweaters in them. In addition, IKEA Swedish-sized curtains did not fit American windows, a mistake about which a senior IKEA manager joked, 'Americans just wouldn't lower their ceilings to fit our curtains.'

As a result of initial poor performance in the US market, IKEA's management realized that a standardized product strategy should be flexible enough to respond to local markets. The company has recently adopted a more balanced strategic focus (giving weight to global and domestic concerns). The current approach puts greater emphasis on global market coordination to limit duplication of activities and capture synergies or economies of scale and scope. In the early 1990s, IKEA redesigned its strategy and adapted its products to the US market. While overall its subsidiaries are still no more than extensions of the corporate head office in Sweden, following instructions provided from the centre, subsidiaries in the US are given more autonomy to respond effectively to the local business environment. A greater customization in the US is made possible by the large size of the US market, which enables IKEA's subsidiaries in the US to produce kits designed specifically for the US market in large quantities and hence keep cost under control. During the period of 1990–4, IKEA's sales in the US increased threefold to $480 million, and rose to $900 million in 1997.

IKEA has learned from its past mistakes in Japan and the United States, paying a lot more attention to local tastes and needs—without sacrificing its basic business model. In 2006, IKEA re-entered the Japanese market, opening five new stores within two years. Meanwhile, the United States has become IKEA's second biggest market after Germany. In 2009, the US market accounted for 11 per cent of IKEA's revenue. The company's CEO, Mikael Ohlsson, is planning further international investments.

*Source*: http://www.ikea.com; 'Furnishing the world', *The Economist*, (19 November 1994): 79–80; H. Carnegy, 'Struggle to save the soul of IKEA', *Financial Times*, (27 March 1995): 12; J. Flynn and L. Bongiorno, 'IKEA's new game plan', *BusinessWeek*, (6 October 1997): 99–102; 'Ikea has designs to furnish the world', *European*, (19 November 1994): 32; B. Solomon, 'A Swedish company corners the business: worldwide', *Management Review*, (April 1991); K. Kling and I. Gofeman, 'Ikea CEO Anders Dahlving on international growth and Ikea's unique corporate culture and brand identity', *Academy of Management Executive*, (February 2003); P. Indu, 'IKEA—the Japanese misadventure and successful re-entry', ICMR Centre for Management Research Case No. 308–270–1 (2008).

## 1.1 **Introduction**

Strategy is about setting a long-term direction for the organization and guiding managers in their decision-making. The purpose of strategy is to achieve success for the organization. IKEA's basic strategy is simple: selling standardized, Swedish designed, self-assembly furniture products at low price. This strategy helps IKEA to maintain low costs and to appeal to a very wide range of customers—which, in turn, helps IKEA to stay ahead of competitors.

As the opening case study illustrates, firms with a successful strategy do not have to change their core strategy significantly when they move beyond their home market. IKEA does not significantly change its corporate strategy and operations to adapt to local markets in foreign countries unless there is a compelling reason for this. By so doing, it reaps the benefits of economies of scale and scope. Economies of scale are cost savings that accrue from increases in volume of production. Economies of scope are savings that accrue from cross-business cost-saving activities.

However, international or global strategies are much more complex than domestic strategies. IKEA's initial strategy in Japan and the United States demonstrates that, even the most successful formula in the home market can fail if a multinational firm does not respond effectively to local business realities. While IKEA's strategy worked well in Sweden, Scandinavian countries, and the rest of Europe, it initially failed in the United States and failed in Japan. The company had to reconsider the perceived universal appeal of its products, and adjusted its activities to local markets without compromising the huge benefits gained from sourcing and selling standardized products. IKEA's example shows that some form of adaptation to local markets does not always require the complete and radical change of the core strategy. A key challenge for managers is to be able to determine the extent to which adaptation to local markets is achieved without compromising the core strategy. Put differently, the secret of success of a global strategy is to strike the right balance between the benefits and costs of providing subsidiaries with the flexibility to react to local business realities they encounter, and the benefits and costs of coordinating a global strategy from the centre.

## 1.2 **Defining the strategic management field**

In this book, we take the view that global strategic management is a subcategory—albeit different and distinct—of domestic or single-country strategic management (henceforward, referred to as strategic management). Therefore, our readers will need to learn a number of core concepts of strategic management, so as to be able fully to understand the process and content of global strategic management. Whenever necessary, these prerequisite core concepts of strategic management will be presented and explained in this book.

Before we proceed to discuss the field of global strategic management, it would be beneficial to define strategic management. What, then, is strategic management? We start with a fairly simple definition of strategic management so that we may bring attention to its important characteristics. Strategic management is *the process of setting long-term direction for the organization*. The central thrust of strategic management is achieving a sustainable competitive advantage. The term 'advantage' refers to the superior benefit, or superior position or condition, resulting from a course of action taken by the firm. 'Competitive' refers to a position in relation to an actual or potential rival. Finally, 'sustain' means to keep up a position over a long period of time. A sustainable competitive advantage is therefore the prolonged benefit gained from developing and implementing some unique value-adding strategy that is not simultaneously (or shortly thereafter) being imitated by current or potential rivals (Bharadwaj et al. 1993; Grahovac and Miller 2009).

The above definition of strategic management suggests that strategic management is the process of strategic decision-making. A *process* is a systematic way of carrying out interrelated activities in order to obtain desired goals and objectives. Strategy-making process involves 'key decisions' made for and on behalf of the entire organization. For firms operating in several countries, the strategy process consists of the *analysis*, *development*, and *implementation* steps taken by firms in order to manage the global network of subsidiaries in different parts of the world. These three steps form the framework used in this book (see Exhibit 1.1). We offer this framework with some reservations, since any framework simplifies reality. However, we believe that a successful strategy involves each of these steps.

Although, in practice, the above three phases—analysis, development, and implementation— take place simultaneously, in this book, for reasons of clarity, we are going to examine them sequentially. This may give the false impression that managers should first analyse the environment and that only after completing this activity should they develop the appropriate strategy and finally implement it. In a fast-changing and turbulent global competitive environment, by the time managers complete the analysis of the environment and start the development stage, a new competitive environment emerges and may render the first analysis absolute. Imagine what would have happened to a meticulous analysis of the global banking industry just before the financial crisis started in 2008. The financial crisis rendered the analysis useless. Or imagine a multinational firm with a well-developed strategy to enter the Greek market just before Greece faced the risk of going bankrupt in 2009. The multinational firm would have been forced to change the implementation plan or delay its entry altogether.

Nonetheless, while circumstances may sometimes change, systematic analysis is crucial to the strategy-making process. Without analysis, managers may not have enough information for taking the best decisions at any given time. This book provides various frameworks for helping managers to analyse the main factors relevant to the strategy-making process. The purpose of strategic analysis is to help managers understand the issues and to ask the right questions

**Exhibit 1.1** Strategic management steps

## Benefits of a single-country strategy

It should be noted that extending a firm's business scope from a single country to several countries is not always the best strategy. Some firms are better off staying at home.

- First, despite the pressure to globalize, some firms can still achieve high returns on investment without relying on foreign markets. Solberg (1997) argues that there is no need for firms operating in a growing non-global industry—such as construction, primary and secondary education, or health services—to operate globally. He suggests that the best strategy in this case is to stay at home. That is, if a firm has a strong competitive strength at home and the pressure for global competition in the sector in which it operates is low, then concentration on the home market is a good strategy option. By staying in the home market, the firm is able to capitalize astutely on its local identity; and its strong familiarity to local customers puts it in an advantageous position vis-à-vis firms operating from far away countries.

- Second, if a firm has limited international experience and has a weak position in the home market, it should try first to improve its competitive position at home before expanding its activities to foreign markets (Solberg 1997; Yip 2002). Without an effective strategy at home, it is unlikely that IKEA would have been able to succeed outside Sweden. Firms like IKEA engage in the process of competing and operating in different countries to capitalize on their strengths in their home market.

## Risks of a single-country strategy

Operating in a single country entails several risks, especially when the business environment in that country is unstable.

- First, since the organization is dependent on one market, it is putting all of its eggs in one country basket, and adverse changes in its one and only market could affect its performance. If the country where the organization operates becomes unattractive due to market saturation, political instability, or erosion of competitive advantage by rivals, then the survival of the company becomes doubtful.

- Second, if managers focus only on competitors in their home market, they run the risk of being surprised by global competitors offering far superior products or technology that could make their firm uncompetitive. As a result, they will at best be forced to reduce their market share or be relegated to serve a small niche segment of the market. At worst, if they engage in price wars with large multinational firms offering superior-quality products and services at lower prices, they might be forced to withdraw from the marketplace.

- Third, since organizations operating in a single country have experience in only one country, they have limited ability to move quickly to other countries when times become tough in the home market. Consequently, they may hurt their performance further by moving outside their home country hurriedly, without proper planning.

1.3.2 **Export strategy**

Before a firm establishes subsidiaries outside its home market and becomes directly involved in their management, it may start by exporting its products and services outside its home market. This stage will be fully covered in Chapters 5 and 10. In most exporting firms, the domestic strategy remains of primary importance. While an exporting firm makes strategic decisions to select appropriate countries to export to, determines the appropriate level of product modification to meet local market peculiarities, and sets and manages export channels, the thrust of its strategy deals with the management of the firm in the home country. For this reason, this phase could be considered as a domestic strategy with an export strategy attached to it.

1.3.3 **International strategy**

When firms first establish subsidiaries outside their home market, they move from a domestic strategy phase to an international strategy phase. Firms that manufacture and market products or services in several countries are called 'multinational firms'. During this phase, each subsidiary is likely to have its own strategy, and will analyse, develop, and implement that strategy by tailoring it to its particular local market. At this phase, adaptation of products to fit local market peculiarities becomes the main concern for multinational firms. Internationally scattered subsidiaries act independently and operate as if they were local companies, with minimum coordination from the parent company. This approach leads to a wide variety of business strategies and a high level of adaptation to the local business environment.

1.3.4 **Global strategy**

As multinationals mature and move through the first three stages, they become aware of the opportunities to be gained from integrating and creating a single strategy on a global scale. A global strategy involves a carefully crafted single strategy for the entire network of subsidiaries and partners, encompassing many countries simultaneously and leveraging synergies across many countries. The term 'simultaneous' is used here to indicate that most of the activities of the different subsidiaries are coordinated from headquarters in order to maximize global efficiency, which allows multinational firms to achieve the economies of scale and scope that are critical for global competitiveness (Doz 1980; Ghoshal 1987; Prahalad and Doz 1987; Ghemawat 2007).

Moving from a domestic or international strategy to a global strategy is not an easy process and creates various strategic challenges. The main challenge is how to develop a single strategy that can be applied throughout the world while at the same time maintaining the flexibility to adapt that strategy to the local business environment when necessary.

---

**KEY CONCEPT**

A *global strategy* involves the carefully crafted single strategy for the entire network of subsidiaries and partners, encompassing many countries simultaneously and leveraging synergies across many countries. This stands in contrast to an *international strategy*, which involves a wide variety of business strategies across countries and a high level of adaptation to the local business environment.

---

## 1.4 International strategy and global strategy: what is the difference?

What differences are there between global strategy and international strategy? There are three key differences. The first relates to the degree of involvement and coordination from the centre. Coordination of strategic activities is the extent to which a firm's strategic activities in different country locations are planned and executed interdependently on a global scale to exploit the synergies that exist across different countries. International strategy does not require strong coordination from the centre. Global strategy, on the other hand, requires significant coordination between the activities of the centre and those of subsidiaries.

The second difference relates to the degree of product standardization and responsiveness to local business environment. Product standardization is the degree to which a product, service, or process is standardized across countries (Zou and Çavusgil 2002). An international strategy assumes that the subsidiary should respond to local business needs, unless there is a good reason for not doing so. In contrast, the global strategy assumes that the centre should standardize its operations and products in all the different countries, unless there is a compelling reason for not doing so.

The third difference has to do with strategy integration and competitive moves. 'Integration' and 'competitive moves' refer to the extent to which a firm's competitive moves in major markets are interdependent. For example, a multinational firm subsidizes operations or subsidiaries in countries where the market is growing with resources gained from other subsidiaries where the market is declining, or responds to competitive moves by rivals in one market by counter-attacking in others (Yip 2002). The international strategy gives subsidiaries the independence to plan and execute competitive moves independently—that is, competitive moves are based solely on the analysis of local rivals (this issue will be discussed in Chapter 3). In contrast, the global strategy plans and executes competitive battles on a global scale. Firms adopting a global strategy, however, compete as a collection of globally integrated single firms. Yip (2002: 7) notes that international strategy treats competition in each country on a 'stand-alone basis', while a global strategy takes 'an integrated approach' across different countries.

However, on the basis of analysis of foreign direct investment (FDI) flow across borders, Alan Rugman argues that most economic activity is regional—not global. Rugman and associates studied the activities of a large number of the Fortune 500 companies, and measured their activities against the flow of FDI. Rugman's work shows that most of what is called globalization activity is, in fact, based within a triad of Europe, Asia, and the United States (Rugman 2005; Rugman and Hodgetts 2001; Rugman and Verbeke 2008). He argues that most FDI is largely intra-firm and industry, and that the key driver is regional- and local-based economic activity, not a global one. Accordingly, multinational firms are often advised to have a regionally oriented strategy in addition to a global strategy. John Menzer, vice chairman of Walmart, told employees that global competition is like 'playing 3-D chess—at the global, regional, and local levels' (quoted in Ghemawat 2005: 100).

## 1.5 Defining global strategic management

Having examined the broad field of global strategic management, we are now able to define it more accurately. Because, as stated earlier, global strategic management is a subset of strategic management, any definition of global strategic management has to be built on basic definitions of strategic management, with an added explanation of the global dimensions. So, what are these global dimensions? We use the three differences between international strategy and global strategy to define global strategic management. In section 1.4, it was suggested that global strategy dimensions can be categorized into three main dimensions: the configuration and coordination, standardization, and integration dimensions (see Exhibit 1.3). The discussion that follows describes the three sets of dimensions in more detail.

**Exhibit 1.3** The three dimensions of corporate globality

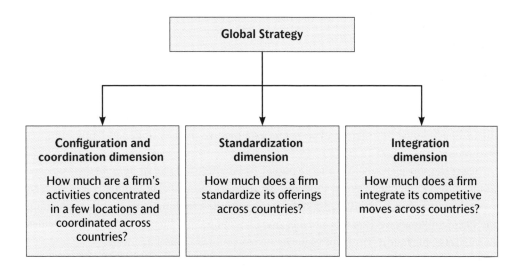

*Source:* Adapted from S. Zou and S. T. Çavusgil (2002), 'The GMS: a broad conceptualization of global marketing strategy and its effect on firm performance', *Journal of Marketing* 66: 40–57.

- The first major dimension of global strategy is *configuration* and *coordination* of the multinational firm's activities across countries. According to this view, global strategy is the process of exploiting the synergies that exist across different countries, as well as the comparative advantages offered by different countries (Zou and Çavusgil 2002). Comparative advantages offered by different countries include resources that are inherited—such as a country's location, climate, size, or stock of natural deposits—and resources that are the subject of sustained investment over a considerable period of time—such as a country's education system and specific skills, its technological and organizational capabilities, its communication and marketing infrastructures and its levels of labour productivity. According to the *configuration and coordination* perspective, multinational firms must configure their operations to exploit the benefits offered by different country locations, and coordinate their activities across countries to capture synergies derived from economies of scale and scope (Zou and Çavusgil 2002).

- The *standardization* dimension expressed by Levitt (1983) defines global strategic management as the process of offering products across countries. According to this view, multinational firms pursuing a standardization strategy have a *global strategy*, while multinational firms pursuing an adaptation strategy should be referred to as implementing an *international strategy*. It is important to note that, for strategy to be global, absolute standardization across countries is not necessary. Rather, it suffices if core elements of the product or service are applied consistently across countries with minor adaptations to local peculiarities. For example, IKEA offers its standard products worldwide but makes necessary adjustments to satisfy local customers and meet different legal standards.

- The third perspective is *integration*. According to this view, global strategy is concerned with the integration of competitive moves across country markets (Zou and Çavusgil 2002). Here, a firm makes competitive moves, not because they are best for the particular country or region involved, but because they are best for the firm as a whole. The ability of a firm to coordinate activities globally across markets depends on its ability to cross-subsidize, explicitly or implicitly, across markets. Yip (2002: 15) noted that in a global competitive strategy, competitive moves are made in a systematic way across countries, and that a competitor could be 'attacked in one country in order to drain its resources for another country, or a competitive attack in one country is countered in another country'.

Each of the above dimensions offers a partial explanation of global strategy. In this book, we adopt a broad definition of global strategy that integrates the above three dimensions. We take it that the pursuance of one dimension does not preclude a multinational firm from pursuing another. A multinational firm may provide globally standard products, coordinate its activities globally, and integrate its competitive moves across countries, simultaneously.

It must be noted that a global strategy is the process towards one, two, or all three dimensions, as opposed to the extreme points of the perspective (Zou and Çavusgil 2002). For a strategy to be global, it does not require absolute standardization across countries, complete coordination between countries, and fully integrated competitive moves. Rather, as the IKEA case study shows, it suffices for the main elements of the core strategy to be standardized, coordinated, and integrated consistently across countries, with varying degrees of adaptation to local market peculiarities when required. That is, multinational firms look for the appropriate level at which each dimension or all dimensions can be pursued. In addition, one cannot pigeonhole multinational firms into global and non-global firms. Rather, as Govindarajan and Gupta (2000) noted, 'globality is a continuous variable along a spectrum', with some firms highly global and others less so.

On the basis of the above analysis, a global strategic management definition must take into consideration all three dimensions. Thus, we define global strategic management as a process of designing a coherent, coordinated, integrated, and unified strategy that sets the degree to which a firm globalizes its strategic behaviours in different countries through standardization of offerings, configuration and coordination of activities in different countries, and integration of competitive moves across countries.

For the purpose of this book, we will occasionally use the term 'global strategic management' to refer to the broad field of managing across countries. This is because the term 'global strategic management' has become the preferred term of academics and managers. For example, both the Academy of International Business and the Strategic Management Society have 'global strategic management' research tracks which deal with strategic management issues across countries. In fact, the term 'global strategic management' was chosen as the title for this book, not to neglect international strategies (or even single-country strategies), but to indicate that a significant part of the book deals specifically with global strategies.

While we restrict the use of the term 'global strategy' to strategies that relate to the specific phenomenon of global strategy, we use the term 'multinational firm' (or 'multinational' for short) to refer to any firm that has extensive operations outside the home market, including producing and marketing in at least two different countries.

---

**KEY CONCEPT**

Global strategic management is the process of designing a coherent, coordinated, integrated, and unified strategy that sets the degree to which a firm globalizes its strategic behaviours in different countries through standardization of offerings, configuration and coordination of activities in different countries, and integration of competitive moves across countries.

---

## 1.6 Drivers for a global strategic perspective

The extent to which a multinational firm adopts a global strategy is determined by three broad factors: *macro globalizing drivers*, namely globalization and information and communication technology; *industry globalizing drivers*, namely market drivers, cost drivers, government drivers, and competitive drivers; and *internal globalizing drivers*, namely global orientation and international experience. The macro globalizing drivers have an overall impact and are not specific to certain industries or organizations. The industry globalizing drivers determine the

**Exhibit 1.4**  Drivers for a global strategic perspective

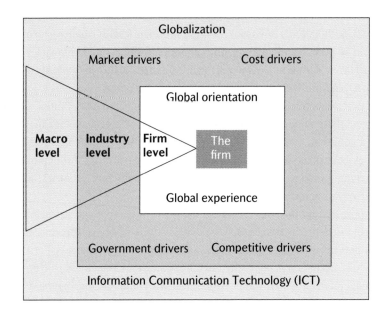

globality of a sector, industry, or market. The internal globalizing drivers determine how a firm responds to its globalizing business environment (see Exhibit 1.4).

The combination of these drivers will be unique for each sector. For example, globalizing drivers are very strong in the petroleum sector and auto sector; 21 out of the world's 100 largest multinational firms are from these two sectors. In contrast to auto and oil/gas sectors, globalizing drivers are relatively weak for postal services, educational providers, and newspapers. Globalizing drivers also impact different firms in the same industry differently. For instance, in the electronics sector, 90% of the assets of Nokia are foreign, whereas the share of foreign assets to total assets is only 25% for Hitachi (see Exhibit 1.5).

### 1.6.1 Macro globalizing drivers

As Exhibit 1.4 shows, there are two key macro globalizing drivers: globalization and information communication technology.

### Globalization

Globalization is inescapably a multifaceted process. There is fundamental disagreement about what globalization is and, indeed, what it is not. For the purpose of this book, we see globalization as being a composite of three interrelated elements: the creation of a global economy, political globalization, and a globalization of ideas and values. Globalization is simultaneously accelerating and deepening these three elements.

**Exhibit 1.5** The world's 100 largest non-financial multinational firms, ranked by foreign assets, (US$ millions and number of employees), 2008

| Foreign assets | TNI[b] | Corporation | Home economy | Industry[c] | Assets | | Sales | | Employment | | TNI[b] (Percent) |
|---|---|---|---|---|---|---|---|---|---|---|---|
| | | | | | Foreign | Total | Foreign | Total | Foreign | Total | |
| 1 | 75 | General Electric | United States | Electrical & electronic equipment | 401290 | 797769 | 97214 | 182515 | 171000 | 323000 | 52.2 |
| 2 | 32 | Royal Dutch/Shell Group | United Kingdom | Petroleum expl./ref./distr. | 222324 | 282401 | 261393 | 458361 | 85000 | 102000 | 73.0 |
| 3 | 6 | Vodafone Group Plc | United Kingdom | Telecommunications | 201570 | 218955 | 60197 | 69250 | 68747 | 79097 | 88.6 |
| 4 | 20 | BP PLC | United Kingdom | Petroleum expl./ref./distr. | 188969 | 228238 | 283876 | 365700 | 76100 | 92000 | 81.0 |
| 5 | 74 | Toyota Motor Corporation | Japan | Motor vehicles | 169569 | 296249 | 129724 | 203955 | 121755 | 320808 | 52.9 |
| 6 | 42 | ExxonMobil Corporation | United States | Petroleum expl./ref./distr. | 161245 | 228052 | 321964 | 459579 | 50337 | 79900 | 67.9 |
| 7 | 27 | Total SA | France | Petroleum expl./ref./distr. | 141442 | 164662 | 177726 | 234574 | 59858 | 96959 | 74.5 |
| 8 | 67 | E.On | Germany | Utilities (Electricity, gas and water) | 141168 | 218573 | 53020 | 126925 | 57134 | 93538 | 55.8 |
| 9 | 89 | Electricite De France | France | Utilities (Electricity, gas and water) | 133698 | 278759 | 43914 | 94044 | 51385 | 160913 | 42.2 |
| 10 | 10 | ArcelorMittal | Luxembourg | Metal and metal products | 127127 | 133088 | 112689 | 124936 | 239455 | 315867 | 87.2 |
| 11 | 53 | Volkswagen Group | Germany | Motor vehicles | 123677 | 233708 | 126007 | 166508 | 195586 | 369928 | 60.5 |
| 12 | 64 | GDF Suez | France | Utilities (Electricity, gas and water) | 119374 | 232718 | 68992 | 99377 | 95018 | 196592 | 56.4 |
| 13 | 8 | Anheuser-Busch Inbev SA | Netherlands | Food, beverages and tobacco | 106247 | 113170 | 18699 | 23558 | 108425 | 119874 | 87.9 |

(Continued)

**Exhibit 1.5** (*Continued*)

| Foreign assets | TNI [b] | Corporation | Home economy | Industry [c] | Assets | | Sales | | Employment | | TNI [b] (Percent) |
|---|---|---|---|---|---|---|---|---|---|---|---|
| | | | | | Foreign | Total | Foreign | Total | Foreign | Total | |
| 14 | 59 | Chevron Corporation | United States | Petroleum expl./ref./distr. | 106129 | 161165 | 153854 | 273005 | 35000 | 67000 | 58.1 |
| 15 | 33 | Siemens AG | Germany | Electrical & electronic equipment | 104488 | 135102 | 84322 | 116089 | 295000 | 427000 | 73.0 |
| 16 | 71 | Ford Motor Company | United States | Motor vehicles | 102588 | 222977 | 85901 | 146277 | 124000 | 213000 | 54.3 |
| 17 | 62 | Eni Group | Italy | Petroleum expl./ref./distr. | 95818 | 162269 | 95448 | 158227 | 39400 | 78880 | 56.4 |
| 18 | 39 | Telefonica SA | Spain | Telecommunications | 95446 | 139034 | 54124 | 84778 | 197096 | 251775 | 70.3 |
| 19 | 78 | Deutsche Telekom AG | Germany | Telecommunications | 95019 | 171385 | 47960 | 90221 | 96034 | 227747 | 50.3 |
| 20 | 37 | Honda Motor Co Ltd | Japan | Motor vehicles | 89204 | 120478 | 80861 | 99458 | 111581 | 181876 | 72.2 |
| 21 | 70 | Daimler AG | Germany | Motor vehicles | 87927 | 184021 | 108348 | 140268 | 105463 | 273216 | 54.5 |
| 22 | 76 | France Telecom | France | Telecommunications | 81378 | 132630 | 36465 | 78256 | 83795 | 186049 | 51.0 |
| 23 | 87 | ConocoPhillips | United States | Petroleum expl./ref./distr. | 77864 | 142865 | 74346 | 240842 | 15128 | 33800 | 43.4 |
| 24 | 63 | Iberdrola SA | Spain | Utilities (Electricity, gas and water) | 73576 | 119467 | 19785 | 36863 | 17778 | 32993 | 56.4 |
| 25 | 18 | Hutchison Whampoa Limited | Hong Kong, China | Diversified | 70762 | 87745 | 25006 | 30236 | 182148 | 220000 | 82.0 |
| 26 | 36 | Eads NV | France | Aircraft | 66950 | 105989 | 57890 | 63299 | 73969 | 118349 | 72.4 |
| 27 | 11 | Nestlé SA | Switzerland | Food, beverages and tobacco | 66316 | 99854 | 99559 | 101466 | 274043 | 283000 | 87.1 |
| 28 | 77 | BMW AG | Germany | Motor vehicles | 63201 | 140690 | 62119 | 77830 | 26125 | 100041 | 50.3 |
| 29 | 55 | Procter & Gamble | United States | Diversified | 62942 | 134833 | 47949 | 79029 | 99019 | 135000 | 60.2 |

| | | Company | Country | Industry | | | | | | | |
|---|---|---|---|---|---|---|---|---|---|---|---|
| 30 | 96 | Wal-Mart Stores | United States | Retail & Trade | 62514 | 163429 | 98645 | 401244 | 648905 | 2100000 | 31.2 |
| 31 | 21 | Roche Group | Switzerland | Pharmaceuticals | 60927 | 71532 | 42114 | 42590 | 45510 | 80080 | 80.3 |
| 32 | 95 | Mitsubishi Corporation | Japan | Wholesale trade | 59160 | 111295 | 6634 | 61063 | 18027 | 60095 | 31.3 |
| 33 | 48 | Sony Corporation | Japan | Electrical & electronic equipment | 57116 | 122462 | 58185 | 76795 | 107900 | 171300 | 61.8 |
| 34 | 56 | Nissan Motor Co Ltd | Japan | Motor vehicles | 57080 | 104379 | 60693 | 83819 | 81249 | 160422 | 59.2 |
| 35 | 40 | Grupo Ferrovial | Spain | Construction and real estate | 54322 | 67088 | 13156 | 20667 | 64309 | 106596 | 68.3 |
| 36 | 91 | RWE Group | Germany | Utilities (Electricity, gas and water) | 53557 | 130035 | 26710 | 71617 | 26688 | 65908 | 39.7 |
| 37 | 1 | Xstrata PLC | United Kingdom | Mining & quarrying | 52227 | 55314 | 25215 | 27952 | 37883 | 39940 | 93.2 |
| 38 | 50 | IBM | United States | Electrical & electronic equipment | 52020 | 109524 | 66944 | 103630 | 283455 | 398455 | 61.1 |
| 39 | 57 | Sanofi-aventis | France | Pharmaceuticals | 50328 | 100191 | 22636 | 40334 | 69990 | 98213 | 59.2 |
| 40 | 3 | Nokia | Finland | Electrical & electronic equipment | 50006 | 55090 | 73662 | 74192 | 101559 | 125829 | 90.3 |
| 41 | 16 | Lafarge SA | France | Non-metallic mineral products | 50003 | 56518 | 23865 | 27846 | 65520 | 83438 | 84.2 |
| 42 | 72 | Pfizer Inc | United States | Pharmaceuticals | 49151 | 111148 | 27861 | 48296 | 49929 | 81800 | 54.3 |
| 43 | 45 | Mitsui & Co Ltd | Japan | Wholesale trade | 48653 | 85262 | 23299 | 54991 | 37810 | 39864 | 64.8 |
| 44 | 58 | Hewlett-Packard | United States | Electrical & electronic equipment | 48258 | 113331 | 81432 | 118364 | 209708 | 321000 | 58.9 |
| 45 | 84 | Rio Tinto Plc | United Kingdom | Mining & quarrying | 47064 | 89616 | 21649 | 58065 | 54156 | 105785 | 47.0 |
| 46 | 9 | Anglo American | United Kingdom | Mining & quarrying | 44413 | 49738 | 21766 | 26311 | 95000 | 105000 | 87.5 |

(Continued)

**Exhibit 1.5** (*Continued*)

| Foreign assets | TNI [b] | Corporation | Home economy | Industry [c] | Assets | | Sales | | Employment | | TNI [b] (Percent) |
|---|---|---|---|---|---|---|---|---|---|---|---|
| | | | | | Foreign | Total | Foreign | Total | Foreign | Total | |
| 47 | 47 | Veolia Environnement SA | France | Utilities (Electricity, gas and water) | 43990 | 68373 | 31723 | 52971 | 220106 | 336013 | 63.2 |
| 48 | 99 | CITIC Group | China | Diversified | 43750 | 238725 | 5427 | 22230 | 18305 | 90650 | 21.0 |
| 49 | 35 | Compagnie De Saint-Gobain SA | France | Non-metallic mineral products | 43597 | 60397 | 45834 | 64082 | 153614 | 209175 | 72.4 |
| 50 | 41 | Novartis | Switzerland | Pharmaceuticals | 43505 | 78299 | 40928 | 41459 | 48328 | 96717 | 68.1 |
| 51 | 66 | BASF AG | Germany | Chemicals | 43020 | 70786 | 50925 | 91154 | 49560 | 96924 | 55.9 |
| 52 | 52 | Fiat Spa | Italy | Motor vehicles | 40851 | 85974 | 65931 | 86876 | 115977 | 198348 | 60.6 |
| 53 | 83 | General Motors | United States | Motor vehicles | 40532 | 91047 | 73597 | 148979 | 127000 | 243000 | 48.7 |
| 54 | 75 | Johnson & Johnson | United States | Pharmaceuticals | 40324 | 84912 | 31438 | 63747 | 69700 | 118700 | 51.8 |
| 55 | 19 | Cemex S.A. | Mexico | Non-metallic mineral products | 40258 | 45084 | 17982 | 21830 | 41586 | 56791 | 81.6 |
| 56 | 93 | Statoil Asa | Norway | Petroleum expl./ref./distr. | 37977 | 82645 | 28328 | 116318 | 11495 | 29496 | 36.4 |
| 57 | 17 | Volvo AB | Sweden | Motor vehicles | 37582 | 47472 | 43946 | 46047 | 73190 | 101380 | 82.3 |
| 58 | 14 | Astrazeneca Plc | United Kingdom | Pharmaceuticals | 36973 | 46784 | 29691 | 31601 | 54183 | 65000 | 85.4 |
| 59 | 79 | Vivendi Universal | France | Telecommunications | 35879 | 78867 | 13789 | 37150 | 30135 | 44243 | 50.2 |
| 60 | 61 | BHP Billiton Group | Australia | Mining & quarrying | 34393 | 78770 | 34784 | 50211 | 24733 | 40990 | 57.8 |
| 61 | 13 | Liberty Global Inc | United States | Telecommunications | 33904 | 33986 | 10561 | 10561 | 13128 | 22300 | 86.2 |
| 62 | 54 | National Grid Transco | United Kingdom | Utilities (Electricity, gas and water) | 33680 | 63761 | 17373 | 26379 | 17429 | 27886 | 60.4 |
| 63 | 23 | BAE Systems Plc | United Kingdom | Aircraft | 33285 | 37427 | 25249 | 30583 | 61200 | 94000 | 78.9 |

| | | Company | Country | Industry | | | | | | | |
|---|---|---|---|---|---|---|---|---|---|---|---|
| 64 | 80 | Repsol YPF SA | Spain | Petroleum expl./ref./distr. | 32720 | 68795 | 43970 | 84477 | 18403 | 36302 | 50.1 |
| 65 | 24 | Philips Electronics | Netherlands | Electrical & electronic equipment | 32675 | 45986 | 37122 | 38603 | 83946 | 121398 | 78.8 |
| 66 | 4 | Pernod Ricard SA | France | Food, beverages and tobacco | 32237 | 35159 | 8845 | 9850 | 16260 | 18975 | 89.1 |
| 67 | 5 | WPP Group Plc | United Kingdom | Business services | 31567 | 35661 | 11966 | 13717 | 88467 | 97438 | 88.9 |
| 68 | 60 | Thyssenkrupp AG | Germany | Metal and metal products | 31422 | 59557 | 51441 | 80207 | 114277 | 199374 | 58.1 |
| 69 | 46 | Vattenfall | Sweden | Electricity, gas and water | 31288 | 56829 | 16079 | 24952 | 23675 | 32801 | 63.9 |
| 70 | 85 | Deutsche Post AG | Germany | Transport and storage | 30765 | 365990 | 55170 | 79699 | 283699 | 451515 | 46.8 |
| 71 | 38 | Unilever | United Kingdom | Diversified | 30236 | 50302 | 40483 | 59287 | 144000 | 174000 | 70.4 |
| 72 | 7 | Linde AG | Germany | Chemicals | 29847 | 33158 | 16574 | 18527 | 44278 | 51908 | 88.3 |
| 73 | 26 | BG Group Plc | United Kingdom | Electricity, gas and water | 29832 | 36437 | 18239 | 23053 | 3639 | 5395 | 76.1 |
| 74 | 43 | Pinault-Printemps Redoute SA | France | Retail & Trade | 29362 | 37617 | 18056 | 29555 | 55169 | 88025 | 67.3 |
| 75 | 34 | TeliaSonera AB | Sweden | Telecommunications | 29067 | 33688 | 10265 | 15707 | 19885 | 30037 | 72.6 |
| 76 | 73 | Samsung Electronics Co., Ltd. | Korea, Republic of | Electrical & electronic equipment | 28765 | 83738 | 88892 | 110321 | 77236 | 161700 | 54.2 |
| 77 | 51 | Metro AG | Germany | Retail & Trade | 28729 | 47077 | 60410 | 99424 | 161925 | 265974 | 60.9 |
| 78 | 98 | Petronas - Petroliam Nasional Bhd | Malaysia | Petroleum expl./ref./distr. | 28447 | 106416 | 32477 | 77094 | 7847 | 39236 | 29.6 |
| 79 | 92 | Hyundai Motor Company | Korea, Republic of | Motor vehicles | 28359 | 82072 | 33874 | 72523 | 22066 | 78270 | 36.5 |

(Continued)

**Exhibit 1.5** (*Continued*)

| Foreign assets | TNI [b] | Corporation | Home economy | Industry [c] | Assets | | Sales | | Employment | | TNI [b] (Percent) |
|---|---|---|---|---|---|---|---|---|---|---|---|
| | | | | | Foreign | Total | Foreign | Total | Foreign | Total | |
| 80 | 82 | China Ocean Shipping (Group) Company | China | Transport and storage | 28066 | 36253 | 18041 | 27431 | 4581 | 69648 | 49.9 |
| 81 | 65 | Carrefour SA | France | Retail & Trade | 28056 | 72487 | 71688 | 127238 | 363311 | 495287 | 56.1 |
| 82 | 22 | CRH Plc | Ireland | Non-metalic mineral products | 27787 | 29396 | 28926 | 30559 | 46248 | 93572 | 79.5 |
| 83 | 44 | Holcim AG | Switzerland | Non-metallic mineral products | 27312 | 42487 | 14323 | 23225 | 63156 | 86713 | 66.3 |
| 84 | 88 | EDP Energias De Portugal SA | Portugal | Utilities (Electricity, gas and water) | 27104 | 49699 | 7679 | 20328 | 4543 | 12245 | 43.1 |
| 85 | 49 | Alcoa | United States | Metal and metal products | 26973 | 37822 | 12566 | 26901 | 57000 | 87000 | 61.2 |
| 86 | 68 | Glaxosmithkline Plc | United Kingdom | Pharmaceuticals | 26924 | 57424 | 28030 | 44674 | 54326 | 99003 | 54.8 |
| 87 | 2 | ABB Ltd. | Switzerland | Engineerig services | 26875 | 33181 | 33166 | 34912 | 113900 | 119600 | 90.4 |
| 88 | 12 | Air Liquide | France | Chemical/Non-metallic mineral products | 26647 | 28678 | 15292 | 19170 | 37876 | 43000 | 86.9 |
| 89 | 69 | United Technologies Corporation | United States | Aircraft | 26451 | 56469 | 30729 | 58681 | 145015 | 223100 | 54.7 |
| 90 | 90 | Sumitomo Corporation | Japan | Wholesale trade | 26448 | 70890 | 18238 | 35470 | 26397 | 70755 | 42.0 |
| 91 | 30 | LVMH Moët-Hennessy Louis Vuitton SA | France | Other consumer goods | 26377 | 43949 | 21549 | 25154 | 57350 | 77087 | 73.4 |

| Rank | | Company | Country | Industry | | | | | | TNI (%) |
|---|---|---|---|---|---|---|---|---|---|---|
| 92 | 86 | Bayer AG | Germany | Pharmaceuticals | 25696 | 73084 | 24979 | 48161 | 53100 | 108600 | 45.3 |
| 93 | 81 | Kraft Foods Inc. | United States | Food, beverages and tobacco | 25638 | 63078 | 20765 | 42201 | 59000 | 98000 | 50.0 |
| 94 | 28 | SAB Miller | United Kingdom | Food, beverages and tobacco | 25139 | 31619 | 12585 | 18703 | 52362 | 68635 | 74.4 |
| 95 | 29 | Coca-Cola Company | United States | Food, beverages and tobacco | 25136 | 40519 | 23930 | 31944 | 79400 | 92400 | 74.3 |
| 96 | 94 | Marubeni Corporation | Japan | Wholesale trade | 25049 | 47985 | 13824 | 39762 | 653 | 3856 | 34.6 |
| 97 | 25 | Schlumberger Ltd | United States | Other consumer services | 24821 | 31991 | 20483 | 27163 | 67502 | 87000 | 76.9 |
| 98 | 97 | Hitachi Ltd | Japan | Electrical & electronic equipment | 24282 | 95858 | 32956 | 99350 | 127277 | 361796 | 31.2 |
| 99 | 31 | Diageo Plc | United Kingdom | Food, beverages and tobacco | 24264 | 29965 | 17086 | 19603 | 12379 | 24270 | 73.0 |
| 100 | 15 | Teva Pharmaceutical Industries Limited | Israel | Pharmaceuticals | 24213 | 32904 | 10609 | 11085 | 32146 | 38307 | 84.4 |

Source: United Nations Conference on Trade and Development (UNCTAD) (2008), from the UNCTAD website at http://www.unctad.org. Reprinted with permission of UNCTAD.

[a] All data are based on the companies' annual reports unless otherwise stated.

[b] TNI, the Transnationlity Index, is calculated as the average of the following three ratios: foreign assets to total assets, foreign sales to total sales and foreign employment to total employment.

[c] Industry classification for companies follows the United States Standard Industrial Classification as used by the United States Securities and Exchange Commission (SEC).

[d] In a number of cases foreign employment data were calculated by applying the share of foreign employment in total employment of the previous year to total employment of 2008.

making governments and economic policies more integrated, and interdependent on each other; and, to some degree, social and cultural policies are interpenetrating each other. The extent of globalization refers to the geographical spread of these intensifying tendencies. The two movements—intensity and extent—are leading to the compression of the world, universalization of managerial values and practices, and homogenization of customers' needs, wants, and behaviours.

---

**KEY CONCEPT**

Globalization is a diverse process embracing economic, political, and cultural change which is deepening the integration of the world economy, strengthening political interdependence between countries, and causing values to converge across countries.

---

## Information communication technology (ICT)

Both popular and academic literature claims that, as a result of the information communication technology (ICT) revolution, the 'conduct of global business will be changed in fundamental ways' (de la Torre and Maxon 2001: 617). The ICT revolution, it is believed, is shrinking distances, eliminating intermediaries between producers and consumers, and bringing about closer integration of the world economy. For instance, thanks to ICT, geographical distance is not significant for the transportation of information, and, hence, global firms are able to collect information about their global activities faster and cheaper. In the past, exchange of information among the global firm's partners was done through paperwork, such as paper documents and faxes. This often caused delays in information-sharing and miscommunications among the different partners. This was an enormous problem for firms operating on a worldwide scale, because out-of-date and/or incomplete data could translate into a poor understanding of what customers actually needed and what suppliers actually had in their warehouses.

ICT makes the information flow more complete, and makes the information more accurate, timely, and accessible. It helps multinational firms to reduce uncertainties, such as demand, delivery times, quality, and competition in the global supply chain. For instance, ICT has helped Dell Computers eliminate inventory from its manufacturing plants, and has been a key in establishing ultra-close ties with its suppliers (Hagel and Brown 2001). As a result, Dell has been able to cut inventory to just three to five hours. The reduction has been so profound, that Dell has been able to turn factory storage space into production lines. Additionally, the company now uses ICT to link suppliers with manufacturers so that suppliers can eliminate excess inventory.

The Dell example shows that ICT enables managers to develop and analyse new and effective ways to improve competitiveness through successful management of global supply chains—through, for example, instant access to information—and information-sharing between different supply-chain parties in order to meet increasing global customer demands for responsiveness, quality, and low prices. It is believed that, thanks to ICT, managers are now able to coordinate their entire global business, including procurement, inventory, manufacturing, logistic, distribution, sales, and after-sales service, to reduce costs, and to achieve high speed and precision in delivering their products and services. Multinational firms are doing this through, for example, having one data entry form for all partners in the network, one data structure for all partners, and a common means of access, often via a tightly secured and controlled intranet. This is enabling firms to collect necessary information to trace in 'real time' the history of every single part in the transformation process. By so doing, ICT provides firms with greater assurance of product quality and specifications, and enables quick identification of problems throughout the global network.

### 1.6.2 Industry globalizing drivers

There are four industry globalization drivers: market globalization drivers, cost globalization drivers, government globalization drivers, and competitive drivers.

#### Market globalization drivers

There is a general belief that several markets are converging around the world. There are several reasons for this (Yip 2002). First, the convergence of Gross National Product (GNP) per capita in the developed world is leading to a convergence in markets sensitive to wealth and level of income, such as passenger cars, television sets, and computers. In other words, a consumer in the United States and Japan can afford to buy the same product.

Second, there is evidence to suggest that in some industries, customers' tastes, perceptions, and buying behaviours are converging globally (e.g., products such as blue jeans, PlayStation, iPod etc.), which has given rise to a global consumer culture (Cleveland and Laroche 2007; Zhou et al. 2008). As a result of this global convergence, the world is moving towards a single global market, where consumption patterns are usually diffused from Western and Asian developed countries throughout the entire world (e.g., hamburgers and sushi as fast food) (Levitt 1983; Akaka and Alden 2010). A global consumer culture does not mean that cultural traditions and values are converging around the world, as some have previously believed (Levitt 1983); a global consumer culture means that there is a worldwide demand for the same global brands such as Levi's and iPod.

Third, in the quest to build a global brand and company image, multinational firms are increasingly favouring a global standardization of marketing and advertising efforts (Zou and Çavusgil, 2002; Powers and Loyka 2007). This does not mean identical marketing and advertising campaigns, but the use of similar themes that send the same message across the world. Recent developments in broadcast media, particularly direct-broadcast satellite and international media, are making this more possible. CNN, for example, broadcasts standard advertisements around the world. Recent research suggests that global standardization of marketing and advertising efforts helps multinational firms to improve performance (Schilke et al. 2009).

#### Cost globalization drivers

Several key cost drivers may come into play in determining an industry globalization level (Nachum 2003; Pontes and Parr 2005; de Backer and Sleuwaegen 2005). One key factor is global scale economies. That is, the costs of producing a particular product or service are often subject to economies or diseconomies of scale. Generally, economies of scale arise when a product or a process can be performed more cheaply at greater volume than at lesser volume. This is often the case when the product or service is standardized. Hence, it becomes hard for multinational firms to differentiate themselves, and cost becomes key in achieving and sustaining a competitive advantage. Producing different products for different countries leads to higher cost per unit. This is because multinational firms serving countries with separate products may not be able to reach the most economic scale of production for each country's unique product. Multinational firms could reduce the cost by using common parts and components produced in different countries.

Another factor is sourcing efficiencies. Global sourcing efficiencies may push multinational firms towards a global strategy. The prices of key resources used in the production process have a strong impact on the cost of the product or service. As will be discussed in Chapter 3 (section 3.3.2), the cost of inputs depends on the bargaining power of the firm vis-à-vis suppliers. For example, large firms purchasing large volumes have more clout with their suppliers than their small rivals. Hewlett-Packard (HP) is a good example. In the past, country-level subsidiaries used to solicit bids for insurance coverage independently. Each subsidiary chose the local provider who bid less than the competition. However, HP now belongs to a global insurer–insured pool which provides rebates based on business volume.

In addition, as noted earlier, some countries provide a cost advantage because of low cost of raw material, low cost of labour, or low cost of transport because of location. Thus, multinational firms locate their activities in different countries to benefit from these advantages. Furthermore, in sectors where transportation cost is low, closeness to customers is not important, and urgency to distribute the product is low, multinational firms tend to concentrate their production in large plants producing large-scale products. Finally, high cost of product development drives multinational firms to focus on core products that have universal appeal to control cost.

### Government globalization drivers

Governments can encourage globalization of industries by lowering trade barriers and reducing regulations. The intensity of government globalization drivers differs between different industries because governments have different policies for different industries. The impact of government drivers on industries will be fully examined in Chapters 2 and 3.

In addition to trade barriers and regulations, governments can influence technical standards. Common international technical standards help multinational firms to standardize their operations across the world. For example, different countries have accepted new international accounting norms and standards. In Europe, the International Accounting Standards (IAS) are quickly becoming the norm. This will allow direct cross-border comparison of financial statements and facilitate communication between subsidiaries and the centre. Companies such as Nokia, the Allianz group, and Novartis are working to bring about a convergence of US accounting standards with IAS.

### Competitive drivers

Because of tight interlinks between key world markets, intense competition across countries, and the continuous increase in the number of global competitors, multinational firms are adopting a 'globally centred' rather than 'nationally centred' strategy (Yip 2002). According to George Yip, the increase in interactions between competitors from different countries requires a globally integrated strategy to monitor moves by competitors in different countries. He notes that by pursuing a global strategy, competitors create competitive interdependence among countries (Yip 2002: 57). This interdependence forces multinational firms to engage in competitive battles and to subsidize attacks in different countries. Cross-subsidization is only possible if the multinational firm has a global strategy that monitors competitors centrally rather than on a country-by-country basis.

Globalized competitors drive industries to adopt a global strategy. Yip noted that when major competitors, especially first movers, use a global strategy to introduce customers to global products, late movers adopt the same strategy so as to achieve economies of scale or scope and other benefits associated with adopting a global strategy.

Last, the ability to transfer competitive advantage globally drives multinationals to adopt a global strategy. For example, IKEA succeeded in transferring its locally developed advantage to a global market. Conversely, in sectors where the competitive advantage is 'locally rooted' and hard to transfer across countries, multinationals tend to adopt an international strategy rather than a global one.

### 1.6.3 Internal globalizing drivers

Two key internal factors significantly influence the extent to which a multinational firm adopts a global strategy: global orientation and international experience.

#### Global orientation

Global orientation is a part of a multinational firm's culture, and is essentially the belief that success comes from a worldwide globally integrated strategy rather than from one operated on a country-by-country basis (Murtha et al. 1998; Harvey et al. 2009). Multinational firms with global orientations look for similarity between markets and synergies across countries, and make globally integrated moves. In these multinationals, managers have a global mindset and tend not to tolerate differences across countries. For example, the global orientation of Lotus is articulated by the vice president's question: 'How can I manage an organization in which I am getting different answers to the same question depending on location?' Multinational firms with a global orientation have the desire to raise corporate strategy above subsidiary strategy. This is illustrated by a Hewlett-Packard manager's comment: 'We want one solution for the world rather than fifty-four country solutions. We optimize at the company rather than the country level.'

#### International experience

There is evidence to suggest that the most experienced multinationals are likely to adopt a global strategy, whereas the less experienced are less likely to do so (Douglas and Craig 1989). Experience gained over the years enables the multinational to take advantage of the comparative advantages of various countries, to spot and capitalize on synergies between subsidiaries in different countries, and to establish common needs among the customer segments worldwide so that core product features are kept intact (Hill 1996). While the multinational may depart from total standardization, as shown in the case of IKEA in the US, it will keep the core product features to simplify global operations, develop consistent image globally, and achieve scale economies, synergies, and efficiencies.

---

**KEY CONCEPT**

The extent to which a multinational firm adopts a global strategy is determined by three broad factors: *macro globalizing drivers*, namely, globalization and information communication technology; *industry globalizing drivers*, namely, market drivers, cost drivers, government drivers, and competitive drivers; and *internal globalizing drivers*, namely, global orientation and international experience.

The macro drivers have an overall impact and are not specific to particular industries or organizations. The industry globalizing drivers determine the globality of a sector, industry, or market. The internal globalizing drivers determine the globality of a firm.

---

## 1.7 Organization of the book

The book is structured around the three key strategic management phases: strategic analysis, strategy development, and strategy implementation. It is divided into five parts. Part I is the introduction.

In Part II, we deal with the analysis of the environment within which a multinational firm operates. To be able to design and implement an effective global strategy, the multinational firm must first conduct a global situation analysis by analysing the external (Chapters 2 and 3) and internal (Chapter 4) business environment of the firm and its subsidiaries to identify the key factors that have, or could have, an influence on the multinational firm's competitive advantage. This phase of strategy development forms the basis for developing and selecting the most appropriate strategy and for proposing actions to implement it.

In Part III, we deal with the strategy development phase. Once the internal and external environments have been analysed, managers then turn their attention to developing and selecting the appropriate strategy for the firm. Managers need to choose the mode of entry and location in different countries (Chapter 5), to establish and manage relationships with global partners (Chapter 6), to develop a subsidiary-level strategy (Chapter 7), and to develop a headquarter-level strategy (Chapter 8).

In Part IV, we deal with the implementation phase. To be able to implement the strategy successfully, managers must design a structure that fits the selected strategy (Chapter 9) and implement change (Chapter 10).

In Part V, we discuss strategic innovation and knowledge management (Chapters 11 and 12). In a fast-changing global market, the most successful multinational firms are those that manage knowledge successfully, introduce new ideas, and differentiate themselves from competitors.

## 📖 Key readings

- For further discussion of the phases of global strategy, see Doz (1980), and Ghoshal (1987).

- For an extensive discussion of industry globalizing drivers, see Yip (2002).

- For further insight into the three dimensions of global strategy, see Zou and Çavusgil (2002).

- For useful tools and advice for global managers, see Ghemawat (2007).

## 💬 Discussion questions

**1.** Discuss the differences between global strategic management and strategic management in the domestic context.

**2.** List and discuss the main differences between international strategy and global strategy.

**3.** Select a multinational firm that follows a global strategy and discuss the key phases of its global strategy.

**4.** Which do you think would be the most relevant factors driving the globalization of mobile phones, automobiles, and pop music?

**5.** Explain why some industries are more global than others and why, in the same industry, some firms are more global than others.

**6.** Select an industry of your choice and analyse its globalization drivers as they are today and as they are likely to be in five years' time.

---

**Closing case study** Walmart v. LVMH—two retailers, two different global strategies

---

### Walmart—the retailer of the Americas

Walmart is the world's biggest company in terms of sales revenues, with revenues of US$405 billion for the 2010 tax year. In 2010, Walmart had 8,446 retail stores in fifteen countries, employing more than 2.1 million associates.

Walmart's original motto, 'everyday low prices', coined by the company's founder Sam Walton fifty years ago, is behind the company's success. Walmart's success depends on economies of scale: huge volume of business allows low prices. Walmart can also reduce costs thanks to lower development costs (building stores and distribution centres on cheap land, away from city centres), choice of products (selling many own brands), and standardization (offering the same products in different regions and seasons of the year).

**Exhibit A**  Walmart's international stores, 2010

| Country | Number of stores | Market entry |
|---|---|---|
| Mexico | 1,479 | November 1991 |
| Canada | 317 | November 1994 |
| Brazil | 438 | May 1995 |
| Argentina | 44 | August 1995 |
| China | 284 | August 1996 |
| United Kingdom | 374 | July 1999 |
| Japan | 371 | March 2002 |
| Costa Rica | 170 | September 2005 |
| El Salvador | 77 | September 2005 |
| Guatemala | 164 | September 2005 |
| Honduras | 53 | September 2005 |
| Nicaragua | 55 | September 2005 |
| Chile | 254 | January 2009 |
| India | 1 | May 2009 |

*Source:* Walmart's website at http://walmartstores.com/ (accessed July 2010).

Walmart's international expansion started in 1991, when it entered into a joint venture with Cifra, S.A., a successful Mexican retailer, in which it held 50% interest in its partner's retail operations. In 1998, Walmart purchased a controlling interest in Cifra and changed the company's name to Walmart of Mexico. Since 1991, Walmart has expanded into 13 other international markets (see Exhibit A). Walmart focused on markets in North and South America: 3,051 out of 4,081 Walmart international stores are based in the Americas. Walmart only has 12% of its stores outside of the Americas.

Walmart was less successful outside the Americas. The company entered Europe in the late 1990s, by purchasing the Wertkauf and Interspar supermarkets in Germany, and by purchasing ASDA in the UK. However, Walmart was losing money in Germany and it withdrew from the country in 2006. There are different reasons for Walmart's lack of success in Europe. First, Walmart is not well known in Europe. This is why Walmart has chosen to retain the ASDA name in the UK market. The European consumer is also more quality oriented, and a strategy that relies solely on low prices is not as successful. Second, many European competitors follow the same strategy as Walmart by focusing on cost reduction and supply chain management, which limits Walmart's relative competitive advantage in the European markets. Third, Europe has a different cost structure. Real estate development is more costly and wages are also higher.

Similarly, Walmart has been less successful in Asia. The company entered Korea in 1999 but withdrew from the country in 2006, and it is struggling to make money in Japan. The company ignored the different tastes of Asian consumers (e.g., dislike of frozen foods in Korea), different shopping styles (e.g., frequent shopping trips by foot or bicycle in Japan), and different types of marketing (e.g., Walmart decided in 2004 to abandon daily newspaper inserts called *chirashi*, which were read by millions of housewives in Japan).

Walmart cannot benefit from economies of scale in Europe and Asia because the company has too few stores. In contrast, Walmart stores in Mexico and Canada are much more successful because they can rely on US suppliers and Walmart's established distribution system.

Walmart's senior managers have learned that you can't please all of the people all of the time all over the world. However, they think that the company's basic low-cost strategy is still right and that Walmart can be successful internationally by learning to adapt to foreign markets. 'We need to be obsessed with understanding customers in every market we operate in,' says Walmart's CEO Mike Duke, 'And we need to serve customers however they want to shop—whether it's on a mobile phone, a laptop, or in a local store.'

**LVMH—the global retailer with a decentralized structure**

LVMH is the world's leading luxury goods company, with total revenues of €17 billion in 2009. A luxury good can be defined as, 'a good at the highest end of the market in terms of quality and price'. The company's luxury brands include Louis Vuitton, Hennessy, Givenchy, Dior Watches, Loewe, Sephora and over fifty other brands. Since its creation in 1987, LVMH has expanded into a global network of more than 2,400 stores and 77,000 employees, 75% of whom are based outside France.

LVMH is a truly global company. Only 14% of LVMH revenues come from its home base in France. The international markets are as follows: other European countries 21%; United States 23%; Japan 10%; the rest of Asia 23%; and the rest of the world 9%.

Customers everywhere recognize LVMH's famous brand names such as Dior Watches and Moët & Chandon. This universal appeal of luxury goods helps LVMH to be successful around the world. For example, in marked contrast to Walmart, LVMH has been very successful in Japan. Louis Vuitton sells almost one-third of its handbags in Japan—Louis Vuitton's biggest market. LVMH sets aside over 10% of all global sales income to be used exclusively for advertising, in order to maintain the global recognition of its brand names.

LVMH strategy is to focus on the development of global 'star' brands. Bernard Arnault, the company's chairman and CEO, defines 'star' brands as 'timeless, modern, fast-growing and highly profitable'. Bernard Arnault says, 'There are fewer than 10 star brands in the luxury world, because it is very hard to balance all four characteristics at once.' LVMH 'star' brands such as Louis Vuitton and Dior Watches generate over 80% of LVMH global revenues.

The profit margin on luxury goods is very high, so control over production, distribution, and advertising are central to profitability. In the manufacture of its high-quality merchandise, for example, LVMH ensures that the highest production standards are always used. LVMH enjoys a home country advantage because France is widely perceived as a home of fashion and haute couture, hence LVMH uses the 'Made in France' label to appeal to global customers. LVMH mainly sources in France, Italy, and Switzerland to emphasize its global reputation for high quality.

LVMH is structured into five strategic business units (SBUs):

- Fashion & Leather Goods (37% of revenue in 2009)

- Wines & Spirits (16% of revenue)

- Perfumes & Cosmetics (16% of revenue)

- Watches & Jewelry (4.5% of revenue)

- Selective Retailing (26.5% of revenue)

These five SBUs are decentralized into production and distribution subsidiaries. Some of the major brands also have their own national subsidiaries. LVMH also operates differently in different parts of the world. For example, in Japan, the LVMH subsidiary centralizes the human resources function, but each brand operates independently in all areas of business activities.

The decentralized structure helps LVMH to encourage creativity and value from its brands, but it can sometimes hinder efficiency in its global operations. Therefore, a key challenge for LVMH is how to share costs and create synergies across all brands, for example, by obtaining large discounts in advertising thanks to centrally negotiating most of the advertising contracts for its brands. On a centralized basis, LVMH also uses a common laboratory for cosmetics research, and integrates the operations for all of the branch offices in each group to ensure maximum efficiency.

Bernard Arnault's vision of a totally integrated global company is necessary to remain a global industry leader, which also requires innovative management and new international investments. 'The key drivers of our strategy will continue to be innovation and the expansion of our presence worldwide,' Bernard Arnault says. 'The future holds excellent potential, in historic markets as well as in emerging markets, for brands which know how to continually inspire their contemporaries, regardless of where they are in the world, and are committed to quality, beauty and authenticity.'

*Source:* A. M. Rugman and S. Girod (2003), 'Retail multinationals and globalization: the evidence is regional', *European Management Journal* 21(1): 24–37; Rugman (2005), ch. 5; A. Toussaint (2009), 'You can't please all of the people all of the time—Wal-Mart's adventures in Japan', Sophia University Case No. 309–046–1; A. Som (2007), 'LVMH—Managing the multi-brand conglomerate', ESSEC Case No. 304–274–1; Walmart website at http://www.walmart.com; and LVMH website at http://www.lvmh.com.

### Discussion questions

1. What are the differences between the strategies of Walmart and LVMH?

2. What are the industry globalizing drivers in the global retail industry?

# References

Akaka, M. A., and Alden, D. L. (2010). 'Global brand positioning and perceptions', *International Journal of Advertising* 29(1): 37–56.

Assael, H. (1998). *Consumer Behavior and Marketing Action*, 6th edn (Cincinnati, OH: South Western College Publishing).

Bharadwaj, S. G., Varadarajan, R. P., and Fahy, J. (1993). 'Sustainable competitive advantage in service industries: a conceptual model and research propositions', *Journal of Marketing* 57: 83–99.

Cleveland, M., and Laroche, M. (2007). 'Acculturation to the global consumer culture: scale development and research paradigm', *Journal of Business Research* 60(3): 249–59.

de Backer, K., and Sleuwaegen, L. (2005). 'A closer look at the productivity advantage of foreign affiliates', *International Journal of the Economics of Business* 12(1): 17–34.

de la Torre, J., and Maxon, R. W. (2001). 'Introduction to the Symposium. E-commerce and global business: the impact of the information and communication technology revolution on the conduct of international business', *Journal of International Business Studies* 32: 617–39.

Douglas, S. P., and Craig, S. C. (1989). 'Evolution of global marketing strategy: scale, scope, and synergy', *Columbia Journal of World Business* 24(3): 47–58.

Doz, Y. L. (1980). 'Strategic management and multinational corporations', *Sloan Management Review* 21: 27–46.

Fahey, J. (2002). 'Would you buy a ChevySaab?' *Forbes* 170(12) (9 December): 82.

Ghemawat, P. (2005). 'Regional strategies for global leadership', *Harvard Business Review* 83(12): 98–108.

Ghemawat, P. (2007). *Redefining Global Strategy: Crossing Borders in a World Where Differences Still Matter* (Cambridge, MA: Harvard Business School Press).

Ghoshal, S. (1987). 'Global strategy: an organising framework', *Strategic Management Journal* 8(5): 425–40.

Govindarajan, V., and Gupta, A. (2000). 'Analysis of the emerging global arena', *European Management Journal* 18(3): 274–84.

Grahovac, J., and Miller, D. J. (2009). 'Competitive advantage and performance: the impact of value creation and costliness of imitation', *Strategic Management Journal* 30(11): 1192–1212.

Hagel, J., III, and Brown, S. J. (2001). 'Your next IT strategy', *Harvard Business Review* 79(10): 105–13.

Harvey, M., Fisher, R., McPhail, R., and Moeller, M. (2009). 'Globalization and its impact on global managers' decision processes', *Human Resource Development International* 12(4): 353–70.

Hill, C. W. L. (1996). *International Business: Competing in the Global Marketplace* (Chicago, IL: Richard D. Irwin).

Levitt, T. (1983). 'The globalisation of markets', *Harvard Business Review* 61(3): 92–102.

Mellahi, K., and Guermat, G. (2004). 'Does age matter? An empirical investigation of the effect of age on managerial values and practices in India', *Journal of World Business* 39(3): 199–215.

Murtha, T. P., Lenway, S. A., and Bagozzi, R. P. (1998). 'Global mind-sets and cognitive shift in a complex multinational corporation', *Strategic Management Journal* 19: 97–114.

Nachum, L. (2003). 'International business in a world of increasing returns', *Management International Review* 43(3): 219–45.

Organisation for Economic Co-operation and Development (OECD) (2007). 'Measuring globalisation: activities of multinationals (Vol. I: Manufacturing)' (Paris: OECD).

Pontes, J. P., and Parr, J. B. (2005). 'A note on agglomeration and the location of multinational firms', *Papers in Regional Science* 84(3): 509–18.

Powers, T. L., and Loyka, J. J. (2007). 'Market, industry, and company influences on global product standardization', *International Marketing Review* 24(6): 678–94.

Prahalad, C. K., and Doz, Y. L. (1987). *The Multinational Mission: Balancing Local Demands and Global Vision* (New York: Free Press).

Ralston, D. A., Holt, D. H., Terpstra, R. H., and Yu, K. C. (1997). 'The impact of national culture and economic ideology on managerial work values: a study of the US, Russia, Japan, and China', *Journal of International Business Studies* 27(1): 177–207.

Rugman, A. (2005). *The Regional Multinationals: MNEs and 'Global' Strategic Management* (Cambridge: Cambridge University Press).

Rugman, A., and Hodgetts, R. (2001). 'The end of global strategy', *European Management Journal* 19: 333–43.

Rugman, A., and Verbeke, A. (2008). 'The theory and practice of regional strategy: a response to Osegowitsch and Sammartino', *Journal of International Business Studies* 39(2): 326–32.

Schilke, O., Reimann, M., and Thomas, J. S. (2009). 'When does international marketing standardization matter to firm performance?' *Journal of International Marketing* 17(4): 24–46.

Solberg, C. A. (1997). 'A framework for analysis of strategy development in globalizing markets', *Journal of International Marketing* 5: 9–30.

United Nations Conference on Trade and Development (UNCTAD) (2010). *World Investment Report 2010* (New York and Geneva: United Nations).

Yip, G. (2002). *Total Global Strategy* (London: Prentice-Hall).

Zhou, L., Teng, L., and Poon, P. (2008). 'Susceptibility to a global consumer culture: a three-dimensional scale', *Psychology and Marketing* 25(4): 336–51.

Zou, S., and Çavusgil, S. T. (2002). 'The GMS: a broad conceptualization of global marketing strategy and its effect on firm performance', *Journal of Marketing* 66: 40–57.

**online resource centre**

# Online resource centre

Please visit www.oxfordtextbooks.co.uk/orc/frynas_mellahi2e/ for further information.

# Part two

# Global strategic analysis

**Opening case study** The Brazilian Embraer and the external business environment

The Brazilian aircraft manufacturer, Embraer, is one of Brazil's leading high-technology firms and the largest single Brazilian exporter. Founded in 1969 as a government initiative, Embraer has become the fourth largest commercial aircraft manufacturer in the world behind Boeing, Airbus, and Bombardier. Unlike Boeing and Airbus, Embraer focuses on smaller aircraft with up to 110 seats, which can serve regional airlines. Operating globally, the company has sold thousands of planes to airlines as diverse as Lufthansa in Germany, JAL in Japan, South African Airlink, and Air Caraibes in Guadeloupe.

Throughout its history, the state-owned Embraer has had a friendly relationship with the Brazilian government and the firm was only privatized in 1994. The Brazilian government's support was crucial for Embraer's expansion. The government not only provided financial assistance when the company needed funds, but it also assisted Embraer's exports. Under an exchange rate subsidy scheme called Proex, the Brazilian government provided funds for the purchase of Brazilian aircraft. If a foreign airline wanted to buy an Embraer plane by taking out a loan from a commercial bank, the Brazilian government would subsidize the loan. As a result, the airline would pay a much lower interest rate on the loan, which made Brazilian aircraft more attractive to foreign buyers.

The Brazilian government subsidies helped Embraer quickly to gain a large market share in the global market for regional aircraft in the 1990s. Embraer's rapid expansion was not welcomed by its main rival, Canada's Bombardier, which complained to the Canadian government about Embraer's 'unfair' advantage. The Canadian government subsequently filed a complaint against Brazil to the World Trade Organization (WTO), the world's most important settlement body for trade disputes. In 2000, the WTO ruled that the Proex-assisted sales of Embraer aircraft were unlawful and could not proceed. The WTO then gave Canada permission to impose trade sanctions worth US$1.4 billion on Brazilian products. Canada never imposed the sanctions, instead negotiating with Brazil while matching the export assistance offered to Embraer.

But the WTO ruling was a big setback for Embraer, as the Proex scheme helped to sell some 900 aircraft. An end to the Brazilian government subsidies and the continuation of Canadian subsidies to Bombardier would make it more difficult for Embraer to survive in the global aircraft market.

The Brazilian government launched a counteroffensive against the Canadian government, accusing the Canadians of illegally subsiding Bombardier's aircraft sales. It called on the WTO to prevent Bombardier from receiving Canadian government subsidies. In 2002, the WTO ruled that the Canadian government's financing of Bombardier exports violated WTO rules and had to withdraw any such assistance. In early 2003, the WTO officially announced its decision to allow Brazil to impose US$248 million in counter-trade measures against Canada. The dispute has not yet been resolved. Both Embraer and Bombardier managers are wary as to how the strategic direction of their companies would be affected by the WTO rulings.

While the WTO dispute continued, global events led to a dramatic decline in the demand for aircraft. The attacks on the World Trade Center in September 2001 were followed by a marked decline in global air travel. Faced with fewer air travellers, airlines either cancelled or delayed orders for new aircraft, hitting the sales of aircraft manufacturers. Within only one month of the events of September 11, Embraer announced that about US$1 billion worth of tentative orders (known as options) had been cancelled.

While managers were hoping for a rise in air travel, the war in Iraq in 2003 further worsened the business prospects for airlines and aircraft manufacturers. After the war broke out, the International Air Transport Association (IATA) estimated that the war in Iraq alone could add US$10 billion to airline losses worldwide in 2003. As a result of the events of September 11 and the Iraq War, important Embraer clients such as the US carrier, ExpressJet (a regional carrier for Continental Airlines), and Swiss International Air Lines deferred or cancelled the delivery of aircraft which they had previously ordered, forcing Embraer to revise its business plans.

The aircraft industry enjoyed three years of growth between 2005 and 2008. However, the global financial crisis in 2008 was a new threat. Airlines such as US Airways and Air France-KLM suffered a decline in customers. The global economic slowdown forced airlines to cut costs and cancel or defer orders for new planes. To make things worse, Brazil's currency—the real—lost almost a third of its value in August 2008. As a result of the global financial crisis, Embraer reported a 70% fall in profits in November 2008 and the company was forced to lay off 4,000 of its 21,000 employees in February 2009. A company spokesman said, 'It has become inevitable to revise our cost base and workforce to adapt them to the new reality in the demand for aircraft.'

Competition is also becoming more fierce, as Chinese and Russian companies have entered the market for medium-sized planes. In 2008, the Canadian rival, Bombardier, announced the construction of a new fuel-efficient plane for 110 to 130 passengers by 2013.

Embraer had world-class products on offer, but the WTO dispute, the decline in air travel, and new competition were major challenges to the company. Embraer's president and chief executive, Frederico Fleury Curado, could not predict how the global aircraft market would be affected by external forces outside his control.

*Source:* Embraer website at http://www.embraer.com/english/; T. C. Lawton and S. M. McGuire (2001), 'Supranational governance and corporate strategy: the emerging role of the World Trade Organization', *International Business Review* 10: 217–33; various newspapers and magazines.

## 2.1 Introduction

The Embraer case shows how a firm's strategic direction may be influenced by global developments outside the managers' control. The events of September 11 and decisions of the World Trade Organization are two examples of global developments which could determine a firm's success or failure. Other examples could be the introduction of a new technology, a financial crisis, an armed conflict, or international migration of people. A business firm is not isolated from the environment in which it operates. Its future development, the results it can achieve, and the constraints within which it operates are all functions of the business environment.

The business environment consists of all factors inside and outside the company which influence the firm's competitive success. It is often divided into the external macro environment, the external industry environment, and the internal firm environment (see Exhibit 2.1).

**Exhibit 2.1** Elements of environmental analysis

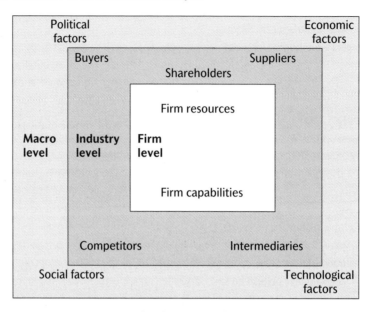

The macro environment consists of political, social, economic, and technological (PEST) factors in the broader society, which are discussed in this chapter. These factors can be specific to an industry or a firm (e.g., the WTO ruling on Embraer) or, more typically, they can influence many different industries (e.g., the events of September 11). The industry environment consists of all factors stemming from actions within a specific industry by buyers, suppliers, competitors, and others which directly influence competitive success within the industry and for the firm (see Chapter 3). The internal firm environment consists of all resources and capabilities found within the firm which influence the firm's ability to act (see Chapter 4). The analysis of these different parts of the business environment allows the firm to understand the context within which strategy needs to be developed and implemented.

---

**KEY CONCEPT**

The business environment consists of all factors inside and outside the company which influence the firm's competitive success. The business environment can be divided into the external macro environment, the external industry environment, and the internal firm environment.

---

## 2.2 The external business environment

The external business environment of the multinational firm can provide both opportunities and threats to firms, so managers must pay adequate attention to them. Opportunities refer to events or processes in the external business environment, which may help the company to achieve competitive success. Threats refer to events or processes in the external business environment, which may prevent the company from achieving competitive success.

### 2.2.1 **Identifying threats and opportunities**

The perception of the external business environment can vary between different managers and between different firms. For instance, Embraer recognized the growth of the Chinese market as an important opportunity much earlier than its main rival, Bombardier. In 2002, Embraer started a joint venture with Harbin Aircraft Manufacturing Corporation, China's fourth largest aircraft manufacturer, and was subsequently able to benefit both from cheap labour costs and the growth of aircraft demand in China. Bombardier previously turned down an offer of a joint venture with Harbin because the company did not perceive the opportunities of the Chinese market.

One multinational firm may sometimes perceive an event as a threat, while another firm may perceive exactly the same event as an opportunity. Perceptions of the external business environment are very important because the labelling of an event as a threat or an opportunity influences the firm's strategic response to changes in the external business environment (Garg et al. 2003; Julian and Ofori-Dankwa 2008).

Studies suggest that, the greater the amount and completeness of information available to firms, the more likely they are to view external events as opportunities. Systematic collection of information from different sources allows firms to feel more positive about changes in the external business environment (Eisenhardt 1989; Kuvaas 2002). In addition, firms are more likely to view external events as opportunities, the more business experience they have of global markets (Denison et al. 1996).

Studies also show that managers from different countries have different interpretations of what is a threat or an opportunity. Managers from cultures with a relatively high propensity to avoid risks, such as Japan and Spain, are more likely to label external events as threats. Managers from cultures with a relatively high readiness to take risks, such as the United States and Britain, are more likely to see external events as opportunities (Sallivan and Nonaka 1988; Barr and Glynn 2004).

### 2.2.2 **Strategic fit and firm performance**

For the most part, the external business environment cannot be easily controlled or changed by the multinational firm (although Chapter 4 suggests that this can sometimes be done). Multinational firms usually have little control over demographic changes, cultural norms, or government policy, so they need to adapt the organization to the external environment. The task of the strategic decision-maker is to develop strategies based on what the multinational firm can do to exploit opportunities and counter threats in the external business environment. Successful strategy, then, is about matching the resources and activities of a firm to the external environment in which it operates—which is known as 'strategic fit'. Organizations which do not possess a minimum degree of 'strategic fit' are bound to fail (Galbraith and Kazanjian 1986).

An organization must achieve a strategic fit with both the macro environment and the industry environment. In this chapter, we deal with the macro environment. But we need to remember that the macro environment should only be considered if it is likely to affect the specific industry and the specific firm. For instance, a new government policy will be of little interest to you if it does not affect your industry or your firm. Studies show that selectivity in external information scanning (that means, collecting data about the external business environment) increases firm performance (Daft et al. 1988; Garg et al. 2003). In other words, managers must focus on what they perceive to be key subsets of the available information, and, by necessity, exclude some other types of information. Therefore, the ability of a manager to recognize the relevant macro environmental factors, understand their implications, and adapt the firm's products and operating methods to the demands of the business environment will influence a firm's success or failure.

Studies show that scanning of the macro environment can especially help firms to improve performance in dynamic business environments, that means when there is a high degree of changes in the external business environment (Garg et al. 2003). Therefore, the scanning of the macro environment is less important in stable business environments such as Denmark and other Northern European countries, and is more important in dynamic business environments such as China and other emerging economies. A common way of exploring the macro environment is through the analysis of political, economic, social, and technological (PEST) factors.

---

**KEY CONCEPT**

Strategic fit is about matching the resources and activities of a firm to the external environment in which the firm operates. Organizations which do not possess a minimum degree of strategic fit are bound to fail.

---

## 2.3 PEST analysis

Managers can conduct a systematic external audit, which surveys all key opportunities and threats faced by the firm. The aim of an external audit is to draw up a list of different types of external forces, which can present either opportunities or threats to the firm. But analysing the macro environment is not easy in practice, for several reasons:

- The macro environment is highly complex, with a vast number of potentially relevant external influences on the firm.

- The macro environment changes over time, which requires an analysis of today's PEST factors and a forecast of future PEST factors.

- A firm's decision to go international entails a movement into new economic, political, and cultural environments, which makes any analysis even more challenging.

- Too much information may lead to an information overload: more information is available than the management of the firm can cope with.

- It is difficult and expensive to monitor constantly the macro environment.

Therefore, we do not suggest that there is a magic formula for making sense of the external business environment. In this chapter, we do not provide detailed advice on how managers should monitor, analyse, or forecast changes in the macro environment. Every firm must decide how far it wants to take systematic analysis, and every firm needs to find its own approach. In particular, small- and medium-sized firms frequently do not have the resources for regular and comprehensive analyses. But it is useful for managers to have a checklist of potential external macro influences. PEST analysis can be used as such a checklist. PEST analysis is not a rigorous analytical tool, but, rather, a broad framework to help managers understand the macro environment. Managers can simply use this framework as a checklist to ask themselves questions as to how political, economic, social, or technological developments can influence their industry and their company.

The importance of political, economic, social, and technological factors differs considerably from one industry to another. Political factors can be crucial for success in industries where governments play an important role, such as the defence industry, which depends on government contracts. Technological factors can be crucial for success in industries where the rate of technological innovation is fast, for instance the electronics industry. So, every industry and every firm will need to focus more attention on those factors which are most relevant to it.

Before the rise of global competition, PEST analysis was more straightforward, as the manager simply had to scan the business environment in his/her own country. For firms operating internationally, the scope of PEST analysis will depend on the location of their operations. A small Indian firm which exports primarily to the United States may want to focus its analysis on the domestic macro environment in that country. A large German firm which operates primarily in the European Union (EU) will want to conduct primarily an EU-wide PEST analysis. A large global firm must scan the entire world for new developments and trends. At the same time, subsidiaries of a multinational firm may still want to conduct a PEST analysis for a specific country or a geographical region. This chapter merely shows what types of external influences firms could encounter in the international marketplace. Exhibit 2.2 summarizes a number of key PEST factors to be considered by international managers; but many other factors could be added to this list. Exhibit 2.3 provides an example of how PEST analysis can be used to help a company make a country selection for exports or investments.

## KEY CONCEPT

**Exhibit 2.2** Summary of key PEST factors in global strategic management

| Political factors | Economic factors |
| --- | --- |
| Regional integration | Cost of production |
| Government legislation | Currency exchange rates |
| Political risk | Cost of capital |
| Corruption | |
| **Social factors** | **Technological factors** |
| Social change | Global technology scanning and technology clusters |
| Global convergence | The knowledge-based economy |
| | The spread of the Internet |

**Exhibit 2.3** Using PEST analysis for country selection at Baser Food

Baser Food is a wholly-owned subsidiary of Baser Holding, one of the leading industrial groups in Turkey. Baser Food is specialized in the production of high-quality olive oil and is one of Turkey's largest exporters of olive oil. Since 1998, Baser Food has expanded internationally, exporting olive oil to the United States, Germany, Russia, and about fifteen other countries.

In the early 2000s, the domestic market for olive oil in Turkey was declining and the Baser Food management decided that the company should continue expanding internationally through exporting. Baser Food was a small company, with an annual turnover of about US$25 million and about fifty employees, and the directors knew that the company had only limited resources and could not expand everywhere. Baser Food had to decide in which countries it should expand.

The company's management decided against expanding in major olive-oil producing and consuming countries such as Spain and Italy because these countries already have intense competition. The company's management considered a number of countries for expansion, including the United States (where the company was already present), as well as Australia, and China. They conducted a PEST analysis for the three countries to help them decide on country selection. PEST analysis ignored technological factors because these were not important for the olive oil market. The main PEST findings are shown below.

| United States | Australia | China |
|---|---|---|
| **Political** | **Political** | **Political** |
| High political stability (O) | High political stability (O) | Corrupt officials (T) |
| | | Government regulations (T) |
| | | Political risk (T) |
| **Economic** | **Economic** | **Economic** |
| High per capita income (O) | High per capita income (O) | High market growth (O) |
| Stability in terms of trade/ currency rates (O) | Stability in terms of trade/currency rates (O) | Low per capita income (T) |
| Low market growth (T) | Low market growth (T) | Changes in terms of trade/ currency rates (T) |
| **Social** | **Social** | **Social** |
| Familiarity with Mediterranean cuisine thanks to immigrants (O) | Familiarity with Mediterranean cuisine thanks to immigrants (O) | Little awareness of health benefits of olive oil (T+O) |
| | Public concern with health and diet (O) | |

*Note:* O means Opportunity; T means Threat.

PEST Analysis potentially shows China to be the least attractive market, with many potential threats. Baser Food management calculated that the company would have to spend at least €1 million on a marketing campaign needed to attempt to change eating habits and encourage olive-oil consumption in China. However, the lack of awareness of health benefits of olive oil in China was also seen as an opportunity because there was relatively little market competition and Baser Food could gain a first mover advantage in a high-growth market. Conversely, there was intense competition and a lack of brand loyalty in the United States, which meant higher costs and lower profit margins. What advice would you give to Baser Food on country selection?

*Source:* V. Sriram and Z. Bilgin (2002), 'Global market opportunity in the olive oil industry: the case of Baser Food', *Case Research Journal* 22(4): 27–41; B. E. Bensoussan and C. S. Fleisher (2008), *Analysis without Paralysis: 10 Tools to Make Better Strategic Decisions* (Upper Saddle River, NJ: Pearson); Baser Food website at http://www.baserfood.com.

PEST analysis (political, economic, social, and technological factors) is a broad framework to help managers understand the environment in which their business operates. Managers can simply use this framework as a checklist to ask themselves questions as to how political, economic, social, or technological developments can influence their industry and their company.

## 2.4 The political environment

Governments can have a major impact on business by imposing regulations on multinational firms. The government can change the levels of taxation or import duties, provide subsidies to certain firms, or impose regulations which require multinational firms to change how they operate (e.g., through anti-pollution regulations). At the same time, business strategies are now also affected by the emergence of new global institutions such as the World Trade Organization and regional economic blocs such as the European Union. In the global economy, therefore, the multinational firm must pay special attention to a complex set of important political issues: regional economic integration, government legislation, political risk, and corruption.

### 2.4.1 Regional integration

The business environment has changed in the last few decades with the emergence of regional economic blocs. The most far-reaching economic bloc is the European Union; other important ones include the North American Free Trade Agreement (NAFTA), the Association of Southeast Asian Nations (ASEAN) Free Trade Area (AFTA), and the Southern Common Market (MERCOSUR) (see Exhibit 2.4).

Regional economic blocs differ widely (Dicken 2007: 190–2):

**Exhibit 2.4**    Important regional economic blocs

**AFTA (Association of Southeast Asian Nations (ASEAN) Free Trade Area)**

Type of regional bloc: Free Trade Area

Member countries: Brunei, Indonesia, Malaysia, Philippines, Singapore, Thailand (Cambodia, Laos, Myanmar, Vietnam from 2012)

**CARICOM (Caribbean Community)**

Type of regional bloc: Common Market

Member countries: Antigua and Barbuda, Bahamas, Barbados, Belize, Dominica, Grenada, Guyana, Haiti, Jamaica, Montserrat, St Kitts-Nevis, St Lucia, St Vincent and the Grenadines, Suriname, Trinidad and Tobago

**EU (European Union)**

Type of regional bloc: Economic Union

Member countries: Austria, Belgium, Bulgaria, Cyprus, Czech Republic, Denmark, Estonia, Finland, France, Germany, Greece, Hungary, Ireland, Italy, Latvia, Lithuania, Luxembourg, Malta, Netherlands, Poland, Portugal, Romania, Slovak Republic, Slovenia, Spain, Sweden, United Kingdom

**MERCOSUR (Southern Common Market)**

Type of regional bloc: Customs Union

Member countries: Argentina, Brazil, Paraguay, Uruguay

**NAFTA (North American Free Trade Agreement)**

Type of regional bloc: Free Trade Area

Member countries: Canada, Mexico, United States

**SADC (Southern African Development Community)**

Type of regional bloc: Free Trade Area

Member countries: Angola, Botswana, Democratic Republic of Congo, Lesotho, Madagascar, Malawi, Mauritius, Mozambique, Namibia, Seychelles, South Africa, Swaziland, Tanzania, Zambia, Zimbabwe

- The *free trade area*, the simplest form of regional economic bloc, whereby member states abolish some trade restrictions between themselves (an example is NAFTA in North America).
- The *customs union*, whereby member states abolish some trade restrictions between themselves and, in addition, establish a common trade policy towards non-member states (an example is MERCOSUR in South America).

- The *common market*, whereby member states abolish some trade restrictions among themselves, establish a common trade policy towards non-member states, and, in addition, allow the free movement of people and capital between member states (an example is the Caribbean Community (CARICOM) in the Caribbean).

- The *economic union*, the most complex type of regional integration, with the EU being the prime example. The EU not only has adopted all the policies mentioned earlier, but also harmonizes government policies of member states on many issues such as anti-competitive behaviour by firms. Furthermore, unlike other regional economic blocs, the EU has developed many common institutions, such as the European Court of Justice and the European Parliament, which exercise supranational control over policies of member states.

Regional economic blocs offer opportunities for international firms. In order to benefit from lower barriers to trade, some firms invest in a given country so as to be able to sell goods and services to other countries in the same regional bloc. For instance, some foreign firms have invested in countries such as Poland and the Czech Republic to benefit from its membership of the EU, while many foreign firms have invested in Mexico in order to be able to export goods to the United States.

Regional integration also poses problems for international firms. One of the key challenges for managers in the EU is to comply with regulations which may apply to their firms. For instance, agricultural firms must comply with different food standards, while the manufacturers of buses and coaches must comply with the Euro 4 standard for emissions. These regulations affect the competitiveness of firms within the EU, for instance, the Euro 4 standard for emissions rendered the production of a bus more expensive by €7,000. In the EU, with its many business regulations, good knowledge of the political business environment can be a distinctive competitive advantage for some firms.

### 2.4.2 Government legislation

While managers must pay attention to the emergence of regional economic blocs, they must furthermore continue to pay attention to government regulations which affect business operations. These include regulations on unfair trade practices (e.g., laws against monopolies), financial regulations, tax codes, environmental regulations, and employment laws. In addition to national regulation by different national governments, firms are also affected by new supranational entities such as the EU. The EU imposes its own laws. These laws are superior to English, Dutch, or Swedish law, so, for example, English courts must apply European law in preference to English law whenever applicable. European laws affect foreign firms which want to do business in any EU country.

The importance of the effect of governments on business is particularly apparent in the 'transition economies', i.e., countries which are experiencing a transition from socialism (where the government made all the important economic decisions) to capitalism (where market forces determine the direction of economic development). Transition economies include two of the world's largest countries—China and Russia—and other states in Eastern Europe such as

Poland, and in Asia such as Vietnam. In those states, the impact of the government on business is still very strong, various large enterprises are state-owned, and good government links can be important for a firm's success (Peng 2000). But political factors are also important in Western Europe or the United States, which continue to impose many regulations and subsidize some sectors of the economy.

Despite globalization, different countries continue to have different rules on the same trade or investment issue. This even applies to the Internet, where a company with a website can theoretically reach customers anywhere in the world. The Internet knows no boundaries; however, Internet firms have to pay attention to regulations in foreign countries. For instance, a new European law in May 2002, required suppliers of digital products from outside the EU to charge value added tax (VAT) on sales of electronically supplied services to private consumers inside the EU. Non-EU suppliers must register with a VAT authority in an EU country of their choice, but to levy VAT at the rate applicable in the country where each customer is resident. So, if a US or Canadian firm sells digital music files or downloadable videos to European consumers through a website, it will have to pay VAT, whether it has any physical presence in Europe or not (Frynas 2002).

Regulations can have both positive and negative effects on firms. For instance, anti-pollution regulations may raise the cost of doing business, since a company may need to install new filters or a waste-treatment facility in order to comply with government legislation. However, anti-pollution regulations can also help certain firms to compete. Porter and van der Linde (1995a; 1995b) suggested that companies based in countries with more stringent environmental laws are able to gain an international competitive advantage over firms in countries with less stringent environmental laws. As more and more countries introduce environmental laws, a firm can gain a head start by introducing a new environmentally friendly product or service before its rivals in other countries. Therefore, government regulations provide both opportunities and threats for multinational firms.

### 2.4.3 Political risk

The above example of environmentally friendly products shows that firms can gain from government regulations. But business writers have usually stressed how governments can create potential problems for firms expanding into new countries. Foreign investors have often suffered at the hands of governments: governments have single-handedly expropriated firms and taken their assets, forced firms out of business by increasing tax rates, and imposed restrictions on transferring profits abroad. Many writers therefore focused on 'political risk' in foreign investment, which is defined as 'the likelihood that political forces will cause drastic changes in a country's business environment that affect the profit and other goals of a particular business enterprise' (Robock and Simmonds 1989: 378). Political risks can include changes in government regulations, war, civil unrest, and politically motivated terrorism.

For instance, the tensions over the US-led war against Iraq have harmed US business interests in the Middle East. While some Arab governments supported the US government, many citizens of Arab countries opposed the war and stopped buying American goods. Coca-Cola was amongst the first companies to suffer from these tensions. Amidst growing anti-US sentiment, Middle Eastern-produced 'Islamic' cola gained popularity at the expense of Coca-Cola sales. Coca-Cola's Middle East and North African operations were based in Bahrain, which was officially an ally of the United States and was home to the US Navy's Fifth Fleet. However, in March 2003, Coca-Cola transferred its regional base from Bahrain to Greece and moved the staff to Greece. It also closed its bottling plant in Riyadh, the capital of Saudi Arabia, to re-equip it to produce other drinks, including water and fruit juices.

Political risks have often been associated with developing countries in Latin America, Africa, and Asia, but there are plenty of examples of risks in Europe, North America, or Japan. It is, nonetheless, correct that political risk is more severe in developing countries (Kobrin 1982). Political risk is also more severe for sectors perceived as important to the country, such as the oil industry and the provision of infrastructure (e.g., water and electricity provision or road construction) (Wells and Gleason 1995).

A key point to remember is that political risk can be different for different companies. Certain companies may be much better able to cope with certain political events than others. For instance, SAB Miller (formerly South African Breweries) is an example of a company which has done well in several politically risky African markets that other brewers have avoided, such as Mozambique and Angola. Frynas and Mellahi (2003) and Frynas et al. (2006) have even argued that political risk itself may be beneficial to specific firms and may assist corporate goals under certain circumstances. Certain firms may have good political connections or experience in politically risky markets, which allow them to weather political risk better than other firms.

### 2.4.4 Corruption

Corruption refers to the misuse of an official position for private gain, normally it involves the payment of a bribe to a government official in return for privileged treatment. Surveys amongst international managers consistently show that some countries are more corrupt than others. The annual reports on corruption by Transparency International show that countries such as Russia and Nigeria are consistently ranked amongst the most corrupt countries in the world, while Denmark and Singapore are ranked amongst the least corrupt countries.

Corruption can negatively affect multinational firms in many ways. A firm's refusal to pay a bribe to a government official may result in the loss of a government contract or a delay in the approval of an investment project. For instance, the Swedish retailer, IKEA, experienced problems with electricity and gas supplies for its Russian stores and with obtaining local government approvals for its investment projects in Russia because IKEA managers refused to pay bribes to Russian officials; as a result, IKEA lost money and was forced to suspend its investments in Russia in 2009.

According to Henriques (2007), corruption can negatively affect the wider external business environment of a country in three ways:

- Macro-economic conditions (for instance, corruption can lead to less foreign investment or higher cost of capital).

- Infrastructure (for instance, corruption can lead to a less effective legal system and less reliable utilities).
- Operational conditions (for instance, corruption can lead to higher crime rates, higher taxes, and higher costs of doing business).

A manager may be tempted to engage in corruption in order not to lose a contract or in order not to lose out to less scrupulous competition. However, engaging in corruption is illegal, unethical, and may have a negative impact on the firm itself. Corruption can lead to a negative reputation for a firm. Studies also suggest that firms engaged in corruption are likely to become less innovative (Desai and Mitra 2004). When an international firm attempts to avoid corruption, it may have to take a strategic decision on whether to expand in a specific country or to engage in a specific investment project.

## 2.5 **The economic environment**

Changes in the economic business environment can influence a firm's expansion. For instance, if economic growth increases, the firm may be able to expand production and open new plants; during an economic recession, when economic activity stagnates or even declines, the firm may need to close down plants and reduce production. Firms have to consider other economic factors, such as the rate of inflation, disposable income, and rates of unemployment. In the global economy, the firm must pay special attention to three important issues: cost of production, currency exchange rates, and cost of capital.

### 2.5.1 **Cost of production**

One of the key global economic issues for companies is the cost of production. Since there are fewer barriers to international trade today and transport costs are not significant for many products, multinational firms can scan the entire world for the cheapest production location. The cost of labour is of key importance and it can differ significantly between countries. In 2007, the average hourly labour costs in textile and textile products manufacturing was US$21 in high-cost United States, US$3 in Mexico, and just over US$1 in the Philippines. But there can be wide differences in labour costs between industries in the same country. In 2007, the labour costs in chemical manufacturing were US$9 in Mexico, compared with US$5 in the auto industry and US$3 in textiles (see Exhibit 2.5).

Firms in labour-intensive industries (where labour accounts for a large part of the total cost of production) have often found that they had to relocate production or services abroad because this allowed them to reduce labour costs and become more internationally competitive. For instance, many American and European call centres are based in India, where wages are low. Since international telephone calls have become relatively cheap, a telephone inquiry from a British or American customer can be rerouted to India, where the service can be performed at lower cost.

**Exhibit 2.5** Global labour cost comparison (in US$, 2007 figures)

### Hourly labour costs in textile and textile products manufacturing

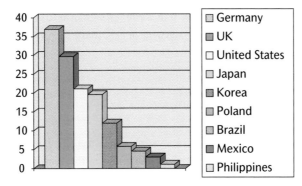

### Hourly labour costs in auto industry

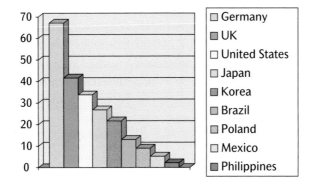

### Hourly labour costs in chemical manufacturing

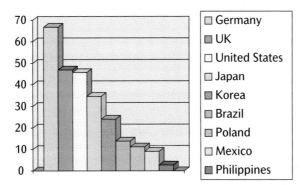

*Source:* US Bureau of Labor Statistics (2009).

But wage rates are not the only determinant of labour costs. Another important factor is labour productivity, which is defined as the amount of output produced per unit of inputs used to produce it. Labour productivity is much higher in Germany than in Sri Lanka. So, the managers have to weigh up the advantages of cheap labour versus other factors such as the necessary skills and efficiency of their workforce, which may not always be available in low-wage countries. For instance, Germany has very high labour costs in the auto industry (see Exhibit 2.5) but the country is a major exporter of cars thanks to the very high efficiency and skills of the German labour force.

### 2.5.2 Currency exchange rates

Cost of production is affected by the currency exchange rate, i.e., the rate at which one country's currency can be exchanged for another's. If the value of the euro goes up relative to other currencies, Dutch or German goods become more expensive to buy for foreigners, and Dutch and German firms may find it more difficult to export their goods. At the same time, firms outside the euro zone will find it easier to export goods to Germany. Similarly, foreign firms will find it less attractive to invest in the Netherlands or Germany, while Dutch and German firms will find it more attractive to invest outside the euro zone. Multinational firms have to monitor currency exchange rates in the global economy in order to spot threats and opportunities for their existing operations in different countries. Political and social events can influence exchange rates. For instance, the threat of a war against Iraq in early 2003, contributed to the depreciation of the US dollar and an appreciation of European currencies such as the euro and the Swiss franc.

In some cases, a firm may need to shift production away from a country where the exchange rates make it too expensive to produce (Froot and Stein 1991; Dewenter 1995). For instance, various Japanese car manufacturers started constructing car plants in the United States in early 1996, as the Japanese yen had become very expensive relative to the US dollar. However, multinational firms face the problem that it can be very difficult to predict future changes in exchange rates. In late 1996 and throughout 1997, the value of the Japanese yen fell against the US dollar, but Japanese car manufacturers had already committed themselves to building plants in the United States.

Currency exchange rates affect different firms differently. Certain industries, such as electrical equipment or precision machinery, are more affected by changes in currency exchange rates than other industries because they rely heavily on globally sourced inputs and are more dependent on exports than, e.g., utilities companies (He and Ng 1998). Firms which operate in many different countries are less affected than others which do not. It has been shown that foreign market participation through direct investment reduces a firm's exposure to exchange rate movements, especially if a firm's investments are widely spread geographically between markets with different currencies (Miller and Reuer 1998).

Currency exchange rates are also less of a problem for firms which resort to 'currency hedging'—the practice of protecting a firm against potential losses resulting from adverse movements in currency exchange rates. For instance, a firm in the Netherlands buys computer equipment from a firm in Singapore at a fixed price and the payment is due in 100 days. If the contract is denominated in Singaporean dollars, the Dutch firm could lose money if the euro were weaker relative to the Singaporean dollar in 100 days. So, the firm could buy a 'forward exchange contract' with a bank, which will deliver foreign currency at a specific exchange rate in 100 days. The firm could also buy a 'currency option'—this gives the firm the right to buy or sell a certain amount of currency at a specified date in the future (an option is more flexible than a forward contract, as the Dutch firm does not have to exercise the option). A firm with a forward exchange contract or with a currency option will be less affected by changes in currency rates in the short term. In the long term, a sustained appreciation of the Singaporean dollar over many years could make imports from Singapore less internationally competitive. In that case, currency hedging will be of little use.

### 2.5.3 Cost of capital

In the global economy, a multinational firm can obtain capital in different countries. But different countries may have different rates for borrowing money. This is important for multinational firms, as the cost of borrowing in the home country affects the firm's ability to raise capital. When the lending rates in the UK increase, the cost of raising capital in the UK increases. In the international marketplace, a firm from a country with high lending rates is at a disadvantage in raising capital compared to a firm in a country with low lending rates (Aliber 1970; Grosse and Trevino 1996). If the cost of borrowing increases in the UK relative to other countries, foreign firms will find it easier to compete in the UK market and their investment in the UK will increase. Conversely, if the cost of borrowing decreases in the UK relative to other countries, firms which raise capital in the UK will find it easier to compete in foreign markets.

In the global economy, large multinational firms are able to raise capital in different countries and they are able to deal with the threat of increasing or decreasing cost of borrowing in any one country. These large multinational firms will need to continuously monitor the global business environment for the cost of borrowing in different countries in order to benefit from the best rates available. When you compete on the world stage, you need to obtain capital from the best available source.

However, raising capital outside the firm's home country may not always be possible, so the home base of a multinational firm still influences the cost of borrowing. The national origin of a firm may thus determine how much money you can raise and at what rate. In the most extreme cases, firms decide to change corporate nationality in order to benefit from lower cost of borrowing. For example, several major South African multinational firms, including SAB Miller, the life assurer, Old Mutual, and the mining firm, Anglo American Corporation, strategically switched their stock exchange listing and headquarters from Johannesburg to London. This allowed the firms to raise significantly greater amounts of capital to finance their international operations. When Anglo American and SAB Miller announced their decision to move to London in late 1998, interest rates in Johannesburg were around 22%, while those in London were close to 6%.

## 2.6 **The social environment**

Social change can have a major influence on firm strategies. Some products and services may become less fashionable and decline. New social trends may open new business opportunities for multinational firms. In the global market, the firm must pay special attention to two key social issues: social change and global convergence of tastes and needs.

### 2.6.1 **Social change**

Firms need to pay attention to new global trends in order to strategically exploit new opportunities. For instance, migration of people can open new business opportunities. The presence of a large ethnic Chinese or Indian population in a foreign country opens new international business opportunities for Chinese or Indian firms. Some small- and medium-sized firms from China and Hong Kong began their international expansion by strategically locating in foreign countries and cities with a large Chinese population, such as Malaysia or Los Angeles (Child et al. 2002). The presence of a large Chinese minority helped to ensure initial demand for goods and services (ranging from Chinese foodstuffs to banking services), and it also helped to reduce transaction costs of setting up a foreign subsidiary. In turn, early expansion into Malaysia or Los Angeles helped Chinese managers to gain international experience and confidence to expand into more challenging international markets.

Firms also need to pay attention to social issues such as changing relations between age groups of consumers. For example, the rising number of old age pensioners in developed countries opens new markets for multinational firms which provide appropriate goods and services for that age group. In order to benefit from this social change, multinational hotel chains such as Marriott and Hyatt constructed special apartment blocks for the elderly, with meals, transportation, and utilities included in the rent. Some social changes are more subtle. Lindstrom (2003) has shown how the brand awareness of small children has changed the buying patterns for many goods. His study on children in fourteen countries suggested that almost 80% of all brands purchased by parents are strongly influenced by their offspring. Children as young as eight or even younger may determine which car or computer their parents buy. The rising influence of children on buying decisions is one example of how social change can have major effects on global marketing, and may require a strategic reorientation of some firms. Other important social changes may relate to changes in lifestyle (e.g., more international travel), the levels of education (e.g., more people with higher education), or income distribution (e.g., greater levels of disposable income amongst certain groups in society). Identifying social change early may allow firms to stay ahead of competitors.

### 2.6.2 **Global convergence**

Some experts claim that the tastes and needs of customers in different countries are becoming increasingly similar, which has been labelled 'global convergence' (Levitt 1983). Thanks to the spread of global communications and transportation, certain social behaviours spread globally.

As people travel abroad, watch the same Hollywood-made films, use the same Internet websites, and play the same video games, they absorb habits from other countries. According to this view, tastes become more similar globally and this global convergence is most visible in young people. Many young people in developed countries drink Coca-Cola, play the Sony PlayStation, and listen to the latest Beyoncé pop songs. As a result of this convergence, multinational firms with a global strategy are increasingly able to offer identical or very similar products in many different countries. In other words, global convergence of tastes and needs can lead to global market convergence, whereby the world becomes one global market for the same products.

At this point in human history, one should be cautious about the idea of 'global convergence', as various experts claim that there are still huge cultural and other differences between countries in terms of doing business (Ghemawat 2007; Witt and Redding 2009; Chang 2009). These differences are sometimes major and sometimes minor; seeming similarities between countries may also be superficial. Even if people use the same or similar products in different countries, they may use them at different occasions, under different circumstances, and for different reasons in each country. Where cultural differences play a major role (as with many types of local foodstuff, clothing, or interior design), global business strategies may not be possible. Convergence facilitates global strategies in some industries; conversely, the absence of convergence hinders global strategies in other industries. So, managers need to be aware of the impact of global convergence on their specific products and services.

Nonetheless, even if there are differences between countries, firms may often be able to introduce relatively small changes to their global products or global marketing campaigns. For example, McDonald's in India sells chicken burgers as the 'Maharaja Mac', while the taste of Coca-Cola varies between some countries, but the overall marketing strategies of McDonald's and Coca-Cola remain largely the same. Similarly, IKEA (the opening case study in Chapter 1) was forced to change some product features for the US market, but it was able to keep the core product features, which helped to simplify global operations.

## 2.7 The technological environment

Technological change can have a major impact on business strategies. In the global economy, technological innovation can spread very quickly around the world and the pace of technological pace is increasing. The Internet, advances in computer technology, genetic engineering, or laser technology revolutionize the ways in which firms operate. An innovation may render a firm's technology obsolete or it can lead to the creation of entirely new industries. Three important issues to consider are global technology scanning and technology clusters, the rise of the knowledge-based economy, and the spread of the Internet.

### 2.7.1 Global technology scanning and technology clusters

In the global economy, a technological innovation may occur anywhere and it may spread quickly around the globe, so managers must constantly monitor the external business environment for new developments (Granstrand et al. 1992). The process of identifying technologies in the external business environment is called 'technology scanning'. The firm may use different methods to learn about new technologies, from attending scientific conferences to pursuing technical partnerships with other technically advanced companies or research centres.

In a large multinational company, technology scanning can be pursued by locating the company's research centres in countries or regions where relevant cutting-edge research is pursued. Technological advances often occur in high-technology 'clusters' where you find many advanced firms from the same sector, often linked to a high-quality university or research centre. The best-known cluster in information technology is Silicon Valley in California, but smaller ones include India's Silicon Valley near Bangalore, the Multimedia Super Corridor in Malaysia, and Silicon Fen near Cambridge in the UK. One key strategy for a multinational firm is to locate inside a cluster to benefit from its advanced knowledge networks. For example, companies such as Olivetti and Oracle (whose research centre was later taken over by AT&T) located some of their research activities in Silicon Fen, where firms benefited from the proximity to the University of Cambridge and from advanced research in information technology by other firms located in the region.

As with PEST analysis in general, technology scanning should be as wide-ranging as possible. Relevant technological innovations may often occur outside the firm's industry: achieved by firms in other industries, by universities, or by specialized research centres. The government may be an important source of innovation—often as a result of government research related to the military. For instance, the development of the flat-panel NXT technology for loudspeakers began in the British military by chance. The military conducted research into reducing noise in helicopter cabins, but the material used in the research amplified the noise instead of reducing it. The research was later continued by NXT—a firm based in Silicon Fen—and was commercialized with the help of the British packaging manufacturer, DS Smith.

### 2.7.2 The knowledge-based economy

The introduction of new information technologies such as computers and the Internet has generally raised the importance of knowledge in the economy. Some experts talk about the rise of the so-called 'new economy'—businesses based on technological innovation. Rifkin (2000) argues that ownership mattered most in the old economy: physical capital was used to make goods which went to market where they were exchanged. In the new economy, intellectual capital is the driving force and the location of the business activities is much less important. The difference between the 'old' and the 'new' economy can be shown by contrasting the oil industry and the computer software industry. In the oil industry, a company's wealth is largely determined by the physical control of oil fields, oil tankers, and petrol stations. In the software industry, a company's wealth is determined by the intellectual ownership of computer programs and the creativity of its staff. The physical location of oil fields and petrol stations plays a huge role, whereas a software programmer can work anywhere.

Some industries increasingly move from the 'old' towards the 'new' economy, for example, movie-making. American movies were largely made in Hollywood in the past, relying on the physical ownership of film studios and proximity to specialized firms which provided stuntmen or film props. But, thanks to technological advancements, computer software can now generate 3D characters which are indistinguishable from live-action film. These technological opportunities were first used extensively by the creators of the movie, *Independence Day*, who made much of the movie with computers in warehouses at perhaps half of the cost of a comparable Hollywood production. The *Lord of the Rings* trilogy and the *Matrix* movies also made extensive use of computer software. As a result of this technological shift, movie-makers depend less on the physical infrastructure of Hollywood. Many of the leading special-effects companies are based outside Hollywood and, indeed, outside the United States, so the infrastructure for movie-making is becoming more global. This example shows how technological advances can reshape an industry in the knowledge-based economy.

A key characteristic of the knowledge economy is that knowledge—unlike physical assets—can often be transferred and used for different purposes on a global scale. Mental Images, a leading German-based company providing 3D modelling software for movie-making, became famous, winning a special award from the prestigious US Motion Picture Academy (the organization behind the Oscars) for its work on movies such as *Star Wars II: Attack of the Clones*. But Mental Images did not only serve film companies such as Disney and DreamWorks. With only about thirty staff based in Berlin and San Francisco, the company was able to use the same intellectual property to serve customers in the video game sector (Nintendo and SEGA), the car industry (DaimlerChrysler and Honda), and aerospace (Airbus and Boeing).

### 2.7.3 The spread of the Internet

The rise of the knowledge-based economy was greatly helped by the spread of the Internet. This made possible new types of product/service (e.g., communications tools and online auctions), operational efficiencies (e.g., savings on distribution costs and improved lead times), and better customer service and relationships (e.g., twenty-four-hour service and personalized marketing and customer service).

Some experts have argued that the Internet has not only brought new products and new distribution channels, but has also transformed the way we do business in general. Don Tapscott (2001) argued that wealth will be largely created through partnerships in future. Since physical assets are less important in the new economy, companies will no longer have to control all stages of research, production, and marketing as oil companies did in the old economy. At the same time, global partnerships between different firms will spread because the Internet can connect people working on the same project in many different countries at a low cost. According to Tapscott, in future managers may simply start with a new idea for a product/service and a blank sheet for the production and delivery system, and then create a network of companies to carry out all necessary activities including research, production, and marketing. One example was the software company, Siebel Systems, Inc.; this had about 8,000 staff in 2001, but 30,000 people worked for the company as consultants, technology providers, system implementers, suppliers, and vendors. A leading firm in the network will identify discrete activities that create value and will parcel them out to appropriate business Web partners. A key ingredient of successful strategy will be Web partnerships; ownership of distinct activities and rivalry will be less important.

Michael Porter (2001) disagrees with Tapscott. Porter does not question that the Internet has brought many changes such as new types of product/service or huge efficiency gains. But he maintains that the logic of old economy strategies, integration of distinct activities, and rivalry has essentially remained the same. According to Porter, the crash in Internet company shares questioned the wisdom of 'new strategies' and ways of assessing the success of online companies (e.g., using click-through rates for websites instead of traditional profitability measures). Porter points out that the big winners of the Internet age are not Internet-based companies. Some Internet businesses such as eBay.com and Amazon.com can claim a huge commercial success. More often, existing companies and industries use the Internet to improve their operations, to offer new products, or to refocus their business strategies. In commercial banking, for example, established institutions like Wells Fargo, Citibank, and Fleet have many more online accounts than Internet banks. Established companies are also gaining dominance over Internet activities in such diverse sectors as online retailing and online brokerage (Porter 2001).

Whether you agree with Tapscott or with Porter, it is clear that the Internet has the potential to reshape old industries and create entirely new businesses. One example is online gaming. The introduction of high-speed broadband Internet connections has led to a boom in online gaming in many countries, which was further helped by improvements in gaming technology such as the introduction of Xbox LIVE. The global online games market has grown to almost US$20 billion in 2010, representing a 90% increase from US$10.4 billion in 2008.

## 2.8 National environmental influences and the Diamond Model

PEST analysis is a useful tool for understanding the external business environment. This understanding can also help to explain why some firms and industries in some countries are more competitive than others. We know that Japanese firms are particularly strong in industries such as cars, consumer electronics, and video games. American firms are particularly strong in sectors such as movie-making, computer software, and defence. Given the existing external business environment in Japan, it would be difficult to develop a world-class movie industry or defence industry there.

Porter (1990) has suggested that there are intrinsic reasons why some nations are more competitive than others and why some industries are very successful in some nations. According to Porter, the national home base of a firm plays a key role in shaping that firm's competitive advantage in global markets. A country's national values, culture, economic structures, institutions, the strength of local rivalry, and challenging local customers all contribute to an industry's economic success. Porter states that the key to global economic success is innovation in the broadest sense—not just technological innovation, but also new skills, new knowledge, or the application of old ideas in new areas. A strong home base of a company often provides the basis for innovation, which can, in turn, lead to global success.

Porter suggests that four characteristics of the home base help to explain why certain nations are capable of consistent innovation in some sectors: (1) factor conditions; (2) demand conditions; (3) related and supporting industries; and (4) firm strategy, structure, and rivalry. These four conditions form the basis of Porter's 'Diamond Model' (see Exhibit 2.6). The Japanese video game industry provides an example of how the Diamond Model can be used to explain the success of a national industry (see Exhibit 2.7).

---

**KEY CONCEPT**

The Diamond Model assumes that the national home base of a firm plays a key role in shaping that firm's competitive advantage in global markets. Four characteristics of the home base help to explain why certain nations are capable of consistent innovation in some industries: (1) factor conditions; (2) demand conditions; (3) related and supporting industries; and (4) firm strategy, structure, and rivalry. The model can be used to analyse the global competitive success of a national industry.

---

**Exhibit 2.6** The Diamond Model

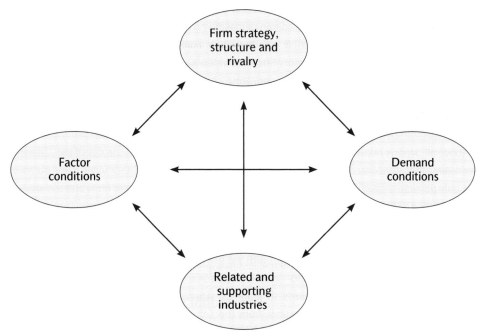

*Source:* M. E. Porter (1990), *The Competitive Advantage of Nations* (Basingstoke: Macmillan). Reprinted with permission of MacMillan (world rights excl. United States and Canada) and reprinted with permission of The Free Press, a Division of Simon & Schuster, Inc. (United States and Canada rights).

development, which can speed up innovation. At the same time, competition among suppliers can result in lower prices of inputs and higher quality of products. In a global economy, a country does not have to be competitive in all related and supporting industries—a multinational firm with a global strategy can source materials, components, or technologies anywhere in the world. But the local availability of high-quality suppliers and related firms in the home base often strengthens the competitive advantage of home-based industries in global markets.

Close relationships between firms, suppliers, and related industries help firms attain global market leadership in many industries. For example, Italian leather footwear firms obtained new styles and manufacturing techniques from domestic leather manufacturers, who helped them to learn about new fashion trends and plan new products.

### 2.8.4 Firm strategy, structure, and rivalry

Porter noted that there are major differences in how firms are created, organized, and managed in different countries, and there are also differences in the nature of domestic rivalry. He found that many globally successful Italian firms were often small in size, privately owned, and operated 'like extended families'. In contrast, many successful German firms had very hierarchical organizations and management practices, and top managers had a technical background. No one country is 'the best' for every industry—some managerial structures are more appropriate for certain industries than for others. Globally successful Italian industries such as footwear and packaging machines were compatible with the character of Italian management structures, emphasizing focus, customized products, niche marketing, and flexibility. The Germans typically excelled in technically demanding and engineering-oriented sectors such as chemicals and complicated machinery, which benefited from precision manufacturing and a careful development process.

An important stimulus to innovation is the extent and character of domestic rivalry. When faced with strong local rivals, firms are forced to lower costs, improve quality, raise productivity, and develop new innovative products or production processes. Firms which face such tough competition at home, often develop the necessary skills enabling them to succeed abroad. Porter et al. (2000) found that the global success of many Japanese sectors such as fax-machine manufacturing was greatly helped by intense local competition, while government intervention and the lack of local competition could help explain the mediocrity of many Japanese sectors such as chemicals.

## 2.9 Criticisms of the Diamond Model

The Diamond Model was not intended as a practical management tool to help specific firms compete more successfully; it was designed to help understand why a particular nation is successful in some industries and not in others. The model has been used by governments to consider how government policies can help foster the competitive advantage of their national industries (e.g., through specific education policies or high-quality standards for certain products). Some industry leaders and managers have also used the Diamond Model to understand better how they can build on their home base to compete more successfully in global markets.

However, the Diamond Model has come under much criticism. It has been said that there are flaws in Porter's methodology and reasoning, that the Diamond Model cannot explain the success of many global industries, and that Porter provided no reliable guide for governments and managers as to how to formulate effective global strategies (Davies and Ellis 2000). Two important criticisms are related to small nations and globalization.

### 2.9.1 The Diamond Model for small nations

Several studies suggested that firms from small countries do not rely on a single home base for their success. Large firms in Austria are dependent on the German industrial base, Mexican and Canadian firms depend heavily on the United States, while New Zealand firms rely on the Australian market. A Canadian or Mexican firm may try out its products in the United States from the start, make intensive use of the US research base, and compete head to head with US-based rivals. Therefore, Rugman and Verbeke (1993) suggested that firms from small nations often depend on a large neighbouring nation to the extent that the distinction between the home base and host nation as a source of economic success becomes blurred.

Regional economic integration has erased many barriers to international trade, so managers in a Canadian firm may perceive the United States as part of their home base and Austrian managers may also think of southern Germany or northern Italy as part of their home market. Rugman and D'Cruz (1991) suggested that we should apply a 'Double Diamond' to explain the success of large firms from small nations. Accordingly, many Canadian firms such as Northern Telecom or Seagram should not be regarded as part of a Canadian diamond but as part of a 'North American diamond'. Canadian managers need to assess the conditions of competitiveness both in Canada and the United States when developing corporate strategies (Rugman and Verbeke 1993).

### 2.9.2 The Diamond Model and globalization

Another criticism of the Diamond Model is that it pays too little attention to the importance of globalization. By their nature, multinational companies can own or generate new assets in a foreign country. We suggested earlier that large global companies can locate the company's research centres in countries or regions where the latest cutting-edge research is pursued such as Silicon Valley or Silicon Fen (section 2.7.1) and obtain innovations from foreign subsidiaries. A global company can also start a strategic alliance with a foreign company (see Chapter 7) or buy a foreign company in order to acquire important resources. In these ways, a company can gain innovation from factor conditions in a foreign location (Dunning 1993; Asmussen et al. 2008).

Globalization also affects demand conditions, supporting and related industries and rivalry. We suggested earlier that the tastes of consumers are becoming increasingly similar (section 2.6.2), so the demand conditions become similar across countries. Since global companies pursue global sourcing strategies and can use any supplier from any country, local supporting and related industries are becoming less important. Finally, local rivalry is becoming less important in the global market, as multinational companies have to compete against the best companies in their sector on a global scale. Therefore, some observers have argued that the Diamond Model no longer makes much sense, since national competitive conditions are now not as important for the success of large global businesses.

### 2.9.3 Response to criticisms

Michael Porter does not deny the importance of international and global strategies. He admits that companies have to compete globally today, but he suggests that the secret of their global success usually lies in the unique mixture of domestic conditions in their home base. At least two further arguments can be made in defence of the Diamond Model.

First, Porter has pointed out that regions are still important despite globalization, and that 'home base' can often refer to a specific region. Technology 'clusters' such as Silicon Valley and Silicon Fen are regional—not national or international—in character. The existence of such clusters shows that, despite globalization and the spread of the Internet, the close physical proximity between firms in the same sector helps to create new ideas and technical innovations. The Internet cannot fully replace the human interaction between engineers, managers, and others. If a Japanese computer software company wanted to invest in the United States, it would be advised to locate in Silicon Valley—not in Florida or Ohio—to benefit from local factor conditions, local suppliers, and domestic rivals in the software sector. Despite globalization, some locations provide a unique mixture of local factors, which facilitates innovation.

Second, in contrast to the view of a truly global economy, Pauly and Reich (1997) showed that firms from different countries continue to differ in their internal governance and long-term financing structures, in their approaches to research and development as well as in the location of core research facilities, and in their foreign investment and intra-firm trading strategies. German and Japanese firms obtain most of their financing through banks (about 60–70%), while US firms rely more on capital markets (bank loans provide only 25–35% of financial liabilities). Foreign research facilities account for less than 15% of the total research and development spending by large American firms; Japanese and German firms spend even less on research abroad. Furthermore, much of corporate research and development spending abroad is used to customize products for local markets or to gather knowledge for transfer back home, not to generate new knowledge. Firms are still largely dependent on innovation in their home country. Therefore, the local conditions in the home base still shape the global strategies of German, Japanese, or American firms.

## 2.10 Summary

The competitive success of organizations is determined by the business environment, which consists of the external macro environment, the external industry environment, and the internal firm environment. The external business environment of the firm provides both opportunities and threats to firms, and the task of the strategic decision-maker is to develop strategies based on what the firm can do to exploit external opportunities and counter external threats. In order to be successful, a firm must achieve strategic fit, i.e., it must match its resources and activities to the external environment in which it operates.

There are no simple recipes for monitoring, analysing, and forecasting external factors, which may influence the firm's development. But it is useful to have a checklist of potential external macro influences—a PEST analysis—which can serve to ask questions as to how political, economic, social, or technological developments can influence a specific industry and a specific firm. If managers ask the appropriate questions relevant to their business, PEST analysis can help to formulate strategies, which aim to exploit external opportunities.

An understanding of the external business environment can also help us to explain why some firms and industries in some countries are more competitive than others. According to Porter, the national home base of a firm plays a key role in shaping that firm's competitive advantage in global markets. Porter suggests that four characteristics of the home base help to explain why certain nations are capable of consistent innovation in some sectors: (1) factor conditions; (2) demand conditions; (3) related and supporting industries; and (4) firm strategy, structure, and rivalry. The model can be used to analyse the global competitive success of a national industry. It demonstrates how the wider business environment can have a major impact on competitive success in the global marketplace.

## 📖 Key readings

- On the external business environment and PEST factors in international business, see Leslie Hamilton and Philip Webster (2009), *The International Business Environment* (Oxford: Oxford University Press 2009).

- On the Diamond Model, see Porter (1990).

- On critique of the Diamond Model, see Davies and Ellis (2000).

## 💬 Discussion questions

**1.** Take one multinational firm of your choice. Conduct a PEST analysis for a country, in which the firm operates.

**2.** What problems do managers face in conducting a global PEST analysis and how might they overcome these problems?

**3.** To what extent has the world experienced 'global convergence' of tastes and needs?

**4.** To what extent did the Internet change the nature of business activity and business strategy?

**5.** Take one national industry of your choice. Can the Diamond Model explain the international success or lack of success of your industry?

---

**Closing case study** Lockheed Martin—from conquering Russia to conquering space

In 1995, two companies—the Lockheed Corporation and the Martin Marietta Corporation—merged to form the Lockheed Martin Corporation. Today, Lockheed Martin is a major global company engaged in the research, design, development, manufacture, and integration of advanced technology systems, products, and services. It employs some 136,000 people worldwide and its reported sales were US$45.2 billion in 2009. Much of the company's business is in the defence sector, and Lockheed Martin's products include tactical aircraft and naval systems. Nearly 80% of the company's business is with the US Department of Defense and the US federal government agencies.

One of Lockheed Martin's main business lines are Space Systems—space launch, commercial satellites, government satellites, and strategic missiles. In the 1990s, a global market for satellite launch services emerged and Lockheed Martin wanted to share in this market growth. The emergence of commercial launch services was made possible by two developments in the external business environment. On the one hand, there was a rapid growth in telecommunications technologies driving significant acceleration of demand for launches of telecommunications satellites; the growth of satellite television channels and mobile phones was dependent on launching new satellites. On the other hand, the political environment changed.

During the Cold War, global access to satellite launch services was tightly regulated, and in many cases controlled, by governments because of the close linkage between satellites and defence requirements. In the 1980s, a global market in satellite launches began to emerge. In 1980, the European Space Agency created Arianespace, the first real commercial space transportation company, which launched its first commercial satellite payload into orbit in 1984 from the European Space Agency's launch site at Kourou, Guyana. Commercial satellites were also launched by NASA from Cape Kennedy during the 1980s. However, commercial launch services remained subject to government control. Soviet and Chinese launch sites remained entirely state-controlled, and were used predominantly for domestic military, scientific, and state telecommunications needs.

In the early 1990s, the global political environment changed radically. The Cold War ended and the Soviet Union disintegrated. The old enemies—the United States and Russia—began to work together on economic and technological issues. In the space sector, NASA and the Russian Space Agency (RSA) cooperated by utilizing the US space shuttle and the ageing Russian Mir space station to prepare for the construction of the International Space Station (ISS). Old barriers to technological transfers in the space sector between Russia and the United States were relaxed.

The US and Russian governments promoted the privatization of Russian firms and commercialization of Russia's space sector to facilitate joint ventures between US and Russian firms. The prospect of joint ventures with Russian firms was attractive for American companies such as Lockheed at a time when the demand for commercial satellite launches had increased. Access to Russia's aerospace assets—launch platforms, rockets, and support services—could help US firms gain new technology and increase capacity for a larger number of satellite launches.

In April 1993, Lockheed formed a joint venture with two Russian aerospace firms—RSC Energia and Khrunichev called Lockheed Khrunichev Energia International (LKEI). Following the merger in 1995, Lockheed Martin established Lockheed Martin Commercial Launch Services Company (LMCLS) to market launch services using Lockheed Martin's Atlas II and III rocket boosters, to be launched from Cape Canaveral in Florida and Vandenberg Air Force Base, California. LMCLS and LKEI then joined forces to form a highly innovative new company, International Launch Services (ILS) to market jointly the commercial launch services of the Russian Proton and American Atlas boosters on a global basis. The first ILS commercial launch using a Proton booster took place in 1996, and business grew steadily.

Lockheed Martin's entry into Russia allowed the company to benefit from the technological base of the country. The company was able to get access to (amongst others) the Proton rocket booster and the RD180 engine, which gave it an advantage in the global market for satellite launches. Most crucially, it benefited from the political situation. The US–Russian cooperation in the space sector gave a privileged position to US companies in Russia. The US and Russian governments actively supported the ILS venture; for instance, the Russian government negotiated with the government of Kazakhstan to allow ILS the use of the Baikonur space facility in Kazakhstan. Political support also helped ILS to cope better with existing government restrictions in the space sector (e.g., pricing restrictions) and to obtain the required government permits (e.g., export licences).

With government support, Lockheed Martin was able to benefit from early market entry in Russia several years before its rivals. Its competitor, Arianespace, only entered Russia in 1996. The early entry into Russia gave Lockheed Martin time to develop a customer base before its rivals obtained the relevant technology. In other words, the conquest of Russia led to Lockheed Martin's conquest of space.

Lockheed Martin continues to be very successful in the design, research and development, production, and launch of satellites. In 2009 alone, the satellite business generated US$5.8 billion in revenues for the company. The global satellite market is forecast to grow by 50% between 2009 and 2018.

*Source:* Lockheed Martin website at http://www.lockheedmartin.com/ and ILS website at http://www.ilslaunch.com/; Frynas et al. (2006); interview with a senior ILS manager.

### Discussion questions

**1.** How did the external business environment influence the success of Lockheed Martin in satellite launch services?

**2.** Michael Porter suggested that a company based in a country with a high level of government intervention will lose out to international competitors. Does the case of Lockheed Martin support his view?

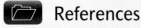 # References

Aliber, R. Z. (1970). 'A theory of foreign direct investment', in C. Kindleberger (ed.), *The International Corporation* (Cambridge, MA: MIT Press).

Asmussen, C. G., Pedersen, T., and Dhanaraj, C. (2008). 'Host-country environment and subsidiary competence: extending the diamond network model', *Journal of International Business Studies* 40(1): 42–57.

Barr, P. S., and Glynn, M. A. (2004). 'Cultural variations in strategic issue interpretation: relating cultural uncertainty avoidance to controllability in discriminating threat and opportunity', *Strategic Management Journal* 25(1): 59–67.

Chang, S. J. (2009). 'When East and West meet: an essay on the importance of cultural understanding in global business practice and education', *Journal of International Business and Cultural Studies* 2: 1–13.

Child, J., Ng, S. H., and Wong, C. (2002). 'Psychic distance and internationalization', *International Studies of Management and Organization* 32(1): 36–56.

Daft, R. L., Sormunen, J., and Parks, D. (1988). 'Chief executive scanning, environmental characteristics and company performance: an empirical study', *Strategic Management Journal* 9(2): 123–39.

Davies, H., and Ellis, P. (2000). 'Porter's *Competitive Advantage of Nations*: time for the final judgement?' *Journal of Management Studies* 37(8): 1189–213.

Denison, D. R., Dutton, J. E., Kahn, J. A., and Hart, S. L. (1996). 'Organizational context and the interpretation of strategic issues: a note on CEOs' interpretations of foreign investment', *Journal of Management Studies* 33(4): 453–74.

Desai, P., and Mitra, P. (2004). 'Why do some countries recover so much more easily than others?' in *Festschrift in Honor of Guillermo A. Calvo* (Washington, DC).

Dewenter, K. L. (1995). 'Do exchange rate changes drive foreign direct investment?' *Journal of Business* 68(3): 405–33.

Dicken, P. (2007). *Global Shift: Mapping the Changing Contours of the World Economy*, 5th edn (New York: Guilford Press).

Douglas, S. P., and Wind, Y. (1987). 'The myth of globalization', *Columbia Journal of World Business* 22(4): 19–29.

Dunning, J. H. (1993). 'Internationalizing Porter's diamond', *Management International Review* 33(2): 7–15.

Eisenhardt, K. M. (1989). 'Making fast strategic decisions in high-velocity environments', *Academy of Management Journal* 32(3): 543–76.

Froot, K. A., and Stein, J. C. (1991). 'Exchange rates and foreign direct investment: an imperfect capital markets approach', *Quarterly Journal of Economics* 106: 1191–217.

Frynas, J. G., (2002). 'The limits of globalization: legal and political issues in e-commerce', *Management Decision* 40(9): 871–80.

Frynas, J. G., and Mellahi, K. (2003). 'Political risks as firm-specific (dis)advantages: evidence on transnational oil firms in Nigeria', *Thunderbird International Business Review* 45(5): 522–41.

Frynas, J. G., Mellahi, K., and Pigman, G. (2006). 'First mover advantage in international business and firm-specific political resources', *Strategic Management Journal* 27: 321–45.

Galbraith, J. R., and Kazanjian, R. K. (1986). *Strategy Implementation*, 2nd edn (St Paul, MN: West).

Garg, V. K., Walters, B. A., and Priem, R. L. (2003). 'Chief executive scanning emphases, environmental dynamism, and manufacturing firm performance', *Strategic Management Journal* 24(8): 725–44.

Ghemawat, P. (2007). *Redefining Global Strategy: Crossing Borders in a World Where Differences Still Matter* (Cambridge, MA: Harvard Business School Press).

Granstrand, O., Bohlin, E., Christer, O., and Sjöberg, N. (1992). 'External technology acquisition in large multi-technology corporations', *R&D Management* 22(2): 111–33.

Grosse, R., and Trevino, L. J. (1996). 'Foreign direct investment in the United States: an analysis by country of origin', *Journal of International Business Studies* 27(1): 139–55.

He, J., and Ng, K. L. (1998). 'The foreign exchange exposure of Japanese multinational corporations', *Journal of Finance* 53(2): 733–53.

Henriques, A. (2007). *Corporate Truth—The Limits to Transparency* (London: Earthscan).

Julian, S. D., and Ofori-Dankwa, J. C. (2008). 'Toward an integrative cartography of two strategic issue diagnosis frameworks', *Strategic Management Journal* 29: 93–114.

Kobrin, S. (1982). *Managing Political Risk Assessment* (Berkeley, CA: University of California Press).

Kuvaas, B. (2002). 'An exploration of two competing perspectives on informational contexts in top management strategic issue interpretation', *Journal of Management Studies* 39(7): 977–1001.

Levitt, T. (1983). 'The globalization of markets', *Harvard Business Review* 61(3): 92–102.

Lindstrom, M. (2003). *BRAND Child* (London: Kogan Page).

Miller, K. D., and Reuer, J. J. (1998). 'Firm strategy and economic exposure to foreign exchange rate movements', *Journal of International Business Studies* 29(3): 493–514.

Norburn, D. (1974). 'Directors without direction', *Journal of General Management* 1(2): 37–49.

Pauly, L. W., and Reich, S. (1997). 'National structures and multinational corporate behaviour: enduring differences in the age of globalization', *International Organization* 51(1): 1–30.

Peng, M. W. (2000). *Business Strategies in Transition Economies* (Thousand Oaks, CA: Sage).

Porter, M. (1990). 'The competitive advantage of nations', *Harvard Business Review* 68(2): 73–93.

Porter, M. (2001). 'Strategy and the Internet', *Harvard Business Review* 79(3): 62–78.

Porter, M., and van der Linde, C. (1995*a*). 'Green and competitive', *Harvard Business Review* 73(5): 120–34.

Porter, M., and van der Linde, C. (1995*b*). 'Toward a new conception of the environment–competitiveness relationship', *Journal of Economic Perspectives* 9(4): 97–118.

Porter, M., Takeuchi, H., and Sakakibara, M. (2000). *Can Japan Compete?* (London: Macmillan).

Rifkin, J. (2000). *The Age of Access* (New York: Tarcher/Penguin Putnam).

Robock, H. S., and Simmonds, K. (1989). *International Business and Multinational Enterprises*, 4th edn (Homewood, IL: Irwin).

Rugman, A. M., and D'Cruz, J. (1991). *Fast Forward: Improving Canada's International Competitiveness* (Toronto: Kodak Canada).

Rugman, A. M., and Verbeke, A. (1993). 'Foreign subsidiaries and multinational strategic management: an extension and correction of Porter's single diamond framework', *Management International Review* 33(2): 60–73.

Sallivan, J., and Nonaka, I. (1988) 'Culture and strategic issue categorization theory', *Management International Review* 28: 6–11.

Stubbs, R., and Underhill, G. R. D. (1994). *Political Economy and the Changing Global Order* (London: Macmillan).

Tapscott, D. (2001). 'Rethinking strategy in a networked world', *Strategy+Business* 24(3): 1–8.

US Bureau of Labor Statistics (2009). 'International hourly compensation costs for all employees, by sub-manufacturing industry, 1996–2007', Bureau of Labor Statistics website at http://www.bls.gov (accessed 4 December 2009).

Wells, L. T., and Gleason, S. E. (1995). 'Is foreign infrastructure investment still risky?' *Harvard Business Review* 73(5): 44–55.

Witt, M. A., and Redding, G. (2009). 'Culture, meaning, and institutions: executive rationale in Germany and Japan', *Journal of International Business Studies* 40(5): 859–85.

# Online resource centre

**online resource centre**

Please visit **www.oxfordtextbooks.co.uk/orc/frynas_mellahi2e/** for further information.

# Global business environment:
## *the industry environment*

**3**

---

## Learning outcomes

After reading this chapter, you should be able to:

➤ Understand the significance of the global industry environment for the strategies of multinational firms.

➤ Apply market segmentation analysis and strategic group analysis.

➤ Apply the Five Forces Model.

➤ Evaluate the importance of industry evolution and the International Product Life Cycle (IPLC) for an industry.

➤ Advise a multinational firm on the techniques for understanding the future of an industry.

**Opening case study** Global economic recession and super luxury cars

The auto industry has suffered heavily as a result of the global economic recession that started in 2008. In January 2009, car sales in Europe fell by 26% and car sales in China fell by 14% compared with January 2008. In the United States, car sales declined by a staggering 37%, and car sales of US companies, General Motors, Ford, and Chrysler fell by about half. General Motors and Chrysler went bankrupt.

However, different market segments were affected differently by the global economic recession. The US companies fared particularly badly because they relied on selling large cars. In contrast, firms that relied on selling small compact cars did better. The US car sales of Subaru and Hyundai actually increased (see Exhibit A).

The market for super luxury cars—depending on definition, cars priced above US$60,000, US$100,000 or US$150,000—fared much worse than the market for small cars. In January 2009, the US sales of Bentley and Ferrari fell by 74% and 52%, respectively. However, senior executives of Bentley and other luxury brands were not very worried about the future. While US companies General Motors and Chrysler faced bankruptcy, Bentley and other luxury brands were expected to recover more quickly than the rest of the auto industry. Christophe George, Bentley's chief operating officer for North America, said: 'The potential for sales is there. Millions of people have more than $30 million in net worth. What we are currently lacking is confidence in the marketplace.' Why were luxury car makers so optimistic about the future?

Luxury car makers were partly optimistic because sales have been growing in some emerging markets, especially in China. China has emerged as the world's second-largest market for luxury cars after the United States. For example, Ferrari sold 212 cars in China in 2008, an increase of 20% compared with 2007.

Luxury car makers were also optimistic because they know that the competitive environment in the super luxury car market is very different from other segments in the auto industry. To begin with, the companies sell a small number of cars with very high value. Maserati, Ferrari, or Bentley sell

**Exhibit A** Growth in US car sales of selected brands, January 2009

| Conventional brand | Annual change (%) | Luxury brand | Annual change (%) |
|---|---|---|---|
| Chrysler | −55 | Bentley | −74 |
| General Motors | −49 | Ferrari | −52 |
| Ford | −40 | Mercedes-Benz | −43 |
| Toyota | −32 | Cadillac | −43 |
| Nissan | −30 | Porsche | −36 |
| Honda | −28 | Land Rover | −34 |
| Subaru | +8 | Acura | −30 |
| Hyundai | +14 | Audi | −26 |

in a year what Ford or Toyota dealers sell in one or two days. The manufacturers of conventional cars talk about building relationships with customers. The senior executives of super luxury brands know many customers by their name.

Luxury car makers produce great cars in small numbers and you sometimes have to wait many months for your car to be delivered. Before the global economic crisis, Ferrari had a long waiting list for its cars. For Ferrari, one benefit of the global economic crisis has been to reduce the waiting list. Maurizio Parlato, Ferrari's director in the United States, says: 'Now we have people who want to own a Ferrari, not people who want to snag one and flip it for profit to someone behind them on the list.'

There are different reasons why people buy a super luxury car. Such cars offer the best performance, the most advanced safety equipment, the most advanced entertainment technology, the most comfortable interior, and most options for individual customization. The newest innovations in the car industry are always first introduced in the super luxury market.

Super luxury cars also offer the intangible value of high status. Not every customer who buys a Porsche or Ferrari is particularly worried about superior performance and safety equipment, some customers just want to be seen driving them. 'It's about emotional connections that people can make with a brand and how it makes you feel,' said one luxury car expert. Senior Bentley and Ferrari executives know that their market is run by different rules of the game than other parts of the auto industry.

*Source:* J. B. White (2009), 'Yes, people buy Ferraris in a recession', The Wall Street *Journal* (31 March); H. Elliott (2009), 'Ten reasons to buy a luxury car', *Forbes* (27 February); various newspapers and magazines.

## 3.1 **Introduction**

The last chapter demonstrated the importance of political, economic, social, and economic (PEST) factors in the external business environment. But a manager needs to understand how PEST factors affect the firm's specific markets. For example, the global economic recession affected different parts of the auto industry differently. The opening case study shows that it is important to understand how changes in the external industry environment affect or do not affect your business.

Managers need to understand the industry environment in which they operate and understand the external opportunities and threats, and to adapt the organization to the industry environment. In order to achieve 'strategic fit' (see Chapter 2, section 2.2), the firm needs to understand the structure of its industry, no matter whether it is a domestic or multinational firm.

Above all, managers need to understand their customers—their preferences, lifestyles, shopping habits, etc. The firm must also understand competition in the industry—who its competitors are, how much they charge for their products, and how easily new competitors can enter the market. Finally, managers need to understand the suppliers—how to form business relationships with them, or how suppliers deliver their goods. Together, customers, competitors, and suppliers are the main elements of the industry environment. This is the topic of this chapter.

## 3.2 Understanding and adapting to industry environment

What industry are you in? On the surface, the question seems very simple, but it is not that simple in real life. Porsche and Ford are both in the car industry. But an increase in the price of Porsche Cayenne cars does not mean more sales of the Ford Focus. The customers for the Porsche Cayenne and for the Ford Focus are different groups of people. The skills and resources necessary to produce a Porsche Cayenne car are different from those needed to produce a Ford Focus. The nature of advertising, product development, and pricing policies are different for the two products. Indeed, using the word 'industry' may be unhelpful because it is very broad. A focus on a broad industry may lead to an inaccurate understanding of the market and the nature of competition: it does not tell you who your competitors are and which are the key competing products for your firm. You need to identify your precise market, which can be achieved by conducting a 'market segmentation analysis' and 'strategic group analysis'.

### 3.2.1 Market segmentation analysis

When identifying the market, the firm should—above all—identify the customers who buy the firm's product or service. For instance, luxury cars have very different customers compared with other types of cars. But even within the luxury car segment, there may be big differences between customers for super luxury cars with a price of US$100,000 and luxury cars with a price of less than US$60,000. Several simple questions can help firms to understand better the markets they serve.

'Market segmentation analysis' aims to identify similarities and differences between groups of people who buy and use your firm's goods and services. To aid market identification, firms can ask questions such as:

- Which other products with similar perceived attributes do my (current) customers rate as highly as mine?
- How price-sensitive are my customers? How much can we increase the price of our goods without losing customers to another firm?
- How far will my (current) customers travel to buy this or that alternative?
- Why do customers buy the product, and what is its value to them?
- How should it best be produced and distributed, and at what cost? That is, does it cost more than the value it creates for customers?
- Who is willing to purchase the good or service?

Such a long list may be confusing, so Doyle (1997) suggested that strategists should concentrate on three questions:

- Customer segmentation. Which customer segments are to be served by the strategy?
- Customer needs. What is the range of customer needs to be met?
- Technology. Which technologies are required in order to pursue customers?

Doyle argued that a focus on these three points helps to identify the relevant market in a way which is relevant to developing strategy. For instance, personal care products could be divided according to customer needs: oral care, grooming, infant hygiene, feminine hygiene, or senior hygiene—all of these would present separate markets for companies.

An added difficulty in global business strategy is that your competitors and customers may differ between countries. So, as part of a market segmentation analysis, a multinational firm may try to identify its main competition by listing all of its main product categories and all of its main geographical markets. For example, Unilever has three principal product categories—foods, personal care, and fabric care—and operates in three main geographical areas—the Americas, Europe, and Asia Pacific–Africa. In most of these product groups and most geographical areas, Unilever's main competitor is the US firm Procter & Gamble (makers of Folgers Coffee, Pampers diapers, and Tide laundry detergent). In order to identify the firm's other important international competitors, Unilever could scrutinize each product group (e.g., personal care products according to oral care, grooming, etc.) and list the main competitors by geographical region. It could ask simple questions, like 'Who is our key competitor for oral care in Europe, in the Americas, in Asia Pacific–Africa?' (MacMillan et al. 2003). Such questions could help the firm gain a picture of its global competitive position in the broader industry.

## KEY CONCEPT

Market segmentation analysis is about identifying similarities and differences between groups of people who buy and use your goods and services.

## 3.2.2 Strategic group analysis

Market segmentation analysis focuses on understanding customers. But it is not always the perceptions of customers that define the market. Sometimes, markets may be defined by the long history of the industry or by the requirements of technology used to manufacture goods. For example, the Japanese steel industry is divided into two main groups: the integrated steel mills and the 'mini-mills', despite the fact that they may share the same customers. The two groups are distinct because of the use of technology: integrated mills use basic-oxygen furnaces and mini-mills use electric-arc furnaces, which require very different inputs in the production of steel. Furthermore, the two groups have been shaped by different histories, different government policies towards them (as Japan's government supported integrated mills), and different economic forces (integrated mills require larger production capacities to become profitable due to the steel-melting technology used) (Nair and Kotha 2001).

The Japanese steel industry or the global car industry are examples of industries divided into two or more strategic groups. A strategic group is defined as 'a group of firms within the same industry making similar decisions in key areas' (Porter 1980: 129). Strategic group analysis aims to identify firms with similar strategies or competing on similar bases. Such an analysis helps in understanding who your main competitors are and what strategies your main competitors are likely to pursue. For example, Audi and BMW concentrate on competing against each another in the global luxury car market, while Fiat and Renault mainly compete against each other in the European small car market (see Exhibit 3.1). Neither strategic group pays much attention to what the other is doing because, from a supply point of view, there is little competition between companies in different strategic groups. Even within the luxury car market, one can distinguish two distinctive strategic groups: 'luxury cars' that often cost less than US$60,000 (e.g., Audi, BMW) and 'super luxury cars' that often cost more than US$100,000 (e.g., Ferrari, Porsche).

**Exhibit 3.1** Strategic groups in the global car industry

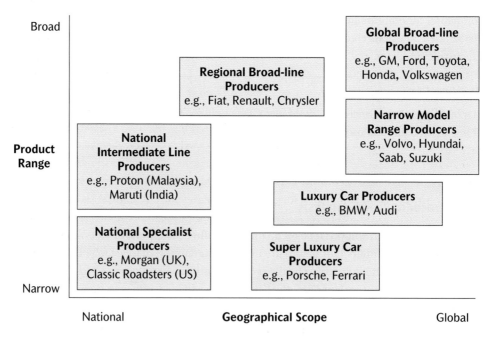

*Source:* Adapted from R. M. Grant (2005), *Contemporary Strategy Analysis,* 5th edn (Malden, MA: Blackwell), 125. Reprinted with permission of John Wiley & Sons.

It has been shown that strategic groups differ in profitability (Short et al. 2007; Fang and Lie 2006). For instance, Japanese integrated steel mills were more profitable than mini-mills in the 1980–7 period but less profitable after 1987 (Nair and Kotha 2001). Strategic group analysis can therefore help us understand the nature of competition and profitability within an industry subgroup; this gives managers better information about where to invest or what type of strategic action to expect from competitors (see McGee and Thomas 1986).

There are no easy prescriptions as to how to identify a strategic group within an industry. As we said earlier, strategic groups are sometimes created because customers perceive certain types of product as distinct, or they can be created as a result of different industry histories, government intervention, or different use of technology. A good predictor of strategic groups is 'mobility barriers', barriers which prevent other firms entering the strategic group and threatening the existing members (McGee and Segal-Horn 1990). In the case of Japanese steel, the key mobility barrier is expensive core-melting technology, which prevents steel firms from switching groups. In the case of the global car industry, the major mobility barriers are brands and specialist skills.

A key problem is that the boundaries between strategic groups can be blurred: sometimes, a multinational firm can be unique and may not easily fit into any strategic group. Mobility barriers are not always very tight, while the external business environment may change (e.g., technology change). The objective criteria cannot always tell us what constitutes a strategic group. Therefore, the most important determinants of strategic groups are perceptions by the senior managers in the industry. Research shows that managers like to partition the external business environment in order to cope with the demands of an uncertain globalizing world where you cannot follow developments in every conceivable market. Therefore, managers create mental pictures of where the boundaries of strategic groups lie, and these imagined boundaries are often shared with managers of other firms in the same strategic group (Peteraf and Shanley 1997; Greve 1998).

One problem with creating and using mental pictures of strategic groups is that this may lead to 'strategic myopia', a human tendency to reject unfamiliar or negative information. This threat is especially present when industries become more international, while the managers' mental picture of the boundaries of their industry remains rooted in national strategic groups. For instance, Scottish knitwear manufacturers did not recognize Japanese or Italian knitwear firms as competitors for a long time, despite the obvious similarities of the foreign products, as managers had always focused on their domestic competition. A rigid focus on a strategic group reduces opportunities for cooperation with firms outside the strategic group and makes firms vulnerable to surprise competitive attacks from outside the group (Peteraf and Shanley 1997).

## KEY CONCEPT

Strategic group analysis is about identifying firms with similar strategies or those competing on similar bases.

- Economies of scale exist in terms of providing high-level customer service, and Amazon.com has been building distribution capacity ahead of expected demand. (+)

- Differentiation plays an important role thanks to Amazon.com's ability to use technology and thanks to its strong brand image. (+)

- Amazon.com developed proprietary software such as its patented '1-Click®' system (Amazon.com sued its rival, BarnesandNoble.com, in court for using a similar system). (+)

- Amazon.com makes intensive use of technology and very specialized skills. (+)

**Power of buyers**

- Buyer information is high as buyers can easily compare prices on the Internet. (−)

- Buyers have low switching costs when shopping on the Internet. (−)

- Amazon.com focuses on value-added activities aimed at reducing the buyer's propensity to switch. Combined with a strong brand, this has increased the loyalty of Amazon.com customers, resulting in very high repeat purchasing rates. (+)

- Improved customer services reduce customer switching to rivals; Amazon.com uses information on prior purchases to predict or prompt additional purchases. (+)

**Power of suppliers**

- For a long time, Amazon.com's book supplies came from only three vendors; while switching costs in e-commerce are relatively low, switching from one of the suppliers would be costly due to the volumes required. (−)

- There is little differentiation in terms of products, so there is limited power of suppliers in terms of the uniqueness of the product. With the growing range of products offered by Amazon.com, the power of the suppliers has diminished. (+)

- The threat of vertical integration is high due to the low capital requirements for traditional firms. (−)

**Threat of substitutes**

- With very low switching costs, buyers can easily shop elsewhere. (−)

- Amazon.com has mitigated the threat of substitutes by offering new products such as CDs, toys, and gifts. It also provides an easy-to-use shopping guide for finding anything for sale online, so one can continue shopping without leaving the Amazon.com website. (+)

- Amazon.com uses information on customer buying habits to recommend other products that the customer might enjoy which can be bought from its website. (+)

*Source:* M. Porter (2001), 'Strategy and the Internet', *Harvard Business Review* 79(3): 63–78; D. Street and G. J. Stockport (2000), 'Amazon.com: from startup to the new millennium—teaching note', Case Study at the Graduate School of Business, University of Cape Town; J. G. Frynas (2002), 'The limits of globalization: legal and political issues in e-commerce', *Management Decision* 40(9): 871–80.

Like PEST analysis in Chapter 2, the Five Forces Model can be used to understand the industry environment within one country, one geographical region, or the entire world. But the competitive forces may be very different in countries and regions, so an international manager may be advised to conduct several Five Forces analyses for different countries or regions and then compare the results. It is also very important that the Five Forces are analysed for a specific market segment or similar market segments or even a specific project, not for an entire industry (Grundy 2006). It would make little sense for Ford or Volkswagen to analyse the Five Forces for the entire car industry because the great number of industry factors would be of little use to managers. On the other hand, a car company might find it useful to analyse a specific market, for example, super luxury cars. The following sections discuss the Five Forces in more detail.

---

**KEY CONCEPT**

The Five Forces Model assumes that industry attractiveness and the firm's competitive position in an industry are influenced by five competitive forces: the entry of new competitors; the threat of substitutes; the bargaining power of buyers; the bargaining power of suppliers; and the rivalry amongst existing competitors. The model can be used to analyse a firm's competitive position in a specific market segment or similar market segments.

---

### 3.3.1 Barriers to entry

Barriers to entry are obstacles which potential newcomers would encounter when entering the market. If there are many barriers to entry, it is less likely that the firm will face new competitors. New entrants could lead to lower sales for the firm, they could force the firm to lower prices, or they could force the firm to spend more money on innovation or new distribution channels. As a result, new entrants could mean lower profits for the established firm, so high barriers to entry help to maintain the firm's profitability. Studies by Bain (1956) and Mann (1966) have shown that profitability is greater in industries with higher entry barriers. There are several different types of barrier to entry, which are discussed below.

#### Capital requirements

Entry into a new industry requires a firm to have resources to invest in, for example, inventories, advertising, and equipment. The capital requirements of entering a new industry vary between industries. Entry into some markets such as large passenger planes is so prohibitive that it is unlikely that Airbus or Boeing will face any new competitors in the foreseeable future. In other markets such as Internet food delivery the costs are much lower and market entry is much more realistic. But the general rule applies: the higher the capital requirements in an industry, the less likely is the entry of new competitors.

However, the barrier of capital requirements can be overcome by new entrants. Research by George Yip (1982) has shown that new entrants can overcome entry barriers. Large multinational firms can use resources from established businesses to fund market entry protection from competition (Deephouse 1999). Similarly, when switching costs are high for the buyer, the firm will also be protected to some extent. Conversely, when products are perceived as 'commodities' (i.e., they are regarded as virtually the same), price wars may occur. Even multinational firms with a strong brand name may face intense price competition because their products are seen as commodities (e.g., films made by Kodak and Fuji).

### Industry growth

When industry growth is high, firms can expand by winning new customers. When industry growth is slow, firms are under more pressure to fight over the existing customers of their competitors, which increases rivalry. A good predictor of industry growth is the Product Life Cycle Model (see section 3.5).

### Fixed costs and storage costs

If the firm's fixed costs are high as a proportion of total costs (e.g., aluminium production), or if the product is perishable (and therefore the storage costs are high, e.g., fresh prawns), firms may be tempted to cut prices. For a firm with high fixed costs, it would be expensive to reduce production, so there is a greater pressure to maintain or increase production even if prices decrease. For a firm with high storage costs, products lose value very quickly, so it may be better to sell them cheaply rather than not selling them at all. As a result, both high fixed costs and high storage costs lead to more intense price rivalry.

### Exit barriers

Barriers to exit are obstacles which established firms would encounter when leaving the market. If there are many exit barriers, it is less likely that an established firm will leave the market, which may result in more intense rivalry. Exit barriers can include: the presence of specialized assets (assets which are of little value outside the particular business or location); fixed costs of exit (e.g., the cost of laying off staff); government restrictions (e.g., environmental clean-up costs); or emotional barriers (e.g., management loyalty to a firm's traditional line of business). Exit barriers can also have an effect on entry into the industry. When exit costs are high, firms will be more cautious about entry into the market, especially if the probability of success is low or uncertain (Rosenbaum and Lamort 1992).

### Excess capacity

Excess capacity may result from a fall of demand during a recession, over-investment, or when production capacity in an industry comes in large increments (e.g., bulk chemicals). When faced with over-capacity, firms may be tempted to cut prices (Baden-Fuller 1990).

## 3.4 Criticisms of the Five Forces Model

Porter's Five Forces Model has come under criticism. It has been said, for example, that the model cannot help firms cope with the fast-changing business environment; that it cannot be used for analysing the position of charitable organizations or government bodies; and that it disregards the importance of human resource management (Lynch 2000: 131). Two key criticisms relate to the 'static' nature of the model and to the ability of firms to earn profits.

### 3.4.1 Static v. dynamic competition

The Five Forces Model has been criticized for being too 'static', leading managers to make wrong assumptions about the business environment. Managers are expected to decide on their firm's strategy based on an analysis of the Five Forces, assuming that these normally change slowly. But it has been said that competition is not 'static' but 'dynamic': the industry environment is constantly changing, so firms cannot make strategic choices by assuming that the threats of entry will not grow or that no new substitutes will be developed.

Some authors even speak of 'hyper-competitive behaviour' today: 'the process of continuously generating new competitive advantages and destroying, obsoleting, or neutralizing the opponent's competitive advantage' (D'Aveni 1994: 217–18). This hyper-competition is said to be driven by globalization and to be greatest in industries that have moved into the global arena (Harvey et al. 2001). In industries with hyper-competition, it does not necessarily make sense for firms to concentrate on building up strength in specific sectors where higher profits can be made; a firm has constantly to improve and innovate, and cannot hide behind entry barriers or its bargaining power towards existing suppliers. This view would suggest that the Five Forces Model could be of only limited value to managers.

### 3.4.2 Industry profitability

Porter assumes that a firm's profitability depends on how attractive the industry is. If competition is intense in an industry, firms will earn low profits no matter how skilful the firm's managers are. But business research has suggested otherwise. Several studies have compared the relative significance of industry-specific influences and firm-specific influences on firm profitability, and discovered that only a small proportion of firms' profitability could be ascribed to the industry in which the firm operated (compare section 5.2.3). According to this research, firm profitability seemed to depend primarily on how skilful individual units of the firm were (Rumelt 1991; Mauri and Michaels 1998). By implication, an analysis of the Five Forces cannot provide a good guide to profitability.

### 3.4.3 Response to criticisms

Firm-specific, rather than industry-specific, influences on firm profitability are becoming more important in the global market (see Chapter 4). But research has suggested that in many industries, changes in barriers to entry (Masson and Shaanan 1982; 1987) or changes in seller concentration (Caves and Porter 1980) have been very slow. Therefore, when industry structure changes slowly, the industry's influence on the firm's profitability only changes very slowly.

Certainly, there are some highly visible industries where change is very fast (e.g., certain types of consumer electronics) but—for most industries—the industry environment does not change quickly. Brian Arthur (1996) has argued that firms usually have the ability to influence industry structure in the early stages of a technological wave. But once a specific product, process, or technology wins over the alternatives, the development of the industry becomes locked into a specific path of development and firms can do little to change the Five Forces. Examples here include Microsoft's Windows operating system, when the introduction of the product at an early stage led to an enduring industry structure. As a result of the early domination of the market by Microsoft, other firms could not challenge the superior bargaining power of the company and could not easily overcome the entry barriers in the market for operating systems (see closing case study). The Five Forces Model would have been of relatively little use to managers when computer operating systems were first introduced, but it is very useful to give an understanding of that market today.

Ultimately, whether you accept the above criticisms of the Five Forces Model depends on your point of view. What does it mean, for example, that an industry is 'static' or 'dynamic'? Porter recognized a long time ago that industries change, sometimes in fundamental ways which could not have been expected. Firms can also help to change the Five Forces in an industry; for example, a firm's innovations in marketing can raise brand identification and differentiate the product, which in turn will increase the firm's bargaining power.

## 3.5 Industry evolution

The Five Forces and market conditions change over time as a result of industry evolution, which has important consequences for the formulation of strategy. Industry evolution can make an industry more or less attractive as an investment opportunity, and it often forces firms to adjust their strategies. Industry evolution is only important for strategy if it changes the underlying Five Forces. If these are not modified, the firm needs to change only some day-to-day practices, but the strategy can remain the same. The easiest way to analyse industry evolution is by asking the question: are there any changes occurring in the industry that will affect any element of the Five Forces Model? For instance, do any changes imply a change in entry barriers or a change in the bargaining power of suppliers? If this question is asked systematically for each of the Five Forces and the causes underlying industry change, the most significant issues will emerge (Porter 1980).

The concept of the Product Life Cycle is useful in understanding the course of industry evolution. The basic idea of this cycle is that every product evolves through a cycle of roughly four stages—introduction, growth, maturity, and decline—which correspond to the rate of growth of industry sales. There are few sales in the introduction stage: customers may be reluctant to buy a new product, and sales prices for newly developed products are initially high. Once buyers learn to appreciate the value of a product, sales increase rapidly and prices decline as a result of larger production runs and new competition. After a period of time, the market becomes saturated and rapid growth comes to an end; as demand for a product slows down, firms are under more pressure to fight over the existing customers and rivalry increases. Eventually, demand for a product declines as substitute products emerge (Levitt 1965).

The Product Life Cycle has major implications for international strategies of firms as industry change may force firms to relocate parts of their business to other countries. Vernon (1966) first argued that advanced countries, which have the necessary financial, technological, and human resources to innovate, and high wages and plenty of disposable income to spend on new products, are the first to introduce new products. However, the innovating country tends to lose its exports initially to other developed countries and subsequently to less developed countries, and eventually could become an importer of these products. According to Vernon, many products go through an international life cycle, during which the United States (and nowadays Japan or other developed countries) is initially an exporter, then loses its export markets, and finally could become an importer of the product. Many industrial products such as televisions have conformed to this pattern (see Exhibit 3.4). Advocates of this International Product Life Cycle (IPLC) model argue that, although there are certainly exceptions, new products tend to evolve along similar international paths, creating more or less predictably five stages or phases (Vernon 1966; Wells 1968; Jacobs et al. 1997). There are five phases of the IPLC model (see Exhibit 3.5).

## Exhibit 3.4 The International Product Life Cycle (IPLC) and TV manufacturing

Electronic television broadcasting began in Britain and Germany in 1936. In 1939, the first American TV sets went on sale. The United States emerged as the unrivalled innovating country. By 1950, there were only 344,000 British homes with a TV set, but the annual sales of TV sets in the United States reached over 7 million. The American TV sets were designed for the US market but some production was exported, mainly to Europe.

Until 1962, the United States was self-sufficient in TV production. In 1962, the first Japanese black-and-white TV sets were imported into the United States; the first colour TV sets were imported in 1967. From 1970, foreign imports rose quickly, despite import restrictions by the US government. By 1982, 68% of black-and-white TV sets and 13% of colour TV sets sold in the United States were imported. In 1965, when US output was almost 3 million colour TVs, Japan produced less than 100,000. By 1980, Japan produced over 10 million colour TVs per year.

As the product matured, TV production moved from developed to developing countries. In the 1970s, the remaining American TV manufacturers relocated production activities to Mexico and Far East Asia, including Korea and Taiwan. But the importance of Japanese TV production also began to decline soon, as Japanese firms relocated some production activities to Korea and Taiwan to obtain lower labour costs. Until 1978, most US imports came from Japan; thereafter, imports from developing countries such as Korea exceeded Japanese imports.

In the last twenty years, countries such as Korea and Taiwan have become more developed themselves and production has once again been relocated, this time to China and other developing countries. Today, China is the world's largest supplier of TV sets, with an annual production of over 90 million units in 2008.

The shift of TV manufacturing from the United States to Japan and other Asian countries was accompanied by major shifts in the ownership of the leading TV manufacturing firms. As early as 1971, five of the ten largest consumer electronics producers in the world were Japanese, led by Matsushita. In 1978, the world's ten largest manufacturers of colour TV sets were as follows:

| Company | Market share (%) |
| --- | --- |
| Matsushita (Japanese) | 12.5 |
| Philips (Dutch) | 12.1 |
| RCA (US) | 6.9 |
| Zenith (US) | 6.8 |
| Sanyo (Japanese) | 6.8 |
| Sony (Japanese) | 5.9 |
| Toshiba (Japanese) | 5.2 |
| Grundig (German) | 4.8 |
| Hitachi (Japanese) | 4.3 |
| GTE-Sylvania (US) | 4.2 |

Since then, US-owned manufacturers of TVs have vanished completely. Their number declined from sixteen in 1966 to three by 1980; later, all three remaining firms disappeared. The last surviving American firm was Zenith, an early pioneer of radio and TV technology. In November 1999, Zenith became a wholly-owned subsidiary of a South Korean firm, LG Electronics.

*Source: International Competitiveness in Electronics* (1983) (Washington, DC: US Congress, Office of Technology Assessment, OTA–ISC–200, November), ch. 4, pp. 107–62; P. Dicken (1998), *Global Shift: Transforming the World Economy*, 3rd edn (London: Sage); various online resources.

### 3.5.1 The five phases of the International Product Life Cycle (IPLC)

**Phase 1: Introduction in the Home Market** According to the IPLC Model, most new products are first introduced in rich developed countries. This is because, it is argued, firms located in such countries have more capability to innovate than firms in poor developing countries. In addition, people in developed countries have more money to spend on newer products than people in developing countries. In this phase, the total production of the new product takes place in the country of origin (often the US) because the speed of adjusting the product to the home market demand is very important for the success of the new product.

This stage is characterized by high unit production costs, but these costs are less significant because the demand for innovative products is price inelastic (demand does not vary with

**Exhibit 3.5** The International Product Life Cycle (IPLC)

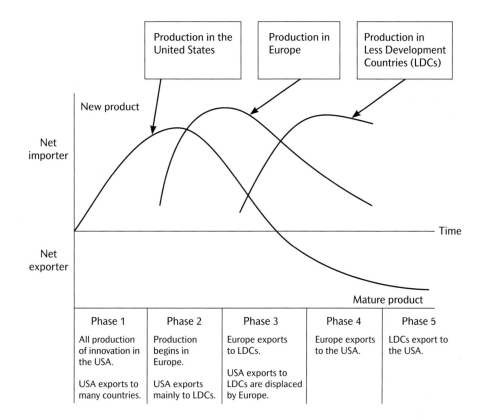

*Source:* L. T. Wells, Jr. (1968), 'A product life cycle for international trade?' *Journal of Marketing*, 32 (July): 1–6. Reprinted with permission of *Journal of Marketing*, published by the American Marketing Association.

price) at this phase. The price is inelastic when, with all other factors held constant, the change in the quantity demanded to a change in price is very small or nonexistent. Initially, the new product goes through a slow sales growth and profits are nonexistent because of the heavy expenses in production and marketing. At some point, the product becomes well-known in the home market, and customers from other developed and high-income countries start buying the product. This leads to the second phase.

**Phase 2: Export to developed countries** The market for the product widens as demand develops in other high-income countries. The production of the product becomes fairly standard, and the widening of the market makes economies of scale possible. As a result, price decreases. This causes the market for the product to widen further, as customers in low- and medium-income countries are able to afford the new product. As the production of the product becomes standard, firms in other developed countries imitate the product and start production in their own countries.

**Phase 3: Export by developed countries to developing countries**  The low price attracts more customers from developing countries. As the demand for the product increases in developing countries, late movers from developed countries begin to export and even produce the new product in developing countries.

**Phase 4: Export by developed countries to the home country**  Eventually, the increasing international distribution of the product, and the relatively lower costs of production, will result in developed countries exporting back to the country where the product was originally introduced.

**Phase 5: Export by developing countries to developed countries**  At this stage, demand for the product declines in the home market and other developed countries as customers demand new products. The standardization of the production process makes it possible to produce the product in developing countries. Because of the cost advantage developing countries have over developed countries due to cheap labour costs, production moves to developing countries. Finally, the country in which the product was first introduced and produced becomes the importer of the product.

---

### KEY CONCEPT

The concept of the 'Product Life Cycle' suggests that every basic product evolves through a cycle of roughly four stages—introduction, growth, maturity, and decline—which correspond to the rate of growth of industry sales. The concept of the 'International Product Life Cycle' suggests that many products go through an international life cycle, during which a developed country is initially an exporter (when innovation is central to product success), then loses its export markets, and finally could become an importer of the product from developing countries (when production costs become central to product success).

---

### 3.5.2 Criticisms of the IPLC model

The IPLC model has helped explain the flows of foreign direct investment and international trade for many different products as diverse as televisions and ships. However, there are several criticisms of the model.

#### Duration of life cycles

The duration of a life cycle varies widely between industries, and the shift from one stage to the next stage may not always be clear. Furthermore, industry growth does not always seem to go through all the stages of the model. Sometimes, industry growth resumes after a period of decline (e.g., in the growth of the motorcycle and bicycle industries). So, the value of the IPLC model as a planning tool for strategists is limited (Porter 1980).

#### Applicability of the model in the global economy

The applicability of the model to explain the behaviour of multinational firms in the current global business environment is questionable. As speedy introduction of new products is often important in the global economy, various industries may skip the slow takeoff of the introductory stage altogether (Porter 1980). As discussed in Chapter 2, the current global business environment allows multinational firms to introduce their new products simultaneously in different countries. The introduction of new generation mobile phones or new computer software is launched simultaneously in the home market, in other developed countries, and in developing countries. For example, on 30 January 2007, Microsoft launched the company's new product, Windows Vista, across the world. While Windows Vista was produced in the United States, it was available the same day in more than seventy countries in nineteen languages, for immediate purchase from more than 39,000 retail outlets and online. Most of the first customers who were able to purchase the new product at commercial outlets were in Japan, as computer shops in Tokyo's technology-centred Akihabara district opened their doors at midnight to sell the new product. By the end of 2007, Windows Vista was available in almost 100 different languages. Therefore, if products no longer move from the innovating country to other developed countries and then to developing countries, the model becomes of more limited use.

### Importance of innovation

The IPLC model focuses on entirely new innovations or products, and does not include products that emerge from a continual process of technological innovation. Even with new innovations and products, firms in developing countries could imitate the products innovated in developed countries very quickly (Grossman and Helpman 1991). When imitation is possible, quick, and cost-effective, firms in other developed countries and in developing countries could charge less than the original innovators, and thus capture the home market before innovators from developed countries start exporting.

### Non-standard industrial products

The IPLC model deals with standard products, and may not explain the evolution of certain non-standard industrial products. Luxury products may not follow the IPLC, because demand for them depends on their being associated with rich developed countries. For example, the demand for French perfume or Italian leather depends on being associated with France or Italy. As the price of luxury goods is of little concern to rich customers, it is not so important for production to be relocated to developing countries. Similarly, IPLC may not apply to products which require specialized knowledge to link present output with the training of technical labour and the development of the next generation of technology. For example, medical equipment is still mostly produced in major developed countries. Production is not generally transferred to developing countries because these countries may not have the skills and organization to produce them. Production may also depend on physical proximity to the research centres, where constant improvements are made.

## 3.6 Anticipating the future

Understanding industry evolution and anticipating future change is crucial, as the cost of changing strategy increases as the need for change becomes more obvious (Porter 1980). For instance, if you are aware that a new technology may become widespread, your firm may be able to reap major profits by introducing the technology before its rivals. There are two generic techniques for learning about the future business environment: forecasting and scenario analysis.

### 3.6.1 Forecasting

Forecasts are educated assumptions about future trends and events such as future demand for specific products, future changes in currency exchange rates, or future shifts in technology. They may be used by firms in different ways. A firm may, for instance, use monthly sales forecasts to fine-tune the distribution of products to its warehouses. We are not interested in 'operational forecasts' of this type here but rather 'strategic' forecasts—forecasts used to understand the future changes in the industry environment which may require a change in the firm's use of resources.

Major surveys of the world's largest multinational firms have shown that the most widely used form of forecasting is 'trend extrapolation' (Klein and Linneman 1984; Reger 2001). On the most basic level, trend extrapolation is the extension of present trends into the future. Trend extrapolation typically uses past quantitative data to predict future economic trends. It can also help managers understand trend patterns—for instance, that sales have been on average declining or increasing over a period of time, or that sales are cyclical (i.e., they repeatedly move up and down, according to some pattern). Making forecasts based on trend extrapolation has become relatively easy, even for small firms: managers can use relatively cheap and user-friendly computer software to analyse a firm's data.

Trend extrapolation can aid strategic decisions about future investments or product development. For instance, forecasts have shown that the demand for chilled drinks is seasonal; above all, warm weather helps to push up sales. Using information about seasonal trends, Bass plc has attempted to smooth out the highs and lows of customer demand for beverages by introducing different versions of its Hooper's Hooch at different times of the year in limited editions: Smooch on Valentine's Day or Ho Ho Hooch at Christmas.

But trend extrapolation has weaknesses: it implicitly assumes that historical relationships will continue into the future, without examining causal relationships between the different factors. Historical trends depend on many different factors: change in one factor could markedly alter the future direction of the trend. Trend extrapolation is of little use in business environments which are prone to a high degree of uncertainty (e.g., the oil industry) or where little historical data exists (e.g., new products, such as the iPad).

The Delphi survey is an example of a forecasting technique, which can help forecast the future in uncertain business environments or where new innovations may emerge (Duboff 2007; Nielsen and Thangadurai 2007). The basic idea of a Delphi survey is to ask the opinion of experts (typically 5–20) on the future of a specific subject (e.g., new technical innovation, specific product market or risk assessment for a country). Questionnaires are sent out to the chosen experts with specific questions, and the returned questionnaires are analysed. At the second stage, a new, refined questionnaire is sent out to the experts, which takes into consideration the previously collected expert opinions about the future; after the experts have filled in the second questionnaire, the results are once again analysed. A Delphi survey consists of at least two stages, but it can have many more, especially if the experts disagree.

Delphi surveys can be very useful to international managers by engaging experts with different perspectives from different countries, learning about new global markets and forecasting the future 'big questions' for global business (Nielsen and Thangadurai 2007). For example, a Delphi study sponsored by four TV and semiconductor manufacturing companies in the 1990s (AT&T, Thomson, Philips, and Zenith), forecasted that HDTV (high-definition television) will be a niche product and will diffuse more slowly than originally expected, partly due to the lack of TV programming. Thanks to the study, the companies avoided making unnecessary early investments in this market (Gupta et al. 1999).

However, Delphi surveys normally do not consider the causes of new trends and interrelationships among new trends, and they normally do not estimate the various alternative futures that may develop. An alternative technique for multinational firms is the so-called scenario analysis.

---

### KEY CONCEPT

Forecasts are educated assumptions about future trends and events such as future demand for specific products, future changes in currency exchange rates, or future shifts in technology. 'Strategic forecasts' are used to understand the future changes in the industry environment which may require a change in the firm's use of resources.

---

### 3.6.2 Scenario analysis

Herman Kahn and A. J. Weiner, who pioneered the use of scenario analysis, defined a scenario as 'a hypothetical sequence of events constructed for the purpose of focusing attention on causal processes and decision points'. Scenarios explore possible future events by looking at particular causes and seek to understand and explain why certain events might or might not occur. Scenario analysis is very different from forecasting techniques, as it does not try to predict what will actually happen. Rather, scenario analysis tries to identify several possible futures (typically, two to four different scenarios), each of which is plausible but not assured (see Exhibit 3.6). The value of scenarios lies in increasing awareness of possibilities and exploring 'what if' questions. By offering different forecasts and offering them in the form of a narrative/description, scenarios provide managers with a better understanding of the relationships between different factors and assumptions underlying different forecasts. Scenario analysis recognizes the shortcomings of most forecasts by considering a number of different and plausible assumptions about the future, rather than a single assumption which may prove wrong (Schnaars 1987; Verity 2003).

The use of scenarios increased markedly after the oil crisis of 1973, when the world economy was disrupted by an Arab oil embargo. Using scenario planning from the late 1960s, managers at Royal Dutch/Shell were able to anticipate major disruptions in the global oil

Global strategic analysis

**Exhibit 3.6** Main difference between a forecast and a scenario analysis

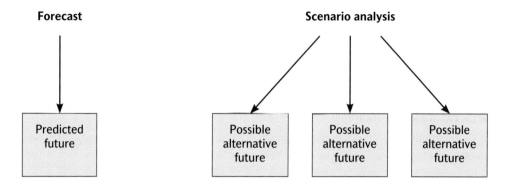

supplies in the 1970s, although scenario analysis did not specify in which year a crisis would happen. As a result of using scenarios, Shell was much better prepared to deal with the 1973 oil crisis than its international competitors, and the company improved its competitive position in the oil industry during the crisis (Wack 1985*a*; 1985*b*). Shell has continued to apply the technique with great success using three different types of scenario analysis: 'global scenarios' (identifying global trends and informing global strategies); 'focused scenarios' (identifying issues relevant to specific countries or specific business strategies); and 'project scenarios' (identifying issues relevant to a specific project) (Cornelius et al. 2005). Multinational firms that have used scenario planning included 3M, British Airways, and Hewlett Packard.

In comparison with most forecasting techniques such as trend extrapolation, scenario analysis is able to look into the long-term prospects of an industry. Trend extrapolation based on historical data typically looks five years ahead; more frequently, forecasts are made for much shorter periods, such as monthly or quarterly forecasts. Such studies fail to assist strategic decision-makers in industries, where investments are made with much longer investment horizons, such as the oil and gas industry, where investments may take longer than five years to pay off. Shell's scenarios allowed managers to look fifteen years ahead and more. However, the main problem of scenario analysis is that the further you look into the future, the more unreliable the scenarios become.

### KEY CONCEPT

Scenarios are hypothetical sequences of events constructed for the purpose of focusing attention on causal processes and decision points. Scenarios explore possible future events by looking at particular causes and seek to understand and explain why certain future events might or might not occur. Scenario analysis does not forecast what will actually happen—it identifies several possible alternative futures.

### 3.6.3 **Anticipating the future and globalization**

Globalization makes it difficult to anticipate future change, in that it is difficult to anticipate changes in distant markets from central company headquarters. This challenge is greatest when it comes to anticipating uncertain events such as the development of new technologies. Using Internet sources or merely interviewing foreign managers, may not always allow a firm to pick up 'weak signals' of important future trends. In order to address this problem, multinational firms can use foreign subsidiaries, foreign partners, or scouts in a foreign market to help anticipate the future.

In technology forecasting, the most effective forecasting can be achieved when it is performed by the firm's research centres around the world, which collect information on the spot. Cheaper alternatives to establishing research centres include international 'listening posts' or 'technology scouts'. For example, the German pharmaceutical firm, Bayer, employed over a dozen technology scouts in addition to its research centres in Europe and elsewhere: two in Japan, six in the United States, and six in Europe; their task was to detect new research results, new technologies, or partners worldwide (Reger 2001).

At the same time, it is important that central company headquarters have an overview of different forecasts or scenarios, and that international information gathering activities are fed into strategic decision-making at the company's headquarters. It makes no sense for a company to have technology scouts around the world if top management is unable to act on the information which scouts provide. In order to coordinate forecasting activities across its worldwide subsidiaries, Bayer formed a central forecasting group, which resides in the strategic analysis department.

## 3.7 **Summary**

This chapter has demonstrated that it is important to understand how changes in the external industry environment affect or do not affect a firm. The first step is to identify your precise market, because a focus on a broad industry may lead to an inaccurate understanding of the market and the nature of competition. In order to identify the precise market, firms can conduct a market segmentation analysis and a strategic group analysis.

A more comprehensive understanding of an industry can be gained through an analysis of its underlying economic and technical characteristics. Michael Porter suggested that managers should understand the rules of competition in their industry so that they become aware both of industry attractiveness and of their firm's own competitive position within the industry. In order to uncover these underlying rules, Porter suggested that managers should understand the five competitive forces in their industry: the entry of new competitors; the threat of substitutes; the bargaining power of buyers; the bargaining power of suppliers; and the rivalry amongst existing competitors.

The Five Forces and market conditions change over time as a result of industry evolution, so managers need to understand the causes underlying industry change. The concept of the

Product Life Cycle can help to understand industry evolution. An extension of the concept, known as the International Product Life Cycle Model (IPLC), helps explain why industry change may force firms to relocate parts of their business to other countries. The model suggests that advanced countries are the first to introduce new products; then, the innovating country tends to lose its exports initially to other developed countries and subsequently to less-developed countries; eventually, the innovating country may cease producing a specific product.

Ultimately, the strategic decision-maker would like to know what could happen to his/her industry in the future. Understanding industry evolution and anticipating future change is crucial, since the cost of changing strategy increases as the need for change becomes more obvious. Multinational firms can use 'strategic' forecasts (forecasts used to understand the future changes in the industry environment which may require a change in the firm's use of resources) or scenarios (hypothetical sequences of events constructed in order to explore possible alternative futures). A thorough understanding of the industry environment and its likely future should help the strategic decision-maker develop more appropriate strategies.

## Key readings

- On strategic group analysis, see McGee and Thomas (1986); and J. Rafferty (2008), *Exploring Strategic Groups* (Milton Keynes: Europrime Publishing).

- On the Five Forces Model and industry evolution, see Porter (1980); and Grundy (2006).

- On the International Product Life Cycle, see Jacobs et al. (1997).

- On scenario planning, see Verity (2003).

## Discussion questions

**1.** What is the difference between market segmentation analysis and strategic group analysis? How can strategic group analysis help managers in formulating a firm's strategy?

**2.** Take an industry of your choice. Conduct a Five Forces analysis of that industry. What are the key forces at work in that industry? What are the key drivers for change?

**3.** What problems do managers face in conducting a global Five Forces analysis?

**4.** To what extent does the IPLC model help or hinder our understanding of how an industry evolves?

**5.** Give five examples of situations when it would be suitable for a firm to use trend extrapolation to forecast its global industry environment, and five examples of when it would be suitable to use scenario planning.

## Closing case study The rise of Linux—the battle for the operating system market

The operating system (OS) is the master control program that runs your computer. It is usually the first program loaded when you switch on your computer. The OS usually controls only one computer, but it can also control groups of computers or even entire local area networks. The global OS market is dominated by Microsoft Windows, which was first introduced in 1983, and most computers today run on a Microsoft-produced OS such as Windows XP or Windows Vista. By the early 1990s, Microsoft was in an ideal global position:

- Microsoft suppliers had insignificant bargaining power (if you count, for instance, firms which supplied hardware on which Windows was developed and computer engineers who supplied their skills).

- There were very few competing or substitute products, such as Macintosh OS (which did not run on PCs) or Unix OS for networks.

- Entry barriers were very high: the development costs for a new widely available OS were enormous and Windows was protected through intellectual property rights. Due to early adoption of Windows in the entire market, the financial and psychological costs of switching to a different OS were enormous and a large number of companies in related sectors (from chip-maker, Intel, to software developers) developed products which worked in combination with Windows.

- Customers had little bargaining power, as most computers had Windows pre-installed on them. Average consumers only had the choice between Windows-operated computers or the much less common Macintosh.

But a new OS has challenged the dominant position of Windows: Linux. Linux was written by a Finnish graduate student called Linus Torvalds, who posted the first version of the OS on an Internet discussion group in August 1991. Torvalds invited other amateur programmers to suggest improvements to his OS, and by December 1991 he had already released the tenth Linux version. By May 1992, Linux was in its ninety-sixth edition.

The main difference between Windows and Linux was that the source code of Windows was a closely guarded secret, while Linux was 'open-source' (i.e., all the basic information on the OS was publicly available). Indeed, a key driving force for Torvalds and his colleagues was to create an OS that did not cost anything, in contrast to the expensive Microsoft system. Since Linux was open-source, amateur programmers around the world were able to continue its development, frequently by using the Internet and email to exchange technical details.

For several years, Linux was mainly used by a small group of computer enthusiasts, and there were barriers to its widespread adoption. There were only a few software applications which could run on Linux, and it was arduous to instal it on a computer. But then small commercial companies such as Red Hat and Caldera began to sell application software for Linux; the companies distributed copies of Linux free, but charged for additional applications and customer support services. Until the arrival of Linux, OS producers such as Microsoft, Novell, and Sun were protected from new competitors through high development costs and the intellectual property rights on their products. Since the introduction of Linux, new firms can enter the market with a low capital investment, since Linux is not protected through patents, and production costs such as plant and machinery account for only a very small part of the cost structure of Linux distributors. With the quick growth of Linux distributors such as Red Hat, Linux began to be used for running entire clusters of computers.

By the late 1990s, large firms and government departments began to replace Windows with Linux to save costs. At the same time, multinational computer firms such as IBM and Oracle started to invest in Linux as an alternative to Windows. In 1998, Oracle started offering Linux versions for its software. In 1999, IBM started participating in the development of Linux and the company declared that it would invest US$1 billion in Linux development. In November 2003, Novell—a Microsoft rival and the maker of the NetWare OS—announced the takeover of the German firm SuSE, one of the companies distributing Linux, for US$210 million.

Despite the success of Linux, Windows still dominates the global OS market today. But there are major differences between the desktop OS market (OS for individual computers) and the server OS market (OS for computer networks). According to research analysts, Windows had a market share of well over 90% within the desktop OS market at the end of 2009, compared with a Linux market share of only 1%. Within the server OS market, Windows only had a 41.6% market share, compared with a Linux market share of over 14.7% (see Exhibit B). Observers suggest that these figures greatly underestimate the use of Linux on computer servers. 'Market share' refers to the sales of new servers by companies such as IBM and Hewlett-Packard, while Linux has been installed on many old Windows servers. Linux may actually be used as operating system on as many as one-third of all servers.

There are several reasons why Linux was less successful in the desktop OS market. Individual customers found it cumbersome to instal Linux on their computers. Despite the introduction of new software applications such as OpenOffice (which competes with Microsoft Office) and Firefox (which competes with Microsoft Internet Explorer), some popular applications do not run on Linux. There are also high switching costs for individual customers who are accustomed to using Microsoft software; it takes time to familiarize yourself with a new OS and—if all your colleagues and friends use Windows applications—it makes sense to continue using the same software (e.g., when you want to swap text files written with Microsoft Office). But even if Linux were more user-friendly, Microsoft still has the advantage of a strong brand name, and it would require a gigantic marketing and sales effort to replace Windows with Linux. The perception that Windows is a superior product helps Microsoft

**Exhibit B**  Global market share for operating systems, fourth quarter 2009

| Desktop operating systems (%) | Server operating systems (%) |
| --- | --- |
| 92.4 Windows | 41.6 Windows |
| 5.2 Mac | 29.9 Unix |
| 1.0 Linux | 14.7 Linux |

*Source:* http://marketshare.hitslink.com and http://www.idc.com/.

to differentiate itself from Linux. Microsoft can spend hundreds of millions on marketing. Smaller Linux software companies such as Red Hat or Novell have limited resources to fight Microsoft.

Large companies and government agencies found it easier to replace Windows with Linux for their computer networks. Because they had a large number of computers, the switching costs per computer unit were much lower than for an individual user. The low cost was a key attraction, while—at the same time—Linux proved to have some technical advantages over Windows. While Windows frequently 'crashed' for no apparent reason, Linux is said to allow more stable operations, which was of greater importance for computer networks than for individual users. Since Linux is open-source, it also allows technicians to amend certain parts of the program or add new ones, so that upgrades can be easily completed without the involvement of Microsoft.

The low cost of Linux was also a key attraction for computer firms such as IBM. The development cost for Windows Vista was reportedly more than US$6 billion, so Microsoft needed to sell a vast number of copies to recover its investment. In comparison, the cost of developing Linux was very low, as many amateur programmers donated their time for free and many companies shared development costs. IBM's research and development costs for Linux-related systems were much lower than for Windows-run systems, and the company was able to reduce its dependence on Microsoft. By 2008, IBM had assigned over 600 IBM employees to work on Linux and other open source projects, all IBM servers supported the Linux operating system, and over 500 IBM software products ran on Linux. In 2008, IBM began a partnership with leading Linux software companies Novell and Red Hat to build and sell desktop PCs preloaded with Linux.

The domination of the OS market by Windows is likely to continue for some time. But Linux sales have benefited from the global economic recession, as the installation of Linux offered savings for cost-cutting companies. According to a 2009 forecast by the research analysts, IDC, Linux-related software spending is expected to triple from US$12.3 billion in 2008 to US$35.5 billion in 2013, with an average annual growth rate of 23.6%.

Microsoft is clearly worried about the threat from Linux. The company earns fewer revenues from Windows as a result of Linux and it even offered Windows for free to some companies in order to persuade them to discontinue using Linux. One major problem for Microsoft is that it does not simply face one rival (e.g., Novell, which in the 1990s was Microsoft's main rival in network OS), as there are many firms distributing and developing Linux. As James Allchin, the group vice president of Microsoft's Windows business, already observed many years ago: 'We're used to competing with products and companies. It's different than anything else we've dealt with before.'

*Source:* K. Subhadra and S. Dutta, 'Linux—gaining ground', case study at ICFAI Center for Management Research (ICMR), Hyderabad, India, 2003; R. Madapati and V. K. Thota, 'Linux vs Windows', case study at ICMR, Hyderabad, India, 2003; various articles and websites.

### Discussion questions

**1.** Outline briefly how the five forces in the OS market affected Microsoft before and after the introduction of Linux.

**2.** What can Microsoft do to counteract the threat from Linux?

# References

Arthur, W. B. (1996). 'Increasing returns and the new world of business', *Harvard Business Review* 74(4): 100–9.

Baden-Fuller, C. (ed.) (1990). *Strategic Management of Excess Capacity* (Oxford: Blackwell).

Bain, J. S. (1956). *Barriers to New Competition* (Cambridge, MA: Harvard University Press).

Caves, R., and Porter, M. (1980). 'The dynamics of changing seller concentration', *Journal of Industrial Economics* 29(1): 1–15.

Cornelius, P., van de Putte, A., and Romani, M. (2005). 'Three decades of scenario planning in Shell', *California Management Review* 48(1): 92–109.

D'Aveni, R. (1994). *Hypercompetition: Managing the Dynamics of Strategic Maneuvering* (New York: Free Press).

Dean, T., and Brown, R. (1995). 'Pollution regulation as a barrier to new firm entry: initial evidence and implications for future research', *Academy of Management Journal* 38: 288–303.

Deephouse, D. L. (1999). 'To be different, or to be the same? It's a question (and theory) of strategic balance', *Strategic Management Journal* 20: 147–66.

Doyle, P. (1997). *Marketing Management and Strategy*, 2nd edn (New York: Prentice Hall).

Duboff, R. S. (2007). 'The wisdom of (expert) crowds', *Harvard Business Review* 85(9): 28.

Fang, C.-L., and Lie, T. (2006). 'The effect of strategic group membership on the operational performance of leisure farms in Taiwan', *International Journal of Management* 23(3): 640–5.

Ghemawat, P., and Ghadar, F. (2006). 'Global integration ≠ global concentration', *Industrial and Corporate Change* 15(4): 595–623.

Greve, H. R. (1998). 'Managerial cognition and the mimetic adoption of market positions: what you see is what you do', *Strategic Management Journal* 19(10): 976–88.

Grossman, G., and Helpman, E. (1991). 'Endogenous product cycles', *Economic Journal*: 1214–29.

Grundy, T. (2006). 'Rethinking and reinventing Michael Porter's five forces model', *Strategic Change* 15(5): 213–29.

Gupta, S., Jain, D. C., and Sawhney, M. S. (1999). 'Modeling the evolution of markets with indirect network externalities: an application to digital television', *Marketing Science* 18(3): 396–416.

Harvey, M., Novicevic, M. M., and Kiessling, T. (2001). 'Hypercompetition and the future of global management in the twenty-first century', *Thunderbird International Business Review* 43(5): 599–616.

Jacobs, L. W., Wills, J. R., Samli, A. C. and Bullard, W. R. (1997). 'Internationalization of domestic product life cycles: an exploration of causality', *International Marketing Review* 14(1): 75–87.

Klein, H. E., and Linneman, R. E. (1984). 'Environmental assessment: an international study of corporate practice', *Journal of Business Strategy* 5(1): 66–75.

Levitt, T. (1965). 'Exploit the product life cycle', *Harvard Business Review* 43(6): 81–94.

Lieberman, M. B. (1987). 'Excess capacity as a barrier to entry', *Journal of Industrial Economics* 35(June): 607–27.

Lustgarten, S. H. (1975). 'The impact of buyer concentration in manufacturing industries', *Review of Economics and Statistics* 57: 125–32.

MacMillan, I. C., van Putten, A. B., and McGrath, R. G. (2003). 'Global gamesmanship', *Harvard Business Review* 81(5): 63–71.

Mann, H. M. (1966). 'Seller concentration, entry barriers, and rates of return in thirty industries', *Review of Economics and Statistics* 48: 296–307.

Masson, R. T., and Shaanan, J. (1982). 'Stochastic dynamic limit pricing', *Review of Economics and Statistics* 64: 413–22.

Masson, R. T., and Shaanan, J. (1987). 'Optimal pricing and threat of entry', *International Journal of Industrial Organization* 5: 1–13.

Mauri, A. J., and Michaels, M. P. (1998). 'Firm and industry effects within strategic management: an empirical examination', *Strategic Management Journal* 19(3): 211–19.

McGee, J., and Segal-Horn, S. (1990). 'Strategic space and industry dynamics', *Journal of Marketing Management* (3): 173–93.

McGee, J., and Thomas, H. (1986). 'Strategic groups: theory, research, and taxonomy', *Strategic Management Journal* 7(2): 141–60.

Nair, A., and Kotha, S. (2001). 'Does group membership matter? Evidence from the Japanese steel industry', *Strategic Management Journal* 22(3): 221–35.

Nielsen, C., and Thangadurai, M. (2007). 'Janus and the Delphi Oracle: entering the new world of international business research', *Journal of International Management* 13: 147–63.

Oster, S. (1982). 'The strategic use of regulatory investment by industry sub-groups', *Economic Inquiry* 20: 604–18.

Peteraf, M., and Shanley, M. (1997). 'Getting to know you: a theory of strategic group identity', *Strategic Management Journal* 18 (summer special): 165–86.

Porter, M. (1980). *Competitive Strategy: Techniques for Analysing Industries and Competitors* (New York: Free Press).

Porter, M. (1985). *Competitive Advantage: Creating and Sustaining Superior Performance* (New York: Free Press).

Prahalad, C. K., and Lieberthal, K. (2003). 'The end of corporate imperialism', *Harvard Business Review* 81(8): 109–17.

Reger, G. (2001). 'Technology foresight in companies: from an indicator to a network and process perspective', *Technology Analysis and Strategic Management* 13(4): 533–53.

Rosenbaum, D. I., and Lamort, F. (1992). 'Entry, barriers, exit, and sunk costs: an analysis', *Applied Economics* 24(3): 297–305.

Rumelt, R. P. (1991). 'How much does industry matter?' *Strategic Management Journal* 12: 167–85.

Schmalensee, R. (1988). 'Inter-industry studies of structure and performance', in R. Schmalensee and R. D. Willig (eds), *Handbook of Industrial Organization*, 2nd edn (Amsterdam: North-Holland).

Schnaars, S. P. (1987). 'How to develop and use scenarios', *Long Range Planning* 20(1): 105–14.

Short, J. C., Ketchen Jr., D. J., Palmer, T. B., and Hult, G. T. M. (2007). 'Firm, strategic group, and industry influences on performance', *Strategic Management Journal* 28(2): 147–67.

Verity, J. (2003). 'Scenario planning as a strategy technique', *European Business Journal* 15(4): 185–95.

Vernon, R. (1966). 'International investment and international trade in the product cycle', *Quarterly Journal of Economics* 80 (May): 190–207.

Wack, P. (1985a). 'Scenarios: uncharted waters ahead', *Harvard Business Review* 63(5): 72–89.

Wack, P. (1985b). 'Scenarios: shooting the rapids', *Harvard Business Review* 63(6): 139–50.

Wells, L. T. Jr. (1968). 'A product life cycle for international trade?' *Journal of Marketing* 32 (July): 1–6.

Yip, G. (1982). 'Gateways to entry', *Harvard Business Review* 60(5): 85–93.

## Online resource centre

**online
resource
centre**

Please visit www.oxfordtextbooks.co.uk/orc/frynas_mellahi2e/ for further information.

# Global business environment:
*analysis of the internal environment*

4

## Learning outcomes

After reading this chapter, you should be able to:

➤ Understand the significance of the internal environment and core competencies for the strategies of multinational firms.

➤ Distinguish between the positioning perspective and the resource-based perspective.

➤ Conduct a resource audit and apply the VRIO framework to a firm.

➤ Conduct a value-chain and value-system analysis.

➤ Conduct a comparative analysis for a multinational firm.

## Opening case study Google.com

The Internet search engine Google has become one of the world's best-known brands since its launch in 1998. Ten years later in 2008, Google had over 20,000 employees and annual revenues of almost US$22 billion. In 2009, Google was ranked the world's most valuable brand with a value of US$100 billion in the '2009 BrandZ Top 100' rankings by Millward Brown Optimor, ahead of Microsoft and Coca-Cola. With a search index in ninety different languages and over twenty offices around the world, the company's global market share for internet searches increased from less than 60% to over 85% in the five-year period of 2005–10. Google's market share in countries such as the UK, France, and Germany was over 90% in 2010, which means that nine out of ten people in France or Germany use Google's Web page when they are looking for information on the Internet. How did Google overtake its rivals to become the world's most popular Internet search engine (see Exhibit A)?

When Google entered the market in 1998, the company was a latecomer to the search engine world and its success was by no means guaranteed. There were many established search engines, including AltaVista, HotBot, Lycos, Yahoo, WebCrawler, and others. It was believed that first movers would triumph, as Internet users would usually stick with the first search engine that they used. Google proved that this belief was wrong.

It all started when Sergey Brin and Larry Page, friends at Stanford University, began to collaborate on a new search engine in January 1996. Initially, they did not want to start their own company, and they approached existing companies such as Yahoo with the aim of selling their search engine technology. But no one was interested. One business executive told them: 'As long as we're 80% as good as our competitors, that's good enough. Our users don't really care about search.' Brin and Page then decided to go on their own.

From its launch in September 1998, the word quickly spread that Google was different from all the other search engines. The search results were more helpful to users and Google had the largest number of indexed pages—the search index grew to over a billion Web pages by June 2000. Google introduced a number of innovations such as the Google Toolbar, which made it possible to use the search engine without visiting the Google home page by using the Toolbar's search box or clicking on text within a Web page; another improvement was the highlighting of keywords in

**Exhibit A** Global market share for Internet searches in 2010

| Company | Market share (%) |
| --- | --- |
| Google | 85.57 |
| Yahoo | 5.88 |
| Bing | 3.23 |
| Baidu | 3.00 |
| Ask | 0.68 |

*Source:* http://marketshare.hitslink.com, data for the first half of 2010.

search results. Finally, Google was faster than many competitors such as AltaVista, as search results were returned more quickly.

Another source of Google's success was simplicity. The Google team realized that the simple, stripped-down Web page design and easy use were reassuring both to new and old users. The home page barely changed over the years, even though the direction of the company had progressively changed. While new functions were added to the website, Google kept away from adding new tools or features which would make it look less user-friendly or would require much new learning by the user.

Since its launch, Google has changed, as the company has become more business-oriented and has concentrated more on generating revenue through advertisements. Google sought business partners and advertising clients to boost its revenues, announcing the first profits in late 2001—a major achievement for an Internet firm at that time. However, the company founders, Brin and Page, refuse to compromise Google's search usefulness in pursuit of profits. In contrast to its chief rival, Yahoo, Google refuses to charge for search inclusion. Google charges for paid searches, but those results are separate from its main search results and clearly differentiated for users, appearing in a distinct style under the heading 'Sponsored Links'. Yahoo includes paid placements with other search results without telling the users. The refusal to accept money for manipulating search results helps Google foster its market leadership. 'We feel very strongly that user trust is key to our success,' says Tim Armstrong, the vice president of advertising sales at Google.

Google is likely to remain the undisputed market leader for some time thanks to its wide distribution network, strong consumer brand, and continuous product innovation. Google's chief rivals, Yahoo and Microsoft, have unsuccessfully tried to improve their market position by buying up other search engines, offering new services to customers, and improving technology. In the period, 2005–10, the global market share of Yahoo fell from 18.5% to less than 6%, while the market share of Microsoft's search engine (previously MSN, now Bing) fell from 14% to about 3%. Google is aware of what competitors are doing and it stays ahead of them. For instance, Google introduced an improved 'related links' feature in 2009 ahead of a planned launch by Microsoft.

However, Google managers do not plan their business strategies by looking at what competitors do. The company's executives continue to do things differently to other companies. In 2009, the company started Google Ventures, a US$100 million venture capital fund to invest funds in other new Internet start-ups, which was a highly unusual move for an Internet company. Even more unusually, Google Ventures would be open to ideas that could eventually even prove disruptive to Google itself. 'We're trying to shine a light and find start-ups and entrepreneurs and people doing amazing things at a time when a general malaise has gripped the economy and people,' said Bill Maris, one of two managing partners of Google Ventures.

The Google executives believe that it is very important to concentrate on how Google can leverage its resources, rather than on what the rivals are doing. Sergey Brin, the Google co-founder, commented: 'I've seen companies so obsessed with competition that they keep looking in their rear view mirror and crash into a tree.'

*Source:* Various newspaper articles and Internet sources.

## 4.1 **Introduction**

The last two chapters have outlined the characteristics of the external business in which firms operate and stressed that the organization should adapt the strategy to the business environment. In contrast, the example of Google shows that international success can be achieved by focusing on the firm, rather than the external business environment. Many business writers—just like Google executives—believe that strategic decision-makers should focus on how a firm can leverage its resources, rather than on what the competitors and other stakeholders are doing.

Just as the external business environment is important, managers need to understand the unique strengths and weaknesses of their firm. They need to understand in what way the firm has unique resources and capabilities, what and who creates value within the firm, and how the firm resources compare with those of other firms. In short, they need to appreciate the 'internal' firm environment, which is the topic of this chapter.

The chapter starts by contrasting the view that the external business environment should be the starting point for formulating strategy with the view that the internal firm environment should guide strategy formulation.

## 4.2 **Positioning perspective v. resource-based perspective**

In Chapter 3, we introduced the concept of strategic fit, which suggests that firms must adapt their resources and activities to take advantage of external business opportunities. But, some writers have suggested that firms sometimes put too much emphasis on strategic fit. Hamel and Prahalad (1993) argued that the concept of fit is unbalanced, and should be supplemented by the idea of strategy development by 'stretch'.

While a firm must ultimately affect a fit between firm resources and the opportunities it pursues, the concept of 'strategic stretch' suggests that managers should try to identify and leverage the resources and competencies of the organization to yield new opportunities or to provide competitive advantage. Creating stretch relates to a misfit between resources and aspirations, and means going beyond what the business environment offers at a particular moment in time. The idea of stretch encourages managers to have high aspirations, and to exploit firm resources and capabilities in ways which rivals find difficult to match, or in genuinely new directions, or both.

The contrast between 'strategic fit' and 'strategic stretch' exemplifies different views on how firms should compete in global markets. Should strategies be developed by looking outward to the external business environment? Or, should they be developed by looking inward, to the firm resources? The focus on the external business environment is associated with the 'positioning perspective' on strategy. The focus on firm resources is associated with the 'resource-based perspective' on strategy.

---

**KEY CONCEPT**

Strategic stretch is about identifying and leveraging the resources and competencies of the organization to yield new opportunities or to provide competitive advantage. Strategy development by stretch suggests that managers should exploit firm resources and capabilities in ways which rivals find difficult to match, or in genuinely new directions, or both.

---

### 4.2.1 The positioning perspective

The positioning perspective assumes that the external business environment determines a firm's freedom to manoeuvre. The successful firm must pay attention to the needs of customers and the actions of competitors, by adapting the company's strategy to its external environment. Firms must be market-driven and externally oriented (Day 1990; 1994). These assumptions underline the Five Forces Model presented in Chapter 3. Michael Porter (1985) argues that a thorough understanding of the five competitive forces will allow strategists to position the firm in a particular strategic group or market niche, which yields sustained profitability: 'Competitive strategy is the search for a favourable competitive position in an industry.'

The key to successful positioning is a thorough and continuous monitoring of the external business environment, which can be done, for instance, using the Five Forces Model. Understanding the business environment will allow the firm to anticipate future changes in market trends. Once a firm positions itself in an attractive market, it needs to respond to challenges by rival firms, react to shifts in customer needs, and deal with product and price changes by suppliers.

Advocates of the positioning perspective do not deny that firm resources matter; if the firm does not have the necessary resources to exploit a specific business opportunity, it will not be able to develop a strategy to take advantage of that opportunity. Nonetheless, the external business opportunity—not the internal resource—is considered the starting point for developing successful strategies.

### 4.2.2 The resource-based perspective

The resource-based perspective distinguishes between firms in terms of their strategic and resource endowments and stresses the uniqueness of every firm in contrast to previous emphasis on the opportunities and threats in the external business environment. This approach assumes that a firm can use superior resources and capabilities to modify the industry structure and/or change the rules of the competitive game (Wernerfelt 1984; Peteraf 1993; Hoopes et al. 2003). The Google founders in our opening case study were not worried about competitive forces in the external environment such as entry barriers and industry profitability, but instead focused on their unique strengths; they have changed the search engine market rather than try to adapt to the market.

**Exhibit 4.1** Competence as a tree metaphor

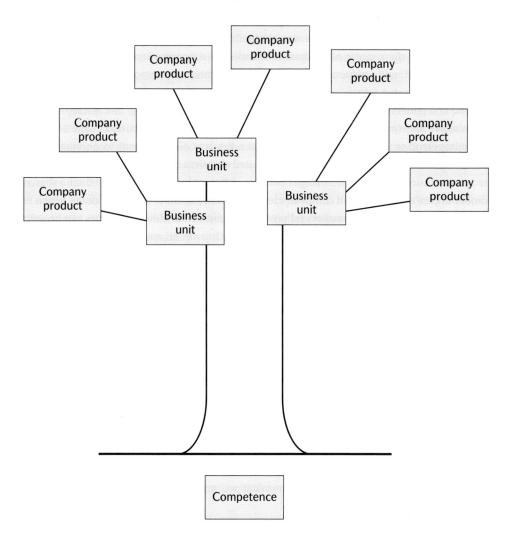

1. A core competence provides potential access to a wide variety of markets.
2. A core competence should make an important contribution to the customer's benefits of the end product.
3. A core competence should be difficult for competitors to imitate.

A more practical tool for identifying core competencies is the VRIO framework devised by Barney (1997: ch. 5), which asks four questions: whether a firm's resources and capabilities are valuable, rare, costly to imitate, and are exploited by the organization.

- The question of value. Do a firm's resources and capabilities enable the firm to respond to environmental threats or opportunities? (A valuable resource or capability helps to neutralize environmental threats or to exploit opportunities to create value for the customer.)

- The question of rareness. How may competing firms already possess particular valuable resources and capabilities? (A rare resource or capability is only possessed by few existing or potential competitors, and helps to distinguish the firm from other firms.)

- The question of imitability. Do firms without a resource or capability face a cost disadvantage in obtaining it compared to firms that already possess it? (A costly-to-imitate resource or capability cannot easily/cheaply be developed by other firms.)

- The question of organization. Is a firm organized to exploit the full competitive potential of its resources and capabilities?

Asking these questions will allow managers to analyse the potential of a broad range of firm resources and capabilities as sources of competitive advantage. For instance, rival firms may imitate new Sony end products through reverse engineering, but Sony's core competence in designing, manufacturing, and selling miniaturized electronic technology has been valuable, rare, difficult to imitate, and consistently exploited by the firm.

Sustainable competitive advantage only arises if firms have resources which combine *all* of these four attributes (see Exhibit 4.2). For instance, Xerox has possessed many knowledge resources which were valuable, rare, and difficult to imitate. Xerox had 'invented' the idea of a personal computer and made great innovations in copying machines over the years; however, the company was not able to exploit its advances in computing and failed to exploit the full potential of its innovations in copying machines.

The example of Xerox demonstrates that it is not sufficient for a firm to spend vast sums on research and development or to have unique resources and capabilities. A firm must be market-oriented and able to coordinate effectively all its activities to deliver value to the customer. In other words, a firm cannot afford to ignore the business environment, just as it cannot ignore the development of unique resources and capabilities.

**Exhibit 4.2** VRIO framework

| Is a resource or capability ... | | | | | |
|---|---|---|---|---|---|
| Valuable? | Rare? | Costly to imitate? | Exploited by the organization? | Competitive implications | Economic performance |
| No | – | – | No | Competitive disadvantage | Below normal |
| Yes | No | – | | Competitive parity | Normal |
| Yes | Yes | No | | Temporary competitive advantage | Above normal |
| Yes | Yes | Yes | Yes | Sustained competitive advantage | Above normal |

*Source:* J. B. Barney (1997), *Gaining and Sustaining Competitive Advantage* (Reading, MA: Addison-Wesley), 173. Reprinted with permission of Prentice Hall.

---

**KEY CONCEPT**

The VRIO framework asks a set of four questions: whether a firm's resources and capabilities are valuable, rare, costly to imitate, and exploited by the organization. Using the VRIO framework can help managers identify their firm's core competencies, and ultimately their firms' competitive advantage.

---

### 4.3.5 Resources and capabilities in multinational firms

Multinational firms have complex structures, with affiliates scattered around the world. A specific resource or capability may exist in some parts of the multinational firm but not in others. Not all valuable assets are located at the company's headquarters (i.e., in the home country). Furthermore, different resources and capabilities may sometimes be needed to succeed in different countries. For example, Japanese mobile telephone manufacturers have performed poorly in the Chinese market because the capabilities required in the mobile phone market differ between Japan and China; in Japan, mobile phone handsets are sold as a part of a package that combines handsets and telecommunications services, but, in China, they are sold as independent commodities, so different capabilities are required to succeed in China (Marukawa 2009).

A key challenge for a multinational firm is not simply how to acquire and develop resources and capabilities, but how to recognize and grow valuable resources and capabilities in its subsidiaries in different countries, and—if necessary—how to diffuse these resources and capabilities to other parts of the company.

As a result of the globalization of markets, resources and capabilities of subsidiaries of multinational firms have gained in importance (Birkinshaw et al. 1998; Birkinshaw and Hood 1998; Gupta and Govindarajan 2000). Global—as opposed to international—strategies demand a high level of subsidiary specialization, as each subsidiary may concentrate on a specific task or activity on behalf of the entire firm. For instance, we suggested in Chapter 2 that firms may conduct global technology scanning by locating the company's research centres in countries where relevant cutting-edge research is pursued (see section 2.7.1). Indeed, innovation generated in the multinational firm's subsidiaries may be crucial for the firm's overall success (see Chapter 11). As a consequence, the flow of resources and capabilities from the foreign subsidiary back to the firm's headquarters becomes as crucial as the flow of knowledge from the headquarters to its subsidiaries. Managers are therefore advised to monitor closely the development of resources and capabilities in the firm's international subsidiaries.

Some resources and capabilities in subsidiaries are 'location-bound', i.e., their value is limited to a specific country or area of operations. But other resources and capabilities are not location-bound and may be transferred to the company's headquarters or the firm's subsidiaries in other countries. These resources and capabilities have the potential to contribute to the multinational firm's overall competitive advantage (Birkinshaw et al. 1998).

According to Birkinshaw and his colleagues, this potential can translate into international competitive advantage, if three conditions are fulfilled (see Exhibit 4.3):

1. An affiliate has a resource or capability, which is superior to those resources and capabilities found elsewhere in the firm (otherwise, there is no point in transferring that resource or capability to other countries).

2. Corporate managers in other parts of the firm recognize and accept the affiliate's superior resource or capability (otherwise, managers in other countries will not be willing to adopt that new resource or capability).

3. The affiliate's superior resource or capability is effectively transferred and is utilized in other parts of the multinational firm (otherwise, the resource or capability will not contribute to the multinational firm's overall competitive advantage).

**Exhibit 4.3** Link between subsidiary resource and competitive advantage

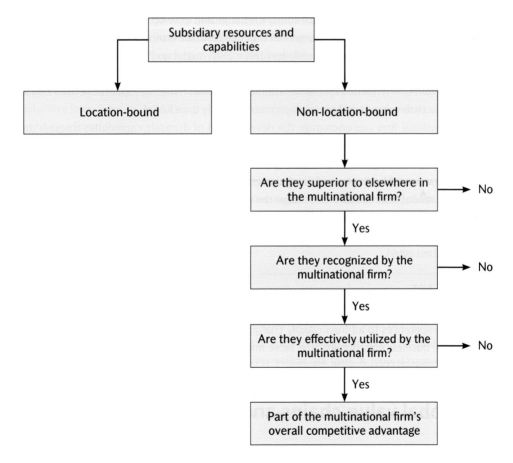

*Source:* Adapted from J. Birkinshaw, N. Hood, and S. Jonsson, (1998), 'Building firm-specific advantages in multinational corporations: the role of subsidiary initiative', *Strategic Management Journal* 19(3): 225. Reprinted with permission of John Wiley & Sons.

**Exhibit 4.4** The product value of South African peaches

| The firm activity | Contribution to final product value (%) |
|---|---|
| **Within South Africa** | |
| Peaches | 12.4 |
| Cans | 11.6 |
| Sugar | 4.2 |
| Canning, of which: | 14.7 |
| 7.4% Labour | |
| 7.3% Other (depreciation, utilities, internal transport, etc.) | |
| Total inside South Africa | 42.9 |
| **Outside South Africa** | |
| Shipping, duties, insurance, landing charges | 24.2 |
| Importer's margin | 6.3 |
| Supermarket margin | 26.7 |
| Total outside South Africa | 57.1 |

*Source:* D. Kaplan and R. Kaplinsky (1999), 'Trade and industrial policy on an uneven playing field: the case of the deciduous fruit canning industry in South Africa', *World Development* 27(10): 1787–801. Reprinted with permission of Elsevier.

South African firms may be further eroded due to the growing rivalry between producers and growing concentration among international supermarket chains. As a result of the changing value added in the global market, two of South Africa's largest fruit manufacturers have moved into the more profitable global sourcing and distribution and have opened offices in Jersey and the UK, respectively, just as they have sought to reduce their processing operations in South Africa (Kaplan and Kaplinsky 1999).

Unfortunately, detailed information on the value added of different business processes is often unavailable in practice, as managers may not have all of the information on the different business activities (e.g., it may prove impossible to put a value on some types of knowledge), or it may be difficult to calculate the value added (e.g., if the firm uses the same overheads to create many different products). But it is important for the strategic decision-maker to have at least a rough idea of the value added of the different activities performed by the firm. For instance, does the firm generate most value added when designing the car, manufacturing the engine, or assembling the final vehicle? Value chain analysis helps to understand where value is created within the firm.

## KEY CONCEPT

Value added is the difference between the cost of inputs and the market value of outputs. It is the value that a firm adds to its bought-in materials and services through its own production and marketing efforts within the firm.

### 4.4.2 Value chain analysis

Most goods and services are produced by a series of vertical business activities, which can include product development, manufacturing, marketing, distribution, and after-sales service. The total economic value created is split amongst them, with some parts of the chain creating more value added than others. Value chain analysis depicts the main activities inside the firm, and aims to reveal the relative value added among the different parts of the firm's operations. Undertaking a value chain analysis helps the firm to understand its cost position and to identify its competitive strengths.

Porter (1985) divided the value chain into primary and support activities (see Exhibit 4.5). Primary activities deal with those activities needed to create or deliver a product or service, while support activities are designed to improve the effectiveness of primary activities. 'Margin' refers to the value added.

Primary activities include:

- Inbound logistics. Receiving goods from suppliers, storing them, and transporting them.
- Operations. Activities needed to convert the inputs into final products and services.

**Exhibit 4.5** The value chain

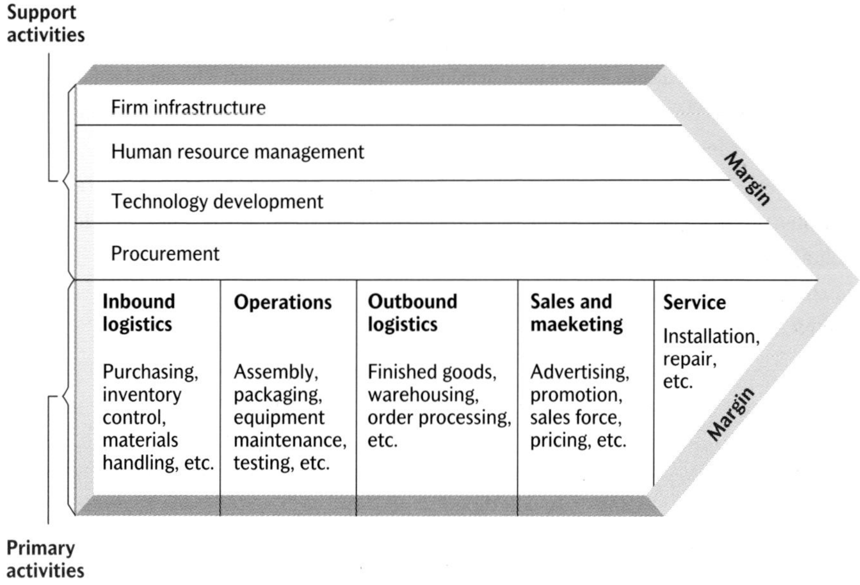


*Source:* Reprinted with permission of The Free Press, a Division of Simon & Schuster, Inc., from *Competitive Advantage: Creating and Sustaining Superior Performance* by Michael E. Porter. Copyright © 1985, 1998 by Michael E. Porter. All rights reserved.

- Outbound logistics. Distributing the final product or service to the customer.

- Marketing and sales. Activities which help make customers aware of the products or services.

- Service. Activities which maintain or enhance the value of the product or service.

Support activities include:

- Firm infrastructure. Planning and control systems which are important to the firm's performance in its primary activities, and which encompass finance, legal support, government relations, corporate strategy, etc.

- Human resource management. Recruiting, training, developing, and rewarding people within the organization.

- Technology development. Knowledge activities needed to improve a firm's products and services or processes used to create products and services, which encompass process equipment, basic research, and product design.

- Procurement. Purchasing the inputs needed to produce the firm's products and services, which may occur in many sections of the firm.

Primary activities differ in each industry. For a car manufacturer, inputs will include specialist manufacturing materials and car components, while inputs of a restaurant chain include meat and vegetables. Vertically integrated firms have more primary activities in the value chain within the boundaries of the firm. For instance, in the petroleum industry, Royal Dutch/Shell and Exxon explore for crude oil, produce crude oil, transport crude oil, refine crude oil into other products, and sell oil products to end consumers. However, even the largest multinational firms do not usually carry out all the activities within the value chain. Smaller multinational firms usually specialize in a particular activity. For instance, the Swiss company, Glencore, specializes in oil trading—the company does not, by and large, engage either in oil production or in the sale of oil products to end consumers (see Exhibit 4.6). Therefore, a firm's value chain is usually part of a larger 'value system' (see Exhibit 4.7).

---

**KEY CONCEPT**

Value chain analysis depicts the main activities inside the firm and aims to reveal the relative value added amongst the different parts of the firm's operations. Undertaking a value chain analysis helps the firm to understand its cost position and to identify its competitive strengths.

---

### 4.4.3 Value system analysis

Since firms do not usually carry out all the primary activities in an industry, it is useful to undertake an analysis of all the different activities inside the firm, as well as the value chain activities not performed by the firm. A firm is part of a wider system of creating value which involves the value chains of its suppliers, distributors, and customers, which is known as a value system. Value system analysis depicts the main activities inside and outside the firm and

**Exhibit 4.6** Examples of value chains in the global petroleum industry

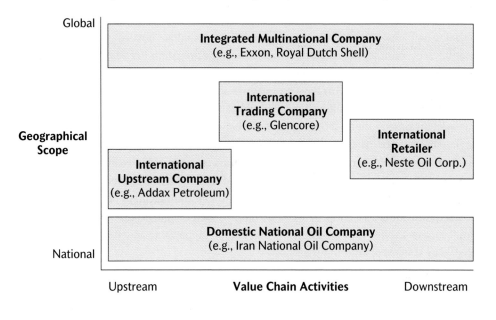

**Exhibit 4.7** Example of a value system in the global petroleum industry

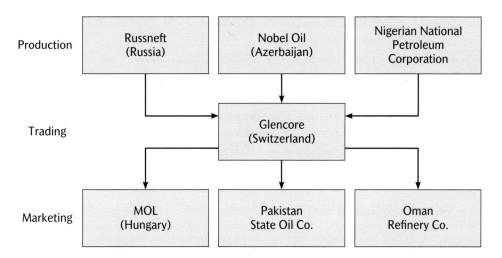

aims to reveal the firm's linkages with its suppliers' value chains and its buyers' value chains. The value system concept is essentially an extension of the value chain concept to inter-firm relationships. While the value chain is specific to each company, different companies may sometimes use similar value systems; two competing firms may use the same suppliers and the same distribution channels. Somewhat confusingly for the student, writers sometimes use other terms, such as 'value chains', 'supply chains', or 'production networks', when referring to value systems.

Globalization of markets has led to the development of global value systems—sometimes referred to as 'global commodity chains' or 'global value chains'—involving many firms from many different countries linked through contracts and partnerships (Gereffi and Korzeniewicz 1994; Sturgeon and Gereffi 2009). Indeed, globalization has led to a shift in value systems in many industries. Global value systems have moved away from vertically integrated firms and value systems based around a lead firm (which gave detailed instructions to its suppliers) towards value systems based around loose connections between firms (Gereffi et al. 2005; Sturgeon and Gereffi 2009). For instance, in the clothing industry (see the closing case study), traditional value systems involving large retailers such as Marks & Spencer and large manufacturers such as Courtauld have given way to new value systems. Globalization has enabled new players such as Chinese and Korean trading firms to become an important element of new global value systems by providing a vital link between US and European retailers and local Asian clothing manufacturers. Exhibit 4.8 shows how the distribution of the value added is changing within global value systems of three industries.

Nonetheless, there is no best way of organizing global value systems. Some multinational firms such as Sony and Samsung benefit from retaining a vertically integrated value chain, as integral product architecture makes it difficult to break the value chain. Similarly, in the clothing industry Zara's success in achieving extremely fast product cycles—biweekly in some cases—has been supported by the firm's in-house textile manufacturing subsidiary and close relationships with sewing workshops which are highly dependent on Zara (see the closing case study). These examples illustrate the point that a firm's value chain and its value system must, above all, match its business strategy.

---

**KEY CONCEPT**

A value system is a wider system of creating value which involves the value chains of the firm's suppliers, distributors, and customers. Value system analysis depicts the main activities inside and outside the firm, and aims to reveal the firm's linkages with its suppliers' value chains, its distributors' value chains, and its customers' value chains.

---

### 4.4.4 Value analysis and cost advantages

Applying value chain and value system analysis allows firms to understand their organization's cost structure, which provides a bridge between strategic management and accounting. Indeed, value analysis was originally introduced as accounting analysis to understand the value added within complex manufacturing processes. An examination of the value added in the different parts of the organization can, for example, help to demonstrate that a firm's cost advantage in the international market comes from a low-cost physical distribution system or a highly efficient assembly process.

Knowledge about where value is created in the firm can further help managers to take important investment decisions. It can help the firm to detect where further investment

**Exhibit 4.8** The changing distribution of value added in three industries

| Sector | Links in value chain | Prime source of profitability | | | Implications for production activities |
|---|---|---|---|---|---|
| | | Past | Present | Future | |
| Fresh fruit and vegetables | Seed design ↓ Growing ↓ Post-harvest processing ↓ Exporting ↓ Retailing | Growing<br><br><br><br>Wholesale | Seed design and new product development<br><br>Coordination of value chain efficiency<br><br>Retail chains | Seed design, new product development | Growing capabilities (climatic specific) are generalized and competition is high<br><br>Profits in intangibles (seed design, growing practices, phyto-sanitary practices, etc.).<br><br>Battle between retail chains and brand names for shelf dominance |
| Footwear | Leather ↓ Design ↓ Assembly ↓ Exporting ↓ Buyers ↓ Retailing | Leather<br><br>Assembly | Design<br><br><br><br>Buying<br><br>Retailing | Design<br><br><br><br>Buying<br><br>Retailing | Design is critical as increasing competition in production forces declining terms of trade<br><br>Buyers play dominant role in global sourcing<br><br>Brand names of growing importance |
| Automotive components | Raw material processing ↓<br><br><br>Design ↓ Forming ↓ Assembly ↓ Exporting ↓ OEM user Spares | Design<br>Forming<br>Assembly | Coordination of value chain<br><br><br>Design<br>Some in forming and assembly<br><br><br>OEM brand name | Coordination of value chain<br><br><br>Design<br><br><br><br>OEM brand name | Manufacturing competencies become widespread; growth of global sourcing, but intense competition leads to falling terms of trade. Profits achieved *by moving to different links* in the chain<br><br>*Within individual links*, profits are increasingly in intangibles (design, knowledge inputs into production, brand names and marketing) |

*Note:* OEM = original equipment manufacturer.

*Source:* R. M. Kaplinsky (2000), 'Globalisation and unequalisation: what can be learned from value chain analysis?' *Journal of Development Studies* 37(2): 133 (http://www.informaworld.com). Reprinted with permission of Taylor and Francis.

**Exhibit 4.10**  The intelligence onion

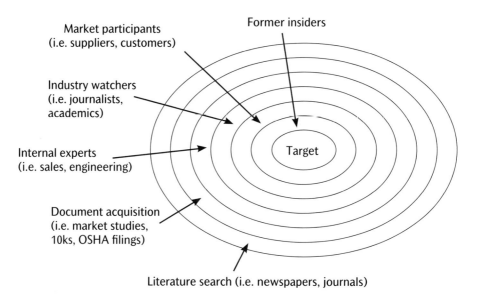

*Source:* C. M. O'Guin and T. Ogilvie (2001), 'The science, not art, of business intelligence', *Competitive Intelligence Review* 12(4): 21. Reprinted with permission of John Wiley & Sons.

### 4.5.2 Benchmarking

When managers lack information about their competitors, they may develop strategies based on wrong assumptions. When low-cost Japanese copiers produced by Canon came to pose a competitive threat to Xerox in the US market in the 1980s, Xerox managers were convinced that Canon sold copiers below production cost to gain high market share at the expense of profits. In order to gain competitor intelligence, Xerox managers travelled from the United States to Japan, where Xerox had a joint venture with Fuji for manufacturing photocopying machines. During their stay in Japan, Xerox managers dismantled a Canon copier and found that it was not only cheaper to make but also of a higher quality than Xerox products. Subsequently, Xerox imitated Canon's materials and methods in order to improve the quality and lower the cost of its own products. This experience led Xerox managers to develop the benchmarking approach, which has since been adopted by many other multinational firms (Cox and Thompson 1998; Camp 1989; Watson 1993). Benchmarking has been defined by Camp (1989: 12) as 'the search for industry best practices that will lead to the superior performance of a company'. The aim of benchmarking is to find better practice processes which show higher levels of performance, and which can be copied or adapted internally by the organization (Cox and Thompson 1998).

The Xerox–Canon case is an example of 'competitive benchmarking', i.e., benchmarking your competitors. Competitive benchmarking can be very successful, for instance, through reverse engineering of a competitor's product. But beyond such simple methods, competitive benchmarking is difficult in practice, as competitors are reluctant to reveal their secrets. An alternative method is 'functional benchmarking' (also called 'generic benchmarking'), which involves benchmarking organizations with regards to specific business activities or processes. This allows firms to benchmark organizations outside the industry or strategic group which may not even share the same value systems, and can help to avoid problems of confidentiality of information (Cox and Thompson 1998). For instance, Xerox benchmarked the direct-mail clothing manufacturer LL.Bean in terms of stock control and warehousing systems and benchmarked Disney's equipment maintenance approaches. British Airways improved aircraft maintenance by studying the processes surrounding Grand Prix racing pit stops, while the English Law Society learned how to improve its phone system from telephone call centres. Indeed, by focusing on the best practice in a specific shared activity (e.g., warehousing or employee training), the organization may learn how 'it is best to do things' in that specific field globally, rather than just learning how 'it is best to do things' in its industry.

---

## KEY CONCEPT

Benchmarking is the search for industry best practices that will lead to the superior perform-ance of a company. The aim of benchmarking is to find better practice processes which show higher levels of performance, and which can be copied or adapted internally by the organization.

---

### 4.5.3 Internal comparative analysis

We have so far concentrated on comparing the firm's resources and capabilities with those of competitors and other external organizations. But it is equally important for the multinational firm to compare different parts of the company. We suggested earlier that globalization has increased the importance of resources and capabilities of subsidiaries of multinational firms (section 4.3.5). So a key challenge for an organization is not simply how to learn from others but also how to diffuse its resources and capabilities within its own boundaries.

Internal comparative analysis can be performed in different ways, such as informal discussions involving subsidiary managers from different countries, a comparison of profitability measures between subsidiaries, or internal benchmarking. It is essentially a top-down process. The headquarters of the multinational firm identifies best practices in specific subsidiaries and then diffuses them to other parts of the company. An alternative to such internal comparative analysis is a bottom-up process, by which the firm's headquarters gives subsidiary managers some freedom to demonstrate their expertise and their willingness to take on additional responsibilities (Birkinshaw et al. 1998). But internal comparative analysis such as internal benchmarking has the advantage of providing the headquarters with an overview of performance by all subsidiaries of the company, and helps it to take strategic decisions on how to develop specific resources and capabilities across the entire firm.

Internal benchmarking can lead to major improvements in a multinational firm (Durst and Binder 2006). For instance, Rank Xerox—the European subsidiary of Xerox—had been less profitable than the US subsidiary for many years. In turn, there were also considerable performance differences between Rank Xerox affiliates in different European countries. While affiliates in countries such as the Netherlands and Portugal could boast a return on assets (ROA) of more than 20% (comparable with Xerox's US affiliate), other affiliates had an ROA of well below 20%. Rank Xerox then identified, documented, and transferred best practices from its best-performing affiliates to other affiliates, which led to revenue improvements of some US$100 million in the first year alone. This example demonstrates that comparative analysis needs to take place at various levels. The challenge for organizations is as much to diffuse best practices as it is to learn from others.

Nonetheless, whether a firm engages in external or internal benchmarking, there will be times when benchmarking may be inappropriate. Even Rank Xerox found that certain practices—such as instituting optimal sales behaviours for salespeople within the company—were difficult to implement in practice. For instance, managers may over-rely on quantitative data rather than trying to understand the reasons for performance measures; it may be very difficult to implement someone else's best practice in a different context; or it may simply not be possible to obtain the relevant data. So, a firm should start by carefully asking questions such as, 'What is to be benchmarked?' and 'Who is to be benchmarked?' (Cox and Thompson 1998). Exhibit 4.11 sets out the Xerox 'Ten-step benchmarking process'.

**Exhibit 4.11** Xerox ten-step benchmarking process

| Planning | 1. Identify what is to be benchmarked. |
|---|---|
| | 2. Identify comparative companies. |
| | 3. Determine method of data collection and do it. |

| Analysis | 4. Determine current performance gap. |
|---|---|
| | 5. Project future performance levels. |

| Integration | 6. Communicate findings and gain acceptance. |
|---|---|
| | 7. Establish functional goals. |

| Action | 8. Develop Action Plans. |
|---|---|
| | 9. Implement specific actions and monitor progress. |
| | 10. Recalibrate benchmarks. |

*Source:* A. Cox and I. Thompson (1998), 'On the appropriateness of benchmarking', *Journal of General Management* 23(3): 4. Reprinted with permission of Braybrooke Press.

### 4.5.4 Comparative analysis in global markets

Some observers believe that competitor analysis and benchmarking are no longer sufficient to be successful in a global market. Competitor analysis may fail to recognize important trends, which may affect the company; for instance, the firm may fail to prepare for the entry of a new competitor because the new competitor comes from outside the recognized strategic group (see section 3.2.2). Imitation of other firms through benchmarking also has pitfalls, since an imitation-based strategy may only lead to reproducing the cost and quality advantages that your competitors already possess in specific activities; it does not lead to a 'competitive revitalization' (Babbar and Rai 1993).

But comparative analysis still has a major role to play in global markets. As the earlier Xerox–Canon example illustrated, a comparative analysis can help to discover best practice, respond to increasing competition, gain a tactical advantage, or to reduce complacency. Since firms can benchmark the best performers from other industries, adopting a new practice from outside the industry can give a specific firm a competitive advantage over the established competitors inside the industry. Furthermore, since multinational firms have resources and capabilities scattered around the world, internal comparative analysis is important to ensure the diffusion of best practices within the organization on a global scale.

Globalization does not mean an end to comparative analysis; it means that firms must constantly develop and transplant their internal resources and capabilities in order to stay ahead of competitors. At the same time as multinational firms need to devote attention to resources and capabilities, globalization means that firms need to look far beyond their established strategic group and must scan the entire world for opportunities and threats.

## 4.6 Summary

Some writers have suggested that managers sometimes put too much emphasis on strategic fit, i.e., matching a firm's resources and activities to the external environment in which it operates. Hamel and Prahalad (1993) argued that the concept of fit is unbalanced and should be supplemented by the idea of strategy development by 'stretch', i.e., identifying and leveraging the resources and competencies of an organization to yield new opportunities or to provide competitive advantage. The contrast between 'strategic fit' and 'strategic stretch' exemplifies different views on how firms should compete in global markets: the positioning perspective and the resource-based perspective.

It is important for strategic decision-makers to understand thoroughly their firm's 'resources', 'capabilities', and, above all, 'core competencies'. 'Core competencies' refers to the combination of individual technologies and production skills that underlie a company's multiple production lines. They can be identified, amongst other methods, using the VRIO framework, which asks four questions regarding value, rareness, imitability, and organization. Prahalad and Hamel (1990) argued that the success of the best multinational firms lay in core competencies underlying all their end products.

Not all resources and capabilities have to be located within the firm's boundaries. In many global industries, there is a strong pressure towards obtaining various value-creating activities from outside the company, either through outsourcing or through strategic alliances. The concepts of value added, value chain analysis, and value system analysis can help strategic decision-makers in identifying where value is created in the firm. This knowledge can aid economic decisions related to the firm's cost structure and strategic decisions related to the selection of activities the firm should focus on.

Resources and capabilities can only be judged to be valuable or rare if a firm compares itself with the competitors. Competitor intelligence and benchmarking can help the firm to compare itself with others, so that managers avoid overestimating their own abilities. However, even if competitor analysis is used properly, one needs to be cautious about over-relying on resources and capabilities. The firm's resources and capabilities may become less rare than they used to be, or they may lose the strategic fit with the external environment. Furthermore, if there is a radical change in the external business environment (e.g., as a result of a major technological shift), the firm's existing assets could become a liability by hindering the firm from adapting to the new external environment. Therefore, managers must pay equal attention to the internal firm environment and the external business environment. Neither the resource-based perspective nor the positioning perspective can guide strategy development by itself.

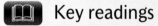

## Key readings

- On the resource-based perspective and firm capabilities in multinational firms, see Augier and Teece (2007); and R. A. Ainuddin, P. W. Beamish, J. S. Hulland, and M. J. Rouse (2007), 'Resource attributes and firm performance in international joint ventures', *Journal of World Business* 42(1): 47–60.

- On value chains, see Porter (1985); and Sturgeon and Gereffi (2009).

- On benchmarking, see Cox and Thompson (1998).

## Discussion questions

**1.** What is the difference between the resource-based perspective and the positioning perspective?

**2.** Take an organization of your choice. Identify the key resources, capabilities, and core competencies of that organization. How easy is it for competitors to imitate your organization's resources, capabilities, and core competencies? What changes in the external business environment can make those resources, capabilities, and core competencies less valuable to the organization?

**3.** Take the same organization. Identify its value chain and value system. Would you advise the managers to improve or change the organization's current value activities?

**4.** To what extent can competitive intelligence and benchmarking help a firm's global strategy?

## Closing case study Clothing industry supply chains and Zara's business model

Global supply chains in the clothing industry can be very complex. Clothing retailers constantly look out for new suppliers of cheaper clothes from foreign manufacturing companies around the world. Retailers often outsource many of the essential supply chain processes including the placing of product orders and quality control.

In many cases, a clothing retailer employs a foreign intermediary, which can range from a foreign agent to an international trading company with wholly-owned or controlled clothing factories. The foreign intermediary can, at one extreme, merely facilitate a business deal between a buyer and a manufacturer or, at the other extreme, can offer a range of services including placing orders with the foreign producer as well as managing the quality control process. The services of an intermediary may reduce the profit margins for the retailer or the manufacturer but they offer a number of advantages, especially in terms of providing the retailer with local knowledge and contacts. The intermediary may buy or facilitate a purchase from a manufacturer. In some cases, the manufacturer may sub-contract part or all of the output (see Exhibit B).

In contrast to other companies in the clothing industry, Zara—a Spanish clothing retailer—has a different business model. Zara's manufacturing is vertically integrated. Zara owns a group of factories in Spain to carry out the initial capital-intensive work such as dyeing and cutting cloth. The cut fabric is sown into clothes in small workshops in Spain and Northern Portugal. All finished clothes are sent to a Zara facility where they are ironed, inspected, tagged, and sent to a retail outlet (see Exhibit C).

### Benefits of Zara's business model

A vertical supply chain allows Zara to introduce new items throughout the year. It also allows Zara to keep short lead times. Vertical integration allows the company to move from clothes design to production to sales in three weeks. The structure of its supply chain allows Zara to respond more quickly to changing customer tastes and new fashions.

Like other clothing retailers, Zara introduces a winter and a summer collection. In contrast to other companies, Zara also introduces new items throughout the year, including changes to existing clothes (e.g., a skirt in a new colour) and entirely new clothes. In a typical year, a typical competitor introduces 2,000 to 4,000 new items. Zara introduces 11,000 new items every year.

Since Zara does not depend on a complex global supply chain, the company does not have to make accurate sales forecasts. Instead, Zara's design teams simply make an initial guess for the number of items needed and communicate the number to the factories. Once the clothes arrive in the retail stores, the sales figures tell the company whether production levels should be quickly reduced or increased. The local factories can adjust to these needs very quickly. Therefore, in contrast to other companies, Zara does not even have to predict how much it will sell in a month or two. It can continuously monitor what customers want at a particular time.

### Internal organization

Zara's internal organization supports its flexible supply chain. Every major sector of a Zara retail store places orders twice a week. Store managers calculate the order quantities by walking

**Exhibit B** Typical global supply chain in the clothing industry

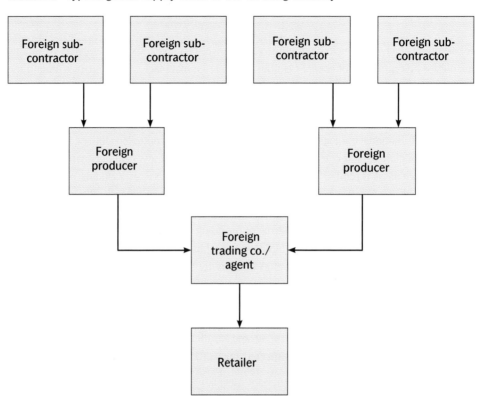

around the shop with a hand-held device, which records the needed clothes, and by talking with other staff.

Zara's marketing team sometimes sends new clothes to stores, which the store manager did not order. These are normally new designs, for which Zara wants to estimate popularity.

The company's distribution centres have kilometres of conveyer belts for receiving clothes from factories and arranging them into shipments for each retail store. Deliveries to retail store normally arrive within one or two days after the order was placed. The clothes are quickly placed on the shelves without delay.

Zara decided not to sell on the Internet. First, the distribution centres were not designed for shipping small orders. Second, the company felt that it was too complicated to manage returns of clothes purchases on the Internet. The lack of Internet sales reduced potential sales but it helped the company streamline operations.

### Local supply chains—global expansion

The first Zara store opened in La Coruña (Spain) in 1975. The first Zara store outside Spain opened in 1988 in Oporto (Portugal). Over the following decade, Zara expanded mainly in Europe, the Americas, and the Middle East. In 2006, Zara opened its first store in China—Zara had retail stores in eleven Chinese cities by 2009.

**Exhibit C** Zara's supply chain

When Zara expanded globally, it continued to rely on its distribution centres in Spain. Retail stores in France or Germany were supplied by lorry from Zara's Spanish distribution centres. More remote retail stores in Northern Europe and the Middle East were supplied by air from the company's Spanish distribution centres. In the Americas and in Asia, where the company was unable to rely on Spanish distribution centres, Zara replicated its business model, using smaller foreign-based distribution centres.

Zara's business model proved very successful. In 2010, Zara had a network of 1,444 retail stores in prime locations of over 400 cities in seventy seven countries around the world.

*Sources* : A. McAfee, V. Dessain, and A. Sjöman (2007), 'Zara: IT for fast fashion', Harvard Business School Case No. 9–604–081; Zara website at http://www.zara.com; Inditex Group website at http://www.inditex.com; J. G. Frynas (2003), 'The transnational garment industry in South and South-East Asia', in J. G. Frynas and S. Pegg (eds), *Transnational Corporations and Human Rights* (Basingstoke: Palgrave), 162–87.

**Discussion questions**

**1.** Compare and contrast Zara's supply chain with the typical supply chain of other clothing retailers.

**2.** To what extent can Zara's business model be replicated by other clothing retailers?

 # References

Augier, M., and Teece, D. J. (2007). 'Dynamic capabilities and multinational enterprise: Penrosean insights and omissions', *Management International Review* 47(2): 175–92.

Babbar, S., and Rai, A. (1993). 'Competitive intelligence for international business', *Long Range Planning* 26(3): 103–13.

Barney, J. B. (1991). 'Firm resources and sustained competitive advantage', *Journal of Management* 17(1): 99–120.

Barney, J. B. (1997). *Gaining and Sustaining Competitive Advantage* (Reading, MA: Addison-Wesley).

Birkinshaw, J., and Hood, N. (1998). 'Multinational subsidiary evolution: capability and charter change in foreign-owned subsidiary companies', *Academy of Management Review* 23(4): 773–95.

Birkinshaw, J., Hood, N., and Jonsson, S. (1998). 'Building firm-specific advantages in multinational corporations: the role of subsidiary initiative', *Strategic Management Journal* 19(3): 221–41.

Camp, R. C. (1989). *Benchmarking: The Search for Industry Best Practices that Lead to Superior Performance* (Milwaukee, WI: ASQC Quality Press).

Campbell, A., and Luchs, S. K. (1997). *Core Competency Based Strategy* (London: International Thomson Business Press).

Chen, M. J. (1996). 'Competitor analysis and interfirm rivalry: toward a theoretical integration', *Academy of Management Review* 21(1): 100–34.

Child, J., and Faulkner, D. (1998). *Strategies of Cooperation: Managing Alliances, Networks, and Joint Ventures* (Oxford: Oxford University Press).

Cox, A., and Thompson, I. (1998). 'On the appropriateness of benchmarking', *Journal of General Management* 23(3): 1–19.

Day, G. S. (1990). *Market Driven Strategy: Processes for Creating Value* (New York: Free Press).

Day, G. S. (1994). 'The capabilities of market-driven organizations', *Journal of Marketing* 58 (October): 37–52.

Durst, S. M., and Binder, M. (2006). 'Improving efficiency through internal benchmarking', *International Journal of Business Performance Management* 8(4): 290–306.

Fahey, L. (1998). *Competitors: Outwitting, Out-maneuvering, and Outperforming* (New York: Wiley).

Fleischer, C. S., and Wright, S. (2009). 'Examining differences in competitive intelligence practice: China, Japan and the West', *Thunderbird International Business Review* 51(3): 249–61.

Fuld, L. M. (2006). *The Secret Language of Competitive Intelligence* (New York: Crown Business).

Gereffi, G., and Korzeniewicz, M. (eds) (1994). *Commodity Chains and Global Capitalism* (Westport, CT: Praeger).

Gereffi, G., Humphrey, J., and Sturgeon, T. (2005). 'The governance of global value chains', *Review of International Political Economy* 12(1): 78–104.

Gupta, A., and Govindarajan, V. (2000). 'Knowledge flows within multinational corporations', *Strategic Management Journal* 21(4): 473–96.

Hall, C. (2001). 'The intelligent puzzle', *Competitive Intelligence Review* 12(4): 3–14.

Hamel, G., and Prahalad, C. K. (1993) 'Strategy as stretch and leverage', *Harvard Business Review* 71(2): 75–84.

Hoopes, D. G., Hadsen, T. L., and Walker, G. (2003). 'Why is there a resource-based view? Toward a theory of competitive heterogeneity', *Strategic Management Journal* 24(10): 889–902.

Hsu, C.-W., and Chen, H. (2009). 'Foreign direct investment and capability development—a dynamic capabilities perspective', *Management International Review* 49(5): 585–605.

Insinga, R. C., and Werle, M. J. (2000). 'Linking outsourcing to business strategy', *Academy of Management Executive* 14(4): 58–70.

Kaplan, D., and Kaplinsky, R. (1999). 'Trade and industrial policy on an uneven playing field: the case of the deciduous fruit canning industry in South Africa', *World Development* 27(10): 1787–801.

Kaplinsky, R. M. (2000). 'Globalisation and unequalisation: what can be learned from value chain analysis?' *Journal of Development Studies* 37(2): 117–46.

Kogut, B. (1985). 'Designing global strategies: comparative and competitive value-added chains', *Sloan Management Review* (Summer): 15–28.

Leonard-Barton, D. (1992). 'Core capabilities and core rigidities: a paradox in managing new product development', *Strategic Management Journal* 13(S1): 111–25.

Liesch, P., and Knight, G. (1999). 'Information internationalization and hurdle rates in small and medium enterprise internationalization', *Journal of International Business Studies* 30(2): 383–94.

Marukawa, T. (2009). 'Why Japanese multinationals failed in the Chinese mobile phone market: a comparative study of new product development in Japan and China', *Asia Pacific Review* 15(3): 411–31.

McGahan, A. M., and Porter, M. (1997). 'How much does industry matter, really?' *Strategic Management Journal* 18 (Special Issue): 15–30.

O'Guin, C. M., and Ogilvie, T. (2001). 'The science, *not art*, of business intelligence', *Competitive Intelligence Review* 12(4): 15–24.

Peteraf, M. A. (1993). 'The cornerstones of competitive advantage: a resource-based view', *Strategic Management Journal* 14(3): 179–91.

Porter, M. (1985). *Competitive Advantage: Creating and Sustaining Superior Performance* (New York: Free Press).

Prahalad, C. K., and Hamel, G. (1990). 'The core competence of the corporation', *Harvard Business Review* 68(3): 79–93.

Rumelt, R. P. (1991). 'How much does industry matter?' *Strategic Management Journal* 12(3): 167–85.

Schmalensee, R. (1985). 'Do markets differ much?' *American Economic Review* 75: 341–51.

Stalk, G., Evans, F., and Shulman, L. (1992). 'Competing on capabilities', *Harvard Business Review* 70(2): 57–70.

Sturgeon, T. J., and Gereffi, G. (2009). 'Measuring success in the global economy: international trade, industrial upgrading, and business function outsourcing in global value chains', *Transnational Corporations* 18(2): 1–35.

Sugasawa, Y. (2004) 'The current state of competitive intelligence activities and competitive awareness in Japanese business', *Journal of Competitive Intelligence and Management* 2(4): 7–31.

Takeishi, A. (2001). 'Bridging inter- and intra-firm boundaries: management of supplier involvement in automobile product development', *Strategic Management Journal* 22(5): 403–33.

Tampoe, M. (1994). 'Exploiting the core competences of your organization', *Long Range Planning* 27(4): 66–77.

Teece, D. J., Pisano, G., and Shuen, A. (1997). 'Dynamic capabilities and strategic management', *Strategic Management Journal* 18(7): 509–33.

Teece, David J. (2007). 'Explicating dynamic capabilities: the nature and microfoundations of (sustainable) enterprise performance', *Strategic Management Journal* 28(13): 1319–50.

Watson, G. H. (1993). 'How process benchmarking supports corporate strategy', *Planning Review* (January–February): 12–15.

Wernerfelt, B. (1984). 'A resource-based view of the firm', *Strategic Management Journal* 5(2): 171–80.

**online resource centre**

## Online resource centre

Please visit www.oxfordtextbooks.co.uk/orc/frynas_mellahi2e/ for further information.

# Part three

# Global strategic development

# Managing the internationalization process

## 5

## Learning outcomes

After reading this chapter, you should be able to:

➤ Understand the motives for internationalization.

➤ Apply the theories underpinning the internationalization process.

➤ Explain the Psychic Distance and Born Global concepts.

➤ Advise a multinational firm on choosing an appropriate entry mode for internationalization.

➤ Advise a multinational firm on de-internationalization.

**Opening case study** Internationalization of a
French retailer—Carrefour

In 1960, Carrefour opened its first supermarket in France. In 1963, Carrefour invented a
new store concept—the hypermarket. The hypermarket concept was novel, and revolutionized
the way French people did their shopping. It moved daily shopping from small stores to enormous stores where customers find everything they want under one roof, in addition to self-
service, discount price, and free parking space. The first Carrefour hypermarket store was
established at the intersection of five roads—hence the name, Carrefour, which means
'crossroads'. Carrefour is the leading retailer in Europe and the second largest worldwide, with

**Exhibit A** International development of Carrefour

| Year | Country and mode of entry | No. of stores (2009) | Formats |
|------|---------------------------|----------------------|---------|
| 1969 | Belgium—Carrefour's first hypermarket outside France | 120 | 57(HM), 63(SM) |
| 1973 | Spain | 2,241 | 162(HM), 96(SM), 1,972(HD), 11(CS) |
| 1975 | Brazil—Carrefour's first hypermarket in the Americas | 476 | 162(HM), 39(SM), 267(HD), 8(CS) |
| 1982 | Argentina | 518 | 67(HM), 112(SM), 339(HD) |
| 1989 | Taiwan—Carrefour's first hypermarket in Asia | 59 | HM |
| 1991 | Greece | 544 | 31(HM), 209 (SM), 271 (HD), 33(CS) |
| 1993 | Italy | 494 | 66(HM), 236(SM), 178(CS), 14(C&C) |
| 1993 | Turkey | 578 | 22(HM), 125(SM), 431(HD) |
| 1994 | Malaysia | 16 | HM |
| 1995 | China | 443 | 134(HM), 309(HD) |
| 1996 | Thailand | 31 | HM |
| 1997 | Poland | 303 | 78 (HM), 225(SM) |
| 1997 | Singapore | 2 | HM |
| 1998 | Colombia | 59 | HM |
| 1998 | Indonesia | 43 | HM |
| 2000 | Japan | 0 | |

*Note:* HM = hypermarkets, SM = supermarkets, HD = hard discount stores, CS = convenience stores,
C&C = cash and carry stores.

*Source:* P. Kamath and C. Codin (2001), 'French Carrefour in South-East Asia', *British Food Journal* 103(7):
479–94; E. Colla and M. Dupuis (2002), 'Research and managerial issues on global retail competition:
Carrefour/Wal-Mart', *International Journal of Retail and Distribution Management* 30(2): 103–11; and
Carrefour's website at http://www.carrefour.com/.

more than 15,000 stores in thirty countries. In 2009, almost 55% of its revenues came from its international stores.

In 1969, Carrefour opened its first hypermarket store outside France, in Belgium. Although French consumers welcomed the hypermarket concept, smaller stores lobbied against the spread of hypermarket stores in the late 1960s and early 1970s, and in 1973, the French legislature passed the Royer Law, which restricted the introduction of more hypermarkets. Carrefour had no choice but to expand internationally. It first moved to neighbouring European countries: Switzerland in 1970; Britain and Italy in 1972; and Spain in 1973. However, Carrefour soon withdrew from the Belgian and British markets, focusing mainly on southern European and Latin American countries where the distribution system was not yet modernized. In 1975, it expanded its format outside Europe, to Brazil. Carrefour's internationalization strategy further accelerated in the 1980s and 1990s (see Exhibit A).

Carrefour's international strategy is based on the hypermarket format with local adaptability. For example, while the store format is the same anywhere around the world, the company sells hot meals to French customers in France and pasta in Argentina and Italy, and has sushi bars in most Asian countries. The success of Carrefour's export of its hypermarket concept is due, at least in part, to its careful choice of countries and to its ability to adapt its format to local business environments. As shown in Exhibit A, most countries are emerging economies with a growing urban middle-class population that find the hypermarket concept appealing.

The international concept of Carrefour is based on:

- A simple and clear idea. People in major cities prefer to do all their shopping under one roof. Carrefour's logic is based on the belief that choice, self-service, free parking, and low prices have universal appeal. Although these principles might seem simple, the introduction of free parking in South Korea and Singapore was considered revolutionary, given the high cost of land in these countries.

- Evolving ideas. Each hypermarket around the world is expected to keep reinventing itself to meet the demands of local customers. For instance, the company has introduced organic food in France, optical shops and tyre fitting in Taiwan, and petrol stations in Argentina.

As shown in Exhibit A, different formats are present in different countries. While the hypermarket model is the only format in emerging economies in South America (with the exception of Brazil and Argentina) and Asia, different formats exist in European countries. This is mainly due to: (1) planning restrictions on building hypermarkets in Western European countries; and (2) historical growth through acquisition of small outlets. In addition, in contrast to its standard entry mode by ownership, Carrefour entered several countries—the United Arab Emirates, Madagascar, Qatar, Romania, the Dominican Republic, and Tunisia—through a franchise partnership.

Most Carrefour stores are still located in Europe. However, the importance of non-European markets has been steadily increasing. For instance, the number of Carrefour stores in Belgium fell from 483 to 120 in the ten-year period of 1999–2009, while the number of stores in Italy fell from 912 to 494. At the same time, the number of Carrefour stores in Brazil increased from 193 to 476, while the number of stores in China increased from 23 to 443.

## 5.1 **Introduction**

Understanding the motives behind a firm's decision to internationalize its business activities helps to explain why and how firms should engage in international business activities. For example, Carrefour was compelled to make its first international move in the 1970s because of the introduction of the Royer Law, which restricted its growth in France. Later on, it was attracted by opportunities in South American, Asian, and Middle Eastern markets. In this chapter, we discuss factors that push and pull firms to internationalize their business activities.

In addition to the motives for internationalization, we need to understand the different modes of entering a foreign country or a region. There is no best way to enter a foreign market. For example, Carrefour's mode of entry differed from one country or region to another. The company started its first international experience cautiously, expanding to countries it knew quite well and in moves which involved small risks. As it gained more experience in foreign markets and confidence in its ability to operate effectively outside its home market, its attitudes towards operating and risk in foreign markets changed. This resulted in further expansions into more challenging and unknown markets, such as the Middle Eastern and Asian markets.

## 5.2 **Decision and motives to internationalize**

In addressing the question of why certain firms are engaged in international business activities while others are not, researchers have focused on the elements stimulating a firm's decision to initiate foreign market entry (Albaum 1983). Internationalization stimuli can be defined as those internal and external factors that influence a firm's decision to initiate, develop, and sustain international business activities.

Two sets of factors lead firms to consider the possibility of operating outside their home market: organizational factors arising from within the firm, and environmental factors which are outside the firm's control (see Exhibit 5.1) (Aharoni 1966).

### 5.2.1 **Organizational factors**

Organizational factors can be split into two forces: decision-maker characteristics and firm-specific factors.

#### Decision-maker characteristics

Recognition by the top manager, or the top management team, of the importance of international activities is an essential part of the process of internationalization. The top manager's (or top management team's) exposure to foreign markets is a critical component in the decision to internationalize (Karafakioglu 1986; Jaw and Lin 2009). Management characteristics such as

**Exhibit 5.1** Factors behind the decision to internationalize

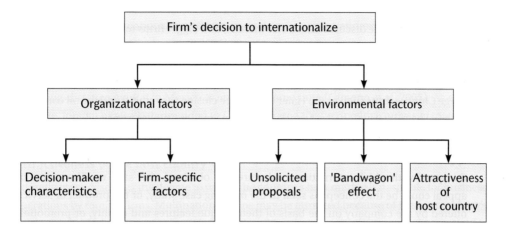

perceptions of risk in foreign operations have a strong influence on management perceptions of international business activities. Reid (1981) found the following characteristics positively influenced the internationalization decision:

- Foreign travel and experience abroad. Managers who travel abroad extensively are more open-minded and interested in foreign affairs, thus being more able and willing to meet foreign managers and form business partnerships. They also have more opportunities to observe first-hand the advantages that foreign partnerships and foreign countries may offer, have a foreign business network in place, and are able to attract and negotiate with managers from different cultures.

- Foreign language proficiency. The number of languages spoken by the top manager is a good indication of his or her interest in international activities. Managers who speak several languages tend to travel more to foreign countries and thus are more able to establish social and business contacts, understand foreign business practices better, are better placed to negotiate a good deal for the company, and communicate not only with top managers of foreign affiliates who could speak the home country's language but with line managers and employees as well.

- The decision-maker background. Having been born abroad, lived abroad, or worked abroad could influence one's view of risks and opportunities in foreign markets. For example, international work experience exposes managers to foreign opportunities, and therefore makes it easier for them to take the first step into foreign markets.

- Personal characteristics. Natural risk-takers are more likely to engage in an international activity than risk-averse managers. Similarly, managers with high ambitions tend to internationalize more than managers with low personal ambitions.

- Efficiency seeking. A company may seek to invest in a foreign country in order to decrease costs through cheaper labour or materials, to locate in a specific industrial cluster or to benefit from better integration of international activities.

- Strategic asset seeking. A company may seek to invest strategically in a foreign country in order to obtain important knowledge resources, accelerate innovation, or learn from different consumer preferences.

The first three motives primarily help a multinational firm to exploit assets in other countries by using the firm's existing capabilities. The last motive—strategic asset seeking—serves to improve the firm's capabilities through learning in foreign locations. Firms can have different motives for foreign investments. For example, Carrefour (see opening case study) was primarily market seeking, while the Haier Group (see closing case study) was primarily strategic asset seeking but the company was also market seeking.

## 5.3 The internationalization process

The previous section explained *why* firms internationalize (the internationalization stimuli). Once a firm decides to expand internationally, it must decide *when* and *how* to internationalize (the internationalization process).

### 5.3.1 Timing of market entry

The environmental factors in the previous section explain why many firms enter a market at a particular time: when a firm is approached by a customer; when competing firms enter an important market; or when a market is growing very fast. For instance, Carrefour decided to expand in emerging markets such as Poland and China at the very time when the economies of these countries were quickly expanding and consumers had increasingly more money to spend on shopping.

Firms may also decide to enter a market at a particular time for wider strategic reasons. Previous research highlighted the strategic importance of the timing of market entry, suggesting that first movers in foreign markets perform better than later market entrants (Mascarenhas 1992, 1997; Isobe et al. 2000; Geng and Hon-Kwong 2005; Frynas et al. 2006). The concept of a first mover advantage suggests that pioneering businesses are able to obtain higher profits and other benefits as the consequence of early market entry (Lieberman and Montgomery 1988).

Early entry into a foreign market can have five generic advantages (Kerin et al. 1992; Lieberman and Montgomery 1998; Frynas et al. 2006):

- Cost advantages (e.g., allowing the firm to have larger economies of scale and accumulating experience about the foreign market before the entry of competitors).

- Pre-emption of geographic space (e.g., pre-empting competitors by securing a specific geographic space or marketing channel).

- Technological advantages (e.g., adapting products and processes to the local market and implementing new innovations before competitors enter the market).

- Differentiation advantages (e.g., higher switching costs for buyers or reputational advantages of established brands).

- Political advantages (e.g., the support of foreign government in raising barriers to entry for late movers).

For instance, Lockheed Martin has been able to reap considerable first mover advantages by expanding into Russia in the late 1990s before the company's competitors did so (see closing case study in Chapter 2). The entry into Russia greatly helped the company to gain a leading position in the global market for satellite launch services ahead of competitors. Lockheed Martin benefited from joint marketing of satellite launches with the best joint-venture partners available in Russia (pre-emption of geographic space), obtaining new technology from Russian joint-venture partners (technological advantages) and benefiting from the Russian and American government support in raising barriers to entry for late comers (political advantages) (Frynas et al. 2006).

However, some studies suggested that there can also be considerable first mover disadvantages and early market entry does not automatically endow pioneers with higher profitability (Tellis and Golder 1996; Shankar et al. 1998; Shamsie et al. 2004). The timing of market entry is clearly as important as the firm's ability to fully exploit the early market entry. Studies show that first mover advantages in foreign markets depend on several internal and external factors, including the strategic importance of an investment, the close linkage of an investment to core business activities, the rate of technological change in the industry, and the policies of the host country government (Isobe et al. 2000; Goerzen and Makino 2007; Frynas et al. 2006).

---

**KEY CONCEPT**

First mover advantages are benefits related to the ability of pioneering businesses to obtain profits as the consequence of early market entry. There are five generic first mover advantages: cost advantages; pre-emption of geographic space; technological advantages; differentiation advantages; and political advantages.

---

### 5.3.2 Obstacles to internationalization

Many companies have discovered that it can be very difficult to expand internationally, even if you offer a superior and cheaper product or service compared with your competitors. For instance, Carrefour faced government restrictions on opening hypermarkets in different countries, problems of adapting its organization to different national contexts, and logistical problems in countries with underdeveloped transport infrastructure. In 2008, some Chinese nationalists called for a boycott of Carrefour following controversial comments of the president of France about China, on the ground that Carrefour is a French-based company.

Carrefour and other multinational firms are aware that expanding internationally can produce 'liabilities'. Foreign companies may be disadvantaged by the government (e.g., restrictions on investment), discriminated against by consumers (e.g., consumer boycotts), unable to transfer their competitive advantages to foreign markets (e.g., inability to replicate a low-cost base due to logistical problems), lack the essential knowledge to operate successfully in a country (e.g., lack of understanding of consumer preferences and distribution networks) (Cuervo-Cazurra et al. 2007). Studies show that internationalizing firms face additional costs in foreign markets, increased failure rates and problems of coordinating operations in different countries (Zaheer 1995; Hitt et al. 1997; Cuervo-Cazurra et al. 2007).

The difficulties of internationalizing firms can be the consequence of at least four different types of 'liabilities':

- Liability of foreignness. The difficulties as a result of the different norms and rules that constrain human behaviour, including culture, language, religion, and politics; companies may lack the knowledge and social networks to understand the different norms and rules of how to operate successfully in a foreign country (Zaheer 1995; Mezias 2002).

- Liability of expansion. The difficulties as a result of an increase in the scale of a firm's activities; domestic companies may also face problems of increased transportation, communication, and coordination as a result of expansion but these problems are usually greater for multinational firms because of the high costs of coordinating international operations (Hitt et al. 1997; Cuervo-Cazurra et al. 2007).

- Liability of smallness. The difficulties as a result of small company size; in particular, small- and medium-sized enterprises (SMEs) may have fewer financial resources for foreign investments, limited information about the characteristics of foreign markets, a lack of human resources to conduct relevant business development work, and less negotiating leverage vis-à-vis potential business partners and foreign governments (Aldrich and Auster 1986; Child et al. 2009).

- Liability of newness. The difficulties as a result of being new to a market; new domestic market entrants also suffer disadvantages compared with established firms but these problems are larger for internationalizing firms because they lack experience of foreign transactions or lack certain resources needed in foreign markets (Freeman et al. 1983; Cuervo-Cazurra et al. 2007).

When Carrefour expanded in China, for example, it faced *the liability of foreignness* (Carrefour was targeted in a consumer boycott by Chinese nationalists in 2008 because it was a French company); *the liability of expansion* (Carrefour faced transportation, communication and coordination problems because of China's vast geographical size, therefore it needed to establish eleven regional procurement centres); and *the liability of newness* (Carrefour did not initially know where to find the best local suppliers and how to deal with local government authorities, therefore it had to rely on the knowledge of local Chinese joint venture partners).

### 5.3.3 **Perceptions of managers**

The previous section demonstrated that there are many *objective* reasons why it can be very difficult for companies to expand internationally. However, *subjective* perceptions of managers about foreign markets are often the key reasons why companies decide to expand internationally in a certain direction.

Managers—like any other human beings—tend to avoid unfamiliar situations compared with familiar ones. They do not like uncertainty and prefer to invest in markets they are familiar with rather than in unfamiliar markets. Their decisions are influenced by their subjective perceptions of how easy it will be to operate in a new market. The concept of psychic distance helps to understand why these perceptions affect the internationalization process of firms.

Psychic distance can be defined as the distance that is *perceived* to exist between characteristics of a firm's home country and a foreign country with which that firm is, or is contemplating, doing business or investing (Child et al. 2009). High psychic distance (that is, *subjective perceptions* of large differences between countries) can discourage the firm's international expansion into a given country because it generates uncertainties among business decision-makers.

Despite the tendency of some previous studies to regard psychic distance as purely cultural differences (e.g., Kogut and Singh 1988), studies show that managerial perceptions are influenced by many different factors. Factors which influence managerial perceptions of psychic distance include: geographical distance, language, religion, education levels, levels of industrial development, logistics infrastructure, political systems, legal systems, and government regulations, among others (Johanson and Wiedersheim-Paul 1975; Ghemawat 2001; Dow and Karunaratna 2006; Child et al. 2009).

---

**KEY CONCEPT**

Psychic distance can be defined as the distance that is *perceived* to exist between characteristics of a firm's home country and a foreign country with which that firm is, or is contemplating, doing business or investing. High psychic distance can discourage the firm's international expansion into a given country because it generates uncertainties among business decision-makers.

---

### 5.3.4 **Psychic distance and internationalization**

An influential explanation of the internationalization process was offered by Swedish researchers (Johanson and Wiedersheim-Paul 1975; Johanson and Vahlne 1977, 1990). Johanson and his colleagues developed the proposition that internationalization proceeds through stages of decreasing psychic distance.

Johanson and Wiedersheim-Paul (1975) made two observations about the way in which firms internationalize. First, firms start expanding to neighbouring countries or countries with small psychic distance. A firm's international expansion depends on its experiential knowledge of foreign markets. Experiential knowledge is knowledge obtained from experience. By implication, there is a direct link between market knowledge and market commitment. The better the knowledge of a market, the stronger the commitment to that market.

Second, firms expand their international operations step by step. In other words, a firm's international expansion occurs as a result of incremental decisions. Johanson and Wiedersheim-Paul (1975) studied the internationalization process of four large Swedish multinationals, and found that the internationalization patterns of these firms were marked by a number of small incremental changes. They identified four successive stages in the firm's international expansion:

1. No regular export activities.
2. Export activities via independent representatives or agents.
3. The establishment of an overseas subsidiary.
4. Overseas production and manufacturing units.

These two observations form the basis of the Uppsala Model, which suggests that a firm's international expansion is a gradual process dependent on experiential knowledge and incremental steps. Johanson and Wiedersheim-Paul's (1975) work was further developed and refined by Johanson and Vahlne (1977), who formulated a 'dynamic' Uppsala Model—a model in which the outcome of one cycle of events constitutes the input to the next (see Exhibit 5.2).

### 5.3.5 The Uppsala Model

The Uppsala Model suggests that firms proceed along the internationalization path in the form of logical steps, based on their gradual acquisition and use of information gathered from foreign markets and operations, which determine successively greater levels of market commitment

**Exhibit 5.2** The Uppsala Model

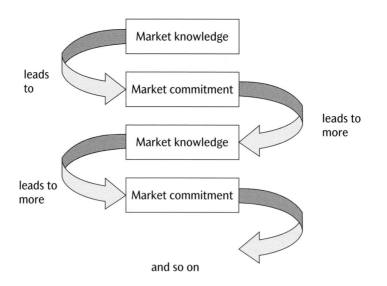

to more international business activities. The concept of market commitment suggests that resources located in a particular market present a firm's commitment to that market, so foreign direct investment means higher market commitment than exporting or licensing. Market commitment is composed of two factors: the amount of resources committed and the degree of commitment. The amount of resources refers to the size of investment in a given market. The degree of commitment refers to the difficulty of finding an alternative use for the resources and transferring them to the alternative use.

The Uppsala Model assumes that the more the firm knows about the foreign market, the lower the *perceived* market risk will be, and the higher the level of investment in that market. The *perceived* risk is primarily a function of the level of market knowledge acquired through one's own operations (Forsgren 2002). So, over time, and as firms gain foreign commercial experience and improve their knowledge of foreign markets, they tend to increase their foreign market commitment and venture into countries that are increasingly dissimilar to their own. This, in turn, enhances market knowledge, leading to further commitment in more distant markets.

The model helps to understand a firm's initial choice of international location and its mode of entry into foreign markets. For example, French firms such as Carrefour initially expand to other Western European countries such as Belgium and Spain, before making direct investments in Turkey, the United States, or China. At the same time, firms initially export to other countries or engage in strategic alliances with foreign firms, before committing capital towards wholly-owned foreign investments.

It should be pointed out that there are three exceptions to the Uppsala Model. First, firms that have large resources and experience can take larger internationalization steps. This helps to explain why small—and medium-sized enterprises follow the Uppsala Model more closely than very large multinational firms. Second, when market conditions are stable and homogeneous, relevant market knowledge can be gained from sources other than experience. Third, when the firm has considerable experience of markets with similar conditions, it may be able to generalize this experience to any specific market.

---

**KEY CONCEPT**

The Uppsala Model suggests that a firm's international expansion is a gradual process dependent on *experiential knowledge* and *incremental steps*. It assumes that firms proceed along the internationalization path in the form of logical steps, based on the gradual acquisition and use of information gathered from foreign markets and operations, which determine successively greater levels of market commitment to more international business activities.

---

# 5.4 Criticisms of the Uppsala Model

Despite the intuitive appeal of the Uppsala Model, there is much concern about its current usefulness. The model does not explain what triggers the first internationalization step. The model largely explains the international expansion of firms in the early stages of internationalization and does not explain the behaviour of large established multinational firms that already have extensive international experience and operations across the world (Melin 1992). Above all, the Uppsala Model cannot explain why some firms do not follow the logical sequence of steps suggested in the Model and why some firms are born global from the start.

### 5.4.1. Firms not following Uppsala Model

Multinational firms do not always expand in countries with low psychic distance before entering more distant countries. Sometimes, a firm's international expansion is not the outcome of a learning process (as the Uppsala Model suggests), but the outcome of a rational strategic choice (i.e., a conscious choice to enter a specific foreign market). For example, if a European firm makes a deliberate decision to relocate its manufacturing production to a low-cost country, it may be more likely to invest in distant China than in a neighbouring European country. This helps to explain, for instance, why many Norwegian firms did not make initial foreign investments close to the home country and would not necessarily internationalize in incremental steps (Benito and Gripsrud 1992).

Furthermore, the Uppsala Model may not always explain the international expansion of firms from emerging markets. Firms from countries such as China may seek to 'catch up' with established multinational firms through the accelerated learning that entry into psychically distant countries can entail. Studies show that companies from emerging markets seek to learn new skills or acquire new technologies from their strategic partners or their subsidiaries in psychically distant developed countries (Child and Rodrigues 2005; Lyles and Salk 2007; Liu et al. 2008). Therefore, some companies from emerging markets may take a strategic decision to expand to the United States or Europe as early as possible in order to enhance their capabilities.

### 5.4.2 The Born Global firm

There are firms which do not follow the traditional internationalization process at all, but which are multinational firms from the very start. In 1993, the consultants, McKinsey, published the findings of a survey for the Australian Manufacturing Council on the internationalization of small and medium firms in Australia (McKinsey 1993). The report put forward evidence that a large number of the surveyed firms in Australia viewed 'the world as their marketplace from the outset and see the domestic market as a support for their international business' (p. 9). One example of such a firm is Tyrian Diagnostics (see closing case study in Chapter 6). The McKinsey report referred to these firms as 'Born Global' firms.

Other researchers observed the Born Global phenomenon, but used different terms to describe it, including international new ventures (McDougall et al. 1994; Oviatt and McDougall 1994), born internationals (Kundu and Katz 2003), and early internationalizing firms (Rialp et al. 2005*a*). In essence, the terms Born Global firm or International New Venture describes firms that, right from their birth, seek competitive advantage by using resources from different countries and by selling their products in multiple countries. The terms, Born Global firm or International New Venture, can be defined as:

> *a business organization that, from inception, seeks to derive significant competitive advantage from the use of resources and the sale of outputs in multiple countries. The distinguishing feature of these start-ups is that their origins are international, as demonstrated by observable and significant commitments of resources (e.g. material, people, financing, time) in more than one nation. (McDougall et al. 1994: 49)*

Born Global firms generally share three characteristics (Knight and Çavusgil 1996; Kotha et al. 2001; Rialp et al. 2005*b*):

- Company size. Born Global firms are usually small- and medium-sized enterprises (SMEs), which have recently started operations.

- Hi-tech focus. Born Global firms are usually hi-tech firms that are able to offer very specialized products or services in global niche markets. The fact that they are hi-tech enables Born Global firms to sell their product or service to global customers with minimum adjustments.

- Decision-maker characterictics. Born Global firms are managed or founded by people who have either greater international experience or access to better international business and personal networks, compared with managers of gradually internationalizing firms. In addition, the managers of such firms may have higher risk tolerance than managers of gradually internationalizing firms.

Firms originating from small countries such as Nordic countries are more likely to adopt a Born Global strategy than firms from large countries such as the United States. For example, Lindmark et al. (1994) reported that nearly 50% of hi-tech start-ups in the Nordic countries began exporting within two years of establishment. The small size of the home market forces firms to sell their products globally from the start in order to be competitive.

---

**KEY CONCEPT**

A Born Global firm is a business organization that, within a short period from inception, seeks to derive significant competitive advantage from the use of resources and the sale of outputs in foreign markets.

---

### 5.4.3 Response to criticisms

The Uppsala Model cannot explain the expansion of Born Global firms. The criticisms of the Uppsala Model might therefore be thought to undermine the analytical contribution offered by the Model and the psychic distance concept. However, recent research suggests that there are relatively few Born Global firms, even among start-up technology firms (Lopez et al. 2009). Indeed, what the criticisms of the Uppsala Model actually undermine is the assumption that psychic distance generates uncertainties which business people *are unwilling or unable to tackle* (cf. Child et al. 2009).

The attractiveness of some foreign markets in terms of their size, growth rate or technological development might be sufficient to offset, in the judgement of business decision-makers, the uncertainties and risks associated with psychic distance. This can help to explain why European firms seeking new markets or Chinese firms seeking new technologies jumped over stages in the Uppsala Model. Johanson and Wiedesheim-Paul (1975) themselves admitted that foreign market size may independently influence decisions in the internationalization process. Johanson and Vahlne (2009: 1421) point out: 'There is nothing in our model that indicates that international expansion cannot be done quickly.'

Born Global firms and firms from emerging markets such as China also face the same problems of psychic distance like other firms (Child et al. 2002; Isenberg 2008). However, instead of expanding to psychically close countries first, these firms sometimes use different methods to help them cope with psychic distance. They use social networks, rely on a local agent or partner, hire local professionals, or expand in foreign cities with a high number of migrants from their country of origin, which in turn helps these firms to obtain tacit knowledge of foreign regulations, culture, and business practices (Zhou et al. 2007; Child et al. 2002, 2009). This does not necessarily suggest that the Uppsala Model and the psychic distance concept are out of date, but rather that smart managers may find ways of bridging distance and exploiting market opportunities (see Exhibit 5.3).

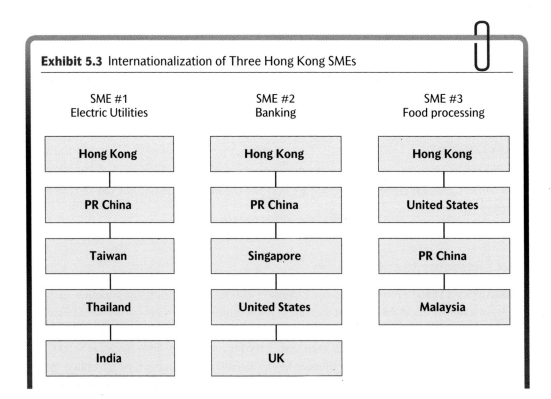

**Exhibit 5.3** Internationalization of Three Hong Kong SMEs

| SME #1 Electric Utilities | SME #2 Banking | SME #3 Food processing |
| --- | --- | --- |
| Hong Kong | Hong Kong | Hong Kong |
| PR China | PR China | United States |
| Taiwan | Singapore | PR China |
| Thailand | United States | Malaysia |
| India | UK | |

The figure above represents the first internationalization steps by three different small- and medium-sized enterprises (SMEs) from Hong Kong.

SME #1—an electric utility firm—followed the Uppsala Model very closely. The firm expanded first to Chinese-speaking neighbouring territories, and then to other Asian countries. SME #2—a family bank—first expanded to two Chinese-speaking countries close to home; however, the company then expanded very quickly to very distant countries. SME #3—a food processing firm—appeared to defy the Uppsala Model and expanded first to the distant United States, before expanding closer to home.

How can the internationalization of SME #2 and SME #3 be explained? The companies' motives for investment allow some reconciliation with the psychic distance concept. In both cases, the overseas investments in the United States were established, not to cater to Western consumers, but to a large overseas Chinese community. In other words, the Chinese overseas community provided a ready market for the two firms.

The managers' perceptions were also crucial for their decision to expand in a distant country. The managers were less worried about the distance to the United States because of the presence of social networks (a trusted friend, a loyal staff member, or a local partner) among the Chinese community in the United States, who helped them bridge the psychic distance between Hong Kong and the United States. In the case of SME #3, the managers preferred the United States as they perceived the country to have a 'stable' environment, safeguarded by the rule of law. In other words, the managers did not perceive the psychic distance to be so large and they were able to find ways to bridge psychic distance between their home country and the host country.

*Source:* J. Child, S.-H. Ng, and C. Wong (2002), 'Psychic distance and internationalization: evidence from Hong Kong Firms', *International Studies of Management & Organization* 32(1): 36–56.

When companies expand internationally, business networks are the best method for bridging psychic distance. Business networks are much more important today than twenty or thirty years ago. The Uppsala Model was originally based on the assumption that a firm accumulates experiential knowledge through its own international expansion. However, the proponents of the Uppsala Model now admit that knowledge about foreign markets can often come from business networks: strategic partners, customers, suppliers, etc. (Johanson and Vahlne 2003, 2009). Business partners can provide information, for example, about the best local suppliers and how to deal with local government authorities. For example, when expanding in China, Carrefour initially relied on the knowledge of local Chinese joint venture partners to help the company bridge psychic distance.

It is certainly true that the speed of international expansion is much faster today than twenty or thirty years ago. For instance, the Japanese company Matsushita waited for almost thirty years between the start of international exports and the establishment of an overseas plant. The Chinese company, Haier Group (see closing case study), achieved this step in less than ten years. It took Matsushita twelve years from building its first overseas plant to its first acquisition of a foreign company, while the Haier Group achieved the first acquisition after only five years. However, while Matsushita and the Haier Group started their international expansion at different times and at different speeds, their internationalization process was similar and broadly followed incremental steps (Yang et al. 2009).

Recent studies provide evidence that the Uppsala Model and the psychic distance concept can still explain the international expansion of firms (Barkema and Drogendijk 2007), including new multinational firms from emerging markets (Elango and Pattnaik 2007; Erdilek 2008; Child et al. 2009; Yang et al. 2009). International managers cannot ignore issues related to psychic distance. Rather, they need to learn how to bridge psychic distance in order to speed up their firms' international expansion.

## 5.5 Entry mode strategies

We have previously referred to modes of entry into foreign markets. When firms decide to enter a foreign market, they are faced with a large array of choices of entry mode, which could be grouped into five main categories: export, licensing, franchising, international joint venture, and wholly-owned operations. This section will only focus on four modes of entry, leaving aside international partnerships between firms. Because of the importance and complex nature of international joint ventures and strategic alliances, we have allocated a whole chapter to this issue (see Chapter 6).

### 5.5.1 Export

A simple definition of exporting is the action by the firm to send produced goods and services from the home country to other countries. This can be ascribed to the fact that exporting does not need the commitment of large resources and is thus less costly than alternatives such as joint ventures (Morgan and Katsikeas 1998). It is also easier for the multinational firm to withdraw its operations with minimum damage (see Exhibit 5.4). Because of the physical distance, however, the export strategy does not enable the multinational firm to control its operations abroad.

Export is a frequently employed mode of internationalization and one of the simplest and most common approaches adopted mainly by small- and medium-sized firms in their endeavour to enter foreign markets.

There are three different exporter categories according to firms' level of export involvement: *experimental involvement*, where the firm initiates restricted export marketing activity; *active involvement*, where the firm systematically explores a range of export market opportunities; and *committed involvement*, where the firm allocates its resources on the basis of international marketing opportunities (Çavusgil 1984).

As shown in Exhibit 5.4, generally firms export for two reasons. First, firms need experiential knowledge, and exporting has the potential to provide firms with international experience without their taking high risk or strong commitment. Second, firms use exporting to expand their sales in order to achieve economies of scale.

**Risks of exporting**

Export strategy, compared with the other modes of entry, is a low-risk strategy. The major risks of exporting are:

- When countries experience major political instability, export could be disrupted, with consequential delays and other defaults on payments, exchange transfer blockages, or confiscation of property.

- The multinational firm has no control over some costs, such as costs of land transport to the port, transfers, shipping costs, insurance, and foreign exchange risk.

## 5.5.2 Licensing

International licensing is 'the transfer of patented information and trademarks, information and know-how, including specifications, written documents, computer programs, and so forth, as well as information needed to sell a product or service, with respect to a physical territory' (Mottner and Johnson 2000: 171).

Licensing does not mean duplicating the product in several countries. Most products going into foreign countries require some form of adaptation: labels and instructions must be translated; goods may require modification to conform with local laws and regulations; and marketing may have to be adjusted.

Benefits of licensing include speed to market, especially when a firm lacks sufficient skills, capital, or personnel to enter a foreign market quickly (see Exhibit 5.4). For instance, German home appliance manufacturers Liebherr and Bosch-Siemens entered several emerging markets such as China and Turkey through licensing agreements for manufacturing refrigerators and other white goods. In turn, emerging market firms such as the Haier Group of China (see closing case study) and Arçelik of Turkey used the foreign licensing technology to expand internationally through exporting.

In addition to being used as an entry mode to foreign markets, licensing may also be used as a step towards a more committed mode of entry such as a joint venture or a wholly-owned form. For example, when in 1997, Phoenix AG, a German manufacturing concern, agreed to license the production of its automotive and railway components in India to Sigma Corp. of Delhi, the licence agreement was no more than a step towards establishing a joint venture, which would integrate Sigma's manufacturing capability into Phoenix's global strategy (Mottner and Johnson 2000).

**Risks of licensing**

Several risks are associated with international licensing. Mottner and Johnson (2000) identified the following risks:

- Sub-optimal choice. This risk is associated with the possibility of licensing being not the best possible choice and or selecting the wrong partner—hence not realizing the full potential of the partnership.

- Risk of opportunism. The possibility that the licensee takes the opportunity to appropriate the technology or process that has been licensed to it and internalizes it.

**Exhibit 5.4** Advantages and disadvantages of different modes of entry

| Mode of entry | Advantages | Disadvantages |
|---|---|---|
| Export | • Does not require a high resource commitment in the targeted country<br>• Inexpensive way to gain experiential knowledge in foreign markets<br>• Low-cost strategy to expand sales in order to achieve economies of scale | • Hard to control operations abroad<br>• Provides very small experiential knowledge in foreign markets |
| Licensing | • Speedy entry to foreign market<br>• Does not require a high resource commitment in the targeted country<br>• Can be used as a step towards a more committed mode of entry<br>• Low-cost strategy to expand sales in order to achieve economies of scale | • Hard to monitor partners in foreign markets<br>• High potential for opportunism<br>• Hard to enforce agreements<br>• Provides a small experiential knowledge in foreign markets |
| International franchising | • Speedy entry to foreign market<br>• Requires a moderate resource commitment in the targeted country<br>• Moderate-cost strategy to expand sales in order to achieve economies of scale | • High monitoring costs<br>• High potential for opportunism<br>• Could damage the firm's reputation and image<br>• Does not provide experiential knowledge in foreign markets |

| | Advantages | Disadvantages |
|---|---|---|
| Wholly-owned ventures Greenfield strategy | • Low risks of technology appropriation<br>• Able to control operations abroad<br>• Provides high experiential knowledge in foreign markets<br>• Low level of conflict between the subsidiary and the parent firm<br>• Does not have the problem of integrating different cultures, structures, procedures, and technologies<br>• Managers of foreign subsidiaries have a strong attachment to the parent firm | • Could not rely on pre-existing relationships with customers, suppliers, and government officials<br>• Potential difficulty in accessing existing managers and employees familiar with local market conditions<br>• Adds extra capacity to the existing market<br>• The firm is seen as a foreign firm by local stakeholders |
| Mergers and acquisitions | • Low risks of technology appropriation<br>• Able to control operations abroad<br>• Provides high experiential knowledge in foreign markets<br>• Could rely on pre-existing relationships with customers, suppliers, and government officials<br>• Access to existing managers and employees familiar with local market conditions<br>• Does not add extra capacity to the market | • Problem of integrating foreign subsidiaries into the parent's system<br>• Managers of acquired foreign subsidiaries may have a weak attachment to the parent firm |

the 1980s and 1990s, Japanese firms adopting a global strategy structure preferred to clone their home country structure and strategy in foreign markets through greenfield strategies (Harzing 2002).

Generally, greenfield investments are preferred when specific technical and organizational skills define a firm's ability to compete. For example, Japanese multinationals with weak competitive advantage tend to use mergers and acquisitions (M&As), while those with strong advantages prefer greenfield investments to transfer their advantages to foreign markets (Hennart and Park 1993).

**Risks of the greenfield strategy** The greenfield strategy is a high-risk strategy. In addition to the above risks associated with other modes of entry, such as political instability in the host country, other risks specific to the greenfield strategy (see Exhibit 5.4) include:

- The risk of not being able to build relationships with customers, suppliers, and government officials in the new country.

- The risk of not being able to recruit managers and employees familiar with local market conditions.

- The risk of being seen as a foreign firm by local stakeholders.

## The mergers and acquisitions (M&As) strategy

An international merger is a transaction that combines two companies from different countries to establish a new legal entity. International acquisition refers to the acquisition of a local firm's assets by a foreign company. In an acquisition, both local and foreign firms may continue to exist. Barkema and Vermeulen (1998: 405) noted that, 'for companies to prefer acquisition to greenfield entry, the cost of constructing new facilities, installing equipment, and hiring and training new labour force must exceed the costs of purchasing and recasting existing properties.'

In the short-term, cross-border M&As can have positive benefits for the shareholders of the acquired firm. In the longer term, however, profitability gains through are often limited or nonexistent (King et al. 2004). There are three types of M&A:

- Horizontal M&As involve two competing firms in the same industry. This type of M&As is more common in industries where consolidation is required, such as automobile, petroleum, and pharmaceutical industries.

- Vertical M&As involve a merger between firms in the supply chain. This involves, for example, a distributor or a supplier merging with a manufacturer.

- Conglomerate M&As involve a merger of two companies from two unrelated industries. Conglomerate M&As were very popular in the late 1980s, but have been declining ever since as firms retreated to their core business during the 1990s and 2000s.

The motives for M&As can be classified into three types (Hopkins 1999: 212):

- Strategic motives aim to improve the overall strategic position of the multinational firm. This includes the intention to create synergy, to strengthen market power, and to gain speedy access to foreign markets (Hopkins 1999: 212). Synergy is the potential ability of two firms to be more successful as a result of a merger or an acquisition. If synergy is achieved, the combined firm's value after the merger or acquisition should be higher than the combined value of the two firms operating independently.

- Economic motives can include the desire to achieve economy of scale by joining productive forces, cost reduction by eliminating redundant resources after the M&As and entry of firms from slow-growing economies into high-growth economies (Gonzalez et al. 1998).

- Personal motives can sometimes guide business decision-makers even if there are no significant economic gains from an international M&A for the firm. A top management team or a chief executive of a multinational firm may simply seek an M&A to satisfy their hubris and ego through 'empire-building', or for motives of self-interest such as increasing their reward package and job security.

**Risks of the M&A strategy** The major risks associated with the M&A strategy (see Exhibit 5.4) include:

- The different corporate and national cultures, structures, technology, and procedures may cause great problems for integrating the acquired subsidiary into the parent company's system. This may result in inferior performance and, in some cases, the subsequent failure of the acquired subsidiaries.

- Managers of the acquired foreign subsidiary may not accept the parent company, which results in a weaker degree of attachment between the managers of the acquired foreign subsidiary and the parent firm.

## 5.6 **Entry modes and risk v. control**

Each of the five entry modes has its advantages and drawbacks. Therefore, multinational firms have to make trade-offs when they decide on the most suitable entry mode strategy. *Control*—the desire to influence decisions, systems, and operations in the foreign affiliate— and *risk* are the two most important factors in the decision formula when deciding on the type of entry mode (see Exhibit 5.5). The two factors often go hand in hand. To obtain control, the multinational firm must commit resources to, and take responsibility for, the management of its foreign plants. In other words, more control requires high risk and vice versa (Anderson and Gatignon 1986).

When selecting the appropriate entry mode, multinational firms have to answer two questions: what level of resource commitment are they willing to make? And, what level of control over the operation do they desire? The firm has to look at the risks in the general environment, risks in industry, and firm-specific risks. For markets where total perceived risk is low, firms use entry strategies that involve a high level of resource commitment,

## 5.8 **Summary**

Different types of internationalization stimuli can lead firms to consider the possibility of operating outside their home market: organizational factors arising from within the firm, and environmental factors that are outside the organization's control. In addition, firms may have four different motives for establishing an investment in a foreign location: (1) natural resource seeking motive; (2) market seeking motive; (3) efficiency seeking motive; and (4) strategic asset seeking motive. These different factors combined lead a firm to a decision to internationalize its business activities.

In addition to the initial decision and the motives to internationalize, one needs to understand the different modes of entry into a foreign country or a region. When firms decide to enter a foreign market, they are faced with a large array of choices of entry mode, ranging from export to wholly-owned operations. There is no best way to enter a foreign market and the mode of entry may differ from one country or region to another, as the opening case on Carrefour demonstrates. Multinational firms have to make trade-offs when they decide on the most suitable entry mode strategy. *Control*—the desire to influence decisions, systems and operations in the foreign affiliate—and *risk* are the two most important factors in the decision formula when deciding on the type of entry mode.

The Uppsala Model seeks to explain the internationalization process by suggesting that a firm's internationalization proceeds through stages of decreasing psychic distance. Its main argument is that firms generally proceed along the internationalization path in the form of logical steps, based on their gradual acquisition and use of information gathered from foreign markets and operations, which determine successively greater levels of commitment to more international business activities. They start with no regular export activities, then move to export activities via independent representatives or agents; after that, they tend to establish an overseas subsidiary; and, finally, they commit themselves to overseas production and manufacturing units.

Multinational firms do not only enter new markets. They sometimes withdraw from a foreign country or region, or de-internationalize, as a result of company failure (a forced process) or strategic decision-making (a voluntary process). The de-internationalization process can be more complicated than the internationlization process.

### 📖  Key readings

- J. P. Buckley and P. N. Ghauri (1999), *The Internationalization of the Firm: A Reader* (London: Thompson Business Press) is a collection of some of the key articles on internationalization.

- On the Uppsala Model, see Johanson and Vahlne (2009).

- On entry modes and risk and control, see Brouthers (1995); and K. Brouthers and L. E. Brouthers (2001), 'Explaining the National Cultural Distance Paradox', *Journal of International Business Studies* 32(1): 177–89.

## Discussion questions

**1.** Select a multinational firm and identify and discuss the internationalization stimuli. Was the firm pushed or was it pulled?

**2.** To what extent do multinational firms follow the Uppsala Model? Justify your answer with examples.

**3.** Identify a Born Global firm and discuss its internationalization process.

**4.** 'There is no one best way to enter foreign markets. It is a case of horses for courses.' Discuss this statement.

**5.** Why is the de-internationalization process sometimes more complex than the internationalization process?

---

**Closing case study** Internationalization of a Chinese firm—the Haier Group

---

The Haier Group began as a nearly bankrupt refrigerator company called Qingdao General Refrigerator in Qingdao, China. In 1984, Zhang Ruimin was appointed as plant director and he has remained the company's CEO until today. In 1992, the company was renamed the Haier Group. Under the leadership of Zhang Ruimin, the Haier Group rose to become the third largest home appliance manufacturer in the world, with 240 subsidiary companies and over 50,000 employees around the world. In the period 1995–2005, the company's global revenue increased from RMB4.3 billion to RMB103.4 billion (see Exhibit B). In 2008, the Haier Group was ranked as No. 13 on *Forbes*' Reputation Institute Global 200 list. The company also ranked as No. 1 among Chinese enterprises on the *Financial Times* 2008 list of the most respected global companies.

Zhang Ruimin had an international outlook from the start. Already in 1984, soon after becoming the company's director, he introduced technology and equipment from the German company, Liebherr, to produce refrigerators in China. In 1990, the company started exporting its products to Europe as a contract manufacturer for multinational brands such as Liebherr's 'Blue Line' brand. Zhang Ruimin said: 'We started exporting to developed markets first because if your products are good enough for consumers in Europe and in the US, you will have better products in developing markets.' Zhang Ruimin's ambition was to create China's first multinational firm.

The company's exports to the United States started in 1994. Michael Jemal, a partner in the import company, Welbilt Appliances, contacted Haier in order to buy 150,000 refrigerators for the US market. All the refrigerators sold within a year, helping Haier to capture 10% of the US market for small compact refrigerators. Following on from this success, the company collaborated with Jemal to market a wider range of products in the US market.

In the 1990s, the company acquired many other Chinese companies. The product range expanded beyond refrigerators to include other home appliances such as washing machines, televisions, air-conditioners, and telecommunications equipment. The company improved its products by acquiring foreign technology through joint ventures with companies such as Mitsubishi of Japan and Merloni of Italy. Zhang Ruimin said: 'First we observe and digest. Then we imitate. In the end, we understand it well enough to design it independently.'

By 1998, the Haier Group had a market share of over 30% in refrigerators, washing machines, and air-conditioners in the Chinese market. But the Chinese home appliances market was saturated and there were few opportunities for further domestic expansion. The Chinese government encouraged the company to expand internationally. Furthermore, the company faced greater domestic competition, as foreign companies began to expand aggressively in the Chinese market. In the mid 1990s, a fierce price war broke out among home appliance manufacturers in China. The Haier Group's CEO, Zhang Ruimin, saw an urgent need for international expansion in 1996: 'Only by entering the international market can we know what our competition is doing, can we raise our competitive edge. Otherwise, we will lose the Chinese market to foreigners.' Therefore, the Haier Group began setting up operations overseas.

Zhang Ruimin pursued a different internationalization strategy to other Chinese companies, which were satisfied with exporting low-cost products from China as contract manufacturers for foreign firms' multinational brands. In contrast to other Chinese companies, the Haier Group emulated the strategies of successful Japanese and Korean firms such as Sony, Samsung, and LG in terms of taking its own brand to foreign markets and in terms of establishing production in foreign markets.

Zhang Ruimin believed that, by setting up manufacturing plants overseas, the Haier Group could gain advantages from avoiding import tariffs and reducing transport costs. He also believed that the company's products would appeal more to consumers in developed countries, if the products were no longer regarded as Chinese imports. 'All success relies on one thing in overseas markets – creating a localized brand name. We have to make Americans feel that Haier is a localized U.S. brand instead of an imported Chinese brand,' said Zhang Ruimin.

**Exhibit B** Revenue of the Haier Group

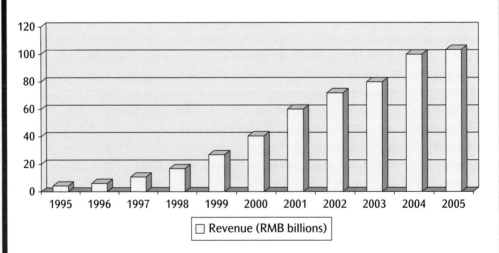

The Haier Group started its international expansion in developing countries. In 1996, the company established a manufacturing plant for refrigerators and air-conditioners in Indonesia. In 1997, further expansions took place in the Philippines, Malaysia, Iran, and Yugoslavia. Once the company gained some international experience, it decided to expand to developed countries. In 1999, the Haier Group expanded to the United States: a refrigerator plant was established in South Carolina and a design centre was established in Los Angeles, California. The company's investment of US$30 million was the largest foreign investment by a Chinese company in the United States. In 2001, the Haier Group purchased a refrigerator plant in Italy and the company opened research and development (R&D) centres in Germany, Denmark, and the Netherlands. In 2006, the company expanded to Japan (see Exhibit C).

Initially, the Haier Group expanded internationally through joint ventures with local firms in Indonesia, Yugoslavia, and other countries. Within three years, the company decided to expand through wholly-owned investments (see Exhibit C). But the company's executives are flexible when taking decisions on international market entry. The entry into the Japanese market through

**Exhibit C** Milestone foreign direct investments by the Haier Group

| Country | Year of entry | Mode of entry |
| --- | --- | --- |
| Indonesia | 1996 | Joint venture |
| Philippines | 1997 | Joint venture |
| Malaysia | 1997 | Joint venture |
| Iran | 1997 | Joint venture |
| Yugoslavia | 1997 | Joint venture |
| India | 1999 | Joint venture |
| United States | 1999 | Wholly-owned |
| Bangladesh | 2001 | Joint venture |
| Pakistan | 2001 | Wholly-owned |
| Italy | 2001 | Wholly-owned |
| Germany | 2001 | Wholly-owned |
| Denmark | 2001 | Wholly-owned |
| Netherlands | 2001 | Wholly-owned |
| Jordan | 2005 | Wholly-owned |
| Japan | 2006 | Joint venture |

*Source:* D. Yuping (2003), 'Haier's survival strategy to compete with world giants', *Journal of Chinese Economics & Business Studies* 1(2): 259–66; Yang et al. (2009); G. Duysters, J. Jacob, C. Lemmens, and Y. Jintian (2009), 'Internationalization and technological catching up of emerging multinationals: a comparative case study of China's Haier Group', *Industrial and Corporate Change* 18(2): 325–49; K. Palepu, T. Khanna, and I. Vargas (2006), 'Haier: taking a Chinese company global', Harvard Business School Case No. 9–706–401; and Haier Group website at http://www.haier.com/.

a wholly-owned investment would be difficult, so the company set up a joint venture with the Japanese company Sanyo in October 2006 as a means for entering the Japanese market.

The Haier Group used its international expansion, not only to sell products overseas, but also to learn new knowledge and skills in foreign markets. The company established research and design centres in the United States, Canada, Japan, and France, among others. It also engaged in strategic alliances with companies such as Mitsubishi, Philips, and Sanyo. Zhang Ruimin had the ambition to create a truly innovative global company that competes on the basis of new product innovations, not on the basis of low costs.

As a result of the Haier Group's international success, the company now faces global competitors. When the Haier Group expanded to the United States, it focused on niche markets such as small, compact refrigerators for students and offices, in order to avoid direct competition with companies such as Whirlpool and GE. But foreign competitors have now formulated strategies to counteract the Haier Group's international expansion. Whirlpool and Electrolux have invested tens of millions of dollars to establish a manufacturing and distribution base in China. These competitors hope that aggressive competitive moves in the Chinese market will prevent the Haier Group from earning more profits that the company would otherwise use to expand further internationally.

The Haier Group executives are ready to face the challenge of global competition. 'We are number three in the world for white goods,' said Yang Mianmian, the company's group president. 'We want to be number one.'

### Discussion questions

1. Why did the Haier Group expand internationally?

2. To what extent did the expansion of the Haier Group follow the Uppsala Model?

 # References

**Aharoni, Y.** (1966). *The Foreign Investment Decision Process* (Boston, MA: Graduate School of Business Administration, Harvard University).

**Albaum, G.** (1983). 'Effectiveness of government export assistance for smaller-sized manufacturers: some empirical evidence', *International Marketing Review* 1(1): 68–75.

**Alexander, N., Quinn, B., and Cairns, P.** (2005). 'International retail divestment activity', *International Journal of Retail & Distribution Management* 33(1): 5–22.

**Aldrich, H., and Auster, E.** (1986) 'Even dwarfs started small: liabilities of size and age and their strategic implications', in **B. Staw and L. L. Cummings** (eds), *Research in Organizational Behavior*, Vol. 8 (Greenwich: Jai Press), pp. 165–98.

**Anderson, E., and Gatignon, H.** (1986). 'Modes of foreign entry: a transaction cost analysis and

propositions', *Journal of International Business Studies* 17(Fall): 1–26.

**Barkema, H., and Vermeulen, F.** (1998). 'International expansion through start-up or through acquisition: a learning perspective', *Academy of Management Journal* 41(1): 7–26.

**Barkema, H., and Drogendijk, R.** (2007). 'Internationalising in small, incremental or larger steps?' *Journal of International Business Studies* 38(7): 1132–48.

**Benito, G. R. G., and Gripsrud, G.** (1992). 'The expansion of foreign direct investments: discrete rational location choices or a cultural learning process?' *Journal of International Business Studies* 23(3): 461–76.

**Benito, G. R. G., and Welch, L. S.** (1997). 'De-internationalization', *Management International Review* 37(2): 7–25.

Bilkey, W. J., and Tesar, G. (1977). 'The export behaviour of smaller Wisconsin manufacturing firms', *Journal of International Business Studies* 8: 93–8.

Brouthers, K. (1995). 'The influence of international risk on entry mode strategy', *Management International Review* 35(1): 7–28.

Brown, J. R., Dev, C. S., and Zhou, Z. (2003). 'Broadening the foreign market entry mode decision: separating ownership and control', *Journal of International Business Studies* 34(5): 473–88.

Burt, S. L., Mellahi, K., Jackson, P., and Sparks, L. (2002). 'Retail internationalisation and retail failure: issues from the case of Marks & Spencer', *International Review of Retail, Distribution and Consumer Research* 12(2): 191–219.

Cairns, P., Doherty, A., Alexander, N., and Quinn, B. (2008). 'Understanding the international retail divestment process', *Journal of Strategic Marketing* 16(2): 111–28.

Çavusgil, S. T. (1984). 'Differences among exporting firms based on their degree of internationalisation', *Journal of Business Research* (12): 195–208.

Child, J., Ng, S.-H., and Wong, C. (2002). 'Psychic distance and internationalization: evidence from Hong Kong Firms', *International Studies of Management & Organization* 32(1): 36–56.

Child, J., and Rodrigues, S. B. (2005). 'The internationalization of Chinese firms: a case for theoretical extension?' *Management and Organization Review* 1(3): 381–41.

Child, J., Rodrigues, S. B., and Frynas, J. G. (2009). 'Psychic distance, its impact and coping modes: interpretations of SME decision makers', *Management International Review* 49(2): 199–224.

Cuervo-Cazurra, A., Maloney, M. M., and Manrakhan, S. (2007). 'Causes of the difficulties in internationalization', *Journal of International Business Studies* 38(5): 709–25.

Cui, L., and Jiang, F. (2009). 'FDI entry mode choice of Chinese firms: a strategic behavior perspective', *Journal of World Business* 44(4): 434–44.

Dikova, D., and Van Witteloostuijn, A. (2007). 'Foreign direct investment mode choice: entry and establishment modes in transition economies', *Journal of International Business Studies* 38(6): 1013–33.

Dow, D., and Karunaratna, A. (2006). 'Developing a multidimensional instrument to measure psychic distance stimuli', *Journal of International Business Studies* 37(5): 578–602.

Dunning, J. (1993). *Multinational Enterprises and the Global Economy* (Harlow: Addison-Wesley).

Elango, B., and Pattnaik, C. (2007). 'Building capabilities for international operations through networks: a study of Indian firms', *Journal of International Business Studies* 38( ): 541–55.

Erdilek, A. (2008). 'Internationalization of Turkish MNEs', *Journal of Management Development* 27(7): 744–60.

Eroglu, S. (1992). 'The internationalisation process of franchise systems: a conceptual model', *International Marketing Review* 9(5): 19–30.

Ferdows, K. (1997). 'Making the most of foreign factories', *Harvard Business Review* 75(2): 73–88.

Forsgren, M. (2002). 'The concept of learning in the Uppsala internationalisation process model: a critical review', *International Business Review* 11(3): 257–77.

Freeman, J., Carroll, G. R., and Hannan, M. T. (1983). 'The liability of newness: age dependence in organizational death rates', *American Sociological Review* 48(5): 692–710.

Frynas, J. G., Mellahi, K., and Pigman, G. (2006). 'First mover advantages in international business and firm-specific political resources', *Strategic Management Journal* 27: 321–45.

Geng, C., and Hon-Kwong, L. (2005). 'Order of entry and performance of multinational corporations in an emerging market: a contingent resource perspective', *Journal of International Marketing* 13(4): 28–56.

Ghemawat, P. (2001). 'Distance still matters: the hard reality of global expansion', *Harvard Business Review* 79(8): 137–47.

Gimeno, J., Hoskisson, R. E., Beal, B. D., and Wan, W. P. (2005). 'Explaining the clustering of international expansion moves: a critical test in the U.S. telecommunications industry', *Academy of Management Journal* 48(2): 297–319.

Goerzen, A., and Makino, S. (2007). 'Multinational corporation internationalization in the service sector: a study of Japanese trading companies', *Journal of International Business Studies* 38(7): 1149–69.

Gonzalez, P., Vasconcellos, G. M., and Kish, R. J. (1998). 'Cross-border mergers and acquisitions: the undervaluation hypothesis', *Quarterly Review of Economic Finance* 38(1): 25–45.

Harzing, A.-W. (2002). 'Acquisition versus greenfield investments: international strategy and management of entry mode', *Strategic Management Journal* 23(3): 211–27.

## 6.1 **Introduction**

The last chapter has demonstrated how companies can expand internationally by using exporting, franchising, or wholly-owned investments. The opening case study in this chapter demonstrates that companies do not necessarily have to 'go it alone'—strategic partners can help them to achieve strategic objectives. Strategic partnerships helped Fiat achieve global expansion at lower cost and faster speed than the company would have been able to do on its own.

Over the past twenty years, international strategic alliances have become a very popular instrument in global competition in many different industries. In 2009, for example, Fiat and Chrysler created a global strategic alliance in the car industry, Microsoft and Yahoo entered into an alliance in the Internet search and online advertising business, and—in the financial sector—the UK's FTSE group started an alliance with MCX-SX, India's new stock exchange.

The growth in international strategic alliances was prompted by a range of drivers. In a global business environment characterized by fierce competition, rapidly changing technologies, shorter product life cycles, and high research and development (R&D) cost, one of the sources of sustainable competitive advantage for multinational firms is their ability to economize on production and research costs, and access intangible assets such as managerial skills and knowledge of different markets more cheaply and faster than competitors.

The above trends are forcing multinational firms to re-examine the feasibility and wisdom of traditional 'go it alone' market development methods, marketing, distribution, and market entry strategies. Inevitably, multinational firms have come to realize that no matter how strong and resourceful a company, there is no way it can have competitive advantage in each and every step of the value-added process in all national markets, nor can it maintain a cutting edge in all the different critical technologies required for the development, production, and marketing of today's sophisticated products and services. Simultaneous competition and cooperation between individual multinational firms are needed to ensure the survival of multinational firms in a dynamic, highly competitive, and increasingly uncertain global business environment.

Consequently, multinational firms now assume that they should forge international strategic alliances unless they can find a good reason not to. If managed properly, international strategic alliances can help multinational firms transform their operations and gain access to new technologies, accelerate time-to-market, and gain insights that would be extremely difficult for the multinational firm to learn and act on its own.

## 6.2 **The concept of international strategic alliances**

What is an international strategic alliance? According to *Webster's Dictionary*, an alliance is an 'association of interests'. In a broad context, the term 'alliance' refers to 'relationships that provide *opportunities for mutual benefit* and results beyond what any single organization or sector could realise alone' (Austin 2000: 47). In a specific business and management context, Gulati and Singh (1998) define an alliance as 'any *voluntarily* initiated cooperative agreement between firms that *involves exchange, sharing, or co-development,* and it can include contributions by partners of capital, technology, or firm-specific assets'. Contractor and Lorange (2002) simply define an alliance as 'any interfirm cooperation that falls between the extremes of discrete, short-term contracts and the complete merger of two or more organizations'.

We define a *strategic alliance* as a strategic cooperative agreement, or agreements, between two or more firms, to pursue a set of agreed upon strategic goals while remaining independent organizations. A strategic alliance is *international* when it involves organizations from at least two different countries.

Therefore, an international strategic alliance has the following three characteristics:

- Cooperative. It is a partnership agreement between two or more firms, which remain independent organizations.

- Strategic. It is a response to strategic challenges or opportunities that the partner firms face.

- International. It is an agreement between firms from at least two different countries.

The above broad definitions comprise a vast array of cooperative arrangements, including joint ventures, cross-licensing, reciprocal distribution and promotion arrangements, technology swaps, information exchange agreements, collaborative research programmes, sharing of complementary assets, and cooperative product development and servicing contracts. At one extreme, two or more multinational firms can have a temporary agreement, for example, a joint marketing campaign. Such agreements tend to last for a short period of time and involve little commitment between partners. At the other extreme, two or more multinational firms may jointly create a new company, an equity joint venture, a legally independent entity where the partners hold certain percentage shares of the new company. Such agreements tend to last for a long time (a joint venture can last indefinitely) and involve greatest commitment between partners (Contractor and Lorange 2002).

Understanding strategic alliances also requires understanding what they are not (Mockler 1999: 5). Mockler argues that 'an agreement through which a firm grants a license for using technology in exchange for a royalty . . . is not considered a strategic alliance *except* when there is continuing contribution and control among two or more independent firms'; in other words, a licencing agreement is often an arm's-length transaction between two firms without any genuine cooperation. Mockler also argues that mergers and acquisitions do not constitute strategic alliances because they 'do not involve two or more independent firms sharing benefits and control over a continuing time period'; in other words, a merger creates a single organization with unified, central control. Finally, it is important to note that international joint ventures (IJVs) 'may or may not be true strategic alliances, depending on the circumstances'. It depends on the importance of the contribution and nature of the relationship. If the contribution of one or all parties is minimal, then they only 'nominally can be considered a strategic alliance'.

## KEY CONCEPT

A strategic alliance is a strategic cooperative agreement, or agreements, between two or more firms to pursue a set of agreed upon strategic goals while remaining independent organizations. A strategic alliance is international when it involves organizations from at least two different countries.

## 6.3 International strategic alliances: external drivers and internal motives

### 6.3.1 External drivers of alliance formation

The main economic argument for strategic alliances is a change in the external business environment, which leads to a perception among managers that the company lacks a specific resource. In turn, the managers may seek to obtain this resource through a strategic alliance (Faulkner 1995; Child et al. 2005). The main changes in the external business environment, which led to a rise in strategic alliances in the last two decades, are technological change and globalization.

Knowledge resources have become more important for firms, technological change has become faster, the sources of knowledge have become more diverse, and the costs of conducting R&D have increased. Technological change was accompanied by the increased strategic importance of speed-to-market, faster rates of product obsolescence, greater number of end applications of the same technologies, and increasing customization (Contractor and Lorange 2002).

At the same time, globalization of markets has provided opportunities for companies to exploit economies of scale, has increased the need for investment, and increased the complexity of operating in an industry. Globalization was accompanied by a reduction in trade and investment barriers and deregulation in many industries, which lowered obstacles to ownership and market entry (Child et al. 2005).

The considerable rise in strategic alliances can be explained as a reaction to technological change and globalization. First, international strategic alliances facilitate access to global markets. Second, in the current global business environment, organic growth alone is often insufficient for meeting a firm's required rate of growth—a strategic alliance can help a firm to grow a business faster than 'go it alone' strategy. Third, strategic alliances greatly reduce speed to market—innovation and new product development. Fourth, as complexity is increasing and no one organization has the required total expertise to best serve the customer, strategic alliances help firms to acquire all of the necessary resources. Fifth, given the global nature of operations, strategic alliances can defray rising R&D costs, as well as production and distribution costs.

### 6.3.2 Internal motives for alliances

Multinational firms entering international strategic alliances may be prompted by one or several external drivers, but they must have a strong internal motivation for an alliance. In other words, the managers must perceive an alliance as a better option for the company compared with an alternative (e.g., licensing or wholly-owned investment). International strategic alliances are relevant only when there is an advantage in combining the capabilities of two or more international firms, and when the combinations of the capabilities yield a total value that is greater than if the capabilities were used separately. For example, in the Fiat-GM alliance, Fiat was primarily motivated by the desire to obtain large cost savings, while GM wanted to increase sales in the European market and to preempt any global competitors from forming an alliance with Fiat. Neither Fiat nor GM could have easily obtained these benefits on their own.

According to Child et al. (2005), there are six main internal motives for strategic alliances:

- Resource need. A company may seek to gain a resource needed to respond to an external threat or external opportunity.

- Learning. A company may seek not simply to gain a resource but to become part of a partnership to create new knowledge.

- Risk limitation. A company may seek to spread financial risk.

- Speed to market. A company may seek to achieve market presence at a faster speed than going it alone.

- Cost minimization. A company may seek to reduce costs.

- Current poor performance. A company may seek an alliance to improve the current poor performance.

Resource need is the most frequent internal motive for a strategic alliance, but a firm may enter an alliance as a result of a combination of different motives. For instance, Fiat sought an alliance with Tata in India for different reasons—Fiat wanted to reduce costs, to obtain knowledge about the Indian market, and to engage in a joint learning process.

## 6.4 **Types of alliance**

Most international strategic alliances can be categorized as *alliances between non-competing firms* and *alliances between competitors* (Ghemawat et al. 1986; Dussauge and Garrette 1999). We can also distinguish different alliances according to their function. Accordingly, alliances between non-competing firms can be divided into: (1) international expansion alliances; (2) vertical integration alliances; and (3) diversification alliances (see Exhibit 6.1). Alliances between competitors can be divided into: (1) complementary alliances; (2) shared supply alliances; and (3) quasi-concentration alliances (see Exhibit 6.2) (Dussauge and Garrette 1999, chapter 4).

### 6.4.1 **International expansion alliance**

An international expansion alliance is a partnership for expanding into a new geographical area. When a company wants to enter a new market, an alliance helps it to learn about the local market conditions. Once the company has learned enough about the local market conditions, it can decide to dissolve the alliance in order to gain operational control and to work autonomously.

**Exhibit 6.1** Alliances between non-competing firms

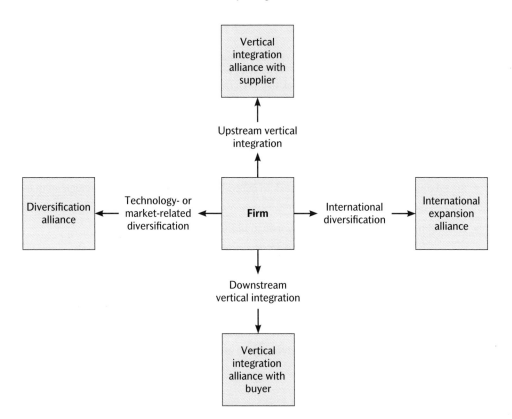

*Source:* Adapted from P. Dussauge and B. Garrette (1999), *Cooperative Strategy: Competing Successfully through Strategic Alliances* (Chichester: Wiley), 51. Reprinted with permission of John Wiley & Sons.

International expansion alliances are particularly helpful for smaller firms that lack the resources or experience to expand internationally on their own. They have also been extensively used by many European or Japanese firms expanding to emerging economies such as China and India; examples are Fiat's alliances with Guangzhou Automobile Industry Group and Tata. Some companies, such as Coca-Cola and Whirlpool, have used international expansion alliances in order to grow into multinational firms.

### 6.4.2 **Vertical integration alliance**

A vertical integration alliance is formed between a supplier and a buyer that agree to use and share their skills and capabilities in the supply chain. Carefully selected suppliers are invited to invest in a long-term collaborative relationship with a customer, instead of being a mere contractor. Vertical integration alliances allow a firm to improve the quality of its goods and services, to innovate or to secure its supply chain—without the need for large investments or acquisitions.

**Exhibit 6.2** Alliances between competitors

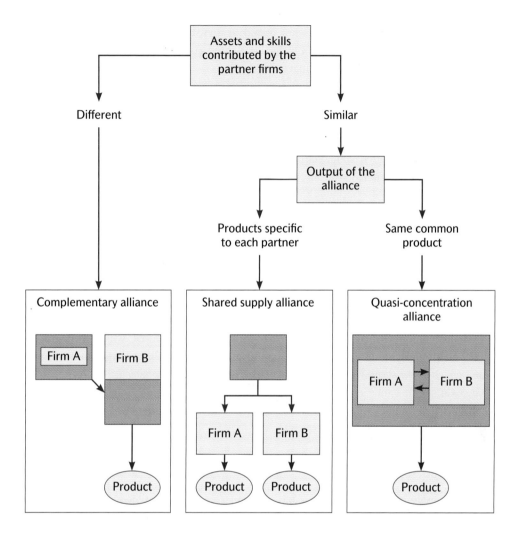

*Source:* P. Dussauge and B. Garrette (1999), *Cooperative Strategy: Competing Successfully through Strategic Alliances* (Chichester: Wiley), 58. Reprinted with permission of John Wiley & Sons.

Vertical integration alliances can be a source of innovation for companies. For instance, the computer manufacturer, Hewlett-Packard, has a long history of collaboration with Intel—supplier of computer processors. The two companies worked together to innovate computer processors and other products such as wireless applications for Hewlett-Packard's handheld products. In 2008, Hewlett-Packard, Intel, and Yahoo started a partnership with research institutes in different countries in order to build a global research network for computer innovations.

### 6.4.3 **Diversification alliance**

A diversification alliance is a partnership between companies in different lines of business. The partners are neither competitors nor linked in a customer/supplier relationship. The aim of a diversification alliance is not to facilitate international expansion, but to facilitate diversification into an unfamiliar product or service.

A key strength of diversification alliances is the ability to combine different competencies and to discover new business opportunities. For instance, Honda (a car manufacturer known for the quality of its car engines) established a joint venture company with General Electric (a manufacturer of aircraft jet engines) to design and manufacture engines for light business jet aircraft, while the coffee chain, Starbucks, formed strategic partnerships with hotel chains, Marriott and Hyatt, to open Starbucks coffee shops in luxury hotels.

### 6.4.4 **Complementary alliance**

A complementary alliance is a partnership between competing firms, which contribute different and complementary assets and capabilities to their joint endeavour. One partner typically contributes a product design or set of critical technologies, while the other provides in-depth knowledge of and access to international markets. In order for partnerships to be successful, the new product should not compete directly with the partner's existing products.

Complementary alliances are often formed between smaller firms, which own unique intellectual property rights but lack international distribution channels, and larger multinational firms, which have access to such distribution channels but lack specific expertise. Such alliances are, for instance, common in the pharmaceuticals and biotechnology sectors, where small companies such as Tyrian Diagnostics have world-leading expertise in a very specific area of knowledge (see closing case study).

### 6.4.5 **Shared supply alliance**

A shared supply alliance is a partnership between competing firms, which collaborate to achieve economies of scale or to share R&D with regard to a specific input within the production process. The scope of such alliance is limited to upstream activities (R&D, parts and components, subsystems), with partner companies normally remaining direct competitors in end products.

Shared supply alliances are formed in the manufacturing sector where economies of scale can be justified. For instance, Fiat formed different shared supply alliances in order to cut costs—Fiat and Tata jointly produced diesel engines and transmission systems in India, while Fiat sourced engines from the Chinese car manufacturer Cherry, among others.

### 6.4.6 **Quasi-concentration alliance**

A quasi-concentration alliance is a partnership between competing firms, which contribute similar capabilities and assets to the alliance in order to develop, manufacture, and market a joint product. It encompasses all functions, from R&D to marketing and the sharing of all development costs and risks. The aim of such an alliance is to benefit from advantages enjoyed by larger rivals without having to merge.

Quasi-concentration alliances are often formed in aerospace and defence industries in order to obtain economies of scale and eliminate competition. One example is International Launch Services, a joint venture between Lockheed Martin and two Russian firms for launching commercial satellites (see closing case study, Chapter 2).

## 6.5 Selecting partners

Once a multinational firm sets the goals and objectives for a strategic alliance, the first step is to select 'the right partner'. Indeed, the success of a strategic alliance can be determined by smart partner selection (Tomlinson 1970; Shah and Swaminathan 2008).

### 6.5.1 Partner selection criteria

The selected partner must fulfil one essential criterion: the partner must help the company towards a competitive advantage. In other words, the partner must have a specific competence (e.g., technology or market knowledge) that will provide the alliance with a competitive advantage that neither partner would have on its own (Porter and Fuller 1986; Child et al. 2005). Beyond this key criterion, there are long lists of possible partner selection criteria (see Exhibit 6.3). Above all, the firm must decide what to look for in a partner for a specific project.

---

**Exhibit 6.3** Possible partner selection criteria

- **Financial Assets.** Resources that reflect financial health (e.g., availability of long-term financial needs or cost of capital).

- **Complementarity of capabilities.** The degree to which a partner's resources can be used in conjunction with those of your firm (e.g., sales of different products or different technical competences).

- **Unique competences.** Resources possessed by a partner but not by other firms (e.g., unique product or unique technological patent).

- **Industry attractiveness.** The degree to which an industry presents a favourable environment in which to achieve a firm's goals (e.g., large profit margins or small number of competitors).

- **Cost of alternatives.** The cost to your firm of alternatives to the alliance (e.g., cost of wholly-owned subsidiary).

- **Market knowledge/access.** The expertise or ability of a partner to operate effectively in a market or industry (e.g., understanding of distribution channels or experience with government regulations).

- **Intangible assets.** Assets which are not reflected in financial statements (e.g., firm reputation or human resources).

- **Managerial capabilities.** The ability of managers to guide their firm efficiently and effectively (e.g., leadership quality of partner firm's CEO or the ability to build consensus among groups).

- **Capabilities to provide quality product/service.** The ability of a partner to provide buyers with the quality of products they desire (e.g., high standards of quality control or quality of manufacturing facilities).

- **Willingness to share expertise.** The degree to which a partner is willing to allow your firm to acquire its capabilities (e.g., share technological or marketing knowledge).

- **Partner's ability to acquire your firm's special skills.** The ability of a partner to learn/ acquire skills which your firm possesses (i.e., experience of learning from partners in alliances or similar corporate culture).

- **Previous alliance experience.** Previous experience of participation in strategic alliances.

- **Special skills that you can learn from your partner.** The ability of your firm to learn/ acquire skills which a partner possesses (e.g., specific technology or marketing know-how that your firm does not possess but wishes to learn).

- **Technical capabilities** The ability of a partner to develop new process or product technologies (e.g., significant R&D operations or the ability to commercialize new products).

*Source:* Adapted from T. M. Dacin, M. A. Hitt, and E. Levitas (1997), 'Selecting partners for successful international alliances: examination of US and Korean firms', *Journal of World Business* 32(1): 3–16; and M. A. Hitt, M. T. Dacin, E. Levitas, J. L. Arregle, and A. Borza (2000), 'Partner selection in emerging and developed market contexts: resource-based and organizational learning perspectives', Academy of Management Journal 43(3): 449–67.

Managers may distinguish two different types of criteria when selecting a partner: partner-related criteria and task-related criteria. *Partner-related criteria* are associated with the efficiency and effectiveness of partners' cooperation, such as partner's corporate culture, compatibility, motivation, commitment, and reliability. *Task-related criteria* are associated with the operational skills and resources which an alliance requires for its competitive success, such as financial resources, marketing resources, customer service, R&D technical resources, organizational resources, and production resources. The complementarity of both the characteristics and the task-related suitability of the chosen partner provides the basis for success or failure, and dictates the level of benefit achievable from the partnership (Geringer 1988; 1991).

The criteria for partner selection can vary significantly between different projects, different industries or different countries. Multinational firms from different countries sometimes look for different criteria. For instance, firms from countries with an Anglo-Saxon business tradition such as the United States and Britain often prioritize financial assets and managerial capabilities, while companies from business environments with a long-term financial planning horizon such as Korea and Japan prioritize technical capabilities and long-term industry attractiveness (see Exhibit 6.4).

**Exhibit 6.4** Partner selection criteria used by Korean and US executives (in order of importance)

| Korean executives | US executives |
| --- | --- |
| 1. Technical capabilities | 1. Financial assets |
| 2. Industry attractiveness | 2. Managerial capabilities |
| 3. Special skills you can learn from partner | 3. Capabilities to provide quality products/services |
| 4. Willingness to share expertise | 4. Complementarity of capabilities |
| 5. Capabilities to provide quality products/services | 5. Unique competencies |

*Source:* T. M. Dacin, M. A. Hitt, and E. Levitas (1997), 'Selecting partners for successful international alliances: examination of US and Korean firms', *Journal of World Business* 32(1): 11. Reprinted with permission of Elsevier.

---

**KEY CONCEPT**

Two types of criteria should be considered when selecting a partner: *partner-related criteria* are associated with the efficiency and effectiveness of partners' cooperation; while *task-related criteria* are associated with the operational skills and resources which an alliance requires for its competitive success.

---

## 6.5.2 Optimal business partner

The previous discussion suggested that different multinational firms may seek different qualities in a partner. Nonetheless, an optimal business partner in a successful international strategic alliance should have two key qualities: strategic fit and cultural fit.

Strategic alliances with low strategic fit have little competitive advantage and have little chance of success. Multinational firms typically seek a partner with high strategic fit, but they attach relatively little importance to finding a partner with high cultural fit. Thus, a typical alliance starts with high strategic fit and low cultural fit, which can lead to future conflicts between partner firms. A key challenge for many strategic alliances is to move towards greater cultural fit during the life of an alliance (see Exhibit 6.5).

### Strategic fit

Strategic fit is the degree to which a potential alliance partner augments or complements a firm's strategy (Jemison and Sitkin 1986). According to Geringer (1988), a firm should seek a partner with strategic fit both in terms of task-related criteria (resources and competences) and partner-related criteria (e.g., size, goals, and operating policies).

Different types of alliance may require a different dimension of strategic fit. In a complementary alliance, where partners contribute different resources and competences in an effort to learn from each other, strategic fit requires the firm to select a partner who can help it

**Exhibit 6.5** Strategic fit and cultural fit

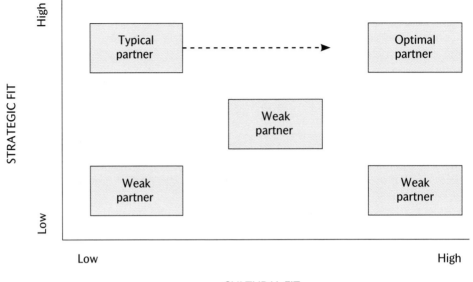

to overcome deficiencies along task-related dimensions. For instance, a small pharmaceutical firm with an innovative new product may seek a large firm with international distribution channels. In contrast, in a quasi-concentration alliance, where partners contribute more or less similar competences in an attempt to maximize the utilization of similar assets, strategic fit requires the firm to seek a partner along partner-related criteria. For instance, a defence company, which plans to design and build a new military aircraft, will seek a partner of similar size and similar goals.

## Cultural fit

There are two types of cultural fit: corporate culture fit and national culture fit.

Corporate culture refers to 'the way we do things around here'. Firms in the same country do things differently. *Corporate culture fit* is the compatibility between partner firms as reflected in the similarity of their organizational management style, which include the levels of employee participation or authoritarian management, delegation of responsibility, and decision-making process—centralized or decentralized (Parkhe 1991). When managers consider corporate culture fit, they should also take into consideration soft issues such as ethics, responsiveness to change, and corporate governance.

National culture refers to patterns of beliefs and values that are manifested in practices, behaviours, and various artefacts shared by members of the same nation. *National culture fit* is the compatibility between partner firms as reflected in the similarity of their national characteristics. Because organizations are, in many ways, embedded in the larger society in which they exist, managers should examine both corporate and national cultures.

International strategic alliances work better when the management practices are compatible with the national culture. International strategic alliances could suffer from problems in communication, cooperation, commitment, and conflict resolution caused by partners' values and behavioural differences, which, in turn, could cause interaction problems and adversely influence the alliance performance. Generally, alliances between culturally similar partners are more likely to be successful than alliances between culturally dissimilar partners. Cartwright and Cooper (1993: 57–60) state that many alliances fail to meet expectations because the cultures of the partners are incompatible, and the degree of cultural fit that exists between combining organizations is likely to be directly related to the success of the alliance.

---

**KEY CONCEPT**

*Strategic fit* is the degree to which a potential alliance partner augments or complements a firm's strategy. *Cultural fit* is the compatibility between partner firms as reflected in the similarity of their corporate culture and their national culture. The most successful strategic alliances are those that achieve both high strategic fit and high cultural fit.

---

### 6.5.3 Strategic alliances in emerging economies

There are many strategic alliances—often joint ventures—between Western multinational firms and firms from emerging economies. However, such strategic alliances can give rise to conflicts. Most Western multinationals are motivated to forge joint ventures with partners from emerging economies because their home markets are saturated and they need to establish a 'bridgehead' in potential foreign markets, and/or to gain access to cheap labour and raw material (Hoon-Halbauer 1999). These motives, however, are not that important for local partners. In most emerging economies, local firms have a customer base and knowledge of local markets, but their technology, management skills, and know-how are outdated. Partners in emerging economies forge alliances with Western multinationals to access financial assets, technical capabilities, and modern technology.

The objectives of a large Western multinational firm and an emerging economy firm can often be entirely divergent. The Western firm may seek access to the local market, safeguard technology, and achieve high quality standards. The local firm may seek to protect the local market, to transfer technology, and save costs rather than invest in high quality standards. Such conflict of objectives may lead to problems in managing the alliance (Hitt et al. 2000). Indeed, strategic alliances between Western multinational firms and firms in emerging economies are often only temporary and the alliance is transformed into a wholly-owned venture after several years—one partner often buys out the other partner (Child et al. 2005, chapter 16; Puck et al. 2009).

As firms from emerging economies themselves internationalize, they also enter into strategic alliances between each other. For instance, the Brazilian aircraft manufacturer, Embraer (see opening case study, Chapter 2), opened its first foreign manufacturing facility through a joint venture in China. Embraer faced conflicts similar to those experienced by Western multinational firms: it wanted to access the local Chinese market and protect its technology, while the Chinese local partner wanted to transfer technology from Embraer and to strengthen the indigenous aerospace industry with a long-term view towards global expansion (Goldstein 2008).

Multinational firms continue to expand through strategic alliances in emerging economies because there are many benefits of doing so. But managers must remember that it is hard to find an equal partner with complementary strategic objectives in an emerging economy. Selecting a partner requires a thorough understanding of the differences between partners and the differences between the countries.

## 6.6 Control in strategic alliances

A successful strategy requires a certain degree of 'control', which can be defined as: 'the process by which one entity influences, to varying degrees, the behaviour and output of another entity through a wide range of bureaucratic, cultural and informal mechanisms' (Geringer and Hébert 1989). In a wholly-owned investment, where the parent company can shape the strategic direction of the subsidiary, control of a subsidiary by the parent company can already be difficult (see Chapter 7). In a strategic alliance, control is even more difficult because the partners jointly share control over the partnership. Insufficient control can limit a firm's ability to align the strategic direction of the partnership with its own strategy, and it can limit a firm's ability to protect its interests in the partnership (e.g., brand reputation or technological know-how) (Geringer and Hébert 1989; Child et al. 2005, chapter 11).

There are two types of control that can be exercised in strategic alliances: strategic control and operational control. *Strategic control* is 'control over the means and methods on which the whole conduct of an organization depends', for instance, control over the use of capital, the setting of strategic priorities, and the making of senior appointments. *Operational control* is 'control over the production process within an organization, in the sense of determining how the employees of an organization perform their work', for instance, control over purchasing, manufacturing, and quality control (Child 1984: 137–8; Child and Yan 1999).

### 6.6.1 Control mechanisms

The simplest mechanism for ensuring control in a strategic alliance is a majority equity share, where one partner has more than 50% equity share in an equity joint venture (Child 2002; Child et al. 2005). For instance, in an international joint venture between Fiat and Premier Automobiles in India, Fiat had a 51% equity share; in a joint venture with Zastava in Serbia, Fiat had a 67% equity share. In both cases, Fiat had a controlling equity share and was able to influence the strategic direction of the partnership.

However, there are three limitations to exercising control through majority equity share. First, it may not be possible for a firm to acquire a majority share—many joint ventures have a 50:50 equity share. Second, this control mechanism only applies to equity joint ventures— many strategic alliances do not involve an equity joint venture. Third, even a minority equity share partner can also exercise control by using 'non-capital resourcing' (Schaan 1988; Child and Yan 1999; Child et al. 2005).

Managers must always remember that control in a strategic alliance can be exercised through both equity capital provision *and* non-capital resourcing. *Equity capital provision* allows the firm to influence strategic control, particularly through the setting of strategic priorities and the appointments of the board of directors in a joint venture. *Non-capital resourcing* allows the firm to influence operational control, particularly through key executive appointments (see Exhibit 6.6). Examples of non-capital resourcing as mechanisms of operational control include: appointment of key alliance managers in R&D, where technological knowledge is shared; appointment of the head of human resources, who can in turn appoint other joint venture employees; reporting mechanisms for alliance employees to the parent company; laying down operational procedures and routines for the alliance; the provision of training and development to the alliance; and regular personal relations with the alliances' senior managers (Frayne and Geringer 1990; Child et al. 2005: 222–3).

Majority equity capital provision does not guarantee full control of a strategic alliance because it cannot necessarily protect a firm's interests in the partnership at the operational level (e.g., sharing of technological know-how between engineers). For instance, Japanese partners often acquired significant technological know-how from strategic alliances with

**Exhibit 6.6** Model of control in international joint ventures

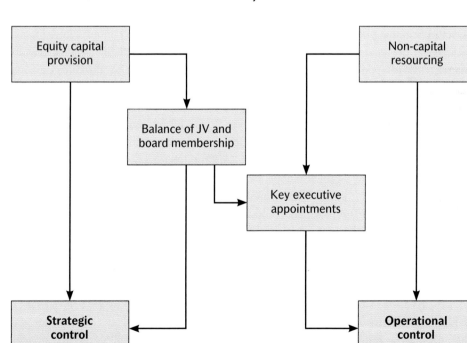

*Source:* Adapted from J. Child and Y. Yan (1999), 'Investment and control in international joint ventures: the case of China', *Journal of World Business* 34(1): 7. Reprinted with permission of Elsevier.

American and European partners by using non-capital resourcing, such as by controlling the manufacturing function of the alliance or by appointing the head of human resources (Hamel 1991; Inkpen 1998). A lack of operational control can have negative consequences for the use of a firm's resources within the strategic alliance. Therefore, the success of an alliance requires both *strategic control* and *operational control.*

---

**KEY CONCEPT**

Control is the process by which one entity influences, to varying degrees, the behaviour and output of another entity through a wide range of bureaucratic, cultural, and informal mechanisms. *Strategic control* is control over the means and methods on which the whole conduct of an organization depends. *Operational control* is control over the production process within an organization, in the sense of determining how the employees of an organization perform their work. The success of an alliance requires both *strategic control* and *operational control.*

---

### 6.6.2 Focus of control

The previous discussion demonstrates that a multinational firm can exercise control in many different ways. The focus of control by a firm can depend on: (1) a firm's strategic priorities; (2) the existing knowledge of alliance partners; and (3) a firm's cultural preferences.

Strategic priorities certainly influence the nature of a firm's operational control over an alliance. A firm that prioritizes profitability in an alliance may seek to appoint senior finance executives in the alliance. A firm that prioritizes learning from an alliance partner may, for instance, seek to appoint senior R&D executives in the alliance or to introduce personal rewards for learning from the alliance (Hamel 1991; Inkpen 1998).

The focus of control by a firm also depends on the existing knowledge of alliance partners. For instance, in joint ventures between Chinese firms and foreign partners in China, the Chinese partner firm would typically appoint the head of human resources because it had the knowledge of local norms and regulations (Child and Yan 1999).

The focus of control by a firm also depends on the firm's cultural preferences. For instance, American and European partner firms tend to prefer formal control mechanisms such as performance-contingent employment contracts, while Japanese firms tend to prefer informal control mechanisms such as developing motivation and loyalty through the promotion of operational practices and cultural symbols (Inkpen 1998; Child et al. 2005).

### 6.6.3 Control and performance

The ultimate objective of control is to ensure successful performance of an alliance in line with the firm's strategy. But 'successful performance' can mean very different things in a strategic alliance. The definition of 'success' depends on the goals of the partner firm—goals can include profitability, sales growth, developing a new product design, learning a new skill from the strategic partner, and so on. Goals can also differ between partners in the same alliance. Bleeke and Ernst (1993) suggest that a strategic alliance is successful if it passes two tests. The first test is that both partners must achieve their own initial strategic goals for the alliance. The second test is that both partners must recover their financial costs of capital.

Various studies have found that the majority of alliances terminate prematurely, which may suggest that the performance of the alliance failed to meet expectations of at least one partner (Child et al. 2005, chapter 17). According to Bleeke and Ernst (1995), the average lifespan for a strategic alliance is about seven years and many strategic alliances end up as an acquisition by one of the partners. However, the eventual termination of an alliance does not necessarily mean failure. A strategic alliance may be terminated because the goals of the alliance partners were met, because the goals of alliance partners have changed over time, or because at least one alliance partner has found better business opportunities elsewhere. For instance, many international joint ventures between foreign firms and local firms in China were transformed into wholly-owned investments over time, either because the foreign partner firm had more local knowledge than before or because the managers of the foreign partner firm perceived China as a safer place to invest than before (Puck et al. 2009). Therefore, the termination of a strategic alliance should not be automatically viewed as a failure and it should be seen as a natural process of business evolution.

From the perspective of a multinational firm, it is crucial to establish effective control mechanisms for measuring and monitoring the performance of its alliances. In particular, research suggests that a dedicated alliance function significantly increases chances of success in international strategic alliances (Dyer et al. 2001; Kale et al. 2001). In other words, a multinational firm with different strategic alliances greatly benefits from a dedicated company director or a department that oversees the performance of its alliances.

The computer manufacturer, Hewlett-Packard (HP) is an example of a company that has been very successful at managing strategic alliances. The firm has a central department that oversees the performance of all its strategic alliances and a 300-page-long manual for managing alliances. HP emphasizes sharing knowledge in order to maximize the learning potential of alliances. One of HP's ground rules is: 'Once you have more than a few alliances, set up systems to ensure that alliance-making know-how is shared.' Thus, HP has a dedicated partner-level alliance-manager to oversee all its alliances with each partner.

## 6.7 International strategic alliances: balancing risks and trust

Multinational firms engaged in international strategic alliances face many different kinds of risk. Because of the nature of international strategic alliances, they are inherently more likely than strategic alliances within the same country to be associated with greater opportunities to cheat, greater behavioural uncertainty, greater instability, and poor performance. Shenkar and Yan's (2002) study of the failure of the Ramada–Guilin Hotel strategic alliance in China found that the lack of a clear legal framework in China, problems dealing with Chinese institutions, partners' politics, and cross-cultural clashes led to the failure of the alliance. Trust between partners can significantly reduce risks associated with a strategic alliance.

### 6.7.1 **Risks in strategic alliances**

Das and Teng (1999) divide risks in strategic alliances into two broad categories: relational risk and performance risk. Relational risks are unique to strategic alliances, as single firms' strategic moves are not subject to such risk. *Relational risk* in a strategic alliance refers to 'the probability and consequences of not having satisfactory cooperation'. Opportunistic behaviours include 'shirking, appropriating the partner's resources, distorting information, harbouring hidden agendas, and delivering unsatisfactory products and services'. Das and Teng (1999; 2001) argue that relational risks are an unavoidable—and quite problematic—element of strategic alliances.

*Performance risk* is the likelihood that 'an alliance may fail even when partner firms commit themselves fully to the alliance' (Das and Teng 1999). This could be due to external factors such as unprecedented fierce competition, political change, government policy change, *force majeure* such as wars, or internal factors such as a 'lack of competence in critical areas'.

Gomes-Casseres (2001) notes that, because alliances are often based on 'incomplete and evolving contracts', alliance agreements are typically open-ended and contain 'gaps' to deal with unforeseen circumstances. Accordingly, each partner runs some risks that the other partner could 'opportunistically' takes advantage of. Gomes-Casseres (2001) argues that partners in strategic alliances practise 'mutual forbearance' by forgoing short-run opportunistic actions in the interests of maintaining the relationship, which partners expect will yield long-run benefits. Exhibit 6.7 provides some basic guidelines in dealing with risks in international strategic alliances.

**KEY CONCEPT**

There are two categories of risks in strategic alliances: relational risk and performance risk. *Relational risk* in strategic alliances is the probability and consequences of not having satisfactory cooperation. *Performance risk* is the likelihood that an alliance may fail even when partner firms commit themselves fully to the alliance.

### 6.7.2 **Trust in strategic alliances**

It is clear from the above discussion that a key challenge for firms in strategic alliances is to protect themselves effectively from relational risks. Trust is a means of reducing risks in inter-organizational cooperation, particularly the likelihood of opportunism.

Trust can be defined as 'the willingness of one party to relate with another in the belief that the other's actions will be beneficial rather than detrimental to the first party, even though this cannot be guaranteed' (Child et al. 2005: 50). Trust stabilizes the expectations partners have of each other under conditions of uncertainty and mutual dependence. Indeed, trust between partners is one of the most important factors for successful international alliances (Parkhe 1998*a*, 1998*b*; Madhok 2006; Child et al. 2005, chapter 4).

Trust has different practical advantages: it makes partners more willing to share information, it makes partners more willing to invest in the alliance, and it reduces the

**Exhibit 6.7** Managing strategic alliance risks

1. Emphasize protection of your own primary resource. Remember that:

   - Risks are relatively low in protecting physical and financial resources, including patents, contracts, logos, and trademarks (ownership protected by law).

   - Risks are high in protecting technological, managerial, and organizational resources. Be careful about unintended transfer of knowledge and imitation; you have little legal protection here.

2. Exercise control through contracts, equity, and management. Employ, as appropriate:

   - Contractual control (specify usage of properties).

   - Equity control (majority or shared ownership).

   - Managerial control (have one's own staff in key positions, regular meetings, frequent interactions and communications).

3. Retain flexibility through short-term recurrent contracts, limiting commitment, and effective exit provisions. You need the ability to adapt, to be free from rigid contracts, and to be able to recover invested resources. Hence:

   - Have contracts specifying an incremental process of alliance-making.

   - Avoid joint ventures and minority equity alliances in favour of less engaging forms such as licensing, shared distribution, and product bundling.

   - Insist on specific costing and pricing formulas and clear property rights, as alliance activities tend to blur ownership contours.

4. Safeguard continued security by limiting exposure to know-how:

   - Maintain the knowledge barrier by forming alliances in which partners work separately, such as funded R&D and outsourcing agreements, unless you are willing to work closely with partners, as in joint ventures.

   - Make clear to partners and your own staff that unauthorized learning will need to be prevented.

5. Ensure increased productivity by emphasizing superior alliance performance:

   - Focus on knowledge productivity, particularly by seeking compatibility of organizational routines and culture of partners.

   - Identify and eliminate internal stickiness and learning barriers that prevent integration with partner's superior knowledge.

*Source:* T. K. Das and S. B. Teng (1999), 'Managing risks in strategic alliances', *Academy of Management Executive* 13(4): 50–62.

temptation for partners to take advantage of the other's goodwill. If the strategic alliance can achieve these advantages, the partners can spend less time and effort checking on the other partner and they can focus their attention on the long-term strategic goals of mutual benefit (Child et al. 2005).

Trust can be an important factor in selecting a partner for a strategic alliance. However, when managers select an alliance partner, they should not put more emphasis on trust than the firm's strategic objectives. For instance, a strategic alliance between General Electric and Cisco was formed because Jack Welch, the CEO of GE, and John Chambers, the CEO of Cisco, knew each other very well; Jack Welch and John Chambers trusted each other and privately discussed collaboration when playing golf together. However, the GE–Cisco alliance quickly failed because there was no strategic fit between the two companies (Bierly and Gallagher 2007). Therefore, managers must remember that strategic fit (section 7.5.2) should always remain the main criterion for selecting a partner.

Trust between partners can deepen over time, as the alliance develops (see Exhibit 6.8). At the beginning of the alliance, trust may often be based on the calculation that: (1) the partner has the motivation and the competence to deliver on his promises; and that (2) there are deterrents based on law and reputation to prevent the partner from letting you down. As the alliance develops, the partners get to know each other better and develop mutual understanding, which leads to greater trust. If the alliance proves to be commercially successful and if it develops into an organization with its own autonomy and identity, there is a tendency for managers of the partner firms to identify with each other's interests and for emotional ties between managers to develop (i.e., bonding). Commercial success and bonding can accompany each other, leading to greater trust and further cooperation between partners (Child et al. 2005, chapter 4).

**Exhibit 6.8** Phases in the evolution of trust in strategic alliances

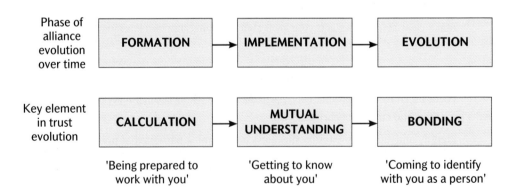

Source: J. Child, D. Faulkner, and S. Tallman (2005), *Cooperative Strategy: Managing Alliances, Networks and Joint Ventures* (Oxford: Oxford University Press), 61. Reprinted with permission of Oxford University Press.

**KEY CONCEPT**

Trust is the willingness of one party to relate with another in the belief that the other's actions will be beneficial rather than detrimental to the first party, even though this cannot be guaranteed. Trust stabilizes the expectations partners have of each other under conditions of uncertainty and mutual dependence.

## 6.8 Summary

The current surge in international strategic alliances was prompted by a range of drivers, including fierce global competition, rapidly changing technologies, shorter product life cycles, and high R&D costs. One of the sources of sustainable competitive advantage for multinational firms is their ability to form and successfully manage strategic alliances to reduce R&D costs and to access intangible assets such as managerial skills and tacit knowledge of different markets more cheaply and faster than competitors. With these pressures has come the realization that competitiveness can be enhanced by combining complementary capabilities and competencies of different organizations in close long-, medium-, or short-term relationships rather than opt for the 'go it alone' strategy.

Strategic alliances can serve different objectives and they can take many different forms. There are alliances between non-competing firms: (1) international expansion alliances; (2) vertical integration alliances; and (3) diversification alliances. There are also alliances between competitors: (1) complementary alliances; (2) shared supply alliances; and (3) quasi-concentration alliances.

The success of a strategic alliance can be determined by good partner selection. Therefore, it is of extreme importance that the firm chooses the right partner—a partner that is trustworthy and meets both partner-related criteria, such as partner characteristics, compatibility, motivation, commitment, reliability, and task-related criteria, such as financial resources, marketing resources, customer service, R&D technical resources, organizational resources, and production resources. In addition to selecting the right partner, for strategic alliances to be successful, they should achieve two types of fit: strategic fit and cultural fit. Choosing the wrong partner, or lack of fit between partners, may lead to unintended knowledge leaks and to loss of skills and technology. Furthermore, choosing the right partner is only the first step towards a successful alliance. As an alliance develops, partners need to carefully develop appropriate control mechanisms in order to oversee the alliance performance.

Multinational firms engaged in international strategic alliances face two broad types of risks: relational risk and performance risk. Trust between partners can significantly reduce risks associated with a strategic alliance. Trust has different practical advantages for alliance partners: it makes partners more willing to share information, it makes partners more willing to invest in the alliance, and it reduces the temptation for partners to take advantage of the other's goodwill. However, managers must remember that strategic fit should always remain the main criteria for selecting a strategic alliance partner.

Like all temporary relationships, strategic alliances do and must end. One should not confuse termination with failure. Not all endings are necessarily failures. If the alliance fulfils its strategic purpose, it is a success, even if it ends earlier than expected or planned.

## 📖 Key readings

- A very useful book on all aspects of international strategic alliances is Child et al. (2005).

- Mockler (1999) is useful in providing insights into practical strategies in international strategic alliances.

- A. C. Inkpen and J. Ross (2001), 'Why do some strategic alliances persist beyond their useful life?' *California Management Review* 44(1): 132–48 provides a comprehensive analysis to why managers tend to escalate their commitment to a failing strategic alliance.

- Useful papers on partner selection in emerging economies are: Hitt et al. (2000); and Dacin et al. (1997).

## 💬 Discussion questions

**1.** Identify the drivers and motives for the strategic alliances established by Fiat (refer to the opening case study.)

**2.** Write a short executive brief to the CEO of a multinational firm, explaining how international strategic alliances could be used to develop a new hi-tech product.

**3.** What problems do managers face in selecting the 'right' alliance partner?

**4.** Take a strategic alliance of your choice. Develop control mechanisms for measuring and monitoring the performance of the alliance.

**5.** By using specific examples, explain how multinational firms balance (or not, as the case may be) trust and risks in international strategic alliances.

---

**Closing case study**  Tyrian Diagnostics—dancing with the big pharmas

Sydney-based Proteome Systems (now called Tyrian Diagnostics) is an example of a company whose success can be attributed to international strategic alliances. Established in 1999 by a small number of academics who left Macquarie University in Australia to set up the company, Proteome Systems has quickly become one of the world's major forces in proteomics (the study of entire protein systems). In 2008, the company was renamed, Tyrian Diagnostics. The company is headquartered in Sydney, Australia, and has premises in the Boston area in the United States.

Tyrian Diagnostics is dedicated to the development of proteomics technology, the discovery of biomarkers and drug targets, and to proteomic bioinformatics. The company's business strategy aims to generate near-term revenues 'from collaborating with companies in the Pharmaceutical and AgBiotechnology industries in return for research and development payments and a combination of milestone payments and royalties based on achievement of commercial outcomes'.

Because of the company's small size and shortage of necessary managerial and financial resources, its management quickly realized that it could not achieve its objectives without forming global strategic alliances. Keith Williams, chief executive and founder, noted that 'you have got to dance with the big pharmas but you don't necessarily have to sell to them' (quoted in Ashiya 2000: 6).

The company's first strategic alliance was with Dow AgroSciences in 1999. The two companies signed a multi-year joint research agreement to collaborate on several projects in the area of proteomics. This included research to characterize more completely an entirely new class of proteins being developed by Dow AgroSciences, and to identify new enzymes and novel pathways in the biosynthesis of plant products.

In November 2001, Tyrian Diagnostics finalized another global strategic alliance with IBM, aimed at conducting advanced scientific studies into proteins' role in preventing, causing, and treating diseases. According to the alliance agreement, IBM provided the IT backbone for Tyrian Diagnostics' commercial offerings, including its platform for proteome analysis, called ProteomIQ. The latter offers a comprehensive suite of software, instruments, and technologies for integrating, analysing, and managing a full range of protein data, including images and biological samples.

In addition, the two companies collaborated on research initiatives, as well as marketing programmes designed to drive sales and to deploy solutions to research institutions, biotechnology, and pharmaceutical companies. Further, IBM supplied hardware and software, and services, as needed, for Tyrian Diagnostics' in-house research programmes and databases that address and examine proteins involved in cancer, infectious diseases, and age-related illnesses. Tyrian Diagnostics can also tap into a wide range of sales, education, training, and technical support programmes available through IBM's PartnerWorld for Developers Program—a worldwide programme designed to help software developers reach broader markets faster and lower their costs of doing business.

Another key strategic partner was the Japanese company Shimadzu Corporation, a leading manufacturer of analytical instruments for scientific research. Both companies agreed to develop a new instrumentation for proteomics based on Tyrian Diagnostics' patented technologies and Shimadzu Corporation helped Tyrian Diagnostics gain access to the Japanese market. In April 2007, Tyrian Diagnostics became a reference site for Shimadzu's state-of-the-art mass spectrometry technology (see Exhibit B).

Other successful alliances have been established with Bayer CropScience, a subsidiary of Germany's Bayer AG and one of the world's leading innovative crop science companies, to collaborate on the application of the DiagnostIQ™ test platform for agricultural applications from 2006; and with the American firm BD (Becton, Dickinson and Company), a leading global medical technology company, to collaborate on the development and commercialization of tuberculosis (TB) diagnostic tests from 2007.

## Exhibit B Selected international strategic alliance partners

- IBM. Global strategic alliance with IBM Life Sciences. Collaboration in which IBM supplied information technology infrastructure for ProteomIQ. This includes hardware and software, and services as required.

- **Shimadzu Corporation and Kratos Instruments.** Development and distribution of Xcise, automated instrumentation for the processing of gels for mass spectrometry analysis. Development of the 'chemical printer', an automated solution for high-throughput mass spectrometric analysis of proteins. Partnering on software development for automated high-throughput proteomics analysis on Kratos' Axima mass spectrometer.
- **Sigma-Aldrich.** Manufacturing and distribution of proteomics products developed by Tyrian Diagnostics.
- **Millipore Corporation.** Development and distribution of consumables and kits for proteomics.
- **ThermoFinnigan.** Collaboration in liquid chromatography, ion-trap mass spectrometry for integration into ProteomIQ. This includes development of sample LC-MS preparation kits and integration of informatics into Tyrian Diagnostics, BioinformatIQ, an informatics package.
- **CSIRO (Commonwealth Scientific and Industrial Research Organization).** Collaboration in statistics, data management, software architecture, and industrial image analysis.
- **GeneBio (Geneva, Switzerland).** GeneBio is the exclusive distributor of Tyrian Diagnostics' GlycoInformatic databases and tools.

Since 1999, Tyrian Diagnostics has quickly grown to become one of the world's major forces in proteomics. With over eighty staff, half of whom hold PhDs or MScs, it has developed a suite of novel technologies to make the world's first integrated, high-throughput platform for proteome analysis. This platform is massively accelerating Tyrian Diagnostics' discovery research. Significant commercial opportunities exist in the commercialization of proteomics technology. But the firm's managers know that they cannot 'go it alone' and Tyrian Diagnostics always looks for new partners around the world.

*Source:* M. Ashiya (2000), 'Proteome Systems Limited', Case Study No. 9–602–039, Harvard Business School; Tyrian Diagnostics' website at http://www.tyriandx.com/.

**Discussion questions**

1. Discuss the main drivers and motives for global strategic alliances at Tyrian Diagnostics.

2. Discuss the advantages and disadvantages of Tyrian Diagnostics' global strategic alliance strategy.

## 📁 References

Austin, J. E. (2000). *The Collaboration Challenge: How Nonprofits and Businesses Succeed through Strategic Alliances* (San Francisco, CA: Jossey-Bass).

Bierly, P. E., and Gallagher, S. (2007). 'Explaining alliance partner selection: fit, trust and strategic expediency', *Long Range Planning* 40(2): 134–53.

Bleeke, J., and Ernst, D. (eds) (1993). *Collaborating to Compete: Using Strategic Alliances and Acquisitions in the Global Marketplace* (New York: Wiley).

Bleeke, J., and Ernst, D. (1995). 'Is your strategic alliance really a sale?' *Harvard Business Review* 73(1): 97–105.

Cartwright, S., and Cooper, L. C. (1993). 'The role of culture compatibility in successful organizational marriage', *Academy of Management Executive* 7(2): 57–70.

Child, J. (1984) *Organization: A Guide to Problems and Practice* (London: Harper & Row).

Child, J. (2002). 'A configurational analysis of international JVs drawing upon experience in China', *Organization Studies* 23: 781–815.

Child, J., Faulkner, D., and Tallman, S. (2005). *Cooperative Strategy: Managing Alliances, Networks and Joint Ventures* (Oxford: Oxford University Press).

Child, J., and Yan, Y. (1999). 'Investment and control in international joint ventures: the case of China', *Journal of World Business* 34(1): 3–15.

Contractor, F. J., and Lorange, P. (2002). 'The growth of alliances in the knowledge-based economy', *International Business Review* 11: 485–502.

Dacin, T. M., Hitt, M. A., and Levitas, E. (1997). 'Selecting partners for successful international alliances: examination of US and Korean firms', *Journal of World Business* 32(1): 3–16.

Das, T. K., and Teng, S. B. (1999). 'Managing risks in strategic alliances', *Academy of Management Executive* 13(4): 50–62.

Das, T. K., and Teng, S. B. (2001). 'Trust, control, and risk in strategic alliances: an integrated framework', *Organization Studies* 22(2): 251–83.

Dussauge, P., and Garrette, B. (1999). *Cooperative Strategy: Competing Successfully through Strategic Alliances* (Chichester: Wiley).

Dyer, J. H., Kale, P., and Singh, H. (2001). 'How to make strategic alliances work', *Sloan Management Review* 42(4): 37–43.

Faulkner, D. (1995). *International Strategic Alliances: Co-operating to Compete* (Maidenhead: McGraw-Hill).

Frayne, C. A., and Geringer, M. J. (1990). 'The strategic use of human resource management practices as control mechanisms in international joint ventures', *Research in Personnel and Human Resources Management* (Supplement 2): 53–69.

Geringer, M. J. (1988). *Joint Venture Partner Selection: Strategies for Developed Countries* (Westport, CT: Quorum Books).

Geringer, M. J. (1991). 'Strategic determinants of partner selection criteria in international joint ventures', *Journal of International Business Studies* 22(1): 41–62.

Geringer, M. J., and Hébert, L. (1989). 'Control and performance of international joint ventures', *Journal of International Business Studies* 20(2): 235–54.

Ghemawat, P., Porter, M. E., and Rawlinson, R. A. (1986). 'Patterns of international coalition activity', in M. E. Porter (ed.), *Competition in Global Industries* (Boston, MA: Harvard Business School Press), 345–67.

Goldstein, A. (2008). 'A Latin American global player goes to Asia: Embraer in China', *International Journal of Technology and Globalisation* 4(1): 56–69.

Gomes-Casseres, B. (2001). 'Inter-firm alliances', in *Routledge Encyclopedia of International Political Economy* (London: Routledge).

Gulati, R., and Singh, H. (1998). 'The architecture of cooperation: managing coordination costs and appropriation concerns in strategic alliances', *Administrative Science Quarterly* 43(4): 781–814.

Hamel, G. (1991). 'Competition for competence and inter-partner learning within international strategic alliances', *Strategic Management Journal* 12: 83–103.

Hitt, M. A., Dacin, M. T., Levitas, E., Arregle, J. L., and Borza, A. (2000). 'Partner selection in emerging and developed market contexts: resource-based and organizational learning perspectives', *Academy of Management Journal* 43(3): 449–67.

Hoon-Halbauer, S. K. (1999). 'Managing relationships within Sino–foreign joint ventures', *Journal of World Business* 34(4): 344–69.

Inkpen, A. C. (1998). 'Learning and knowledge acquisition through international strategic alliances', *Academy of Management Executive* 12(4): 69–80.

Jemison, D. B., and Sitkin, S. B. (1986). 'Corporate acquisitions: a process perspective', *Academy of Management Review* 11(1): 145–63.

Kale, P., Dyer, J. H., and Singh, H. (2001). 'Value creation and success in strategic alliances: alliancing skills and the role of alliance structure and systems', *European Management Journal* 17(5): 463–71.

Madhok, A. (2006). 'Revisiting multinational firms' tolerance for joint ventures: a trust-based approach', *Journal of International Business Studies* 37(1): 30–43.

Mockler, J. R. (1999). *Multinational Strategic Alliances* (New York: Wiley).

Parkhe, A. (1991). 'Interfirm diversity, organizational learning, and longevity in global strategic alliances', *Journal of International Business Studies* 22(4): 579–601.

**Opening case study** Dell in China: will the direct sales model crack in China?

Michael Dell founded Dell in 1984 when he was a freshman at the University of Texas, Austin. Dell's business model is based on the belief that firms that sell directly to consumers are better placed to understand and respond to consumers needs than conventional firms that sell indirectly through reseller channels. The direct selling model enabled Dell to bypass the traditional middleman and sell custom-built computers to its consumers at a competitive price. In the 1980s, Dell offered its customers a number of reassurances to overcome the psychological barriers of not buying from a well known retail outlet. Reassurances included risk free return, and next-day-at-home product assistance. Dell was also the first computer firm to send technical staff to homes to service their computers. By dealing directly with customers' requests, Dell was able to forecast demand for personal computers (PC) parts and, as a result, was able to reduce inventory costs and overheads.

**Exhibit A** The five beliefs of Dell's direct sales model

**Most efficient path to the customer.** We believe that the most efficient path to the customer is through a direct relationship, with no intermediaries to add confusion and cost. We are organized around groups of customers with similar needs. This allows our teams to understand the specific needs of specific customers—without customer needs being 'translated' by inefficient resellers and middlemen.

**Single point of accountability.** We recognize that technology can be complex, so we work to keep things easy for our customers. We make Dell the single point of accountability so that resources necessary to meet customer needs can be easily marshaled in support of complex challenges. Our customers tell us they want streamlined and fast access to the right resources; direct provides just that.

**Build-to-order.** We provide customers exactly what they want in their computer systems through easy custom configuration and ordering. Build-to-order means that we don't maintain months of aging and expensive inventory. As a result, we typically provide our customers with the best pricing and latest technology for features they really want.

**Low-cost leader.** We focus resources on what matters to our customers. With a highly efficient supply chain and manufacturing organization, a concentration on standards-based technology developed collaboratively with our industry partners, and a dedication to reducing costs through business process improvements, we consistently provide our customers with superior value.

**Standards-based technology.** We believe that standard technology is key to providing our customers with relevant, high-value products and services. Focusing on standards gives customers the benefit of extensive research and development from Dell and an entire industry—not from just a single company. Unlike proprietary technologies, standards give customers flexibility and choice.

*Source:* Dell website at http://www.dell.com/. © Dell

Today, Dell is a leading global brand. It consistently features in the list of the most admired companies in the US. In 2009, Dell shipped more than one PC every second in the US, which is about 140,000 per day. Dell boasts that every Fortune 100 company does business with it, and it is the leading PC supplier to small and medium business in the US for over a decade.[1]

The direct selling model became the 'soul of Dell'. Michael Dell describes the model as 'the backbone' of Dell and 'the greatest tool in its growth'. The model is based on the five beliefs (see Exhibit A).

Although Dell experimented with indirect distribution channels during the early 1990s, it reverted to its direct selling model in 1994. In 1996, Dell started selling its computers through the Internet via its popular website, dell.com. The latter venture targeted individual consumers who were able to post their specific requirements and request specific add-on parts and software. The Internet enabled Dell to enhance its build-to-order system. Once an order is received from a customer via an email or by phone, Dell would assemble the PC according to the stated specifications, at very short notice, using sophisticated logistic structure.

Dell quickly gained confidence in its business model and started its international venture in 1987. Its initial venture was in the UK market. It then expanded into Ireland, Germany, and then Canada. By the early 1990s, Dell had become the sixth largest desktop PC maker and the seventh largest notebook PC maker, operating in a large number of European countries, including Italy, Sweden, Poland, the Czech Republic, Finland, and Norway. Although a number of experts were sceptical about Dell's direct selling model suitability outside the US, the model proved a success in Europe. To serve its international customers, Dell developed a global distribution network, spanning the US, Europe, and Asia. Regardless of location, Dell strives to assemble the product within six hours of receiving the order and request that its suppliers deliver the item within 90 minutes. To be able to do so, Dell's suppliers set up their warehouses close to its assembling factories.

Dell ventured into China in 1995. The Chinese PC market was experiencing a significant growth in the late 1990s and Dell had to have a strong foothold in it in order to establish itself as world leader. When Dell entered the Chinese market, early movers such as Compaq, IBM, and Legend were the market leaders in the Chinese PC market. They depended on Chinese resellers to sell their products. Initially, Dell imported PCs assembled in its factories in Malaysia and sold them through Chinese distribution channels. However, in order to use its direct selling model, Dell had to manufacture its PCs in China. In 1998, Dell started manufacturing PCs in the Xiamen region, which is close to Taiwan, where most of Dell's suppliers were located and close enough to China's major urban cities such as Beijing and Shanghai.

Dell encountered a number of challenges in the Chinese market. Prices of PCs are too high for the average Chinese buyer—the price of a PC is equal to three months' salary for average Chinese buyers. Chinese average buyers have to save for a year or more to purchase a PC, and would involve friends and family members in the purchasing decision, including visiting a retail shop to learn about the machine before buying it. Furthermore, Dell receives a small number of orders via the Internet because of low Internet usage and perceived risk of financial transactions over the Internet. A number of analysts pointed out that Dell's direct selling model is not suitable for the individual PC market because people in China prefer to purchase from retail shops and 'prefer to

[1] Company facts: http://content.dell.com/us/en/corp/d/corp-comm/Company-Facts.aspx

pay cash and see products before they buy'. The *Financial Times* (2010) reported that, 'the strongest evidence that Dell's model is not yet matched to the China market is the appearance of numerous unofficial "agents" who buy its computers and sell them for a profit'.

Aware of the challenges of penetrating the individual consumer market, Dell has historically focused on institutional, corporate, and urban customers. As a result, in 2010, corporate clients made up more than 60% of Dell's sales in China. However, the Chinese PC market has witnessed a radical shift over the last few years. The urban market is saturated and the corporate market is becoming more competitive as competitors have copied Dell's business model. The market for average individual consumers in Chinese townships and small cities, however, has witnessed significant growth. Despite warnings from experts and local managers about the need for a varied selling approaches, the Dell headquarter's management has stuck to its direct selling model. Michael Dell commented, 'go back and look at the reaction to Dell's entry into any market. What you will see is conventional wisdom that the direct-sale model won't work. The fact is, no one sells more computer systems than us.'

So far, Dell has not been able to penetrate successfully remote markets using its direct sales approach. Lenovo and Founder, Dell's main competitors in China, have been capturing the individual consumer market using their varied distribution approach. By 2006, Lenovo captured more than 35% of the Chinese Desktop market share. Dell's share was just over 8%. Indeed, a number of Dell's executives in China left the company in the late 2000s to join Dell's major competitors such as Lenovo. Observers attributed the flux of Dell's executives to their frustrations with Dell's headquarters in the US sticking to the direct selling model and their refusal to use indirect selling to break into the growing semi-urban and rural market. Dell is under severe pressure to change its golden rule, 'Never sell indirectly.' Will it break the business model that underpinned its success so far?

*Source:* Dell website at http://www.dell.com/; N. Chowdhury (1999), 'Dell cracks China', *Fortune* (21 June): 121; Z. Dongsheng and C. Junsong (2006), 'A decade of adventure of Dell in China', Case No. CC–506–010, China Europe International Business School (CEIBS), Shanghai; H. I. Wang, A. Farhoomand, and P. Ng (2007), 'Dell, selling directly, globally', Asia Case Research Centre, University of Hong Kong, Hong Kong; G. Fairclough and J. Spencer (2005), 'Dell's PC in China marks developing market push', *Asian Wall Street Journal* (22 November): B3; *Financial Times* (2010), 'Dell: in China the agent enters the equation', by M. Dickie and S. Morrison (August 26 2005), downloaded from http://www.ft.com/cms/s/2/770cceb6-1614-11da-8081-00000e2511c8.html. (24 March); and B. Collen (2006), 'Dell debuts new website to enhance online sales and service', *Twice* 21(22): 16.

## 7.1 Introduction

The primary concern of the preceding chapters has been: (1) the broader business environment in which the multinational firms compete; (2) mechanisms through which multinational firms identify, build, and exploit their capabilities to compete successfully in the global market; and (3) a discussion of the different modes of entry into international markets. In this chapter, our focus shifts to the management of the relationship between the headquarters and the different subsidiaries and the role of subsidiaries in the pursuit of the multinational firm goals and objectives (Yeung 2000; Phene and Almeida, 2008).

The opening case study highlights some of the key issues that we will discuss in this chapter. Dell was able to compete successfully in many Western markets through its direct sales model, using its sophisticated supply chain system. Initially, Dell's subsidiary in China treated the Chinese market much like other Western markets—closely following the global strategy set by Dell's headquarters in the United States. But the managers of Dell's subsidiary in China soon realized that Dell's global approach of competing in the marketplace is not as efficient in China as it is in Western markets. Dell in China finds it very hard to compete with local players such as Lenovo and other multinational firms selling directly to consumers. The opening case study shows how Dell's managers in China faced the challenge of adapting Dell's business model to the Chinese business environment. In responding to local pressures for adaptation, Dell managers in China had to deal with a variety of complex domestic challenges, such purchasing decisions, a lack of direct selling experts, and risks over purchasing goods via the Internet. As a result, Dell managers found themselves facing difficult choices as they considered whether to stick with a business model that has been tried and tested and proven successful in a number of countries or develop a new business paradigm suitable to the Chinese business environment. As discussed in Chapter 1, subsidiaries of multinational firms have to balance pressures for adaptation to local needs and exploitation of local opportunities and pressures for global integration. The experience of Dell in China shows that subsidiaries of multinational firms may sometimes have to forsake the global strategy set by the headquarters in order to fit local environments.

In addition to balancing pressures for local needs and global integration, subsidiaries of multinational firms are increasingly playing a prominent role in developing valuable knowledge for the whole multinational firm (Monteiro et al. 2008; Yang et al. 2008; Ambos et al. 2006; Yamao et al. 2009). A number of multinational firms are becoming learning networks, with their foreign subsidiaries playing a valuable role in generating and diffusing new knowledge throughout the multinational firm network. The parent multinational may benefit from knowledge transferred from subsidiaries by introducing new products or processes or by improving existing products and services, saving costs through transfer of best practices from subsidiaries, more efficient decision-making processes as a result of advice obtained from subsidiary managers, and innovation through a combination and cross-pollination of ideas originating from subsidiaries (Hansen and Nohria 2004).

Knowledge flow from subsidiaries is often referred to as 'reverse knowledge transfer'. Reverse knowledge transfer refers to the parent multinational utilization of knowledge developed by its subsidiaries. There are a number of examples where the subsidiary made valuable contributions to the whole firm. For example, McDonald's popular Filet-O-Fish burger was introduced by a franchisee located in Cincinnati and adopted by McDonald's globally. Another example is BP Plc. BP has recently transformed its subsidiaries in over a 100 countries from stand-alone fiefdoms, to a network of collaborative subsidiaries contributing to, and learning from each other.

The ability of subsidiaries to adapt to local pressures and be a source of valuable knowledge is linked to the degree of autonomy the subsidiary has. Evidence suggests that a high level of autonomy is a prerequisite for a subsidiary's ability to develop new knowledge. This is because tight control by the parent firm leaves little room for the subsidiary to develop and diffuse new knowledge. The opening case study shows how Dell's control over its subsidiaries restricted its subsidiary in China from experimenting with new approaches that, if proved successful, could be exported to the headquarters and other subsidiaries facing similar challenges. This chapter discusses the different roles subsidiaries play and the degree of autonomy subsidiaries should have. The chapter also discusses the mechanisms through which subsidiaries transfer knowledge to the parent firm and other subsidiaries.

## 7.2 Global strategy levels

Before we discuss the different roles of subsidiaries and how subsidiaries create and transfer knowledge throughout the multinational firm network, we need to discuss the different levels of strategy within a multinational firm. In multinational firms, strategies are initiated at two distinct levels. There is a strategy for the multinational firm and all its subsidiaries, which is called headquarter or corporate-level strategy. And there is a strategy for each subsidiary, which we refer to as subsidiary-level strategy (see Exhibit 7.1). We will use the terms 'headquarter' and 'corporate-level strategy' interchangeably. At both corporate level and subsidiary level, multinational firms have to deal with specific management functions, such as finance, human resources, marketing, and operations.

Corporate-level strategy deals with the question of *what* business or businesses to compete in, and the overall game plan of the multinational firm. In other words, the corporate-level strategy revolves around the definition of businesses in which the multinational firm wishes to compete, and the acquisition and allocation of resources to its different subsidiaries. The headquarter-level strategy will be discussed in the next chapter.

In contrast, subsidiary-level strategy refers to the game plan of each subsidiary. It is concerned with the question of *how* a subsidiary positions itself among local and international rivals to achieve its strategic goals (Dess et al. 1995: 374). It also deals with the integration of subsidiary-level strategy with the corporate-level strategy. Toward this end, the subsidiary-level strategy is concerned principally with crafting a strategy that is congruent with the overall

**Exhibit 7.1** Levels of global strategy

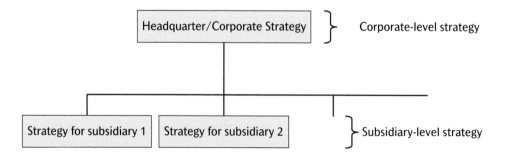

corporate-level strategy, and at the same time with addressing specific strategic issues facing the subsidiary in its particular industry and/or geographical location. This chapter focuses on the subsidiary-level strategy.

---

**KEY CONCEPT**

In multinational firms, strategies are initiated at the corporate/headquarter level and the subsidiary level. Corporate-level strategy deals with the question of *what* business or businesses to compete in, and the overall game plan of the multinational firm. Subsidiary-level strategy refers to the game plan of each subsidiary and is concerned with the question of *how* a subsidiary positions itself among local and international rivals to achieve its strategic goals. Each of the two levels of strategy has an important and distinct role to play in achieving and sustaining competitive advantage.

---

# 7.3 Strategic role of subsidiaries

We broadly define the strategic role of subsidiaries as the significance of the subsidiaries' contribution to the overall global success of the multinational firm. The strategic role of subsidiaries in multinational firms varies, from simply meeting the challenges of implementing the global headquarter-level strategy, to taking the lead in developing a specific strategy for the subsidiary. Some subsidiaries may be given the authority to make strategic and operating decisions autonomously, whereas others may be passive implementers of headquarters-developed strategy (O'Donnell and Blumentritt 1999: 194; O'Donnell 2000).

The degree to which subsidiaries are actively involved in the formulation and implementation of corporate strategy, and the degree to which they are creators or passive users of knowledge within the multinational firm, varies from one multinational firm to another, and sometimes from one subsidiary to another within the same multinational firm.

There are three key drivers for a subsidiary's autonomy. First, corporate-level managers should give the authority to subsidiaries to make strategic decisions when the subsidiary faces conditions of high environmental uncertainty. For instance, when subsidiaries face local uncertainties in their business environment which require quick intervention, headquarter-level managers should give subsidiaries the authority and power to make strategic and operational decisions to deal with these uncertainties (Vereecke and Van Dierdonck 2002).

Second, corporate-level managers should give authority to subsidiaries when the subsidiary production technologies are non-routine and require complex and specific knowledge located at the subsidiary level. Corporate-level managers should keep interference in the strategy of the subsidiary to the minimum because they are not well equipped to respond adequately to local exigencies facing these subsidiaries.

A third major factor determining the degree to which subsidiaries set their own strategy is how much the multinational firm needs to adapt its overall strategy to local conditions. At one extreme, are multinational firms which use a standardized strategy worldwide with little or no modification. At the other extreme, are multinational firms that give absolute power to subsidiaries to tailor their strategy to their local business environment. However, in practice, it is not a case of adopting an entirely standardized strategy or an entirely localized strategy, but a matter of degree.

The subsidiaries of Dell have relatively little autonomy. However, Dell is forced to give more autonomy to its Chinese subsidiary in order to adapt to local conditions. Dell does not have to give up its 'standardized strategy' across the world. Dell only needs to give more autonomy to one or several of its subsidiaries.

## 7.4 Types of subsidiary-level strategy

Subsidiaries typically fall into two broad categories, varying from passive supporter and implementer of the headquarter-level strategy, to subsidiaries with a high level of autonomy. It must be pointed out that it is not a case of either/or, but, rather, of the extent to which the multinational firm is pursuing type 1 or type 2 strategy. Below, we discuss the two types of subsidiary-level strategy.

### 7.4.1 Support and implementation

Under the support and implementation approach, multinational firms have a dominant corporate-level strategy, and the role of the subsidiary is to implement the corporate-level strategy. The centre in this case controls most of the multinational firm's activities and makes most strategic decisions. In brief, a dominant corporate-level strategy occurs when a subsidiary produces a component or a product under assignment from the parent for the multinational firm as a whole. Since the subsidiary is simply making an 'assigned' product, very little strategizing is required at the subsidiary level (Crookell 1986; Vereecke and Van Dierdonck, 2002).

This is an appropriate strategy in industries where consumers worldwide have roughly the same preference. In these industries, firms should avoid the pressure and temptation to produce completely different products for different geographical markets. As discussed in Chapter 1, extreme customization is an expensive strategy, and often the returns do not justify the high cost. Instead, firms are advised to produce variations on the basic products. This will obviously increase design, production, and marketing cost, but will have the advantage of greater acceptability by customers in different geographical locations and therefore higher returns.

The support and implementation role is also appropriate when little strategizing is needed at the subsidiary level in cases where, for example, subsidiaries in different countries face similar competitive environments and use standard processes. The role of subsidiary managers in this case is devoted primarily to improving the efficiency of their existing operations. The success of the subsidiary, therefore, requires an internal focus, specifically on achieving operating efficiencies.

Another minor but critical role of subsidiaries is localization of products. Note that, under the support and implementation role, the subsidiary is involved more in localization than in adaptation. 'Localization' refers to 'the changes required for a product or service to function in a new country'. Adaptation, however, refers to changes that 'are made to customer tastes or preferences' (Johansson 2004: 392). A subsidiary *localizes* its products by, for example, making adjustments to its electrical equipment to make it compatible with local technical requirements such as electrical voltage. It *adapts* its products to local preferences when, for example, it produces shapes and colours that are popular in that country. Subsidiaries pursuing a support and implementation role are involved more in localization than in adaptation.

One must point out that a support and implementation role should not be taken to mean *total* centralized authority at the parent or corporate level, where the parent acts as the sole command and control. Some strategic elements of global corporate strategy are—and, according to many, should be—dispersed across multiple subsidiaries.

Scholars (Nohria and Ghoshal 1994; Vereecke and Van Dierdonck 2002; Shao-Lung and An-Tien 2010) have over the years identified the factors which, if present, the support and implementation role is more likely.

- Degree of local competitive intensity. Low competitive intensity lowers the pressure for local adaptation and pushes the subsidiary to play a support and implementation role.

- Headquarter ownership level. Fully owned and/or substantially owned subsidiaries are more likely to play a support and implementation role than partially owned subsidiaries.

- Market similarities. The more similar the local markets are, the more likely that subsidiaries play a support and implementation role.

Multinational firms adjust the level of delegation to the subsidiary level by weighing the trade-off between the virtues and the vices of decentralization. Below, we discuss the advantages and disadvantages of the support and implementation approach.

## Advantages of support and implementation role strategy

A support and implementation approach, like most strategic business alternatives, involves trade-offs. The benefits of pursuing a support and implementation strategy must be weighed up against possible drawbacks.

Most multinational firms would prefer to have a single standard corporate strategy if their products and services are accepted around the world. Subsidiary managers in this case would not need to redesign their products to suit different customer needs and expectations, or develop a new strategy to compete in their local markets.

Further, from the corporate-level perspective, a sense of unity among its subsidiaries, a willingness to act as part of a single global strategy, is a strategic resource of enormous value, often more valuable than giving subsidiaries the flexibility to design their own strategy with little reference to the global corporate strategy. Having a global corporate strategy means that strategic disagreements and rivalries between subsidiaries are resolved within the context of the global strategy, and once a decision on the direction of a firm has been reached, it will be honoured by all subsidiaries.

Key advantages of the support and implementation role of the subsidiary level strategy include the following:

- A standard global design strategy with a common standard design for the entire market eliminates the sources of additional costs through economies of scale. As explained in Chapter 1, the cost of production tends to decline as the firm gains experience with a particular production process.

- A standard global design strategy with a common standard design for the entire market creates a cost advantage through faster organizational learning. This is because a global design strategy eliminates complexity by focusing on a smaller set of homogeneous tasks, and leads the firm to a faster path of learning through familiarity and repetition.

- A standard global design strategy can enhance efficiency for the multinational firm by producing fewer product varieties in longer production runs in different national plants.

- When subsidiaries focus on implementing and supporting the corporate-level strategy, they are likely to gain strengths in pursuing operational efficiencies.

### Disadvantages of support and implementation role strategy

The support and implementation strategy has several disadvantages. They include the following:

- The strategy is not suitable in industries or regions where customers are increasingly more demanding and less willing to accept standard global products and compromise their specific needs and wants.

- The strategy is not adequate when subsidiaries face conditions of high environmental uncertainty, or when they use non-routine production technologies that require complex and specific knowledge located at the subsidiary.

- The strategy builds a one-sided relationship between the headquarter and the subsidiary and gives the impression that the parent company lacks respect for, and confidence in, the subsidiary managers' ability to manage.

### 7.4.2 Autonomous subsidiaries

There are two types of autonomous subsidiaries. The mini replica which is a small-scale replica of the parent firm, and the global mandate which focuses on a single product or process. Below, we discuss the two types in detail.

### Mini-replica role

Mini-replica subsidiaries operate as small-scale replicas of their parent firms (Young et al. 1988; Beugelsdijk, Pedersen, and Petersen, 2009). In a truly mini-replica role, the subsidiaries are able, not only to select their own strategies in the matters allocated to them, but also to define their own goals with little interference from the corporate headquarters.

In this approach, while subsidiaries have the authority to design their own subsidiary-level strategy unconstrained by corporate dictates, they must do so within recognized boundaries set by the corporate parent. Typically, the subsidiary utilizes the core competences of the parent firm, or processes that the parent firm does exceptionally well as its main competitive weapon in its local market. However, the subsidiary is free to customize its products and services and its marketing campaigns to best meet the needs of its local market. The key challenge here is how to decentralize the strategy-making process to the subsidiary level without breaking the umbilical cord between the corporate parent and the subsidiaries.

The mini-replica approach is particularly effective when the need for local adaptation is high, and when there are significant differences between the customers' needs. Mini-replica subsidiaries often replicate the full range of activities of the value chain.

## Global 'product' mandate

The third approach is the global mandate approach. Global or world 'product' mandates are defined as the full development, production, and marketing of a product line in a subsidiary of a multinational firm (Rugman 1986; O'Donnell and Blumentritt 1999). A global or world product mandate gives the subsidiary global responsibility for a single product line, including development, manufacturing, marketing, and exporting (Crookell 1986; Harzing and Noorderhaven 2006).

The global product mandate grants subsidiaries the power and authority to undertake high value-added activities in the subsidiary, as well as providing subsidiary management with the opportunity to develop and grow the mandate over time (Bouquet and Birkinshaw 2008). In other words, under the global product mandate, the subsidiary acts more like an equal partner of the corporate parent than a subordinate entity. It can also expect a much higher level of operational autonomy under the world mandate arrangement than under dominant corporate-level strategy.

Multinational firms grant subsidiaries a global product mandate when tariffs to operate in certain countries are prohibitively high, or when firms wanting to sell products in particular markets have to make them locally. Because the global product mandate gives the subsidiary the power and responsibility to act beyond its market, the subsidiary has to have an externally oriented strategy, in that it must continually search for untapped or emerging market opportunities for its product. The subsidiary should have a relatively greater freedom to enter and leave markets in a timely fashion.

The global product mandate has several implications for the multinational firm. First, under the global product mandate, functions such as R&D, production, marketing, and strategic management, will be located at subsidiary level (Rugman 1986). Second, because subsidiaries with a global product mandate may have unique control within the multinational firm of certain products, they are both integrated within the corporate firm because they export finished goods to other subsidiaries, and autonomous because they have a high degree of independence over strategic product-related decisions.

## Advantages and disadvantages of the mini-replica and global mandate strategies

When implemented properly, the mini-replica and global mandate strategies have several important advantages.

**Exhibit 7.2** Generic strategies and examples

| Generic strategies | Characteristics | Examples |
|---|---|---|
| Cost leadership | Competitive scope: broad target | Ryanair |
| | Competitive advantage: lower cost | Low fares |
| Differentiation | Competitive scope: broad target | Mercedes cars |
| | Competitive advantage: differentiation on quality, reliability, convenience, or speed of delivery | Quality |
| Focus cost | Competitive scope: narrow target | Charity shops (e.g., Oxfam) |
| | Competitive advantage: very low cost | Affordability |
| Focus differentiation | Competitive scope: narrow target | Ferrari |
| | Competitive advantage: differentiation | Prestige |

---

**KEY CONCEPT**

A firm's relative position within an industry is given by its choice of *competitive advantage*, i.e., cost leadership or differentiation, and of *competitive scope*, i.e., broad target or narrow target. Based on these two distinctions, Michael Porter has distinguished four generic strategies that firms can pursue: cost leadership, differentiation, focused low cost, and focused differentiation.

---

### 7.5.1 Cost leadership strategy

Subsidiaries pursuing a cost leadership strategy appeal to price-sensitive customers. The strategy involves setting out to become the lowest-cost producer relative to local or other foreign rivals in the same market.

The subsidiary's goal in pursuing a cost leadership strategy is to outperform competitors in its market by producing goods and services at a lower cost. As a result, even when all competitors in the market charge the same price for their products, the cost leader makes higher profits because its costs are lower. Furthermore, if price wars develop and competition increases, then it is most likely that high-cost companies will be driven out of the industry before the cost leader.

This strategy requires the subsidiary to be fully and continually devoted to cutting costs throughout the value chain. Porter (1985: 35) noted that, 'Cost leadership requires aggressive construction of efficient-scale facilities, vigorous pursuit of cost reductions from experience, tight cost and overhead control, avoidance of marginal customer accounts, and cost minimization in areas like R&D, service, sales force, advertising, and so on.' Thus, subsidiaries following a cost strategy must vigorously pursue cost minimization activities by tightly controlling overhead costs, and by minimizing costs in activities such as R&D, marketing and advertising, and process innovation. The cost leadership strategy also requires achieving cost advantages in ways that are hard for competitors to copy or match. Dell's strategy of assembling and distributing standard computers through an efficiently managed global supply chain helps it create a low-cost position relative to its rivals.

Multinational firms and subsidiaries must be careful when pursuing a cost leadership strategy. The subsidiary must reduce cost without compromising product features and services that buyers consider essential. Compromising essential product features in the quest to minimize cost may lead to poor-quality products rather than value-for-money products. Ryanair is a case in point here. In its quest to remain the cheapest airline in Europe, Ryanair introduced several innovative cost-cutting initiatives, but a number of innovations were questionable (see Exhibit 7.3).

Cost leadership is appropriate when the industry's product is perceived by buyers to be much the same from one producer to another; when the marketplace is dominated by cut-throat price competition, with highly price-sensitive buyers; when there are few ways to achieve product

---

**Exhibit 7.3** Successful cost leadership strategy at Ryanair: no frills, no toilet, no seats!

Since its foundation in 1985, the airline, Ryanair, has followed a very successful cost leadership strategy. By 2010, Ryanair offered more than 1,100 flight routes across twenty six countries, connecting 155 destinations. With 7,000 staff and 73.5 million passengers per year, Ryanair generated annual revenues of about €3 billion.

Unlike other airlines, Ryanair eliminated cost at every step: it focused on secondary airports with lower airport charges; it eliminated free services to passengers (e.g., no free food), it paid lower salaries to its staff; it entered into contracts with third parties in order to reduce passenger and aircraft handling costs; it eliminated payments to travel agents by selling only directly through a website; and it lowered the cost of buying and maintaining aircraft by relying on one type of aircraft (Boeing 737), amongst others.

However, sometimes, cost-cutting zeal goes a step too far and can backfire badly. Ryanair reported in 2009 that its onboard toilets would become coin-operated, forcing passengers to pay £1 or €1 per visit. The plan was retracted and may never materialize after it attracted negative media attention and became a popular joke. The plan to charge for toilet use was to be introduced with another plan to remove seats and introduce standing room on its aircraft. The plan was to remove toilets as well as a row of seats from the back of the plane and leave one coin-operated toilet at the front of the plane. This would free space up for standing room, and hence more passengers.

The plan to introduce standing room was put on hold until it gets the go-ahead from European Aviation Safety Agency (EASA), which is highly unlikely. Ryanair's plan would require EASA to rewrite its rules which state that, 'a seat (or berth for a non-ambulant person) must be provided for each occupant who has reached his or her second birthday'. Analysts believe that Ryanair went a step too far, but there is also a widespread belief that the two plans were no more than a highly cost-effective publicity campaign by Rynair to highlight how far it is willing to go to cut cost to remain the cost leader.

*Source:* Various newspapers; Ryanair website at http://www.ryanair.co.uk.

differentiation that have much value to buyers; and when switching costs for buyers are low. Examples of cost strategy include retail multinational firms such Kmart, Walmart, Tesco, and fast food chains such as McDonald's, Burger King, Subway, and Kentucky Fried Chicken.

### The cost leadership strategy and the subsidiary–headquarters relationship

Subsidiaries pursuing a cost leadership strategy produce a large volume of fairly standardized products that appeal to large price-sensitive segments of the market. They are often internally focused and their main concern is cost reduction. The multinational firms achieve cost leadership through efficiency which can be obtained through various economies in the production and distribution process.

The parent and other subsidiaries assist the subsidiary achieve its cost leadership strategy by supporting activities that lead to cost reduction, such as scale economy in sourcing and cost-effective management skills (see Exhibit 7.4 below). For example, by sourcing globally, the parent is able to obtain scale economy in purchasing. The high volume of raw materials or parts purchased by the parent allows the subsidiary to take advantage of volume discounts. Further, the parent is better positioned to scan the international market for the least expensive raw materials or parts. The parent can also shift labour-intensive operations from subsidiaries in countries where labour cost is high, to countries where it is low. The subsidiary can also benefit from sharing knowledge and value chain functions with other subsidiaries. For example, a subsidiary located in a country where certain skills for carrying out a specific process are abundant and inexpensive, performs the process for all subsidiaries. Further, when a single global brand name is used worldwide, the subsidiary makes savings in advertising costs and sales efforts. This support enables the subsidiary to produce and market its product at a lower cost and thereby gain a competitive advantage.

---

### KEY CONCEPT

A cost leadership strategy involves setting out to become the lowest-cost producer relative to the firm's rivals.

---

**Exhibit 7.4** Generic strategies and headquarter–subsidiary support

| Generic strategies | Support from headquarters |
| --- | --- |
| Cost leadership | Strong support from headquarters to reduce cost |
| | Strong cooperation between subsidiaries to share best practice to reduce cost |
| Differentiation | Very strong support from headquarters to maintain quality and innovation |
| | Very strong cooperation between subsidiaries to maintain quality and innovation |
| Focus cost | Low support from headquarters |
| | Very low support from and cooperation between subsidiaries |
| Focus differentiation | Very strong support to maintain quality of products and services |
| | Very strong support from and cooperation between subsidiaries to maintain quality of products and services |

7.5.2 **Differentiation strategy**

A subsidiary employing a differentiation strategy seeks to be unique in its industry along some dimensions that are perceived widely as unique and valued by customers. While differentiation typically involves higher costs, the uniqueness associated with its products allows the subsidiary to compensate by appealing to a broad cross section of the market, willing to pay premium prices. Apple, for example, produces products that are unique and valued by its customers. While Dell put a strong emphasis on price, Apple's primary emphasis is on 'non-price' attributes such as design and style, for which Apple's customers are willing to pay a premium. Similarly, while a subsidiary pursuing a low-cost strategy such as Volkswagen's Skoda may produce a car that is safe, reliable, and durable, Volkswagen's Audi subsidiary follows a differentiation strategy and produces cars with extra-quality features, such as expensive leather seats, expensive wood in the dashboard, and so on.

In contrast to the cost leadership strategy, subsidiaries pursuing a differentiation strategy must focus on continuously investing in and developing features that differentiate their products in ways that customers perceive as unique and valuable.

When a subsidiary pursues differentiation, it seeks to distinguish itself along as many dimensions as possible. These dimensions can include prestige and brand image (e.g., Lacoste fashion retailer and most five-star hotels), innovation (Nokia mobile phones and Apple electronic products), physical characteristics of the product such as quality or reliability (BMW cars and DHL express mail services), customer service (John Lewis retail chain), or distribution network (Caterpillar earthmoving machinery). For example, in addition to providing high quality and reliability in its products, Rolex, the Swiss-based watch manufacturer, has created a global network of specialists who alone are qualified to guarantee to Rolex owners the authenticity of their watches and the dependability of the features that ensure its longevity in order to safeguard its reputation.

Uniqueness may also relate to the psychological need of customers, such as status or prestige. For example, high-quality cars such as Audi and quality watches such as Rolex are not just reliable and technologically sophisticated products, but they also appeal to customers' prestige needs. The development of a distinctive competence, such as Federal Express with its fast reliable service, is also a base for uniqueness.

**Differentiation strategy and the subsidiary–headquarters relationship**

Subsidiaries pursuing a differentiation strategy require strong support from the parent and other subsidiaries in terms of sharing technology, process innovation, and product development and marketing (see Exhibit 7.4). The quality of the product produced by the subsidiary is likely to be thoroughly tested by the parent.

Because differentiation requires constant innovation in order to produce unique products suited to local customers' demand preferences, subsidiaries must share knowledge, processes, and technologies with one another. That is, subsidiaries following a differentiation strategy are likely to depend more on support from the parent and continued resource sharing within the corporate group than subsidiaries following a cost leadership strategy. Note that, while in both cost leadership and differentiation strategies the subsidiary requires the support of the parent and other subsidiaries, the type of support the subsidiary needs is different. Subsidiaries following a cost leadership strategy require support that helps them lower cost. In contrast, subsidiaries pursuing a differentiation strategy need support that helps them acquire capabilities necessary for producing differentiated products.

---

**KEY CONCEPT**

A subsidiary employing a differentiation strategy seeks to be unique in its industry along some dimensions that are perceived widely as unique and valued by customers.

---

### 7.5.3 Focused low-cost strategy

A subsidiary following a focus strategy puts emphasis on a niche market segmented by geographical region, income level, and/or product specialization. A focused low-cost strategy is a market niche strategy, concentrating on a narrow, specific, and recognizable customer segment and competing with lowest prices, a strategy which requires the subsidiary to be the cost leader in its niche. This strategy works well when the firm is able significantly to lower cost to a well-defined customer segment.

Examples of firms employing a focused cost strategy include youth and backpacker hostels, which provide cheap accommodation for students and backpackers looking for a place to stay, or low-cost retailers such as charity shops in the UK (e.g., Oxfam) that offer second-hand products at a discount to price-sensitive shoppers.

---

**KEY CONCEPT**

A subsidiary following a focused low-cost strategy selects a narrow, specific, and recognizable segment whose requirement is less costly to satisfy compared to the rest of the market, and tailors its strategy to serve customers in this segment.

---

#### Focused low-cost strategy and the subsidiary–headquarters relationship

Because subsidiaries following a focused low-cost strategy concentrate on a small segment of the market and offer specific products, using well-defined technology and processes, they need only a small degree of support from the corporate parent (see Exhibit 7.4). Further, the link with other subsidiaries may also be weak because subsidiaries following a focused low-cost strategy tend to focus on their local market, which may be served differently from one country to another.

### 7.5.4 Focus differentiation strategy

A second market niche strategy is focused differentiation strategy. The subsidiary here concentrates on a narrow customer segment and competes through differentiating features. For example, Burj Al Arab hotel in Dubai—a seven-star hotel and widely considered the world's most luxurious hotel—promise the ultimate personal service.

To be successful, the subsidiary must be able to offer its target market something they value highly and which is better suited than other firms' products to their specific and unique requirements. Further, the strategy must have a strong brand and the subsidiary must have a thorough understanding of its targeted market's unique tastes and preferences, and the ability to offer products with world-class attributes.

Examples of focus differentiation include high-fashion clothing boutiques in Paris and Milan, and sports car manufacturers such as Ferrari, or makers of prestigious cars such as Rolls-Royce. Customers buying from such companies are willing to pay a high premium for the finest products and services.

### Focused differentiation strategy and the subsidiary–headquarters relationship

In contrast to focused low-cost strategy, subsidiaries following a focused differentiation strategy need strong support from the parent and peer subsidiaries (see Exhibit 7.4). Producing products with world-class features requires specific resources and competencies that develop from cooperating and sharing information with the parent and other subsidiaries. Also, it is imperative that the parent assist subsidiaries to acquire the necessary resources and competencies in order for them to produce and/or offer products that consistently conform to the highest standards. Although the costs associated with the extensive sharing of information and coordination between the parent and subsidiaries and within subsidiaries are quite high, customers are willing to pay a high premium for the product.

---

**KEY CONCEPT**

A subsidiary following a focused differentiation strategy concentrates on a narrow customer segment and competes through differentiating features.

---

### 7.5.5 Integrated strategy or 'stuck in the middle'

Multinational firms sometimes adopt a hybrid strategy—also known as an integrated strategy—balancing the emphasis on cost reduction against an emphasis on differentiation. The hybrid or integration strategy seeks to provide customers with the best cost/value combination. This strategy has a dual strategic emphasis, appealing to value-conscious customers who are sensitive both to price and value. For example, Korean multinational firms in the automobile and electronic industries have been successful in developing and implementing integration strategies. As a result, they have been able to provide high-quality products at a very competitive price.

Several writers have criticized such a hybrid strategy. Michael Porter and several other writers, while accepting that each generic strategy has pitfalls and that there are different risks inherent in each strategy, argue that a hybrid strategy leads to mediocrity. Porter argues that the two basic generic strategies—cost leadership and differentiation—are incompatible and fundamentally contradictory, requiring different sets of resources and competencies and appealing to different customers; that any firm attempting to combine them would eventually end up 'stuck in the middle'; and that, as a result, such a firm will be out-performed by competitors who choose to excel in one of the basic strategies. Porter (1985: 12) noted:

> if a firm is to attain a competitive advantage, it must make a choice about the type of competitive advantage it seeks to attain and the scope within which it will attain it. Being 'all things to all people' is a recipe for strategic mediocrity and below-average performance, because it often means that a firm has no competitive advantage at all.

### 7.5.6 Criticisms of generic strategies

Several writers have challenged Porter's typology and questioned his claims about the exclusivity of the generic strategies. They argued that, contrary to what Porter advocates, sustainable competitive advantage rests on the successful combination of cost leadership and differentiation strategies (Deephouse 1999). One of the key reasons for adopting an integrated strategy is the turbulent global business environment, which requires multinational firms to adopt flexible combinations of strategies. For instance, Shanghai Volkswagen initially concentrated on a cost leadership strategy and produced cars to be used as taxis in the Shanghai area. Through its operations in China, Shanghai Volkswagen gained a strong market position in its market, as well as valuable knowledge on the Chinese car market. Although Shanghai Volkswagen captured leadership in its particular segment, management realized that concentration on a single strategy involved higher than normal risks. New competitors started invading Shanghai Volkswagen's segment by imitating its strategy. There were signs that customers were starting to switch to competitors. As a result, Shanghai Volkswagen expanded its segment, and now follows a multi-segment strategy by pursuing low-cost and differentiation strategies, simultaneously.

To multinational firms such as Volkswagen, a hybrid strategy combining elements of cost leadership and differentiation is not only possible but is the most successful strategy for them to pursue. The hybrid strategy deals with the many inherent disadvantages of cost leadership and differentiation strategies. When properly employed in the right target market, it is likely to have a higher performance than a pure cost leadership or differentiation strategy.

Nonetheless, Porter's generic strategies make a valuable contribution by emphasizing that firms need to make strategic choices between pursuing a certain type of strategy. For instance, when Volkswagen decided to differentiate its products increasingly in China, its costs invariably increased due to extra features offered in its cars. Therefore, firms need to weigh up the benefits of spending more money on more differentiated products, as opposed to cutting costs in order to offer customers a low-cost product.

## 7.6 Summary

In multinational firms, strategies are initiated at two distinct levels. Strategies for the whole multinational firm are formulated at the headquarters level and called 'headquarter-level' or 'corporate-level' strategies. Corporate-level strategy is discussed in the next chapter (Chapter 8). Strategies for each subsidiary are formulated at the subsidiary level, and are termed 'subsidiary-level strategies'. Corporate-level strategy deals with the question of *what* business or businesses to compete in, and the overall game plan of the multinational firm. Subsidiary-level strategy is concerned with the question of *how* a subsidiary positions itself among local and international rivals to achieve its strategic goals, and deals with the integration of subsidiary-level strategy with the corporate-level strategy.

As far as the relationship between headquarters and subsidiaries is concerned, we identified two broad types of subsidiary-level strategy: support and implementation, and autonomous subsidiaries. Each strategy has advantages and pitfalls. The role of managers is to weigh up the advantages against the disadvantages of each strategy before selecting the most appropriate strategy for their organization.

Multinational firms cannot, and should not, target all customers in a particular market or country. They need to target a specific segment, large or small, using three specific strategies called generic strategies—cost leadership, differentiation, and focus. The subsidiary can also combine, or integrate, cost leadership strategy and differentiation generic strategies. The integrated strategy is a challenging strategy and has several risks. However, if implemented properly and successful, such integrated strategy enables the subsidiary to enjoy superior performance and enhance its competitive position.

## 📖 Key readings

- On the relationship between the headquarter and subsidiaries, read O'Donnell (2000).

- On the role of subsidiaries in creating and diffusing knowledge, see Phene and Almeida (2008); and Shao-Lung and An-Tien (2010).

- On the structures of subsidiaries, see Birkinshaw and Morrison (1995).

- On generic strategies, see Porter (1985).

## 💬 Discussion questions

**1.** Briefly describe the two levels of global strategy.

**2.** Identify and briefly describe the roles of subsidiary-level managers.

**3.** Explain the different types of subsidiary-level strategy, and discuss some of the pitfalls associated with each type.

**4.** Briefly describe the three generic strategies—cost leadership, differentiation, and focus—and discuss the pitfalls associated with each of the three generic strategies.

**5.** Explain the relationship between the three generic strategies and the headquarters–subsidiary relationship.

**6.** Can subsidiaries—and multinationals as a whole—combine generic strategies of cost leadership and differentiation? Put forward arguments for and against.

**7.** Choose a multinational firm and identify the different roles of its subsidiaries.

---

**Closing case study** Managing the melamine contamination crisis by Nestlé China

In 2009, Nestlé's subsidiary in China teamed up with China Nutrition Society to launch its Healthy Kids Programme. The aim of the programme is to improve the nutrition, health and wellness of school children aged 6 to 12 years old by raising their awareness about the importance of nutrition and healthy physical activities. The programme has had widespread media coverage and Nestlé's subsidiary in China received significant positive publicity as a result of it. The new positive image of Nestlé China is a far cry from what had been happening to Nestlé China in the previous years.

In 2008, it looked as though there was no end to constant bad news for China's food industry in general and Nestlé China in particular. The bad news started in 2008, with reports of nearly 300,000 children falling ill, thousands of children stricken with kidney problems, and four dying in China after consuming milk products. The contamination was caused by companies adding melamine—used to make plastics—to milk. This initial news was followed by revelations that the contaminated milk was widely used in the production of chocolate, yoghurt, and several other processed food products.

The bad news continued. In October 2008, supermarkets in Hong Kong took Chinese eggs off the shelves when tests revealed high levels of melamine in eggs originating from Hubei Province. The fear that the contamination was spread beyond China was soon confirmed when the Indonesian government ordered the destruction of over 2,000 boxes of Snickers and M&M's chocolates made with Chinese dairy products. This was followed by Taiwanese authorities reporting that Nestlé's infant formula and powdered milk were contaminated with melamine and therefore were banned in Taiwan.

Not surprisingly, the global media reported widely on the issue and the melamine scare spread worldwide. Analysts pointed the finger at the inadequate, and often total absence, of government monitoring of food safety in China which allows unscrupulous 'entrepreneurs' to put public health at risk. Two perpetrators were found guilty and sentenced to death, and a number of individuals were sentenced to lengthy terms of imprisonment. Subsidiaries of multinational firms also took a big share of the blame. It was argued that the inadequate monitoring was an added reason for multinational firms to keep a close eye on every activity of their supply chain production.

The melamine scare forced multinational firms in China to take radical action. In order to ensure the safety of its products, Walmart announced on 22 October 2008 a major overhaul of its Chinese supply chain and soon thereafter pulled certain brands of Chinese eggs off the shelves in China.

Nestlé took the most radical action to deal with the problem in an attempt to restore customer confidence. On 31 October 2008, Nestlé announced that it was opening a world class R&D centre in Beijing that cost in the region of US$10 million. The centre was equipped with the most advanced testing equipments that could detect contaminations such as melamine. Nestlé feared that its US$1 billion investment in China over two decades was at risk and had to make such a big investment to protect one of its key markets. Nestlé mobilized its public relations (PR) machine and went on the offensive to reassure customers and governments and took several actions, including recalling already sold contaminated milk powder, and sending twenty specialists from its headquarter in Switzerland to its plants in China to carry out testing for known dangerous substances such as melamine.

The research centre and Nestlé PR machine not only saved Nestlé China, but also improved its market position. The melamine scare did not go away and there was concern among Chinese customers that the the contamination was more widespread. However, while Nestlé China was able to reassure its customers that its products are safe from contamination by using its powerful PR machine, often referring to the research centre which was reported to detect 'trace amounts of residues and undesirable compounds like melamine or veterinary drugs or natural toxins' and well-publicized safety measures, local rivals did not have such a powerful PR machine to reassure customers, nor did they have world class facilities comparable to that of Nestlé to test their products.

By 2009, Nestlé sales were on the up again. The melamine contamination helped Nestlé China take market share from its rivals. Recent reports suggest that Chinese customers trust Nestlé China more than its local rivals. As put by Patrice Bula, chairman and CEO of Nestlé China: '[as a result of the crisis] we have gained market share, all our businesses, our branding is stronger and we had greater market recognition'. Shaun Rein, a Shanghai-based market research expert, reported that Nestlé's market share increase was 'partly because everybody's fleeing the domestic producers'.

*Source:* F. Balfour (2008), 'Wal-Mart pulls tainted eggs from shelves in China', *Business Week* (October 30) available at http://www.businessweek.com/globalbiz/blog/eyeonasia/archives/2008/10/wal-mart_pulls. html; D. Roberts (2008), 'Nestlé combats China food scandals', *BusinessWeek* (October 31) available at http://www.businessweek.com/globalbiz/content/oct2008/gb20081031_663334.htm; *China Daily* (2005), 'Nestlé China apologizes for unsafe iodine infant milk powder', (6 June); Bloomberg (2009), 'Nestlé China growth may double after evading scandal', (7 September) at http://www.bloomberg.com/apps/news; BBC News Report (2009), 'Chinese milk scam duo face death', BBC World News.

## Discussion questions

1. Discuss Nestlé China's management of the melamine crisis.
2. Discuss Nestlé China's positioning strategy after the melamine crisis.

# 📁 References

Ambos, T. C., Ambos, B., and Schlegelmilch, B. B. (2006). 'Learning from foreign subsidiaries: an empirical investigation of headquarters' benefit from reverse knowledge transfers', *International Business Review* 15(3): 294–312.

Beugelsdijk, S., Pedersen, T., and Petersen, B. (2009). 'Is there a trend towards global value chain specialization? An examination of cross border sales of US foreign affiliates', *Journal of International Management* 15(2): 126–41.

Birkinshaw, J., and Morrison, A. J. (1995). 'Configurations of strategy and structure in multinational subsidiaries', *Journal of International Business Studies* 26(4): 729–53.

Bouquet, C., and Birkinshaw, J. (2008). 'Weight versus voice: how foreign subsidiaries gain the attention of headquarters', *Academy of Management Journal* 51(3): 577–601.

Crookell, H. H. (1986). 'Specialization and international competitiveness', in H. Etemad and L. S. Dulude (eds), *Managing the Multinational Subsidiary* (London: Croom Helm): 102–11.

Deephouse, D. (1999). 'To be different, or to be the same? It's a question (and theory) of strategic balance', *Strategic Management Journal* 20: 147–66.

Dess, G., Gupta, A., Hennart, J.-F., and Hill, C. (1995). 'Conducting and integrating strategy research at the international, corporate, and business levels', *Journal of Management* 21(3): 357–93.

Frynas J. G. (2003). 'The limits of globalization: legal and political issues in e-commerce', *Management Decision* 40(9): 871–80.

Gupta, K. A., and Govindarajan, V. (2004). *Global Strategy and Organization* (New York: Wiley).

Hansen, M. T., and Nohria, N. (2004). 'How to build collaborative advantage', *MIT Sloan Management Review* 46(1): 22–30.

Harzing, W. A., and Noorderhaven, N. (2006). 'Knowledge flows in MNCs: an empirical test and extension of Gupta and Govindarajan's typology of subsidiary roles', *International Business Review* 15(3): 195–214.

Johansson, K. J. (2004). *Global Marketing*, 3rd edn (New York: McGraw-Hill).

Monteiro, F., Arvidsson, N., and Birkinshaw, J. M. (2008). 'Knowledge flows in multinational corporations', *Organization Science* 19(1): 90–107.

Nohria, N., and Ghoshal, S. (1994). 'Differentiated fit and shared values: alternatives for managing headquarters-subsidiary relations', *Strategic Management Journal* 15(6): 491–502.

O'Donnell, S. W. (2000). 'Managing foreign subsidiaries: agents of headquarters or an interdependent network?' *Strategic Management Journal* 21(5): 525–48.

O'Donnell, S. W., and Blumentritt, T. (1999). 'The contribution of foreign subsidiaries to host country national competitiveness', *Journal of International Management* 5: 187–206.

Phene, A., and Almeida, P. (2008). 'Innovation in multinational subsidiaries: the role of knowledge assimilation and subsidiary capabilities', *Journal of International Business Studies* 39(5): 901–19.

Porter, M. E. (1985). *Competitive Advantage* (New York: Free Press).

Rugman, A. M. (1986). 'New theories of the multinational enterprise: an assessment of internalization theory', *Bulletin of Economic Research* 38: 101–18.

Shao-Lung, L., and An-Tien, H. (2010). 'International strategy implementation: roles of subsidiaries, operational capabilities, and procedural justice', *Journal of Business Research* 63(1): 52–9.

Vereecke, A., and Van Dierdonck, R. (2002). 'The strategic role of the plant: testing Ferdows' model', *International Journal of Operations & Production Management* 22(5): 492–514.

Yamao, S., De Cieri, H., and Hutchings, K. (2009). 'Transferring subsidiary knowledge to global headquarters: the role of HR configurations', *Human Resource Management* 48(4): 531–54.

Yang, Q., Mudambi, R., and Meyer, K. E. (2008). 'Conventional and reverse knowledge flows in multinational corporations', *Journal of Management* 34(5): 882–902.

Yeung, H. W.-C. (2000) 'Organising "the firm" in industrial geography I: networks, institutions and regional development', *Progress in Human Geography* 24(2): 301–15.

Young, S., Hood, N., and Dunlop, S. (1988). 'Global strategies, multinational subsidiary roles and economic impact in Scotland', *Regional Studies* 22(6): 487–97.

**online resource centre**

## Online resource centre

Please visit www.oxfordtextbooks.co.uk/orc/frynas_mellahi2e/ for further information.

### 8.3.1 Types of control

Control of subsidiaries can be carried out in two ways: personal or impersonal. Personal control relies on human interaction such as expatriates using methods such as direct supervision, whereas impersonal control is carried out through formal bureaucratic and written rules and procedures such as written manuals (Ferner 2000).

According to Child (1984: 158–60), personal control suits small organizations, whereas impersonal control is more appropriate for larger organizations. Personal control is also a distinctive feature of multinational firms from certain countries such as Britain and Germany, where multinationals from these countries are known for relying more on direct personal than impersonal control. Also, when managing subsidiaries, East Asian firms tend to put more emphasis on personal rather than formal rules and procedures. Tata, for example, relies heavily on personal control. In contrast, French multinational firms usually rely more on impersonal control than personal control (Harzing 1999).

### 8.3.2 Focus of control

In addition to the above two types of control or how control is being carried out, managers need to decide on the content of control or what is being controlled. Scholars have classified control content into three main types: *output control, behavioural control*, and *cultural control* (Ouchi 1980; Baliga and Jaeger 1984). Multinational firms may use a combination of different types of control for different purposes; for instance, the firm's headquarters may use output control to motivate subsidiary-level managers to meet strategic goals, and may use behavioural control to better integrate the subdisiaries' strategics into the firm's overall global strategy (Chang et al. 2009).

Headquarters of multinational firms that employ output-oriented control systems employ formal procedures that specify desired resources to be used in the process and performance targets for each subsidiary, and take corrective actions when deviations from expected levels arise.

Generally, output control is recommended when the centre is able to design a system that produces reliable and verifiable evidence of the performance of the subsidiary without heavy interference in the subsidiary's activities (Ouchi 1977; 1979). When subsidiaries have to adjust their operations to local circumstances, the centre needs to go beyond output control measures and develop more complex control apparatus to tackle the increasing environmental variety and complexity facing them (Doz and Prahalad 1991).

Output control measures include performance metrics such as profitability, market share, growth, productivity, customer satisfaction, employee commitment, and impact on environment. The centre usually rewards subsidiaries that achieve or exceed their targets, and may intervene in the running of subsidiaries that fail to meet their targets.

An alternative to output-based control is the behaviour-based control (Paik and Sohn 2004: 61). Behavioural control refers to control obtained by monitoring the behaviour of staff at the subsidiary level. Ouchi and Maguire (1975) define behavioural control as personal surveillance which enables top management to guide and direct subordinates. Multinational firms use behavioural control when they desire to influence the means to achieve desired outcomes. That is, behavioural control is an *input* control that focuses on the activities and decision-making processes rather than the end result, as in the case of output control. In their quest to achieve behavioural control, multinational firms often appoint expatriate managers that are knowledgeable of, and highly committed to, the corporate parent's decision-making processes and practices to fill key subsidiary positions. This is because, generally, expatriates have a better understanding of the corporate parent's operating procedures and the overall multinational firm's priorities and goals than locally hired employees and managers (Doz and Prahalad 1986).

The centre may control the subsidiary through cultural control. In contrast to output and behavioural control mechanisms, cultural control is not formal and relies on subtle ways to control the subsidiary. It involves the indoctrination of subsidiary managers and employees into the parent firm's norms and value systems. With cultural control, there is little need for direct control because subsidiary managers and employees are expected to buy into the norms and value systems of the parent firm and therefore exercise self-control by controlling their own behaviour.

Jaeger and Baliga (1985) note that cultural control relies 'on internalization of and moral commitment to the norms, values, objectives and "ways of doing things" of the organization'. The aim of cultural control is to ensure that the norms and values of individual employees at the subsidiary level are congruent with those of the overall multinational firm. Similar to behavioural control, cultural control relies on employing expatriate managers as top managers of subsidiaries abroad to enable the parent firm to transmit its visions, values, and norms to subsidiaries (Collings et al. 2008). Multinational firms use informal communication and networks, as well as international management training to enhance control through expatriates in socialization acting as 'bumblebees', flying from plant to plant to spread the corporate parent's norms and value systems (Harzing 2001). In the following section, we discuss in more detail how multinational firms control their subsidiaries by institutionalizing global corporate values and norms.

### 8.3.3 **Control and global values**

Most multinational firms believe that decision-makers throughout the multinational firms need a common foundation upon which they base decisions, ranging from operational issues to ethical and moral dilemmas. To do so, most large multinational firms developed a global set of values in order to achieve some consistency of behaviour across their subsidiaries. In practice, nearly all these global values look similar. They usually include abstract ideals such as justice, integrity, honesty, sincerity, competence, and excellence. Some multinationals are founded on a core set of values and some adopted fundamental values later on. Multinational firms such as Hewlett-Packard (HP) often claim that their core values are timeless. HP boasts that their core values, established over seventy years ago by its founders, Bill Hewlett and Dave Packard, are 'as relevant as they've ever been'. HP values include:

- We are passionate about customers;
- We have trust and respect for individuals;
- We perform at a high level of achievement and contribution;

- We act with speed and agility;

- We deliver meaningful innovation;

- We achieve our results through teamwork; and

- We conduct our business with uncompromising integrity.

*Source:* http://h30434.www3.hp.com/t5/Hardware/Hp-pavilion-Dv6000/m-p/195935.

Global values embody the multinational firm's 'desired' business philosophy and responsibility towards key stakeholders. Multinationals often express them in terms of desirability or avoidance, bad or good, and/or better or worse to evoke emotional reaction from employees, frame their attitudes, and provide behavioural standards against which employees' behaviours can be judged. Global values are often reported to be the foundations that glue the separate parts of the multinational together by developing a shared perspective of the firm's vision. They are often spoken of as the blueprint of the multinational firm's success. Basically, global values systems tell people within the organization how to act in different situations. HP states that its strategy is 'guided by enduring values', listed above. It states that 'Our ethical standards and shared values form the cornerstone of our culture of uncompromising integrity. Our culture of integrity and accountability, and our performance culture go hand-in-hand. We win, both as individuals and as a company, by doing the right thing' (http://www.hp.com/).

In order to translate global values into actions, leaders of multinational firms urge employees and managers to adhere to these core principles and use them as a moral basis in everyday decision-making. Leaders of multinational firms have the responsibility for implementing global values. This makes them essentially stewards of the firm's core principles. One of the most written-about and cited as an example of leadership success in translating global values into practice is the pharmaceuticals multinational firm, Johnson & Johnson's (J&J) leadership by the Credo (see Exhibit 8.2).

---

**Exhibit 8.2** Johnson & Johnson Credo

**Johnson & Johnson**

**Our Credo**

We believe our first responsibility is to the doctors, nurses and patients,
to mothers and fathers and all others who use our products and services.
In meeting their needs everything we do must be of high quality.
We must constantly strive to reduce our costs
in order to maintain reasonable prices.
Customers' orders must be serviced promptly and accurately.
Our suppliers and distributors must have an opportunity
to make a fair profit.

We are responsible to our employees, the men and women who work
with us throughout the world.
Everyone must be considered as an individual.
We must respect their dignity and recognize their merit.
They must have a sense of security in their jobs.
Compensation must be fair and adequate,
and working conditions clean, orderly and safe.
We must be mindful of ways to help our employees fulfill
their family responsibilities.

Employees must feel free to make suggestions and complaints.
There must be equal opportunity for employment, development
and advancement for those qualified.
We must provide competent management,
and their actions must be just and ethical.
We are responsible to the communities in which we live and work
and to the world community as well.
We must be good citizens—support good works and charities
and bear our fair share of taxes.
We must encourage civic improvements and better health and education.
We must maintain in good order
the property we are privileged to use,
protecting the environment and natural resources.

Our final responsibility is to our stockholders.
Business must make a sound profit.
We must experiment with new ideas.
Research must be carried on, innovative programs developed
and mistakes paid for.
New equipment must be purchased, new facilities provided
and new products launched.
Reserves must be created to provide for adverse times.
When we operate according to these principles,
the stockholders should realize a fair return.

*Source:* http://www.jnj.com. Copyright holder: Johnson & Johnson.

J&J's success has often been attributed to the Credo values developed in 1943. Basically, the Credo affirms and reminds managers around the world of their primary 'responsibility to the doctors, nurses and patients, to mothers and all others who use our products and services . . . , to our employees . . . , to the communities in which we live and work . . ., to our stockholders . . .'.

Inspired by the core values described in the Credo, in 2006 J&J executives developed the so-called Global Standards of Leadership programme designed primarily to provide J&J managers around the world with guidance for the development of its leaders and evaluation of its employees. J&J conduct regular surveys of its employees to measure its performance against the Credo principles.

### 8.3.4 Barriers and challenges to headquarter-level control

The role of coordinating the activities of different subsidiaries is fraught with challenges for a number of reasons. We categorize the challenges into cross-cultural challenges, subsidiary-level challenges, and headquarter-level challenges.

**Cross-cultural challenges**　Savvy global leaders at the centre of the multinational firm not only develop and inculcate effective management systems, processes, routines and rules that guide and constrain behaviour for the whole multinational firm, but must adapt them to the considerable prevailing differences in work values and norms across cultures. Leaders of multinational firms have to balance two sources of pressure: conformity to expected norms in each country and developing a global mindset that governs some of the behaviours of employees in different countries. A corporate global mindset represents the values, beliefs ,and practices that undergird a multinational firm's management philosophy and management style. Or, what can be referred to as the multinational firm's DNA. For instance, Walmart pursues cost-cutting zealously wherever it operates, guided by clear ethical practices and the Walmart culture of dedication to customer satisfaction. The task of leaders of multinational firms is to make sure the global mindset of the firm meshes well—or at least does not clash—with local sets of norms, beliefs, and values. Generally, multinational firms that discern when to use global values and norms and when national cultures have to be accommodated, perform better than organizations that adopt a one-size-fits-all approach, ignoring local sensitivities or organizations that over-adapt to cross country differences and by so doing impede the effective execution of its global strategy.

**Subsidiary-level challenges**　Because a typical multinational firm 'consists of a group of geographically dispersed and goal-disparate . . . subsidiaries' (Ghoshal and Bartlett 1990: 603), subsidiary-level managers have the power to influence decisions at the corporate level by controlling the flow of information attended to by managers at the centre. Scholars have argued for a long time that in managing distant subsidiaries, the headquarter suffers from an information asymmetry problem, whereby information available at subsidiary level may not be available to the headquarter (Gong 2003: 728).

Problems may arise as a result of the relationship between the centre and subsidiary because of the agent–principal relationship between the two, where the agent (subsidiary) might have goals and incentives that differ from those of the principal (the centre). Once these goals diverge, subsidiaries may not act according to the overall corporate interests, and, as a result, the cooperative relationship between the centre and subsidiaries turns into a coalition of competing interests. When the latter occurs, subsidiaries may hinder the effective management of the whole multinational firm for the benefit of the subsidiary. Also, given that subsidiaries are usually rewarded for their own performance, it may be in the subsidiary's self-serving interest, for instance, to keep their resources such as financial slack or highly talented individuals, even though they are underutilized, rather than bring them to the attention of the centre.

**Headquarter-level challenges** In addition to an information asymmetry problem, which means that subsidiaries have more or better information about their activities and resources than the centre, corporate-level managers are constrained by their bounded rationality. 'Bounded rationality' refers to the lack of time and cognitive limits headquarter-level managers experience in their ability to process and interpret a large volume of pertinent and complex information on and from a large number of subsidiaries. To cope with their limited ability and time to digest and analyse complex and incomplete information, corporate-level managers may base their decisions on a fragment or subset of available information, resulting in 'good enough' decisions rather than optimal ones which limit their ability to develop and implement effective control mechanisms.

## 8.4 Diversification strategies

Some organizations stick to the business they know well, following what is called a 'concentration strategy' or a 'single-market strategy'. Multinational firms, such as Boeing based in the United States and Airbus based in France, follow a concentration strategy and concentrate their activities on manufacturing aircrafts. In the fast food industry, several large and successful multinational companies, such as Domino's Pizza and McDonald's, are still pursuing a single-market strategy. Indeed, most well-known firms, such as Eastman Kodak and Virgin, began their existence serving a single market in a single country, with a single product or service.

Concentration on a single business entails important advantages as well as dangerous disadvantages. On the one hand, by focusing on a single market, the firm is better positioned to obtain in-depth knowledge of the business in which it operates than are firms operating in several markets. On the other hand, pursuing a concentration strategy is dangerous, especially when risk is substantial; when the product or service the company provides becomes obsolete; or when the industry reaches maturity and starts declining (Amit and Livnat 1988).

The main advice for managers is that the firm should stick to its core business, unless: the risk of operating in that particular business is high; the firm's existing business stagnates or starts to shrink; or the firm acquires or develops unique competencies that are key success factors and valuable competitive assets in other industries. For example, Dell which in the past repeatedly argued against diversification and particularly growth through acquisition, was lately forced—after its value dropped from around US$100 billion in 2005 to US$30 billion in 2009—to consider acquiring other firms to obtain a foothold in the hi-tech service industry. Dell is aiming to reinvent itself—from being a leading PC maker by mastering global logistic and supply-chain processes, allowing it to sell its PCs directly to consumers at a competitive

**Exhibit 8.3** Diversification strategies

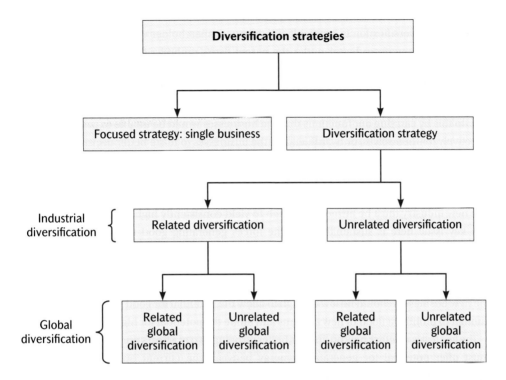

price—to a hi-tech service provider. Dell is hoping that its 'beyond PC' strategy will enable it to expand into services and other PC-related businesses, such as smart phones.

The overwhelming majority of multinational firms operate in more than one business and diversify their operations, either across multiple businesses ('industrial diversification'), or across different national markets ('global diversification'), or both (see Exhibit 8.3). For example, Tata and General Electric operate in a large number of different businesses on a global scale (both industrial diversification and global diversification). The following sections will discuss these two types of diversification strategy.

## 8.4.1 **Industrial diversification**

In the 1960s, most commentators and corporate strategists extolled the virtues of diversification in Western economies and, as a result, a large number of US and European firms adopted industrial diversification strategies. Accumulated evidence, however, suggests that diversification is not always the best strategy (Datta et al. 1991; Delios et al. 2008), and the link between diversification and performance is not clear. As noted earlier, most well-known global companies such as Microsoft, Dell, Nokia, Amazon, McDonald's, Coca-Cola, Gillette, and Xerox all obtained their initial success through a single business. Attempts by some of these companies to diversify failed miserably and they quickly returned to their core business.

The opening case study shows that Tata's diversification into new markets passes all of the three tests. Tata tends to enter into attractive and growing industries (first test), entry to such industries such as the tea market, hotels, and IT requires high initial cost and therefore barriers to entry are not low (second test), and the centre of Tata adds value to its group via the Tata management systems and procedures, and being part of a trusted and highly valued brand name (third test).

### 8.4.2. Types of industrial diversification

Generally, two industrial diversification options are available to the firm. The firm has to choose whether to diversify into closely related business ('related diversification') or into completely unrelated business ('unrelated diversification'). Below, we examine the two types of diversification in more detail.

### Related diversification

A firm diversifies into related business when it enters new businesses that have valuable relationships among the activities constituting their respective value chains (Thompson and Strickland 2003: 295). A related diversification involves adding new businesses that are strategically similar to the existing business (Davis et al. 1992). For example, Johnson & Johnson which started over a century ago producing sterile sutures and dressings and bandages to treat peoples' wounds, broadened its business over the years into human health and well-being and diversified into products such as baby products, first-aid products, women's sanitary and personal care products, skin care, prescription and non-prescription drugs, surgical and hospital products, and contact lenses. Similarly, Gillette which started in 1985 as a safety razor manufacturer, now its portfolio includes—in addition to blades and razors—toiletries, toothbrushes (Oral-B), shavers (Braun), batteries (Duracell), and writing instruments (Parker Pen, Mate Pen). Such portfolios provide firms such as Johnson & Johnson and Gillette with opportunities to share technological and managerial know-how, lower costs, capitalize on common brand names usage, and benefit from cross-collaborations between the different businesses.

Related diversification presents firms with three key potential benefits:

- Economies of scope. Because related businesses often use similar production operations, marketing, and administrative activities, related diversification provides firms with the opportunity to reduce manufacturing costs, share distribution activities, rationalize sales and marketing activities, and rationalize managerial and administrative support activities (Davis et al. 1992). For instance, firms with closely related manufacturing activities can save costs by sharing knowledge on cost-efficient production methods between one business and another. Further, because of the closely related distribution activities, the different businesses can perform better together than apart. By managing all the businesses under one corporate umbrella, the firm saves costs by, for example, centralizing overlapping managerial and administrative activities such as finance, accounting, R&D, customer support centres, and some of the marketing activities. For example, 3M, a global technology company focusing on innovative solutions, leverages its capabilities and competencies in adhesive technologies to several businesses such as automotive, construction, education, and telecommunication.

- Market power. Related diversification enables the different businesses to use common suppliers across the firm. This gives the firm greater power over its suppliers, and as a result it may secure volume discounts because of the large volume ordered from the same supplier.

- Knowledge competencies. Related diversification provides firms with the opportunity to transfer valuable know-how from one business to another, by for example, enabling firms to combine knowledge generated in separate businesses into a single R&D centre. By so doing, the firm saves R&D costs, reduces 'new product-to-market' lead time, and is better positioned to develop new products.

---

### KEY CONCEPT

There are two types of industrial diversification: related diversification and unrelated diversification. Related industrial diversification is the dispersion of a firm's activities into closely related businesses. Unrelated industrial diversification is the dispersion of a firm's activities into completely unrelated businesses. Related diversification measures dispersal of activities across business segments within industries. Unrelated diversification measures the extent to which a firm's activities are dispersed across different industries.

---

### Unrelated diversification

A firm diversifies into unrelated business when it enters businesses whose value chains are so dissimilar that no, or very little, real potential exists to transfer technology or management know-how from one business to another, to transfer competencies to reduce costs, to achieve competitively valuable benefits from operating under the same corporate umbrella, or to combine similar activities (Thompson and Strickland 2003: 295). For example, Virgin—a British conglomerate started in 1968 publishing the *Student* magazine before it launched in 1971 the Virgin Record Shop—diversified over the years into the airline industry (Virgin Atlantic), railway transport (Virgin Trains), soft drinks (Virgin Cola), and music (Virgin Superstores). Similarly, Giorgio Armani has been leveraging its well-known brand and association with fashion and haute couture into everyday clothes, cosmetics, spectacles, watches, and accessories, as well as furniture (Casa Armani), chocolate and food (Armani Dolci), flowers (Armani Fiori), nightclubs (in Milan), and hotels (in Dubai). Although under a common corporate umbrella, these businesses are too dissimilar to present Virgin and Giorgio Armani with any opportunity to share technological knowledge or business processes.

Unrelated diversification, if not managed properly, may lead to what is known as 'contamination'. Contamination occurs when two businesses with different critical success factors are encouraged to work closely together in the name of synergy, and pollute each other's thinking and strategies. For example, when Benetton merged with Benetton Sportsystem in 1998, the 'new' Benetton faced a new form of competition. For instance, while in the casual-wear market, Benetton competes through a special network of relationships with its retailers; in the sports business, the company has to deal with a host of different distributors, from big distribution chains to small specialized shops and retail agents.

If the corporate parent cannot benefit from leveraging its core competencies or sharing its activities across businesses, what motivates a firm to diversify into unrelated businesses? The reason in most cases is the quest for sustained growth or a good profit opportunity. For example, a firm may enter a fast-growing industry or acquire a firm whose assets are undervalued or a firm that is financially distressed, for less than full market value and make quick capital gains by restructuring it and reselling it as one company or separate parts, whichever is more profitable.

Unlike in related diversification, where the corporate parent adds value by exploring synergies *across* the different businesses, with unrelated diversification the corporate parent adds value by exploring synergies *within* the different businesses. The corporate parent does this by using its 'parental advantage' (Campbell et al. 1995). The 'parental advantage' stems from expertise in, and support from, the centre. The corporate parent, in this case, makes positive contributions to the different businesses by providing them with skills and competencies hard to obtain without the help from the parent, such as expert help (otherwise not available to them or available only at very high cost) on strategic moves, use of brand names, legal processes, divestment and downsizing strategies, and human resource policies.

Thompson and Strickland (2003: 303) argue that 'the basic promise of unrelated diversification is that any company that can be acquired on good financial terms and that has satisfactory profit prospects presents a good business to diversify into'. They propose that managers use six key criteria to select an industry into which to diversify. The six questions are listed in Exhibit 8.6.

---

**Exhibit 8.6  Six criteria that firms should use to select an industry into which to diversify**

- Can the new business meet corporate targets for profitability and return on investment?
- Does the new business require substantial infusion of capital to replace out-of-date plants and equipment, fund expansion, and provide working capital?
- Is the business in an industry with significant growth potential?
- Is the business big enough to contribute significantly to the parent firm's bottom line?
- Is there a potential for union difficulties or adverse government regulations concerning product safety or the environment?
- Whether there is industry vulnerability to recession, inflation, high interest rates, or shift in government policy?

*Source:* A. A. Thompson, Jr. and J. A. Strickland (2003), *Strategic Management: Concepts and Cases*, 13th edn (New York: McGraw-Hill), 303.

## Risks and pitfalls of diversification

Since corporate managers must divide their time and energy between a number of businesses in the portfolio, they will always be less close to the affairs of each business than the business's own management team. Inevitably, there is a danger that their influence will be less soundly based than the views of the managers running the business.

Further, central cost has a tendency to creep upwards, as unproductive central interference goes unchecked (Oijen and Douma 2000: 309). Goold and Campbell (2002: 219) warned that parents may destroy some value by incurring overhead costs, slowing down decisions, and making some ill-judged interventions, and that many corporate parents do not add enough value to compensate. In these cases, the net effect of corporate parent's activities is negative, and it would be better to break up the group.

Diversification may also lead to the use of cross-subsidies which allow poorly performing subsidiaries to drain resources from better-performing ones (Berger and Ofek 1995). That is, diversification enables poorly performing subsidiaries to access free resources as part of a diversified firm, rather than being on their own. This may demotivate highly performing subsidiaries. For example, Michael Walsh reported that when he joined Tenneco as CEO, he found that some of its profitable businesses such as auto parts and chemical divisions were not striving as they could have done because their surplus was dumped into the company's money-losing businesses such as farm equipment.

Another major risk of diversification is corporate parents' interference in the running of subsidiaries. Interference from parents may inhibit the initiative of subsidiary managers and impel them to take on tasks for which they are ill-suited. For example, Coca-Cola, under Dough Ivester, CEO from 1997-99, was criticized by subsidiary managers for becoming too centralized. The head of Coke Europe at that time, Charlie Frenette, commented, 'if I wanted to launch a new product in Poland, I would have to put in a product approval request to Atlanta. People who had never ever been to Poland would tell me whether I could do it or not' (*The Economist* 2001).

This is not to suggest that parents should play a hands-off role. On the contrary, as noted in section 8.3, the role of the parent is to develop and communicate clear responsibilities to subsidiaries without excessive detail. Absence of the latter will result in confusion about the specific roles and responsibilities of different subsidiaries, and the danger of a destructive conflict between subsidiaries.

## Diversification in emerging economies

While managers of firms based in Western developed economies are advised to stick to their core business unless they have good reasons to diversify, managers of large firms in emerging economies tend to diversify into different lines of businesses unless they have good reasons not to diversify. This has led to the development of highly diversified companies in emerging economies.

Highly diversified businesses in emerging economies include *chaebols* in Korea, *grupos* in Latin America, and business houses in India such as the Tata group discussed in the opening case study. This is because, in emerging markets, institutions that support key business activities are not yet developed. According to Khanna and Palepu (1997: 3), companies in emerging economies operate in a market without effective securities regulation and venture capital firms and, as a result, focused companies may not be able to raise adequate financing to start or support a new business opportunity. In most cases, they are forced to generate the money from within the firm. To be able to do this, firms in emerging economies have to diversify to generate the financial capital to expand the business internally.

Further, without strong educational institutions, firms in emerging economies struggle to hire skilled employees. For example, Tata, like many large groups in emerging economies, has its own management training schools to develop the necessary skills needed to manage the company.

Also, unpredictable government behaviour can stymie any operation in emerging economies (Khanna and Palepu 1997: 4). To guard against this risk, firms have to pursue a diversification strategy to spread the risk of government behaviour. Khanna and Palepu (1997: 6) found that the larger the size of the group, the easier it is to carry out the cost of maintaining government relationships. For instance, Tata and other large groups in India have 'industrial embassies' in New Delhi, the capital of India, to facilitate interaction with bureaucrats and government officials.

Furthermore, in emerging economies, because of the lack of information and weak law enforcement, it is very hard for customers to verify claims by firms regarding the quality and performance of products. While the cost of building a trusted brand is very high, once the brand becomes credible, the firms can leverage the power of a trusted and well-known quality image to new products and markets across different businesses. For example, a company like Tata, with a reputation for delivering on its promises, can use its trusted brand name to help it enter new businesses quickly at low cost.

Thus, diversification of a large company in emerging economies provides competitive strength in each market it enters, and helps the company deal with market imperfections in these countries (Lins and Servaes 2002). In contrast, as a result of these imperfections, focused firms would find it very hard to survive in emerging markets. For these reasons, Khanna and Palepu (1997: 3) noted that, 'although a focused strategy may enable a company to perform a few activities well, companies in emerging markets must take responsibility for a wide range of functions in order to do business effectively'.

### 8.4.3 Global diversification

Recent commentators have often extolled the virtues of global diversification. The main motivations for global diversification include the search for new foreign markets in an effort to exploit unique assets in foreign markets; gain access to lower-cost, higher-quality input, or both; build scale economies and other efficiencies; and pre-empt competitors who may seek similar advantages in strategic markets (Kim et al. 1989).

On the one hand, increased integration of the global economies and opening of new markets has increased the feasibility of global diversification. On the other hand, heightened global competition has forced more firms to focus on their core line of business. That is, while global diversification has increased over time, industrial diversification has declined over the same period. It must be noted here that global diversification is not replacing industrial diversification. The causes of the recent increase in global diversification are different, and not related to the causes of the decline in industrial diversification. Indeed, research shows that, on average, firms with high global diversification have a higher level of industrial diversification than firms operating in a single country or a very small number of countries (Denis et al. 2002: 1953). For example, in the media industry, large media empires such as Time Warner, News Corp., Bertelsmann, CBS, and Viacom induced by digitization of communication, networking, deregulations of the media industry, and globalization, spread both globally to become global networks and into unrelated businesses to became multimedia corporations.

### Related and unrelated global diversification

There are two types of global diversification: related global diversification and unrelated global diversification. Related global diversification is the dispersion of a global firm's activities across countries within relatively homogeneous clusters of countries (Vachani 1991: 307–8). Unrelated global diversification is the dispersal of the global firm's activities across heterogeneous geographic regions (Vachani 1991: 308). Let us assume that Western European countries can be regarded as a homogeneous cluster. A British firm that operates in five countries, all of which are Western European, would be regarded as having relatively highly related global diversification. However, a British firm that operates in five countries, with one each in Africa, the Middle East, South America, Asia Pacific, and Western Europe, would be regarded as having highly unrelated global diversification. To distinguish between related global diversification and unrelated global diversification, one needs to consider three factors:

**Physical proximity** Buckley and Casson (1976) argue that communication cost in multinationals depends on the physical distance between the countries in which the firm operates. This is because of the costs associated with coordinating and controlling a widely dispersed network of subsidiaries. Accordingly, multinationals that operate in countries clustered physically close to each other should have lower costs of managerial coordination, and their managers may benefit from intimate personal contact.

**Cultural proximity** Multinationals that operate in a cluster of countries with similar cultures and a common language may enjoy efficiencies because of reduced complexities in management operations. These complexities may arise because of dissimilarities in the language, culture, and socio-economic environment (Buckley and Casson 1976). Generally, the larger the cultural distance between the centre and the subsidiary, the harder the task of transferring technical and managerial knowledge.

**Level of economic development** Intangible assets are generally hard to transfer to certain types of countries. For instance, if a multinational's success is associated to a large extent with intangible assets, which are highly valued in Western countries, it may find it easier to operate in similar Western countries than in developing countries, where customers value tangible assets more than intangible assets.

---

**KEY CONCEPT**

There are two types of global diversification: related global diversification and unrelated global diversification. Related global diversification is the dispersion of a global firm's activities across countries within relatively homogeneous clusters of countries. Unrelated global diversification is the dispersal of the global firm's activities across heterogeneous geographic regions.

---

## Benefits of global diversification

Global diversification provides the multinational firm with numerous benefits. It enhances shareholder value by exploiting firm-specific assets, increasing operating flexibility, and satisfying investor preferences for holding globally diversified portfolios (Hitt et al. 1997; Kim et al. 1989; Tallman and Li 1996). The key question here is: What is the optimum level of global diversification? Research shows that, while, generally, global diversification is positively associated with shareholder value, the association may turn negative if the multinational firm over-diversifies. Managers need to identify the level of diversification beyond which global diversification starts having a negative impact on performance and shareholder value.

Global diversification may also enhance value by creating flexibility within the firm to respond to changes in relative prices (Hitt et al. 1997). Global diversification also gives multinational firms the flexibility to shift production to the country in which production costs are low, or shift distribution to the country in which market demand is highest. Furthermore, global diversification gives the multinational firm the ability to lower the firm's overall tax liability by exploiting differences in tax systems across countries, and to raise capital in countries in which the costs of doing so are lowest. Finally, global diversification enables the multinational firm to lower risk by spreading it across markets.

For managers of globally diversified multinationals, global diversification benefits corporate managers in at least two ways. First, managing a large company, with subsidiaries all around the world, confers greater power and prestige on the manager (Jensen 1986). Second, levels of managerial compensation tend, on average, to be positively correlated with firm geographical diversification.

## Costs and risks of global diversification

There are a number of costs and risks associated with global diversification. The structure of a globally diversified firm is more complex than that of a purely domestic firm, which leads to high costs of coordinating a globally dispersed network of subsidiaries. It is possible that the costs of coordinating corporate policies in diversified firms, and the difficulties in monitoring managerial decision-making in globally diversified firms, increase the likelihood that the costs of global diversification outweigh the benefits (Denis et al. 2002: 1976). Global diversification can also lead to the inefficient cross-subsidization of less profitable business units. This often happens when subsidiary managers exert influence to increase the assets under their control. This leads, in some cases, to less profitable divisions being subsidized by more profitable subsidiaries. Finally, because managers may have private benefits from global diversification, they may adopt and maintain value-reducing diversification strategies, even if doing so reduces shareholder wealth.

## 8.5 **Global sourcing strategies**

One of the key roles of the corporate parent is developing and managing a global sourcing strategy (see Exhibit 8.7). Global sourcing is 'the procurement of products and services from independent suppliers or company-owned subsidiaries located abroad for consumption in the home country or a third country' (Çavusgil et al. 2007: 484). Multinational firms are always on the lookout for the best sources of their products and services. Managers at the corporate centre of multinational firms need to identify 'which production units will serve which particular markets and how components will be supplied for production' (Kotabe and Murray 2004). They need to decide which activities should be carried out inside the company (vertical integration) and which ones should be carried out by an external supplier or partner (outsourcing). The rule of thumb here is that proprietary knowledge and business activities and processes that are considered as firms' core competencies do not lend themselves to outsourcing and therefore should not be outsourced (see Chapter 4, section 4.3.3).

**Exhibit 8.7** Outsourcing types

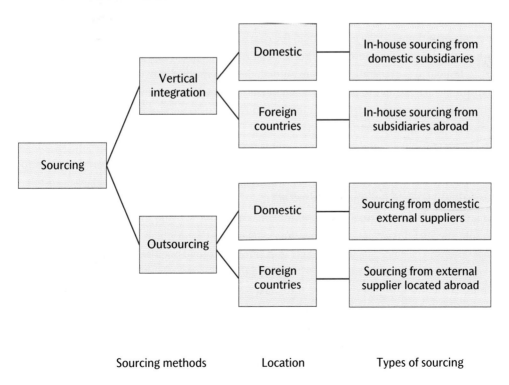

Sourcing methods          Location          Types of sourcing

The global sourcing strategy enables the multinational firm to exploit both its own and its suppliers' competitive advantages as well as the comparative locational advantages of various countries where the suppliers are located (Kotabe and Murray 2004). Multinational firms take advantage of locational advantages by sourcing components from foreign markets to take advantage of low production costs in certain countries or regions, or to take advantage of specific skills and technologies located abroad.

Every time the multinational firm adds a new plant to its global network of subsidiaries, it must develop a sourcing strategy to deliver raw materials and finished and semi-finished goods to and from the new plant to the existing network. This can be done internally through the existing network of subsidiaries on an intra-firm basis or through external suppliers. The former is commonly referred to as vertical integration. The latter is commonly referred to as 'outsourcing' (see Exhibit 8.7). Below, we examine these two sourcing strategies.

### 8.5.1 Vertical integration

Vertical integration represents the expansion of the firm's activities to include activities carried out by suppliers or customers. A vertically integrated firm oversees the flow and processing of raw and finished materials, information, and finances as they move in a process from suppliers, to manufacturers, to wholesalers, to retailers, to consumers.

Vertical or intra-firm sourcing can be domestic or international. Firms source components in-house domestically when the costs of producing them abroad outweigh the benefits of producing them at home. This is the case when the cost of producing and distributing the components domestically is lower than the cost of producing them in foreign markets, and/or where the quality of the components cannot be guaranteed abroad.

To be able to source intra-firm from abroad, the firm needs a network of globally integrated facilities which are able to procure raw materials, transform them into intermediate goods and then final products, and deliver the final products to customers, often in different countries, through an integrated distribution system.

During the 1960s and 1970s, the ability to carry out everything internally at major multinational firms such as IBM, General Motors, and AT&T was considered a powerful competitive advantage. Since the 1980s, however, ample evidence has emerged to suggest that vertical integration may slow multinational firms down and that, in most cases, it is better for multinational firms to outsource non-essential activities than do everything in-house. As a result, successful multinational firms such as Dell and Cisco, which outsource many of their operations to partners, are now held up as exemplars of good practice.

Several successful multinational firms and industries, however, remain vertically integrated. The European package tour business is an example of a vertically integrated sector. Most major European tour operators run their own travel agencies, airlines, hotels, resorts, etc. TUI, the world's largest tourism firm, manages nearly 100 brands, owns over 3,000 travel agencies and nearly 300 resorts, and owns eighty one tour operators; it operates around 100 airplanes and has incoming agencies in seventeen countries. Leading corporations in the global media industry are vertically integrated. The move towards vertical integration in the media industry started in the 1980s, when it became possible and preferable to distribute products such as movies and TV programmes across a wide array of platforms. Time Warner controls both Warner Brothers which accounts for about 10% of the global firm and television production, owns the second largest cable TV operator in the US, nearly fifty regional and international cable channels, as well as the AOL Internet platform over which it distributes its production. Similarly, News Corp., widely considered to be the most vertically integrated news corporation, owns forty seven television stations in the US, the MySpace social networking platform, controls 20th Century Fox Studios and home entertainment, and controls, or maintains a high interest in, several satellite delivery platforms in five continents (Arsenault and Castells 2008: 716).

---

**KEY CONCEPT**

Vertical integration represents the expansion of the firm's activities to include activities carried out by suppliers or customers.

---

Multinational firms will usually follow a vertically integrated strategy just after entering a new country, because of the lack of suppliers able to produce high-quality inputs. For example, when European and US car manufacturers entered the Chinese market in the 1980s, there were no Chinese suppliers capable of producing high-quality auto parts to meet the standards required by multinational firms. As a result, Western car manufacturers had to take control of the supply chain, and often imported complete kits from their home country. As the auto industry grew in China, a network of suppliers capable of producing high-quality parts developed. Consequently, in the early 2000s, most car manufacturers in China were using Chinese suppliers rather than producing the parts in-house.

Multinational firms also carry out activities in-house when competencies needed at the different stages of the value chain are similar, because vertical integration provides the multinational firm with the opportunity to transfer best practices, and helps it secure access to critical knowledge and resources at different stages of the value chain.

### Advantages of vertical integration

Vertical integration provides the multinational firm with a number of advantages. First, vertical integration enables multinational firms to cross-subsidize one stage of the value chain by another in order to squeeze out competitors. For example, European travel giant, TUI AG, is able to subsidize one of its businesses, such as its airline business, to squeeze out more focused competitors. Also, the vertical integration of global media networks facilitates the production, distribution, and consumption of their products and services.

Second, vertical integration provides multinational firms with the opportunity to retain control over proprietary knowledge, thus preventing leakage of proprietary knowledge to competitors and preventing suppliers from becoming competitors. Vertically integrated multinationals can keep proprietary technology and knowledge within the confines of their corporate system without passing it on to competitors or suppliers. In contrast, multinational firms that are not vertically integrated have to disclose and dissipate knowledge that could compromise their competitive position. For instance, many Asian firms have entered Western markets by first entering as a supplier for Western multinationals and subsequently marketing their own brand independently (Gilley and Rasheed 2000).

Third, vertical integration enables firms to foreclose—or at least raise the cost of—input and output markets to competitors (Osegowitsch and Madhok 2003), as well as reduce quality uncertainty by having control over the quality of inputs at all stages of the value chain. For example, focused competitors are not able to use—or must use at a higher cost—hotels and tour operators owned by TUI.

Fourth, vertical integration reduces uncertainties in demand and price (Osegowitsch and Madhok 2003). TUI, like other firms in the tourism industry, often faces fluctuation in demand due to external factors such as wars, epidemics, and changes in the weather. By being able to access data on all phases of the value chain, vertically integrated multinationals are aware of potential problems and are able to plan accordingly.

Fifth, vertical integration enables multinational firms to add value at different stages of the value chain. This is very important in sectors where value has immigrated from one stage of the value chain to another. In some industries, value added has migrated downstream in the value chain. For example, the number of cars in use is much higher than the number of cars produced. This has led to a considerable shift of value added away from manufacturing to servicing existing products. Thus, it makes sense for the manufacturing firm to expand its operations into downstream activities such as after-sales services. Manufacturing firms like IBM, Cisco, GE, and Compaq have moved into computer services and consultancy.

### Disadvantages of vertical integration

Studies have identified a number of disadvantages of vertical integration. First, by engaging in several activities, the multinational firm cannot concentrate on certain core tasks it does best, and, as a result, more focused competitors may outperform a vertically integrated one. Second, vertically integrated multinationals often have higher costs relative to multinationals which pursue an outsourcing strategy. This is because vertical integration requires higher investment in plants and equipment than outsourcing firms. Third, in fast-changing global business environments, and particularly in industries where barriers to exit are high, vertical integration increases inflexibility. For example, when technology or customers' preferences change, vertically integrated multinationals cannot change their technology or product quickly and cheaply. In contrast, outsourcing multinationals can switch their suppliers quickly and at much lower cost than vertically integrated ones.

### 8.5.2 Outsourcing

Outsourcing has become a significant corporate strategy since the 1990s. Organizations large and small, local and global, are turning to outsourcing in an attempt to improve their performance. The global outsourcing market was estimated to be worth around US$373 billion in 2009, with India and China accounting for 44.8% and 25.9%, respectively (*BusinessWeek* 2009). A large number of multinational firms have recently moved their entire production facilities from Western countries to emerging economies. Even firms that traditionally opposed outsourcing, such as the Japanese multinational, Sony, are now increasingly using global outsourcing to cut cost and focus on their core business.

In the 1970s and 1980s, multinational firms from Western countries outsourced primarily low-value work and labour-intensive activities to plants in developing countries. Typical of industries that led the way in outsourcing to developing countries were clothing and shoes, followed by electronics. For example, many clothing companies outsourced their clothes-production activities to plants located in emerging markets. In the late 1980s and early 1990s, several firms in the software development sector in Western developed countries started outsourcing their activities to plants in India, Ireland, Taiwan, and South Korea. By the mid 1990s, largely because of the influence of the Internet, firms around the world were able to transmit, quickly and cheaply, messages containing graphs, images, and audio and video files. This enabled multinational firms to outsource activities that were technically difficult or prohibitively expensive before the advent of the Internet. As a result, firms are now outsourcing activities ranging from basic research to financial analysis. Further, the cost-saving justification for international outsourcing in the 1970s and 1980s has been gradually supplanted by concerns for quality and reliability in the 1990s and 2000s. Large multinational firms such as IBM and Hewlett-Packard all have outsourced their activities to plants in countries such as India and China, because of the low cost of operations as well as the quality and reliability of products produced in these countries.

In addition to the traditional outsourcing of production activities, some of the growing outsourcing businesses are conducted over the Internet, such as information technology processes outsourcing (ITO) and business processes outsourcing (BPO). India is the leading destination for both ITOs and BPO firms. For instance, top Indian outsourcing firm such as Infosys and Wipro provide IT solutions and perform IT support and maintenance for leading European- and US-based multinational firms. It is expected that around 3.3 million office jobs and US$136 billion in wages will be moved from the US to low-cost countries by 2015. Half of these jobs will be for office support, 14% for computer and computer-related jobs, and only 10% for operations—actual processing and production of goods and services.

## Conditions of outsourcing

As discussed above, not all activities can or should be outsourced (also refer to Chapter 4, section 4.4.5 for a further discussion of this issue). To be successful at outsourcing a task in the value chain to an extenal partner, a firm must meet three conditions (Christensen 2001). First, it must be able to specify what attributes it needs from the supplier. If the attributes are not specified, the supplier may add, delete, or modify attributes that are key to the final product.

Second, the technology and processes to measure those attributes must be reliably and conveniently accessible, so that both the company and the supplier can verify that what is being provided is what is needed. Third, if, and when, there is a variation in what the supplier delivers, the company needs to know what else in the system must be adjusted. That is, the company needs to understand how the supplier's contribution interacts with other elements of the system so that the company can take what it procures and plug it into the value chain with predictable effect.

## Types of outsourcing

As shown in Exhibit 8.7, a multinational firm can outsource its activities domestically or abroad. Firms prefer domestic outsourcing when the disadvantages of producing goods abroad far outweigh the advantages. This is the case when the cost of producing and distributing the components by a domestic supplier is lower than the cost of producing them by foreign suppliers, and where foreign suppliers do not possess the necessary skills and technologies needed to produce the components.

In order to reduce production costs under competitive pressure, most multinational firms are increasingly turning to outsourcing of components and finished products from abroad, particularly from emerging economies such as South Africa, India, China, South Korea, Taiwan, Brazil, and Mexico.

The type of relationship with suppliers can be categorized as arm's-length or strategic outsourcing. A firm's decision to pursue arm's-length or strategic outsourcing is often based on the type of component needed and the firm's country of origin. For example, car manufacturers would acquire necessary but not strategic input from independent suppliers on an arm's-length basis to obtain lower cost of these inputs (Kotabe and Murray 2004: 8). Examples here include belts, tyres, batteries, and entertainment equipments. However, inputs of critical components or processes which are customized and which differentiate the firm's product from its competitors are sourced from suppliers based on strategic partnerships that enable the firm to gain access to suppliers' capabilities and to control the quality of products produced by the suppliers (Kotabe and Murray 2004: 8).

National differences also have an impact on the outsourcing strategy. US firms, for instance, tend to manage their suppliers in an arm's-length fashion. In contrast, Japanese firms divide their suppliers according to the type of input. Suppliers of core products that are crucial to differentiate the product are managed through exclusive, long-term relationships called *keiretsu*. Suppliers of standardized, non-core products, however, are managed on an arm's-length basis.

### KEY CONCEPT

Outsourcing by multinational firms comprises the inputs supplied to the multinational firm by independent suppliers from around the world. Firms prefer outsourcing abroad when the advantages of producing abroad far outweigh the disadvantages. This is the case when the cost of producing and distributing the components by a domestic supplier is higher than the cost of producing them by foreign suppliers, and where domestic suppliers do not possess the necessary skills and technologies needed to produce the components.

## Advantages of outsourcing

Outsourcing provides firms with four potential advantages (see Exhibit 8.8):

- Cost saving. On average, outsourcing multinationals achieve cost advantages relative to vertically integrated multinationals (Gilley and Rasheed 2000: 765). Cost saving typically occurs because the cost of accessing suppliers in low-cost countries is lower than investing in manufacturing facilities in these countries. Also, because outsourcing promotes competition between suppliers, thereby reducing cost and increasing quality of inputs.

- Access to proprietary knowledge. Outsourcing enables multinational firms to tap into new knowledge and make use of proprietary knowledge to which the company would not otherwise have access. For instance, when US and European retailing firms entered into partnership with Japanese distribution networks by outsourcing their marketing and distribution activities to them, Japanese distribution networks provided them with valuable knowledge on marketing and distribution in Japan, such as Japanese shopping behaviours and distribution networks. Further, by accessing proprietary knowledge, the multinational may start producing and marketing the product directly.

- Focus on core competence. By outsourcing peripheral activities to outside suppliers, the firm frees up internal resources to concentrate on tasks in which the multinational has distinctive capabilities and does them better than competitors. For example, Nike's core competence is in designing and marketing shoes rather than manufacturing them. Nike has outsourced virtually all its manufacturing tasks to outside manufacturers in the Far East and South America, allowing the company to focus on the design and marketing aspects of the shoe industry.

- Flexibility. Outsourcing makes multinational firms 'footloose', enabling them to switch suppliers and countries as new practices, technology, or processes become available through a new supplier or in a different country.

### Disadvantages of outsourcing

Like all strategies, outsourcing has several disadvantages (see Exhibit 8.8). Below, we discuss the four key disadvantages of outsourcing:

- Damage capabilities. Outsourcing may damages a firm's capabilities, leading in extreme cases to virtual or 'hollow firms', such as Nike offering innovative concepts and designs without investing in physical capital such as manufacturing plants.

**Exhibit 8.8** Advantages and disadvantages of global outsourcing

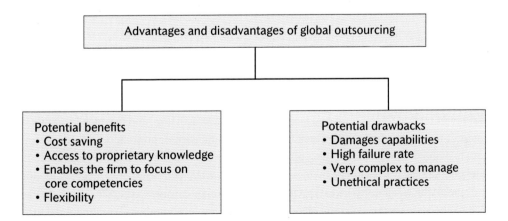

- High failure rate. Outsourcing in general and global outsourcing in particular have high failure rates. Research by Dun and Bradstreet (2000) found that around a quarter of all outsourcing agreements fail within the first two years and around half fail within five years. Results from a survey of Fortune 1000 companies reported several problems with global outsourcing, including unanticipated increases in cost, culture clashes, and service-level failure. In fact, several firms could not cope with outsourcing related problems, and decided to reverse their outsourcing strategy and perform previously outsourced tasks in-house.

- Cultural and operational incompatibilities. Unforeseen operational and cultural problems may arise, primarily when Western firms outsource tasks that require repeated interface with customers in the home market. A case in point is Dell technical support in India. Dell received a large volume of complaints from its customers in the US, who complained that operators in India were very rigid in their response because of the standard scripted answers given to employees in India and the difficulty in understanding Indian accents. As a result, Dell considered reversing its move to base its technical support in India.

- Unethical practices. Outsourcing may damage the multinational firm's ethical image. When multinational firms outsource, parts of their value chain are outside their physical boundaries and difficult to monitor. For example, Marks & Spencer (M&S) was accused in January 1996 by a British TV channel, Granada, in its *World in Action* programme, of deliberately misleading its customers through labelling its St Michael own-brand products with incorrect country-of-origin stickers. Moreover, it was alleged that M&S had used underage workers in the production process. M&S implemented a £1 million action plan by creating a 'hit squad' to audit its suppliers through randomly visiting foreign factories to ensure that they did not employ underage workers. The company also wrote to all its suppliers, reminding them of the strict code of conduct and service obligations of being a part of the M&S supply chain. Similarly, despite its rigorous code of ethics for its suppliers, Ikea has been repeatedly accused of using suppliers that use child labour in India.

## 8.6 Managing global portfolios

In the previous sections, we explained how and why multinational firms expand into different lines of businesses. In this section, we examine how the multinational firm manages its global business portfolio. This task is called global portfolio management. A global business portfolio refers to the set of businesses that make up the firm as well as the different activities carried out by the multinational firm in different locations. Global portfolio management is about how the multinational firm selects (and deselects) which business activities, and in which locations, to invest in to ensure a balance between future growth and current profitability. Multinationals have to manage their global business portfolio because they have limited resources and should not squander scarce resources by investing in unattractive countries. They need to identify truly deserving locations to invest in. Often, multinationals consider today's locations that are likely to become tomorrow's critical locations. For example, a number of multinational firms entered the Chinese market in the 1980s, not because China was an attractive market at the time, but because they expected the Chinese market to grow significantly in the future.

In addition to selecting which countries to move into, multinational firms need to reallocate their resources by exiting unattractive locations. For example, Marks & Spencer, a leading British retailer, exited from a number of Western markets during the early 2000s in order to enter leading emerging markets such as India. In brief, portfolio management aids multinational firms in assessing priorities and in making resource allocation decisions.

Several portfolio models have been proposed over the years to help firms manage their portfolios. However, most of these models were developed for firms operating in a single country, and are not therefore fully adequate to capture the complexity of diversified multinational firms. The Boston Consulting Group Matrix, commonly known as the BCG, is one of the most popular business portfolio management tools. It was developed by the Boston Consulting Group in the 1970s to help highly diversified corporations allocate resources in a systematic way. The core assumption of the BCG is that, for a firm to survive, it must have a balanced portfolio that contains both high growth business lines in need of resources and low growth business generating enough resources for the high growth business. According to BCG, managers should use resources generated by mature and/or low growth business to help the firm gain a market share in fast-growing industries. The BCG helps managers decide which business to fund, which businesses to grow, and which business to exit.

The BCG is more suited to single-country businesses. Diversified multinational firms cover multiple international markets, with multiple related or unrelated product lines. Few writers, however, have attempted to adapt well-known portfolio management tools such as BCG to incorporate the multidimensional nature of diversified multinational firms. For example, the directional policy matrix—which was developed to assist managers to consider a portfolio of businesses in terms of the attractiveness of the industry within which the firm operates and the strength of the business units—was adapted by Harrell and Kiefer (1993) to develop a global market portfolio matrix as a way of considering a portfolio of businesses in different countries in terms of the country attractiveness and the company's compatibility with each country (see Exhibit 8.9). The global market portfolio matrix positions subsidiaries in each country according to country attractiveness and competitive strength.

## Country attractiveness

How attractive is the relevant country in which the firm operates? Factors that are usually used in measuring country attractiveness include the country's market size—measured according to projected average annual sales in units—growth rate of its market, strength and number of competitors, workforce availability, legal business environment, economic indicators, and political risk and stability.

Estimating the true potential of a country market poses serious challenges for managers of multinationals. This is more so in emerging and developing countries, where reliable data is not always available. This may force multinational firms to carry out their own market research to gain an insight into the attractiveness of such markets. Generally, managers start with evaluating market potential of different markets by looking at aggregate country data such as per capita gross domestic product (GDP), the GDP growth rate, and gross national

**Exhibit 8.9** A Global Market Portfolio Matrix

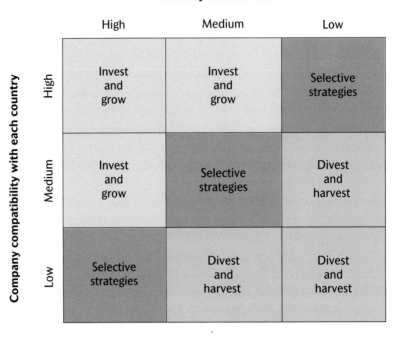

**Country attractiveness**

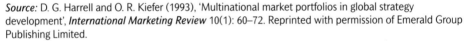

*Source:* D. G. Harrell and O. R. Kiefer (1993), 'Multinational market portfolios in global strategy development', *International Marketing Review* 10(1): 60–72. Reprinted with permission of Emerald Group Publishing Limited.

income (GNI), as well as other market potential indicators such as size of population, income distribution, education system, commercial infrastructure, size of the middle class, degree of political risk, and economic freedom index.

After indentifying the factors that are used as an objective basis for prioritizing the different markets, multinational firms weigh each factor according to its relative importance to their business activity (Harrell and Kiefer 1993). For instance, a multinational firm in extraction industries would put more emphasis on political risk and infrastructure than size of the population and income distribution. On the other hand, a mobile phone firm would put more emphasis on gross national income and size of the population than degree of political risk. Below, we provide an example used by Ford, the car manufacturer, in the mid 1980s to calculate the relative attractiveness of different countries (Harrell and Kiefer 1993). Ford used eight factors to calculate countries' attractiveness:

- Market size. The country population, especially those who are able to afford to buy a car.

- Market growth. The country's GDP growth rate.

- Price control/regulations. The degree to which government intervenes in setting prices and in business activities of businesses.

- Homologation requirements. The set of rules and standards such as safety and environmental impact that the firm has to meet to be able operate in the country.

- Local content and compensatory export requirements. The proportion of locally made inputs and parts in the final production of the vehicle, and required level of export of vehicles and/or parts to earn foreign exchange to pay for a percentage of imported components used in the making of vehicles.

- Inflation. The predicted rise in the level of prices of goods and services in a country over a period of time.

- Trade balance. The difference between the value of exports and imports of the country.

- Political factors. Political factors—such as political risk and fiscal system—that have an influence on the running of businesses in the country.

By incorporating the above eight factors, Ford proposed the following formula for calculating relative country attractiveness:

> Country attractiveness = market size + 2 * market growth + 0.5 * price control/regulation + 0.25 * homologation requirements + 0.25 * local content and compensatory export requirements + 0.35 * inflation + 0.35 * trade balance + 0.3 * political factors.

The weights—represented in the numbers before the factors—represent the relative importance of each variable to Ford's strategic planning efforts. The equation uses market size as a benchmark (weighted as 1), and weights market growth as twice the weight of market size. That is, the importance of market growth for Ford is double that of market size. The weight of price-control regulation is half (0.5) the weight of market size, and compensatory export requirements is one-quarter (0.25) the weight of market size, and so on.

## Competitive strength

How compatible is the company's strength with each country? The firm's competitive strength is measured, among other factors, by relative market share, product fit, contribution margin, and market support.

**Relative market share**  Typically, relative market share of a multinational firm refers to the ratio of the multinational's market share relative to its next biggest competitors in a particular market. It is obtained by dividing the multinational's share of the market in a particular country by that of its largest competitor. For example, if multinational firm A in India has 40% of the market and its next competitor has 20% of the market, the relative market share of firm A is 50%.

**Product fit**  Product fit represents an estimate of how closely the product fits a particular market need. In the tractor industry, for example, 'Ford defines this broadly in terms of horsepower classes and more specifically in terms of unique product features which may or may not match country needs' (Harrell and Kiefer 1993).

**Contribution margin**  This is a measure of profit per unit and profit as a percentage of net dealer cost. Low contribution margins often reflect limited price scope because of competition or government controls. Harrell and Kiefer argue that (1993), while this measure should be reflected in the other three elements, it does serve as a measure of ability to gain profit, an important competitive strength.

**Market support** This includes availability of a high-quality workforce, and the firm's ability to attract the required number of employees to carry out parts service and technical support, and advertising and sales promotion capability within the country to acquire and enhance the company image there.

Ford used the above four factors to compute a single linear scale, reflecting a firm's competitive strength as follows (Harrell and Kiefer 1993):

$$\text{Competitive strength} = 0.5 * \text{absolute market share} + 0.5 * \text{industry position} + 2 * \text{product fit} + 0.5 * \text{profit per unit} + 0.5 * \text{profit percentage of net dealer cost} + \text{market support.}$$

As with the country attractiveness, the weights reflect managers' subjective estimates of the relative importance of each variable in defining the competitive strength required to excel in international markets.

Based on the above two equations, each country is positioned within the $3 \times 3$ global market portfolio according to the above indicators of attractiveness and strength. The matrix thus helps managers consider appropriate corporate-level strategy, as shown in Exhibit 8.9. It suggests that the firm should invest and grow in markets with the highest attractiveness and the highest strength.

Markets in the invest/grow position require further commitment and resources by the corporate level to enable them to strengthen their presence and grow. This can involve such tactics as expanding existing plants, opening new plants, or both.

In contrast, the firm should harvest and divest from markets with the lowest attractiveness and the weakest strength. This can involve such tactics as closing or downsizing existing plants and selling off assets.

## 8.7 Summary

Corporate-level managers have four key roles. First, the corporate parent must determine the overall strategic direction and structure of the firm as a whole, and develop mechanisms to manage and coordinate the different activities of subsidiaries. In particular, it needs to balance the level of control and autonomy by finding out the desirable degree of control, where the benefits of control more than offset the costs of controlling the subsidiaries.

Second, a fundamental task of the headquarters is to manage the multinational's growth strategy. Should the multinational operate in a single business, diversify into related businesses, diversify into unrelated businesses, diversify into geographically related countries, or diversify into geographically unrelated countries? When the multinational firm follows a diversified strategy, corporate managers at headquarters must be able to identify and create synergies among multiple subsidiaries or businesses. The parent must have sufficient skills and resources to implement strategies which take advantage of potential synergies. It should also play an active role, when required, in promoting, guiding, coordinating, and arbitrating between subsidiaries (Goold and Campbell 2002).

Third, effective strategic management at the corporate level of the multinational firm requires a clear understanding, both of the potential for strengthening the competitive position of the multinational through outsourcing, and of the threats posed by outsourcing. Understanding the advantages and disadvantages of outsourcing helps corporate managers to decide whether or not to outsource, and to determine the optimal extent of outsourcing by the multinational firm.

Fourth, the corporate parent must continuously review the performance of the existing mix of businesses and countries in which the multinational operates and explore opportunities for growth.

## 📖 Key readings

- Çavusgil, Knight, and Riesenberger (2007); and Kotabe (1992) are comprehensive books on global sourcing strategy.

- Goold et al. (1998) provides a comprehensive discussion of the challenges of adding value at the corporate level.

- For an excellent review of the relationship between global diversification and firm value, see Denis et al. (2002).

## 💬 Discussion questions

**1.** Select a multinational firm and discuss the advantages and disadvantages of pursuing (or not, as the case may be) a vertically integrated strategy.

**2.** Multinational firms must outsource non-core activities to remain competitive. Discuss this statement, illustrating your answer with examples.

**3.** Critically examine the argument that firms in emerging economies should pursue a diversification strategy.

**4.** Refer to the closing case study and discuss the advantages and disadvantages of Lufthansa's diversification strategy.

**5.** Choose a multinational firm and develop a Global Business Portfolio Matrix.

## Closing case study  Lufthansa's diversification strategy

Deutsche Lufthansa AG is made of a number of separate business groups. Deutsche Lufthansa AG is both a parent company and the largest single operating business in the group. The core values of the group are: quality, reliability, innovation, trust, and proximity to the customer. Each business group is monitored by its own supervisory board.

In the mid and late 1990s, Lufthansa followed a diversification strategy into related and unrelated businesses. The diversification strategy, designed and implemented by its corporate headquarters in Cologne, was hailed as a success and emulated by a number of competitors. The business model was simple: generate higher return by catering for various customers across the value chain. It was also hoped that diversification would make the company less exposed to economic cycles. However, the massive losses accumulated by its non-core businesses in the early and mid 2000s, threw its diversification strategy into sharp relief.

Over the years, the German carrier, Europe's third-largest player behind Air France and British Airways, diversified into a number of unrelated businesses, including Information Technology (IT) services through Lufthansa Systems, Maintenance, Repair and Overhaul (MRO) services through Lufthansa Technik Group, Logistics Services through Lufthansa Cargo, tour operations through Thomas Cook, and Passenger Transportation Services through its well-known LSG SKY Chefs. In the late 1990s and first couple of years of the 2000s, the group provided MRO services for around 600 customers worldwide, and generated, on average, around 10% of its total revenue from its MRO services. It also provided IT services to around 180 regular—aviation and related industries—customers through its IT systems. Furthermore, through its LSG SKY Chef group, it provided services to over 250 regular customers, mainly from Europe, the Middle East, and Africa, and about a third from America.

But things started going pear-shaped for the company in 2002. In March 2003, the airline posted a loss of US$1.22 billion, including an US$850 million write-off covering LSG Sky Chefs. Expectedly, following the September 11 attacks in the US, revenues of LSG Sky Chefs and from the US declined dramatically. Also, several of the Thomas Cook services were substituted by online services which enabled travellers to make their own travel arrangements online. Plagued by the sharp decline in profit, the airline was not able to support Thomas Cook and decided to sell it in 2006. On 22 December 2006, Karstadt bought half of Lufthansa shares in Thomas Cook for €800 million and took control of Thomas Cook.

The decline of revenue from non-core businesses prompted the company to sell off some of its unrelated businesses. Although the Lufthansa group still owns a number of related and unrelated business, the new core business in the group is passenger transportation. This business segment includes Lufthansa Passenger Airlines, SWISS, and Germanwings. The passenger transportation segment also includes equity investment in the following major airlines: British Midland (bmi), JetBlue, and SunExpress. The remaining non-core business—MRO, IT Service, and Catering—are also performing well. Lufthansa Technik is now a global house name in the maintenance, repair, and overhaul of civil aircraft. Its IT Service is one of the world's leaders for providing IT solutions for airlines. Similarly, LSG SKY Chef has bounced back and is now a global market leader in airline catering.

*Source:* Lufthansa website at http://www.lufthansa.com; J. Flottau (2004), 'German plunge: Lufthansa's 2003 results are writ in glaring red ink; non-core businesses, deteriorating markets fingered', *Aviation Week and Space Technology* 160(9) (1 March): 37.

**Discussion questions**

1. Was it wise for Lufthansa to enter into new businesses in the mid to late 1990s?
2. Should Lufthansa keep its non-core businesses?

 # References

Ambos, B., and Schlegelmilch, B. B. (2007). 'Innovation and control in the multinational firm: a comparison of political and contingency approaches', *Strategic Management Journal* 28(5): 473–86.

Amihud, Y., and Lev, V. (1981). 'Risk reduction as a managerial motive for conglomerate mergers', *Bell Journal of Economics* 12: 605–17.

Amit, R., and Livnat, J. (1988). 'Diversification and the risk–return trade-off', *Academy of Management Journal* 31: 154–66.

Andersson, U., Forsgren, M., and Holm, U. (2007). 'Balancing subsidiary influence in the federative MNC: a business network view', *Journal of International Business Studies* 38(5): 802–18.

Arsenault, Amelia H., and Castells, M. (2008). 'The structure and dynamics of global multimedia business networks', *International Journal of Communication* 2: 707–48.

Baliga, B. R., and Jaeger, A. M. (1984). 'Multinational corporations: control systems and delegation issues', *Journal of International Business Studies* 15: 25–40.

Bartlett, C. H., and Ghoshal, S. (1990). 'Managing innovation in the transnational corporation', in C. H. Bartlett, Y. Doz, and G. Hedlund (eds), *Managing the Global Firm* (London, NewYork): 215–55.

Berger, G. P., and Ofek, E. (1995). 'Diversification's effect on firm value', *Journal of Financial Economics* 37: 39–65.

Buckley, P. J., and Casson, M. C. (1976). *The Future of the Multinational Enterprise* (London: Holmes & Meier).

*BusinessWeek* (1986). 'The hollow corporation', (3 March): 53–5.

*BusinessWeek* (2009).'World's outsourcing market worth US$373 billion', available at http://bx.businessweek.com/vietnam-business/worlds-outsourcing-market-worth-373-billion/2441453481264597847-82664d2a16 31b3c3da2e3f5bfdb0a874/ (25 September).

Campbell, A., Goold, M., and Alexander, M. (1995). 'Corporate strategy: the quest for parenting advantage', *Harvard Business Review* 73(2): 120–32.

Çavusgil, T., Knight, G., and Riesenberger, J. (2007), *International Business: Strategy, Management, and the New Realities* (Upper Saddle River, NJ: Prentice-Hall).

Chang, Y. Y., Mellahi, K., and Wilkinson, A. (2009). 'Control of subsidiaries of MNCs from emerging economies in developed countries: the case of Taiwanese MNCs in the UK', *International Journal of Human Resource Management* 20(1): 75–95.

Child, J. (1984). *Organization*, 2nd edn (London: Harper & Row).

Christensen, M. C. (2001). 'The past and future of competitive advantage', *MIT Sloan Management Review* 42(2): 105–9.

Cohen, W. M., and Levinthal, A. D. (1990). 'Absorptive capacity: a new perspective on learning and innovation', *Administrative Science Quarterly* 35: 128–52.

Collings, G. D., Morley, M. J., and Gunnigle, P. (2008). 'Composing the top management team in the international subsidiary: qualitative evidence on international staffing in US MNCs in the Republic of Ireland', *Journal of World Business* 43(2): 197–212.

Datta, D. K., Rajagopalan, N., and Rasheed, A. M. A. (1991). 'Diversification and performance: critical review and future directions', *Journal of Management Studies* 28: 529–58.

Davis, P. S., Robinson, R. B., Pearce, J. A., and Park, S. H. (1992). 'Business unit relatedness and performance: a look at the pulp and paper industry', *Strategic Management Journal* 13: 349–62.

Delios, A., Xu, D., and Beamish, P. W. (2008). 'Within-country product diversification and foreign subsidiary performance', *Journal of International Business Studies* 39(4): 706–24.

Denis, D. J., Denis, D. K., and Sarin, A. (1997). 'Ownership structure and top executive turnover', *Journal of Financial Economics* 45(2): 193–221.

Denis, D. J., Denis, D. K., and Yost, K. (2002). 'Global diversification, industrial diversification, and firm value', *Journal of Finance* 57(5): 1951–79.

Doz, Y., and Prahalad, K. (1991). 'Managing DMNCs: a search for a new paradigm,' *Strategic Management Journal* 12, 145–64.

Doz, Y., and Prahalad, P. K. (1986). 'Controlled variety: a challenge for Human Resource management in the MNC', *Human Resource Management* 25(1): 55–71.

Dun and Bradstreet (2000). 'Dun and Bradstreet sees 25 per cent growth for global outsourcing', http://www.businesswire.com (23 February): 3–4.

*Economist, The* (2001). 'New Formula Coke' (3 February).

Epstein, M. J., and Roy, M.-J. (2007). 'Implementing a corporate environmental strategy: establishing coordination and control within multinational companies', *Business Strategy and the Environment* 16: 389–403.

Ferner, A. (2000). 'The underpinnings of "bureaucratic" control systems: HRM in European multinationals', *Journal of Management Studies* 37(4): 521–39.

Ghoshal, S., and Bartlett, A. C. (1988). 'Creation, adoption, and diffusion of innovation by subsidiaries of multinational corporations', *Journal of International Business Studies* 19: 365–88.

Ghoshal, S., and Bartlett, C. (1990). 'The multinational corporation as an interorganizational network', *Academy of Management Review* 15(4): 603–25.

Ghoshal, S., Korine, H., and Szulanski, G. (1994). 'Interunit communication in multinational corporations', *Management Science* 40(1): 96–110.

Gilley, K., and Rasheed, A. (2000). 'Making more by doing less: an analysis of outsourcing and its effects on firm performance', *Journal of Management* 26(4): 763–90.

Gong, Y. (2003). 'Subsidiary staffing in multinational enterprises: agency, resources and performance', *Academy of Management Journal* 45: 728–39.

Goold, M., and Campbell, A. (2000). 'Taking stock of synergy', *Long Range Planning* 33: 72–96.

Goold, M., and Campbell, A. (2002). 'Parenting in complex structures', *Long Range Planning* 35(3): 219–43.

Goold, M., Campbell, A., and Alexander, M. (1998). 'Corporate strategy and parenting theory', *Long Range Planning* 31(2): 308–14.

Gupta, A. K., and Govindarajan, V. (1986). 'Resource sharing among SBUs: strategic antecedents and administrative implications', *Academy of Management Journal* 29: 695–714.

Gupta, A. K., and Govindarajan, V. (1991). 'Knowledge flows and the structure of control within multinational corporations', *Academy of Management Review* 16(4): 768–92.

Harrell, D. G., and Kiefer, O. R. (1993). 'Multinational market portfolios in global strategy development', *International Marketing Review* 10(1): 60–72.

Harzing, A. W. K. (1999). *Managing the Multinationals: An International Study of Control Mechanisms* (Cheltenham: Edward Elgar).

Harzing, A. W. K. (2001). 'Of bears, bumble-bees, and spiders: the role of expatriates in controlling foreign subsidiaries' *Journal of World Business* 36(4): 366–79.

Hitt, A. M., Hoskisson, E. R., and Kim, H. (1997). 'International diversification: effects on innovation and firm performance in product-diversified firms', *Academy of Management Journal* 40: 767–98.

Jaeger, A. M., and Baliga, B. R. (1985). 'Control systems and strategic adaptation: lessons from the Japanese experience', *Strategic Management Journal* 6(2): 115–34.

Jensen, C. M. (1986). 'The agency costs of free cash flow: corporate finance and takeovers', *American Economic Review* 76(2): 223–9.

Jensen, C. M., and Murphy, J. S. (1990). 'Performance pay and top management incentives', *Journal of Political Economy* 98(2): 225–64.

Khanna, T., and Palepu, K. (1997). 'Why focused strategies may be wrong for emerging markets', *Harvard Business Review* 75(4): 41–51.

Kim, W. C., Hwang, P., and Burgers, P. W. (1989). 'Global diversification strategy and corporate profit performance', *Strategic Management Journal* 10: 45–57.

Kotabe, M. (1992). *Global Sourcing Strategy* (New York: Qurom Books).

Kotabe, M. (1998). 'Efficiency vs. effectiveness orientation of global sourcing strategy: a comparison of U.S. and Japanese multinational companies', *Academy of Management Executive* 12(4): 107–19.

Kotabe, M., and Murray, Y. J. (2004). 'Global sourcing strategy and sustainable competitive advantage', *Industrial Marketing Management* 33(1): 7–14.

Lins, V. K., and Servaes, H. (2002). 'Is corporate diversification beneficial in emerging economies?' *Financial Management* 31(2): 5–32.

Oijen, A. van, and Douma, S. W. (2000). 'Diversification strategy and the roles of the centre', *Long Range Planning* 33: 560–78.

Osegowitsch, T., and Madhok, A. (2003). 'Vertical integration is dead, or is it?' *Business Horizon* 46(2): 24–35.

Ouchi, W. (1977), 'The relationship between organizational structure and organizational control', *Administrative Science Quarterly* 22: 95–113.

Ouchi, W. (1979). 'A Conceptual Framework for the Design of Organizational Control Mechanisms', *Management Science* 25(9): 833–48.

Ouchi, W. (1980). 'Markets, bureaucracies and clans', *Administrative Science Quarterly* 25(March): 86–107.

Ouchi, W., and Maguire, M. A. (1975). 'Organizational control: two functions', *Administrative Science Quarterly* 20: 559–69.

Paik, Y., and Sohn, D. J. (2004) 'Expatriate managers and MNC's ability to control international subsidiaries: the case of Japanese MNCs', *Journal of World Business* 39(1): 61–71.

Simon, H. A. (1979) 'Rational decision making in business organizations', *American Economic Review* 69: 493–513.

Szulanski, G. (1996). 'Exploring internal stickiness: impediments to the transfer of best practice within the firm', *Strategic Management Journal* 17: 27–44.

Tallman, S., and Li, J. (1996). 'Effects of international diversity and product diversity on the performance of multinational firms', *Academy of Management Journal* 39: 179–96.

Thompson, A. A., Jr., and Strickland, J. A. (2003). *Strategic Management: Concepts and Cases*, 13th edn (New York: McGraw-Hill).

Vachani, S. (1991). 'Distinguishing between related and unrelated international geographic diversification: a comprehensive measure of global diversification', *Journal of International Business Studies* 22(Second Quarter): 307–22.

Zander, U., and Kogut, B. (1995). 'Knowledge and the speed of the transfer and imitation of organizational capabilities', *Organization Science* 6(1): 76–92.

# Online resource centre

**online resource centre**

Please visit www.oxfordtextbooks.co.uk/orc/frynas_mellahi2e/ for further information.

# Global structures and designs

**9**

## Learning outcomes

After reading this chapter, you should be able to:

➤ Explain the contingency factors that determine the structure of multinational firms.

➤ List and explain the different ways in which a multinational firm can be structured.

➤ Explain the strengths and weaknesses of each structure in the light of the strategy being adopted.

➤ List and discuss the different forms multinational firms adopt to balance the need for global integration with the pressure for local responsiveness.

➤ Choose a structure that supports the different forms of multinational firms.

## Opening case study  Procter & Gamble (P&G)

When William Procter, a candle maker, and James Gamble, a soap maker, got together in 1837 to start Procter & Gamble (P&G), they did not need a sophisticated structure to run their newly formed business. Their small company produced a very narrow range of soaps and candles for local customers. P&G's structure was simple: the two entrepreneurs, with few supervisors, and several hired workers coordinated their activities without the need for a formal structure. The two entrepreneurs ordered material, supervised production, hired staff, and dealt with all marketing and financial issues.

Soon after its inception, P&G enjoyed enormous success and its size grew significantly. By 1859, P&G had around eighty employees and its sales grew to over US$1 million. To cope with its larger size and high sales volume, P&G needed a more elaborate structure. It established small specialized departments to handle marketing, distribution, operations, finance, and personnel functions.

When P&G won the contract to supply the Union Army with soap and candles during the American Civil War, its size grew much larger and had to reach larger geographical areas. Consequently, P&G, of course, needed more managers to staff the various functional departments. As a result, the simple initial structure evolved into a functional structure, where production and sales departments performed primary activities, and remaining functions such as personnel and finance provided essential information to the top management team to help them run the company.

The company continued to grow in size, and, in the early 1880s, P&G began introducing new products to the market, starting with the famous Ivory soap—an inexpensive soap that floats in water, followed in the early 1900s by the introduction of cooking products such as Crisco, a vegetable-based oil shortening. Very quickly, P&G shortening products became very popular in the US and, as a result, the company started producing them on a mass scale. By the early 1900s, the simple candle and soap manufacturer evolved from a small Cincinnati-based organization into a sophisticated multi-product organization covering a wide geographical area.

By the 1930s, P&G outgrew its US market and expanded internationally, starting in 1930 with an acquisition of a production plant in Newcastle upon Tyne in England. At the same time, P&G continued its product diversification strategy, launching a range of commercially successful products such as the laundry detergent, Tide, in 1946, Perl shampoo in 1947, Crest toothpaste in 1955, and Charmin toilet paper in 1957. As a result of its international growth, P&G established its first international sales department to deal with the large volume of sales in foreign markets. Furthermore, in order to better manage the expanding portfolio of products, in 1954, P&G replaced the functional division with a product division structure.

In the 1960s and 1970s, the company branched out into baby products, such as Pampers—the first disposable diapers—and Downy and Bounce—one of the first fabric softeners. This period also witnessed a number of acquisitions, to give P&G a strong foothold in a number of consumer industries, ranging from perfume to pharmaceuticals. To cope with the challenges of producing multiple products and distributing a wide range of products in multiple markets, P&G had to introduce specialized departments, focusing on specific product lines in different geographical regions.

Within this structure, different products were looked after by different brand managers and their activities were coordinated with managers handling different geographical regions. This geographical-based structure brought together product and geographic areas experts together to share knowledge across different products and capture the benefits of economies of scale, while attempting to make products responsive to different geographical markets. However, P&G remained highly centralized and all strategic decisions were made at the Cincinnati Head Office. Only operational decisions were made by brand and geographical managers. While the structure worked well in the 1970s, the high centralization of strategic decision-making in the hands of the few top managers in Cincinnati hindered the company's ability to respond quickly and effectively to customers' needs in different geographical areas. Although geographical managers were responsible for responding to changes in their global markets, they did not have the formal authority to make such decisions. They had to wait for such decisions to come from the headquarter. By the early 1980s, P&G realized that its centralized geographical structure did not fit its strategy of being innovative and responsive to changes in its market.

To address the shortcoming of its centralized structure, P&G provided more autonomy to its international divisions and developed processes to enhance communications across its subsidiaries located in different countries. This was followed by the development of P&G's Purpose, Values and Principles (PVP) initiative in the mid 1980s, which guided the managers' decision-making process and set out P&G's managers and employees' personal responsibility and expectations. In brief, P&G moved from bureaucratic control to cultural control through the PVP. Guided by the PVP, country managers were granted more authority. It also reduced the number of management layers to speed up the decision-making process. *The Economist*, describing P&G's European structure, noted at the time that:

> Each local manager wears two hats—one for his product, one for his region. The French manager now reports both to his country manager and to a category manager who looks after a basket of related brands. This category manager is a mini-profit centre, reporting to one of P&G's central division managers. So, fewer layers separate the top of the (management) pyramid from the market.

The new decentralized structure helped P&G overcome some of the shortcomings of the old structure by enabling managers to make relatively quicker decisions and respond better to customers' needs in different markets. By 1989, P&G doubled its revenue to US$12.4 billion and increased its revenue from outside the US to 40%.

Since the 1990s, P&G has become a global household name. As the pace of change in the business environment accelerated and competition intensified, P&G needed to respond even quicker and more effectively to changes in the marketplace. Its matrix structure was not able to cope with the complexity of its operations and the speed of change in the global business environment. As a result, the value of its shares dropped significantly in the mid 1990s.

In 1997, P&G's top management came up with the 'Organization–2005' (O–2005) initiative. The O–2005 initiative brought sixteen managers together to identify the kind of organization P&G needed to be in order to succeed in the future. After extensive research, the working group suggested that the matrix structure should be dismantled and be replaced with four interdependent entities. The four entities represented the pillars of the new P&G. They are: Global Business Units (GBU), Market Development Organizations (MDO), Global Business Services (GBS), and Corporate Functions (CF).

This streamlined structure allows P&G to get to market faster by coordinating the activities of the four pillars. GBUs build major global brands with robust business strategies, while MDOs build local understanding as a foundation for marketing campaigns. The two entities are supported by GBSs, which provide business technology and services that drive business success, and CFs, which work to maintain P&G's place as a leader of its industries. Differently put, GBUs are in charge of product development and brand management; MDOs are responsible for taking products to their regional markets; GBSs provide back office services; while CFs focus on developing and leveraging capabilities and governance. A number of processes that were codified in previous structures were left open to the discretion of GBU and MDO presidents. Also, hierarchical layers were reduced from thirteen to seven, providing managers with more authority to make important decisions.

P&G's four-pillar structure is underpinned by the company's strong belief in the need to 'Think Globally' through GBUs and 'Act Locally' through MDOs, while being guided by P&G's commitment to operate efficiently through GBSs, and constantly strive to be the best at what it does through CFs. In 2010, P&G had five GBUs: baby and family care, beauty and feminine care, fabric and home care, snacks and beverages, and health care. They managed over 300 brands around the globe. Guided by the philosophy of 'Think Globally,' GBUs' main roles are to create strong brand equities through product development, and brand design, and new business development through innovation in products, and marketing to build major global brands. By moving from the previous geographical regions structure to few GBUs based on global product lines and by putting the responsibility for strategy and profit on brands rather than on geographical regions, P&G hoped to speed up the decision-making process and achieve greater innovation. Each GBU operates autonomously from other GBUs and is led by a president who reports directly to the CEO and is a member of the global leadership council that overseas P&G's overall strategy.

In 2010, P&G had seven MDOs: North America, Asia/India/Australia, Northeast Asia, Greater China, Central-Eastern Europe/Middle East/Africa, Western Europe, and Latin America. Guided by the philosophy of 'Act Locally,' the MDO's role is to tailor products to local markets, while seeking synergy across programmes to leverage corporate scale. MDOs do not have profit responsibility but are measured by and compensated for sales growth. Like GBU, each MDO is led by a president that reports to the CEO and is a member of the global leadership council.

The third pillar of the P&G structure is its three GBS centres located in Costa Rica (GBS Americas), Manila in the Philippines (GBS Asia), and Newcastle in England (GBS Europe, Middle East and Africa). The main role of GBSs is to standardize and streamline the operations processes. These include providing services and solutions such as IT solutions 'that enable the company to operate efficiently around the world, collaborate effectively with business partners, and help employees become more productive'. The standardization of routine processes enables MDOs and GBUs to focus on their core competencies. The head of each GBS reports to the CEO but is not a member of the global leadership council.

The last leg of the new structure is made up of the ten CFs, covering key functional areas such as marketing, human resources, finance, and operations, guided by the philosophy of 'Be the Smartest and the Best.' CFs aim to 'ensure that the functional capability integrated into the rest of the company remains on the cutting edge of the industry'. P&G aims to be 'thought leader within each CF'.

To illustrate how the four pillars work together, let us take the case of the roll-out of Pantene, one of P&G's international, billion-dollar brands in the US and Latin Americas. The Pantene team had to define the equity and what Pantene's brand stands for. The slogan, 'Pantene gives you healthy, shiny hair,' came out of this process. The Pantene Team within the Beauty Care GBU built the product equity through three basic guidelines: '(1) Product initiatives or upgrades, ideally launched simultaneously worldwide; (2) A marketing campaign communicating the same fundamental benefits worldwide; and (3) Manufacturing product in accordance with global formula and package specifications.'

Different MDOs would ensure that Pantene excels in their region by making adjustments to fit the product to their local market. While the brand equity is the same across the regions, MDOs may implement them differently. For instance, the size of the packaging could be different across the regions. Because US customers prefer, and are able to afford, large-size volumes of Pantene, the MDO in North America had to work with partners to provide large-size packaging. In some of the Latin Americas countries, however, consumers may prefer small-sized packaging, and a large proportion of them are not able to afford to buy large-size bottles, therefore, the Latin American MDO needed to arrange with partners to package the products in small volumes and single-use sachets.

The GBS in the Americas, located in Costa Rica, provides support for both US and Latin America MBOs. These services range from, dealing with financial issues such as accounting, to production operations and distribution processes. The CF provides consulting and advice when and where needed, making sure that best practices are used and that P&G's values and core principles are adhered to.

So far, the new structure has worked well. It has provided P&G with the ability to coordinate its global activities, respond to changes in the business environment quickly and effectively, save cost through the transfer of best practices, enhance the capacity for innovation through the combination and cross-pollination of ideas between different MDOs, and maximize inter-organizational learning and knowledge sharing between the different parts of the organization.

*Source:* Procter & Gamble website at http://www.pg.com; L. Huston and N. Sakkab (2006), 'Connect and develop: inside Procter & Gamble's new model for innovation', *Harvard Business Review* 84(3): 58–66; *The Economist* (1989), 'Perestroika in Soapland', 311(7606): 75–7. *Wikipedia* (2010), 'Procter & Gamble', retrieved January from http://en.wikipedia.org/wiki/Procter_&_Gamble.

## 9.1 **Introduction**

As the P&G case study suggests, the sustainability of success of any organization depends to a large extent on the appropriateness of its structure and design to meet the overall goals of the organization. The P&G example demonstrates that sustained high performance of a multinational firm requires two conditions to be fulfilled. First, the structure of the organization must be aligned with the overall strategy of the multinational firm (Xu et al. 2006). A study by Gokpinar et al. (2010) revealed that a misalignment between the structure of the organization and its product architecture has a negative impact on quality. In the same vein, a study by Willem and Buelens (2009) showed that an aligned organizational structure enhanced knowledge sharing within the organization. Therefore, structures are expected to evolve with the multinational firm's strategy (Day 1999; Xu et al. 2006). The opening and closing case studies show that P&G and Sony had to change their structures several times to meet the demands of ever-changing business environments. Over the years, P&G moved from a simple structure to a sophisticated global matrix-like structure, to have the kind of structure that helps it execute its strategy and handle challenges brought on by its growing size and significant changes in its operating environment.

Second, the structure must fit the prevailing conditions in the multinational firm's markets. For example, in the mid 1990s, P&G came to the realization that its centralized geographical structure needed to change and so it adopted a more sophisticated structure. The new structure enabled P&G to achieve effectiveness by accomplishing its organizational goals, efficiency by producing the maximum obtainable output with the available resources available to it, and innovativeness by enabling it to respond and adapt effectively to changes in its business environment.

This chapter explores the issues highlighted by the P&G case study. The chapter starts with a discussion of the concept of organizational structure and design in domestic and international firms. Next, the chapter turns to structures of domestic firms, before providing a detailed discussion of the various structures of multinational firms. The chapter concludes with a summary of the key issues explored in the chapter.

## 9.2 Organizational structures: what are they?

An organizational structure can be seen as the blueprint depicting the formal reporting relationships within the firm explaining who does what, where, and when. It explains the manner in which the firm organizes its resources and capabilities into specific tasks and achieves coordination among these tasks. As illustrated in the opening case study, the latest structure of P&G sets the duties and responsibilities of each entity and reporting line within the organization. For example, the heads of each GBU and MDO report directly to the CEO and are members of the global leadership council. However, while heads of GBSs report directly to the CEO, they are not members of the global leadership council.

Organizational structures are often represented in diagrams in a form of organizational charts. These are like maps of towns or countries, giving a diagrammatic representation of the reporting relationship within the firm. Such diagrams and charts must be simple—typically emphasizing, generalizing, and omitting certain features. In other words, while an organizational structure, as depicted in an organizational diagram or chart, can be seen as a mirror of the organization's reporting relationships, the content of the structure diagram or chart is intentionally reduced and selectively distilled to focus on one or two particular items, such as formal reporting relationships and responsibility over tasks. By looking at an organizational structure, one could identify the way people and jobs in an organization are arranged so that the work of the organization can be performed, identify internal reporting systems and lines of communication, learn about managerial hierarchy, the level of centralization of power and formalization of roles in an organization, and composition of decision-making processes within a firm.

Choosing the wrong structure has adverse effects on performance. Day (1999: 33) noted that, 'the wrong strategy can doom . . . market-driven initiatives in the organization to failure'. This is because the structure of the organization is a powerful determinant of how people behave within the organization. Also, as illustrated in the opening case study, organizations outgrow their structures overtime, and structures that were appropriate at one point in time may become inappropriate at a latter stage.

Associated with structure is design—the way the major activities of an organization are carried out within the structure—which provides the skeleton for control and coordination. Design includes such matters as where decisions are made, the form of the information systems used, how people are rewarded for their contributions, and how knowledge is transferred within the organization. Together, structure and design have been termed the 'internal architecture' of an organization (Kay 1993: 14).

Management scholars have approached structures and designs of multinational firms from two different perspectives. The first perspective, led by Stopford and Wells (1972), focused on the structural fit between multinational firms' expansion strategies and their organizational structure. This literature dominated structures and designs of multinational firms from the 1960s to the late 1980s. This will form the first part of the chapter (sections 9.3 to 9.4). The second perspective, led by Bartlett and Ghoshal (1989), is generally known as the 'integration-responsiveness literature'. This perspective changed the focus from the issue of structural fit to the question of trade-offs between pressure for global integration and pressure for local responsiveness. This will be discussed in the last part of the chapter (section 9.5). Before we explain these two perspectives, let us look at structures and designs of domestic firms or firms operating in a single country.

## 9.3 Domestic organizational structures

To begin the discussion of structures and design, we will first present the structures common to domestic operations—the operations of a firm before it goes international. We start here because, with the exception of few Born Global firms (see section 5.4.2 in Chapter 5), a firm begins in one country—its home country—and thus in any subsequent international expansion, the domestic structure is the one that is built on and extended.

As the P&G example shows, in the very early stage, firms do not have formal structures whereby specific departments are allocated well-defined tasks. Rather, most likely, the founders with the help of a small team of individuals assume responsibility for the running of the business with no formal control mechanisms. This is because, initially, the size of the firm is small and its activities are simple so that no formal structure is required. As a firm grows in size, it becomes too big for a single entrepreneur or a small team of individuals to handle effectively. As the P&G case study suggests, firms at this stage may split their operations into separate functions. Whilst a business consists of many functions, when considering organizational structures it is convenient to consider a business as being composed of four 'super' functions: operations (including procurement), marketing (including distribution, sales, and after-sales), support services (functions such as personnel, finance, and IT), and

**Exhibit 9.1** Domestic structures

(a) Single business structured by function

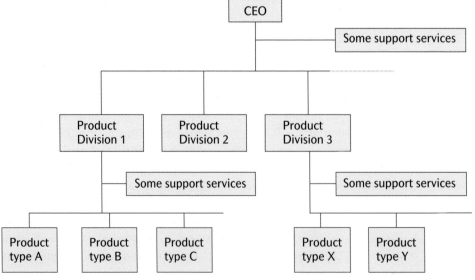

(b) Product group structure

research and development (R&D). The most common way in which a business is structured is by function, as shown in Exhibit 9.1.

The functional structure has many advantages. It makes communication easy among people from the same specialists. For example, marketing staff in the marketing department can easily communicate and share information with each other. This leads to quicker decision-making because people from the same perspective tend to approach problems in a similar way. This is not the case, for example, when marketing and finance staff interact with each other. Marketing staff may focus on customer satisfaction while finance staff may pay more attention to cost and financial returns. In addition to ease of communication, the functional structure makes it easier for people to learn from one another's experiences and improve their skills and abilities. Also, the functional structure makes it easier for supervisors and heads of functional divisions to evaluate staff performance in their divisions because they usually have higher levels of skills in the particular function.

The functional structure, however, does not cope well when the organization produces a wide range of products. As the opening case study illustrates, after P&G added new product lines to its soap and candle products, the various functions had difficulty in servicing efficiently the wide range of products and was compelled to change its structure to address this challenge. To illustrate this point, imagine how difficult it is for an operations department to learn about all the different processes and operations needed to produce a wide range of significantly different products. Also, the marketing department would find it hard to manage its customer base because different products and services attract different customers with different needs and different purchasing behaviour. Further, in a multi-product organization, it is difficult to identify the productivity of each product line using a functional structure.

Organizations with multiple products and services tend to switch to a product structure to overcome the shortcomings of the functional structure discussed above. In a product divisional structure, each division is responsible for one or a portfolio of products. A major consideration in organizational structure is how to group the businesses within a firm. As a general rule, groupings will depend on the degree of relatedness of the activities of the constituent units. Exhibit 9.1(b) illustrates product subdivision. The assumption is that the similarities of the activities in one product division are greater than between those of any other product division. Thus, for example, product types A, B, and C in product division 1 are more similar to each other than to products X and Y in product division 3.

There are a number of potential advantages to the product structure. The product structure provides the organization with the flexibility to exit products with little disturbance to the overall structure of the organization. This is because, in a product structure, each product division is a self-standing unit dealing with a product or a portfolio of products. It provides heads of divisions with a sense of ownership and responsibility for the products they are responsible for. This also makes them accountable for their business results. Also, the product division enables divisions to focus on competences relevant to their products.

The product division, however, has a number of potential limitations. Being a self-standing division reduces the need for cooperation with other divisions. This may lead to isolation between the divisions, causing fragmentation and non-cooperation between the different divisions. In addition to fragmentation and the risk of non-cooperation, the production structure is costly because of the duplication of the various management functions with each division.

## 9.4 Strategy and structure of multinational firms

During the early 1960s, Chandler (1962; 1966) mapped the growth of multi-product companies in the US. He saw the small, local firm move progressively to set up sales organizations in faraway cities; subsequently, production units would follow this expansion. This is similar to P&G's strategy during and soon after the American Civil War. Chandler also observed that after setting up sales departments in different parts of the country, firms tend to diversify into new products and services. Each move led to a different organizational form. For instance, P&G and other firms such as DuPont, General Electric, General Motors, and Matsushita, introduced multidivisional structures during the 1920s and 1930s to handle the growing size of the organization and the growing number of product lines. Chandler's research led him to enunciate the view that *structure follows strategy*, where structure can best be defined as the way in which an organization divides its labour into distinct tasks and then achieves coordination among them. In addition to the view that structure follows strategy, Chandler reached two further conclusions: (1) strategies and structures develop in certain sequential stages; and (2) organizations do not change their structures until provoked by inefficiencies.

Stopford and Wells (1972) applied Chandler's contingency framework to analysing the structures of multinational firms. Using data from 187 large US multinational firms, they suggested that foreign product diversity—measured by the number of products sold internationally—and the level of internationalization—measured by foreign sales as a percentage of total sales, i.e. the importance of international sales to the company—determine the structure of the multinational firm.

Stopford and Wells (1972) suggested that multinational firms have, and go through, four structures: international division, worldwide product division, area division, and matrix division (see Exhibit 9.2). At the early stage of foreign expansion, foreign sales represent a small proportion of total sales and product lines are limited. At this stage, multinational firms tend to support this small level of international expansion with an *international division structure*. Stopford and Wells observed that, after the first stage, some multinational firms expanded their sales abroad without significantly increasing foreign product diversity. These companies tended to adopt an *area division structure*. This structure gives area divisions a responsibility for products sold in their geographical region. While some multinational firms expanded their sales without significantly increasing their product diversity, other multinational firms increased foreign product diversity without expanding their percentage of foreign sales. These multinational firms supported their strategy with a *worldwide product division structure*. This structure gives domestic product divisions a global responsibility for the performance of their product lines worldwide. Finally, when multinational firms expanded both their foreign product

**Exhibit 9.2** The Stopford and Wells model of multinational structures

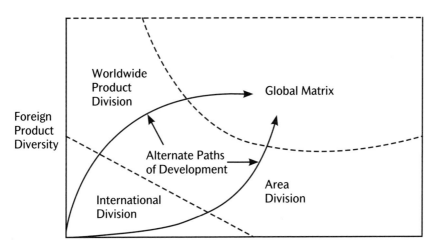

Foreign Sales as a Percentage of Total Sales

*Source:* J. M. Stopford and L. T. Wells, Jr. (1972), *Managing the Multinational Enterprise: Organization of the Firm and Ownership of the Subsidiaries* (New York: Basic Books). Reprinted with permission of Basic Books.

diversity and percentage of foreign sales, they tended to employ a *matrix structure*. A matrix structure is an overlap of the two structures discussed above—product division and area division structures.

---

**KEY CONCEPT**

A structure is the way in which an organization divides its labour into distinct tasks and then achieves coordination among them. There are five basic types of structures for multinational firms: a functional structure; an international division structure; an area or geographic division structure; a product division structure; and a matrix structure.

---

Several management scholars revised the model put forward by Stopford and Wells and added, deleted, or integrated different stages and structures (Egelhoff 1988). Chi et al. (2004: 224) proposed a similar framework to that of Stopford and Wells, but replaced the international division structure with 'functional form'. Franko's (1976) study of eighty five European multinational firms found that European firms follow a different pattern to that reported by Stopford and Wells. In particular, he found that most European multinational firms move from the home structure directly to a global product structure, without going through the international division as an intermediate structure. Similarly, Egelhoff (1982) listed four forms: functional, international, geographical, and product. Thus, we add functional structure to the four structures of Stopford and Wells. We will discuss the characteristics of the five types of structures below.

### 9.4.1 **Functional structures**

A grouping by functions is shown in Exhibit 9.3. Such a structure is likely to evolve as an expansion of a domestic functional configuration, possibly via an international division arrangement. Management control and coordination comes through functional authority, whilst the operation units themselves focus on specific product groups, which are then sold through the mainstream established distribution and sales channels, which are controlled from the centre.

Grouping by function is suitable for a multinational firm with a clear separation in the activities undertaken by each of the foreign subsidiaries. Examples of this are where procurement is from one country and assembly is in another; and where, for example, a production unit is located in a low-cost country but the majority of sales are in Europe. Here, it makes sense to organize functionally, with global operations responsible for product integration and efficiency. This sort of arrangement suits companies where the integration of manufacturing or service operations can achieve economies of scale. Thus, it is a particularly good arrangement for some firms in the European Union at the turn of the twenty-first century, where there was a need to reduce duplication in national operations to match the continental scale required.

Grouping by function also makes sense when there is a need to coordinate marketing and sales efforts, especially where strong central control is required. This is the common practice with international brands such as McDonald's and Coca-Cola, whereby the global marketing function controls many of the marketing and sales features of a product that is sold internationally, although the product offering is likely to be tailored nationally. It also makes sense when there is a particular need to integrate financial activity; for example, where such

**Exhibit 9.3** Functional structure

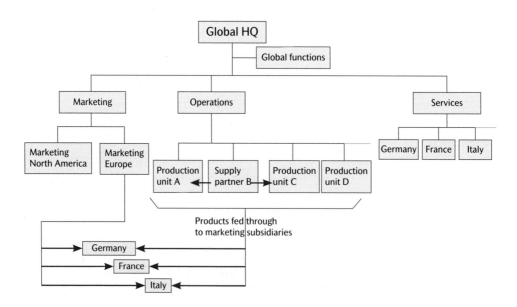

matters as transfer pricing and national taxation regimes require a great deal of expertise to be available to the centre. Grouping by function is also applicable to small companies that cannot afford to duplicate support services and need the centre to provide them.

A functional arrangement can be a problem, however, where one or two powerful units do not accept central authority. Is it likely, for example, that a head office in France can dictate personnel or IT policies in the US or Japan if the units there are large? British American Tobacco has traditionally had difficulty getting its very powerful US and Brazilian companies to follow parental advice: they are too large and too profitable to be dictated to by the centre.

### 9.4.2 International division structure

For the firm that is selling a large proportion of its output in its domestic market and a small quantity internationally, and has low foreign-product diversity, the most common form of organizational structure is the international division structure, as depicted in Exhibit 9.4. That is, the international division structure is appropriate when foreign operations are relatively small.

The international division handles all international activities. Historically, this form of structure is the way in which purely national players dipped their toes into international waters, since it is a low-risk method of servicing overseas markets. An example here is exporting firms, where international markets are still secondary to the domestic market. The international division structure is very common amongst US firms during their early internationalization

**Exhibit 9.4**  International division structure

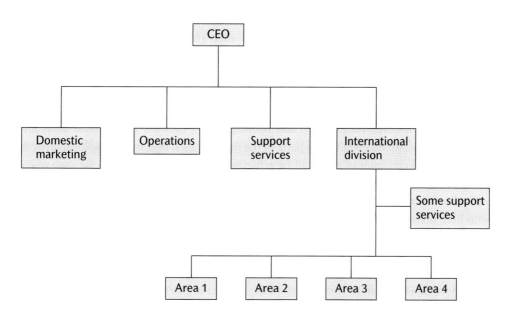

the core products are effectively standard across borders. This means that the core products themselves are central to the organization, with modifications to non-core features made market by market. The Ford Mondeo, as its name suggests, was Ford's first significant attempt to develop a world car—one that could be sold in all its major markets. An example of the same core offering in services is telecommunications.

A product structure based on the primacy of global operations will be organized to achieve economies of scale, often through vertical integration of procurement operations and distribution, utilizing sources of low-cost labour. With marketing activities tailored to the specifics of the market, these consequently tend to be less cost-effective. If the regions are large enough for production and procurement economies, yet homogeneous enough to be considered one broad market, then the product structure will work, with the regional head office taking control both of operations and marketing.

Whilst global marketing is subservient to operations in this sort of organization, each product line has its own dedicated marketing staff, often with their own support services. A representation is shown in Exhibit 9.6. In such a grouping, there appears to be a high degree of duplication: each product group has its own dedicated marketing staff. However, these are not unnecessary duplications if the product groups are distinct. For example, 3M has four major product groups: automotive and chemical, consumer and office, electronics and communications, and industrial. These groups have distinct characteristics and their products are sold to very different customers. This means that, in practice, dedicated marketing staff can be much more knowledgeable than personnel who needed to cover a great range of products.

**Exhibit 9.6** Product structure

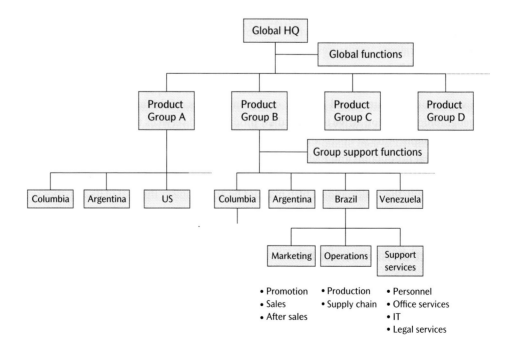

9.4.5 **The matrix structure**

Since the 1980s, large multinational firms have increased both their international sales and operations in foreign markets, and diversification across both products and geographical areas. According to the Stopford and Wells model, a high degree of diversification and foreign sales and operations should lead the multinational firm to adopt a matrix structure. A matrix structure is an overlapping of two or more of the four structures discussed earlier—functional structure, international division structure, area or geographical division structure, and/or product division structure (Egelhoff 1988). Further, each of the four arrangements discussed so far has strengths but also severe weaknesses. Giving primacy to the functions through functional grouping is likely to mean that national responsiveness is weak. Giving primacy to the nations or regions in a geographical grouping is likely to reduce the level of global integration. Giving primacy to operations in product groupings can easily lead to marketing and service duplication, and weaken the role of global marketing and service initiatives.

Given these weaknesses, it makes sense to combine authority over operations, marketing, and geography in some way. Such a combination attempts to coordinate matters so that the organization does not lose any economies of scale or the advantages of locally responsive marketing. The way this is done is to operate a matrix structure in which each operating unit in a region has responsibility both for marketing and the operations that are conducted there. This gives primacy to the geographical regions but with the head of each unit having two reporting lines at regional or global head office—to someone in operations and to someone else in marketing. A matrix structure is shown in Exhibit 9.7, which shows an arrangement whereby products in three product groups are sold in two geographical areas. Picked out is one unit and the responsibilities of the head of the unit: the geographical line of responsibility is to region 1, the functional line of responsibility is to operations, and the product line of responsibility to product group B.

**Exhibit 9.7** Matrix structure

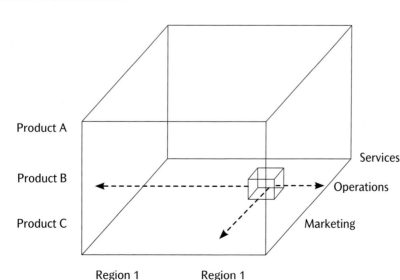

Region 1              Region 1

The matrix structure has certain potential advantages. The sales force is likely to be more efficient, being able to offer a wider portfolio of offers than would be possible if it were working for only one product group (Donaldson 2009). Brand management will be able to maintain the characteristics of the brand over all markets. The downside of this is that the sales force is likely to be less dedicated and less knowledgeable about the products—a significant disadvantage if the products are technically sophisticated. Small decisions can be made locally and large decisions will be more informed, with the decision-makers knowing all sides of the product–market situation and knowing the bigger national or regional picture.

Having responsibility for both product and market and being mindful of the subsidiary's wider regional responsibilities should mean that managers develop into more general managers, but at the cost of the triple chains of responsibility leading to greater management stress levels. Planning and control are likely to be more complex within a matrix structure. Decisions are likely to take longer, as three chains of command are involved. In general, the advantages that might come from adopting a matrix structure seem to be outweighed by the disadvantages—mainly the massive demands on managers, especially having to deal with multiple lines of command. Bartlett and Ghoshal (1989) summed up the practical problems with the matrix structure as follows:

> the matrix prove all but unmanageable—especially in international context. Dual reporting led to conflict and confusion; the proliferation of channels created information logjam as proliferation of committees and reports bogged down the organization; an overlapping responsibilities produced turf battles and a loss of accountability. Separated by barriers of distance, language, time and culture, managers found it virtually impossible to clarify the confusion and resolve the conflicts.

This explains why many multinational firms tried a matrix organization and abandoned it. For example, Texas Instruments found that the structure created too much ambiguity and too little coordination, and abandoned it in favour of product groupings with integrated functional support (Egelhof 1993: 182–210). However, others have successfully adopted a matrix structure—at least for many years. An example here is the Walt Disney Company. Michael Eisner, CEO of the company from 1984 till 2005, commented in 2000 that the matrix structure generates valuable synergy, as he put it:

> We're (also) trying to increase the amount of synergy in our global operations by country. We've just re-organized our international organization into a hybrid type of structure, so the person running movies in Italy, for instance, not only reports to an executive in the movie division, as he or she did before, but also to a country head. (Wetlaufer 2000: 121)

---

**KEY CONCEPT**

A matrix structure is an overlapping of two or more of the following four structures: functional structure, international division structure, area or geographical division structure, and/or product division structure.

---

## 9.5 Balancing integrations and local responsiveness: broad forms of international strategy

Firms will begin in one country and will almost invariably initially have their production facilities and head office located there. They will almost always begin by supplying solely their home market. In wishing to move to supply foreign markets, there are two major and generally conflicting pressures. First, there is the pressure to become and remain responsive to the foreign markets—to satisfy the differing demands as they arise. Second, there is a pressure to use the scope offered by operating abroad—both economies of scale and the ability to tap into the differing expertise that resides abroad (Bartlett and Ghoshal 1989). These two pressures suggest the four broad configurations that are shown in Exhibit 9.8 (Finlay 2000: 539).

### 9.5.1 The export firm

For the firm that is selling a large proportion of its output in its domestic market and a small quantity internationally, the most common form of organizational structure is the incorporation of an export section into the already existing domestic marketing function, as depicted in Exhibit 9.9. Historically, this form of structure is the way in which purely national players experimented with foreign markets, since it is a low-risk method of servicing overseas markets. The marketing and sales functions would be split between 'domestic' and 'export', with the export section possibly organized along national or regional lines (e.g., grouping all European countries in one group and all South American countries in another). The setting up of an export section brings internationally experienced personnel together to handle such

**Exhibit 9.8** International configurations

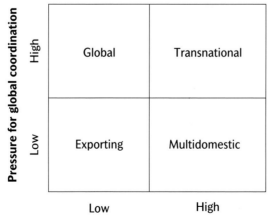

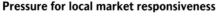

**Exhibit 9.9** Export structure

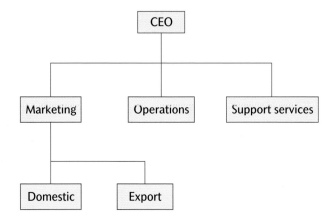

things as export documentation and foreign exchange interactions. An example of an export firm is Baser Food (see Exhibit 2.3 in Chapter 2).

### 9.5.2 The multi-domestic firm

The multi-domestic firm consists of several businesses operating almost independently, each in a home base that is similar to a mother country—having its own production capacity and a country head office. Any concern for international cooperation tends to be muted, since almost all the products of each business are destined for their own home markets. Classic examples of this are retail banking, newspapers, and TV, where the local context is so important. Aviva—the world's fifth largest insurance group—follows a multi-domestic structure. This is because most of its life and pension products in Europe are significantly different from those in Asia Pacific and North America.

#### Organizational structures to support a multi-domestic strategy

The rationale for a firm to choose a multi-domestic strategy is that the nation—or some similar geographical grouping—has a particularly strong influence on activities. Such grouping would almost automatically come about and be preferred where the strategy had involved the acquisition of strong national businesses—as in Europe, especially after the EU was formed. Organizational groupings to fit this strategy will naturally be by geography.

The term 'multi-domestic' indicates what the organizational structure will be like. Within each country, the structure will replicate the domestic arrangements discussed in section 9.5.3. For cases where there is just one product line in each country, the simple structure depicted in Exhibit 9.1(*a*), or something very similar, will be implemented; where there are multi-products, the structure shown in Exhibit 9.1(*b*) would be appropriate. The reporting lines might be directly from country to head office, or there might be regional groupings, as shown in Exhibit 9.4. The grouping shown in Exhibit 9.4 is appropriate where the businesses in each country are totally owned by the organization. However, many such holdings may not be wholly-owned by

**Exhibit 9.10** Holding company structure

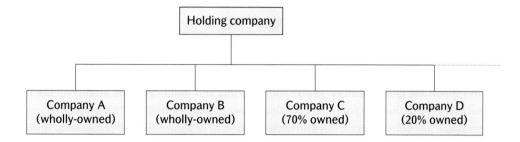

the firm: indeed, alliances that give rise to partly owned joint ventures are a significant way in which firms expand globally. The extreme structural case is where the global head office acts as a holding company, having shareholdings in one or more separate companies. A holding company structure is shown in Exhibit 9.10.

With a holding company structure, the linkages between the parent and its operating companies are kept to the minimum. Such an arrangement suits a diversified organization where the linkages between the businesses are effectively nonexistent. The parent restricts itself to providing very broad strategic direction, generally setting boundaries to the scope of the businesses and setting financial targets for them. The parent will have some financial and legal expertise, but these are unlikely to be offered to the businesses.

A significant weakness of the multi-domestic arrangement is duplication, particularly of support services, and the inability of the units to obtain economies of scale. A further deficiency is that organizational learning is likely to be hindered by the lack of contact between national operations.

---

**KEY CONCEPT**

A firm following a multi-domestic strategy has two possible structures that it can employ. Where it wholly-owns all the businesses in its portfolio, it is most likely to support domestic arrangements in each country with reporting of business performance to the parent. Where ownership of some of its units is shared, the parent may wish to operate as a holding company. In many cases, the two structures may be adopted to run side by side.

Compared to the holding company, the divisionalized structure has high central overheads, because the parent carries out many more of the parenting functions. With such a slim head office, the holding company will put no effort into developing synergies or providing central services.

---

9.5.3 **The global firm**

The global firm has a presence in many countries to take advantage of favourable trading conditions (Porter 1985). A global firm is characterized as selling and/or producing a standard core product in many countries—examples are pharmaceuticals, aircraft, aero engines, and a transnational organization moves away from the single line of responsibility by downplaying the importance of hierarchy. A transnational firm is not dominated by hierarchies: hierarchies remain, but they play nowhere near as strong a role as in other arrangements.

Senior managers in transnational organizations must think in terms of managing a network of associates rather than operating within a hierarchy: a network of centres for each of research, development, component manufacture, assembly, distribution and sales, and marketing. The emphasis is on interdependence rather than independence or hierarchical subservience, and the ability to work with colleagues from many different cultures is important. In the ultimate transnational strategy, there would be no head office and no home country, although for legal reasons an office would have to be nominated as such. There would be a set of units that take the lead in an aspect of marketing, or of operations, or some aspect of services. For example, part of Bombardier, the Canadian engineering firm specializing in railway and tram systems, now operates this sort of structure.

Advances in IT—through the Internet and video-conferencing—support such developments. For example, the Taiwanese-based Giant bicycle company would appear to be acting as a transnational. One of its biggest markets is the EU, and it manufactures in the Netherlands so as to be close to this major market, as well as in China and Taiwan. Three-quarters of the bikes it sells around the world are the same, but the other quarter have a regional flavour. Bikes are as much a fashion item as a mode of transport in some markets: in the mid 1990s Giant introduced five to ten new models a year. As well as spreading its production, it has designers in Taiwan, China, Japan, the US, and the Netherlands. Chinese and Japanese customers seek commuting bikes, the Dutch designers contribute ideas from the European racing scene, and the US designers are working on mountain bike variants. The designers work together using computer-aided design facilities and get together twice a year in Taiwan (Marsh 1997: 16).

Roles in a network structure are much more ambiguous than those in traditional organizations and make it more difficult to define precise responsibilities and duties. However, this ambiguity makes it more important to define roles carefully, not just as a way of telling individuals what their responsibilities are, but also for communicating with the rest of the network. Role definition should be such that it fosters loyalty to the alliance, not to the parent, as this helps to develop the focus and motivation necessary to make the network function.

Interpersonal relationships are key to the success of any network-based structure. Although it is not easy to establish good relationships between members of the network from very different business cultures, it is even harder to sustain it. Operational and cultural differences will emerge after collaboration is under way; and these dissimilarities require working out, with much more communication than anyone could have anticipated (Kanter 1994: 96–108).

A major role for all senior managers in a transnational structure is to manage the relationships between the units in the corporate portfolio. Although some cooperation between units will almost always be desirable, in a transnational organization, the need to facilitate rather than dictate cooperation becomes paramount. There are several ways that units can usefully collaborate:

- Sharing best practice. By which the parent encourages groups of units to use each other as benchmarks and in this way spread best practice. This is spreading knowledge—of process and of technology. In the past, BAT Industries has grouped its worldwide tobacco operations into a set of triplets—for example, Brazil, Germany, and the UK—with each member of the triplet looking at the others' activities to see what they could find of benefit to themselves.

- Sharing skills. Linked somewhat to spreading best practice is the spreading skills. Skills are tacit knowledge that cannot be codified, and the only real way of spreading these is to move the people who have these skills. The parent has the role—through its personnel policies—of moving its personnel around the firm, inculcating others with the skills they have, and learning new ones to pass on subsequently. Nestlé is a company that has acted in this way in its European operations for many years.

- Sharing data. It is useful, particularly in the financial services sector, to use customer data to cross-sell services. For example, someone with a mortgage will have their data available to the unit that is selling insurance. The availability of enterprise resource planning systems is an aid to this.

- Cooperation when dealing with stakeholders. It can be beneficial for units to share distribution channels or to combine when facing a powerful supplier. This allows start-up activities, or activities with low activation rates, to piggyback on the activities of others.

---

**KEY CONCEPT**

In contrast to other structures, a transnational organization is not dominated by hierarchies: hierarchies remain, but they play nowhere near as marked a role. Senior managers must think in terms of managing a network of associates, and must have the ability to work with colleagues from many different cultures. The emphasis is on interdependence, rather than independence.

---

## 9.6 Summary

Organizational structure provides the skeleton on which the organization is designed. Structure has to match the strategy that the organization is following in order to make best use of company resources. A company's resources have been considered to consist of four super functions: operations (including procurement); marketing (including distribution, sales, and after-sales); support services (functions such as personnel, finance, IT); and research and development (R&D). The first three functions are concerned with ongoing activities and the present, whereas R&D is concerned with the future. For ease of discussion, structures to support ongoing activities can be treated separately from those aimed at the future.

There is no one best structure. It is a case of horses for courses (Ghoshal and Nohria 1993). Different strategies require different structures, and different structures may require different strategies. All structures embody trade-offs. As a rule, strategy and structure must match. A mismatch between strategy and structure will ultimately lead to poor communication and

### Restructuring initiated in 1995

In 1995, after the implementation of the divisional company structure in the electronics sector, changes were made in the group management structure, with Sony led by a team that included Ohga, the group president and chief operating officer (COO), and the presidents of the divisional companies. In March 1995, Nobuyuki Idei was appointed the group president and COO.

Given Sony's poor financial performance at this time, the top management decided to integrate the group's various domestic and global business functions such as marketing, R&D, finance, and HR. Thus, many of the functions of the divisional companies were brought under the direct supervision of headquarters. Idei also decided to strengthen the existing eight-company structure and to lay more emphasis on R&D in the IT field.

Accordingly, in January 1996, a new ten-company structure was announced for the electronics sector. Under the new structure, the previous consumer audio and video products company was split into three new companies—display, home audio-video, and personal audio-video. A new company—information technology—was created to focus on Sony's business interests in the PC and IT industries. Infocom products and mobile electronics were merged to create personal and mobile communications. The other companies formed were recording media and energy, and broadcast products. Business and industrial systems was renamed image and sound communications, and components was renamed components and computer peripherals. Semiconductors remained unchanged.

### Further group changes

In order to devise and implement the corporate strategies of the Sony Group, an executive board was created, chaired by Idei. The other members of the board included the chief HR officer, the chief production officer, the chief marketing officer, the chief communications officer, the chief technology officer, the chief financial officer, the executive deputy president and representative director, and the senior managing director.

In an attempt to consolidate the marketing operations of Sony, the marketing divisions that had belonged to the previous organizational setup were spun off to create three new marketing groups: the Japan Marketing Group (JMG), the International Marketing and Operations Group (IM&O), and the Electronic Components and Devices Marketing Group (ECDMG). The JMG was responsible for all marketing activities in Japan for five companies—display, home audio-video, IT, personal audio-video, and image and sound communications. The IM&O was responsible for supporting all overseas marketing efforts for these companies. The ECDMG oversaw the worldwide marketing operations for semiconductors and for components and computer peripherals.

To centralize all the R&D efforts of Sony's electronics sector, the previous R&D structure (in which each company had its own R&D unit) was revamped and three new corporate laboratories were established. The laboratories were: the architecture laboratory (responsible for software, network, and IT-related technologies), the product development laboratory (audio and video), and the system laboratory (system design and the basic components of hardware products). In addition, a new D21 laboratory was established to conduct long-term R&D for future-oriented technology-intensive products.

Sony also gave emphasis to grooming young, talented people to take up top management positions. The company also introduced the concept of 'virtual companies'—temporary groups consisting of people from different divisions for launching hybrid products. Sony applied this idea when developing the latest generation of mini disk players.

## Restructuring initiated in 1998

During the early part of 1998, Sony formed Sony Online Entertainment in the US to focus on Internet related projects. In May 1998, it changed the composition of its board of directors and established the new position of Co-chief executive officer (Co-CEO). Idei was appointed Co-CEO. The new organization separated individuals responsible for policy-making from those responsible for operations.

Under the new system, Idei was responsible for planning and designing Sony's strategies and supervising the growth of e-business. Along with Ohga, he had to supervise the performance of the entire Sony Group. The chief financial officer was made responsible for the company's financial strategies and network businesses.

In the late 1990s, Sony's management felt the need to establish a link between its electronics business (TVs, music systems, computers) and its content-related businesses (music, video games, movies, and financial services) by making use of the Internet. It wanted to use the Internet as a medium for selling its electronics products as well as its content (music, movies, and so on). In order to achieve this, Sony announced another reorganization of business operations—to the unified–dispersed management model.

## Restructuring initiated in 1999

In April 1999, Sony's key electronics and entertainment interests were reorganized into network businesses (see Exhibit A). This involved reducing the ten divisional companies into five; three network companies, Sony Computer Entertainment (SCE), and Broadcasting and Professional Systems (B&PS), as shown in Exhibit A. According to the new structure, each network company was delegated with authority from the corporate headquarters, and was asked to pursue the management of their respective business domains as self-contained, autonomous business units. SCE was responsible for the PlayStation business, while the B&PS supplied video and audio equipment for business, broadcast, education, industrial, medical, and production-related markets. The restructuring aimed at achieving three objectives: strengthening the electronics business, privatizing three Sony subsidiaries, and strengthening management capabilities.

## Strengthening the electronics business

The three network companies created were Home Network, Personal IT Network, and Core Technology Network. Each network company was governed by a network company management committee (NCMC) and a network committee board (NCB). The NCMC was responsible for developing management policies and strategies. Its members included the officers and presidents of the network company concerned. An NCB was responsible for managing the day-to-day operations of the network company, while keeping in mind the overall Sony corporate strategy.

**Exhibit A** Sony Group organizational structure, 1999

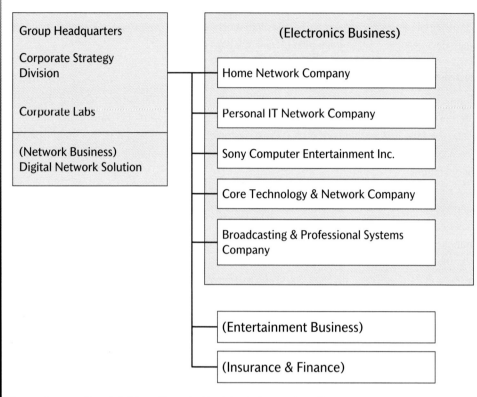

Source: Sony.net/Sony Info/News/Press_Archive/199903/99_038/at1.gif

The new structure aimed at decentralizing the worldwide operations of the company. The corporate headquarters gave the network companies the authority to function as autonomous entities in their business areas. To facilitate more functional and operational autonomy, the corporate headquarters also transferred the required support functions and R&D laboratories to each network company.

### Privatizing Sony's subsidiaries

As part of its strategy to promote functional and operational autonomy and to devote more attention to units which contributed significantly to its revenues and profits, Sony decided to convert three of its companies—Sony Music Entertainment (Japan); Sony Chemical Corporation (which manufactured printed circuit boards (PSBs), recording media, and had battery operations); and Sony Precision Technology (manufactured semiconductor inspection equipment and precision measuring devices)—into wholly-owned subsidiaries of Sony. In addition, Sony converted SCE, jointly owned by Sony and Sony Music Entertainment (Japan), into a wholly-owned subsidiary of Sony.

### Strengthening the management capability

To strengthen the management capability, Sony clearly defined the roles of headquarters and the newly created network companies. In particular, a sharp distinction was made between the strategic and support functions. Sony's headquarters was split into two separate units: group headquarters and business unit support.

The role of group headquarters was to oversee group operations and expedite the allocation of resources within the group. The support functions, such as accounting, HR, and general affairs, were handled by the network companies so that they could enjoy more autonomy in their operations. Significant long-term R&D projects were directly supervised by headquarters, while immediate and short-term R&D projects were transferred to the network companies concerned.

### Restructuring initiated in 2001

At the beginning of the 2000s, Sony faced increased competition from domestic and foreign players (Korean companies like Samsung and LG) in its electronics and entertainment businesses. The domestic rivals, Matsushita and NEC, were able to capture a substantial market share in the Internet-ready cellphone market. Analysts felt that the US-based software giants, like Microsoft and Sun Microsystems, and the networking major, Cisco Systems, posed a serious threat to Sony's home entertainment business.

Sony announced another round of organizational restructuring in March 2001. The company aimed at transforming itself into a personal broadband network solutions company by launching a wide range of broadband products and services for its customers across the world. Explaining the objective of the restructuring, Idei said, 'By capitalizing on this business structure and by having businesses cooperate with each other, we aim to become the leading media and technology company in the broadband era.' The restructuring involved designing a new headquarters to function as a hub for Sony's strategy, strengthening the electronics business, and facilitating network-based content distribution.

Sony's headquarters was revamped into a global hub, centred on five key businesses—electronics, entertainment, games, financial services, and Internet/communication service. The primary role of the global hub (headed by the top management) was to devise the overall management strategy of the company.

Sony's management decided to integrate all the electronics business-related activities under the newly created electronic headquarters. In order to achieve the convergence of audio-video products with IT, Sony devised a unique strategy called the 'four-network gateway'. Under this strategy, the games and Internet/communication service businesses were combined with the electronics hardware business so that innovative products could be developed and offered for the broadband market.

In order to provide support services for the entire group, a management platform was created which consisted of key support functions in diverse fields such as accounting, finance, legal, intellectual copyrights, HR, information systems, public relations, external affairs, and design. The management platform was later split into the engineering, management and customer service (EMCS) company and the sales platform (which comprised the regional sales companies and region-based internet direct marketing functions). The management platform was headed by the chief administrative officer, a newly created position.

Sony's management also converted the product-centric network companies into solution-oriented companies by regrouping them into seven companies. Group resources were allocated among the network companies on the basis of their growth potential.

For the first quarter, ending 30 June 2003, the Sony Corporation stunned the corporate world by reporting a decline in net profits of 98%. In the financial year 2002–3, Sony had spent a massive ¥100 billion on restructuring (on 23 July 2003, €1 = ¥132; US$1 = ¥118). Moreover, in April 2003, the company had already announced its plans to spend another ¥1 trillion on a major restructuring initiative in the next three years.

### Radical restructuring in mid 2006

After seemingly endless strings of restructuring and enduring several rounds of painful quarters of poor performance, Sony's management realized that the company was losing ground fast and radical actions were needed to it. Indeed, some industry observers wrote it off. In 2009, Douglas McIntyre, the editor of *The Wall Street Journal* wrote:

> Sony may be remembered as the largest consumer electronics company failure in history. No other company had the Sony brand at that critical period in the late 1990s and early this decade when most of the products that dominate the market today were born. Sony was not in on the ground floor of a single one of them.

Sony's failure was due to the fact that the business environment was changing much faster than Sony was able to change, and the new competition from the likes of Microsoft, Samsung, Apple, Sharp, Nokia, and Canon to name but a few, was eating up its market share.

To shake up its corporate culture, Sony took a historical decision by appointing, for the first in its history, a non-Japanese CEO. In March 2005, Sony appointed Howard Stringer, a US executive, to run the company and rejuvenate its flagging performance. Stringer was not only the first non-Japanese CEO of Sony, but he also did not speak Japanese, he was not an engineer as his predecessors, and his knowledge of electronics was very limited. But for these very reasons, Sony's board of directors believed he was the right person for the job. Sony's board believed that Sony was in need of someone like Stringer who knew very little about the company to help it break away from its old way of doing things.

Stringer inherited an over-diversified company, plagued with divisional infighting and sagging profits. Soon after his appointment, Stringer moved fast and took radical decisions to revitalize Sony's position in the marketplace. His aim was to end the seemingly never-ending tampering with Sony's structure without going far enough to address the key problems. In addition to cutting costs by eliminating over 5,000 jobs, closing a number of plants, and selling off assets worth over US$700 million—including the chain of 1,200 cosmetics saloons and the Maxim's de Paris restaurant chain—Stringer's other priority tasks included shaking up Sony's culture, and, in particular, breaking down its 'silo culture', which was a side effect of the division structure where different divisions were not communicating with each other. Sony introduced the 'Sony United' initiative to break down barriers between independent departments and encouraged cross-department collaboration. Stringer argued that a modernization of Sony required a cultural revolution.

Also, Stringer scrapped the traditional division structure for a centralized structure, where the headquarter retained decision-making power. This enabled Sony to break down the silo culture; streamline decision-making across the different product areas, overseas R&D spending, and large divisional spending plans; remove overlapping business processes; and focus Sony on high-growth business such as HD and 3D products, game businesses, mobile phone products, and network-enabled products. The new structure, as described by Stringer, was designed to, 'transform Sony into a more innovative, integrated and agile global company and . . . make it possible for all of Sony's parts to work together'. The new structure, as depicted in Exhibit B, has two main groups: the Consumer, Professional and Devices Group and the Network products and services group. The two groups are coordinated by common platforms coordinating marketing, production, and R&D activities at the company level, and a powerful headquarter overseeing strategic decisions and coordinating the activities of the different groups.

### At last Sony bounces back

In 2010, Sony returned to profitability. It reported an operating profit of US$2.3 billion. It seems that the tough restructuring programmes introduced by Stringer have paid off. By 2010, Sony's performance in consumer electronics was solid due largely to significant reductions both in

**Exhibit B** Sony Group organizational chart summary, 2010

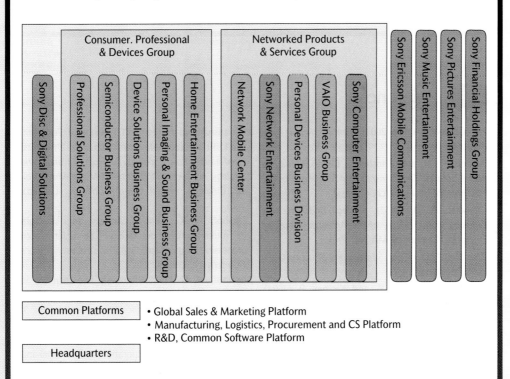

*Source:* http://www.sony.net/SonyInfo/CorporateInfo/Data/organization.html.

# Global management of change

## Learning outcomes

After reading this chapter, you should be able to:

➤ Describe the two types of strategic change and recognize where management and where leadership are required.

➤ Explain the characteristics required of a change agent.

➤ Recognize the three phases of the change process.

➤ Empathize with people when their work processes are changed and thus be able to manage most appropriately the change process.

➤ Select the change-management style that best fits the context under which change is taking place.

## Opening case study  Shanghai Volkswagen

Shanghai Volkswagen Automotive Co. (SVW) is a joint venture between the Shanghai Automotive Industry Corporation (SAIC) and Volkswagen Group. The two companies signed a trial agreement in 1982 for manufacturing the Volkswagen Santana model in Shanghai, and the joint venture (JV)—Shanghai Volkswagen (SVW)—was formally established in October 1984, and started operations in September 1985. The joint venture is located in Anting International Auto City on the outskirts of Shanghai, China. SVW was one of the first Western auto manufacturers in China, and a market leader for a long period of time.

In the early 1980s, the Chinese automobile sector was underdeveloped and the Chinese government had near total control over the sector, deciding who produces what and where. Not surprisingly then, when the SVW JV was established, it needed the help of the regional government in Shanghai and central government in Beijing to operate in China. Indeed, the president of SAIC and SVW's general manager's offices were located directly underneath the office of Shanghai's mayor.

For the two decades of the 1980s and 1990s, SVW worked closely with the Chinese government at the regional and central levels and helped SAIC develop a network of local suppliers. SVW worked patiently with its local suppliers, even when they were not able to meet Volkswagen's stringent quality standards. It regularly dispatched German engineers to serve as technical consultants to local supply firms. By 1997, nearly 93% of the parts used in SVW's cars were produced in Shanghai and about 50% were produced by suppliers belonging to SAIC.

SVW was rewarded handsomely for its cooperation with the Chinese government and, in particular, for helping SAIC build its supply network. Both regional and central governments provided SVW with preferential treatment in taxation, access to foreign currencies, government procurement, and access to institutional market. For example, in 1996, the Shanghai municipal government banned cars that had an engine capacity of less than 1.6 litres from city streets, a move conveniently ruling out cars produced by competing automakers, and, in 1998, it levied an extra US$10,000 licence fee on Citroën cars (ZX/Fukang) made in the nearby Hubei Province. SVW was also offered a lion's share of the auto market for Chinese institutional users—cars for government officials and public organizations—which, at that time, accounted for a large part of the sedan market. A good example of the preferential treatment of SVW is the Shanghai government under Zhu Rongji's leadership decision to reserve the Shanghai city taxi market for SVW by requiring that every Shanghai city taxi be an SVW's Santana model. As a result, SVW captured around 50% of the market share. However, most of its cars were sold to institutional organizations and taxi companies.

SVW's early success, though, came at a cost. When the market for the car industry changed dramatically in the early 2000s, SVW was caught off guard. Its capabilities that made it successful in the previous decades suddenly turned into a liability. By the early 2000s, the institutional market had shrunk significantly on the one hand, while on the other hand, the number of private buyers increased significantly. Between 1996 and 2005, private auto ownership in China increased by 22% annually, and by the end of 2005, 58.5% of China's vehicle fleet was privately owned. However, because SVW served a protected market, its products in terms of both price and quality were not able to serve private consumers who were far more responsive to price than institutional ones, and were more concerned with quality and style.

In addition to changes in consumer profile, several new competitors, including General Motors, Toyota, Nissan, and Ford, entered the Chinese auto markets to serve the ever-increasing private market segment. The increase in the number of competitors caused prices to fall significantly. For example, the price of the basic Santana, which was 200,000 RMB (US$24,096) in the early 1990s, fell to 89,900 RMB (US$10,857) by 2004.

SVW realized that it needed to change in order to compete in the new business environment. Its market share in the passenger car segment declined by nearly two-thirds from 50% to 17% in just four years from 2001 to 2005.

SVW started by trying to change its supply operations by tightening quality and cost control through the supply chain. However, this was met with resistance by its partner—SAIC—the regional government, as well as by its suppliers. Suppliers were used to being paid inflated prices for low-quality parts. For nearly two decades, suppliers within the SAIC group got used to supplying SVW, no matter how high their costs were, and therefore resisted SVW plans to move to a cost-inefficient supply network. SAIC saw SVW's move to change its supply chain operations as a threat to the development of its suppliers and resisted moves by SVW to obtain parts from outside its network of suppliers. The regional government also resisted moves to supply SVW by suppliers located outside the Shanghai municipality.

As competition intensified in the early 2000s, SVW had to deal with stiff resistance from its suppliers, local government, and its local partner. Tensions started appearing in one of the best partnerships that worked perfectly well for over two decades. General Motors, which signed a joint venture with SAIC, became the new market leader in China. Volkswagen and SAIC locked horns and blamed each other for a lack of flexibility. SAIC wanted more up-to-date technology and models and know-how transfer to the IJV. Volkswagen asked for modernization of the supply network and the ability to source parts from the SAIC network when its suppliers do not meet its criteria. However, SAIC had more bargaining power as a number of multinational firms were waiting to take SVW's place. To break the deadlock and help its JV in China regain its competitive advantage, Volkswagen promised the transfer of more technological knowhow to SVW, and to help the IJV introduce new models, and assist it to become a world class car producer rather than a production plant for the Chinese market. SVW also convinced SAIC that an efficient supply chain would be good for all parties concerned.

By the late 2000s, the introduced changes seemed to be paying off. SVW had developed a different relationship with its suppliers. The new relationship is based on hard bargaining and competition with suppliers from outside the SAIC group and Shanghai municipality. On the production side, SVW had been very aggressive and introduced a number of new models, such as the Tiguan sport-utility vehicle, the Audi Q5, and an upgraded Volkswagen Jetta that appealed to private buyers. In 2010, the China Association of Automobile Manufacturers reported that SVW had regained the No.1 position in the Chinese auto market by selling over 700,000 cars in China in 2009, and Winfried Vahland, president and chief executive of Volkswagen China reported that, 'we are practically sold out of many of our models'.

## 10.1 **Introduction**

All types of firms, multinational or single-country, small or large, single-business or diversified, need to undertake operational renewal constantly in order to renew those parts of the organization that are ageing. However, the opening case study demonstrates that the management of change in multinational firms is more complex and involves more stakeholders than just the focal firm, as is the case with single-country firms. Multinational firms operate across several countries, which creates a complex and sometimes chaotic mix of management practices influenced by different national cultures and institutions. As the opening case study shows, SVW had to deal with the regional government in Shanghai, its local partner—SAIC—and its network of suppliers. In addition, some subsidiaries are more aware of the competitive nature of the business environment and its dynamics and, as a result, are less resistant to change. Others are oblivious to the nature of the business environment, perhaps because the subsidiary or the industry is protected or subsidized by the government, and hence may not fully understand the importance of change and may resist it. Further, people's attitudes towards change are also affected by a set of culture-specific factors, such as taken-for-granted behaviour, norms, and values, which adds another layer of complexity to change management in multinational firms. The different behaviours and attitudes of employees and management at subsidiary level towards change increase the potential for conflict between the centre and subsidiaries, and may hinder the success of the change strategy (Andrews and Chompusri 2001).

Due to the inherent instability in today's business environment, multinational firms often find themselves facing the need to undertake strategic renewal in order to pursue a change strategy and/or to adjust to changing environmental factors. Where environmental change is slow and/or small, organizational change is likely to be in small, incremental steps. The changes that the organization needs to undertake are likely to be larger, however, where the environmental changes are larger or because it wishes to change its strategy significantly, as did SVW. Such changes are transformational.

## 10.2 **Types of change**

Multinational firms have to be prepared to undertake both incremental change and transformational change. Change management is the process by which a multinational firm obtains its current and future strategy.

### 10.2.1 **Incremental change**

By far the most frequent sort of change in organizations is incremental change. Incremental change refers to slow and gradual changes which are consistent with an existing strategy of the firm. It alters behaviours in the organization, but generally leaves undisturbed the more deeply held organizational beliefs. Examples of incremental change that aim to produce more of 'something' and/or do things better are the introduction of continuous improvement programmes or quality improvement programmes. Pizza Hut's attempt to emphasize its pasta products can be considered as an incremental change strategy. In 2008, Pizza Hut sent a signal to its existing and potential customers that it is more than a pizza restaurant chain by changing its name for a period of six months from Pizza Hut to Pasta Hut. As described by its CEO, 'we're putting our food above the parapet. We're trying to say to people: "Yes, we're great at pizzas, but we're also great at salads and pasta.'

Incremental change is often a role for management rather than leadership, since management generally continues current activities with a concern for efficiency. Managers deal with the physical resources of an organization—with its capital, raw materials, technology, and with the demonstrable skills of the workforce. They are concerned with efficiency and with mastering routines. They are the people who resolve issues as they arise: they do things right—working within defined policies. However, although incremental change may be sanctioned by managers, much incremental change is originated by the people most intimately connected with the organization's processes, its products/services, and its customers. If they are suitably empowered, they can bring about the required change themselves.

Incremental change does not lead to a change in the implicit fundamental beliefs underpinning the organizational way of working. The characteristics of situations involving incremental change are summarized in the first column of Exhibit 10.1.

## 10.2.2 Transformational change

Transformational change involves changing one or more of the fundamental organizational beliefs, and with it the values of the organization. It often requires a complete abandonment of the old ways of doing things and the adoption of new technologies and/or serving new markets. SVW's move to serve private buyers in the early 2000s is an example of a transformational change. SVW had to renew its technology, introduce new products, and improve its production processes. Examples of transformational change are the changes in the processes associated with doing things very differently, or with undertaking very different activities, as LG did moving to up-market innovative products (see closing case study). Also, BP's 'Beyond

**Exhibit 10.1** Differences between incremental and transformational change

| Incremental change | Transformational change |
| --- | --- |
| Management | Leadership |
| Doing things better or doing more of them | Doing things very differently or doing different things |
| Bottom-up | Top-down |
| Fundamental beliefs unaffected | Fundamental beliefs changed |
| Efficiency | Effectiveness |

*Source:* Adapted from R. D. Stacey (1996), *Strategic Management and Organisational Dynamics*, 2nd edn (London: Pitman).

Petroleum' strategy to transform itself towards sustainable business practice and develop alternative sources of energy is a good example of transformational change.

Transformational change is carried out by leaders of the multinational firm. Leaders are people who are concerned with effectiveness: they do the right things, they make policy. They act on the emotional and spiritual resources of the organization, dealing with its values, commitment, and aspirations (Bennis and Nanus 1985: 21). Kouzes and Posner (2007: xi) note that leadership is 'about the practices leaders use to transform values into actions, visions into realities, obstacles into innovations, separateness into solidarity, and risks into rewards. It's about a climate in which people turn challenging opportunities into remarkable successes.' At the global level, leadership involves 'the ability to inspire and influence the thinking, attitudes and behaviour of people from around the world' (Adler 1997: 236).

The major differences between the situations appropriate for incremental management and those suitable for transformational leadership can be seen by comparing the two lists in Exhibit 10.1. In general, transformational change will be a top-down process, initiated and possibly imposed by the top team.

---

**KEY CONCEPT**

Change management is the process by which a multinational firm obtains its current and future strategy. Two types of change can be recognized: *incremental change*, which takes place without disturbing fundamental organizational beliefs; and *transformational change*, which does change them. In general, carrying through incremental change typically requires management skills with support from the leaders of the multinational firm, whilst carrying out transformational change involves considerable leadership skills.

---

### 10.2.3 Types of change and national cultures

While all types of strategic change, small or large, incremental or radical, are to a varying degree difficult to manage, strategic change in multinational firms is much more difficult to manage than change in firms operating in a single country (Bamford 2006). This is because, in addition to the different stakeholders involved in the change process as demonstrated in the opening case, employees and management in different countries hold different managerial values and are used to different managerial practices.

Some of the differences between different countries are apparent and others are quite subtle. The national management culture is a product of the core values and beliefs that people espouse, ingrained attitudes and behaviours, and the norms of what is ethically acceptable and what is not. Because the psyche of national culture varies widely across cultures, leaders of multinational firms operating around the globe need to adapt their leadership styles to local circumstances during the process of change.

Kay (1995: 15) makes an interesting contrast between US and UK views on leadership and those of the rest of Europe. In the United States and the UK (and to some extent in France), the chief executive is seen as the master of the organization, and business success becomes, in effect, realizing the chief executive's vision. In Japan and most of the rest of Europe, senior executives are seen as the servants of the organization, and success is seen as maximizing the value of an organization's distinctive capabilities.

Harding's (1996: 111) study of strategic change of Lucas Car Braking Systems in Britain and Germany found that during the process of change, the British workforce were stuck in what he called the 'bad practice learning phase'; by contrast, the German workforce were more receptive to learning in the post-shock phase. As a result, management used a different method of change in the two sites. In the case of the British workforce, Harding argues that to overcome the inherent resistance to change, there is a need for a shock or transformational change. In contrast, the German workforce's acceptance of the need for change makes the gradual or incremental change strategy more appropriate. That is, compatibility between the type of change and the cultural values and management practices of the workforce is a necessary ingredient for the success of the change strategy.

### 10.2.4 Organizational change and national culture

Over the years, a number of studies have been carried out to identify the characteristics of national cultures and how they shape managers attitudes, and influence the process of change. These studies found significant differences in key leadership capabilities across cultures and proposed a number of typologies categorizing the different types and styles of leadership. Below, we discuss how national cultures affect behaviours in organizations and influence the process of change.

According to Geert Hofstede, national cultures are differentiated along five key dimensions: individualism–collectivism, power distance, uncertainty avoidance, masculinity-femininity, and time orientation. Hofstede argues that the five dimensions are mirrored in the behaviour of employees in the workplace, the way they interact with their superiors and subordinates, and the behaviour that is held in high esteem by subordinates (Hofstede 1980, 1983; Tang and Koveos 2008). We discuss each of the five dimensions in turn below.

**Individualism–collectivism** Refers to the degree to which individuals in a society are more concerned with one's own needs and interests, as opposed to group-oriented needs and interests. Individuals in cultures high on the individualism dimension, such as the US and Western Europe, have the tendency to be concerned with their own interests, goals, and needs and take responsibility for the consequences of their own behaviour. They feel good about themselves when they perform well and accomplish something and guilty when they underperform. In these cultures, people think of the self and immediate family and the right of the individuals are often of higher importance than that of the group. Therefore, in the management of change, leaders need to emphasize the short-term impact of the change on employees' immediate concerns, such as job security, rather than the long-term implications on the wider community. That is, in individualist culture, people care more about how the change affects *them* rather that its wider impact on their community (see Exhibit 10.2).

**Exhibit 10.2** National culture and management of change

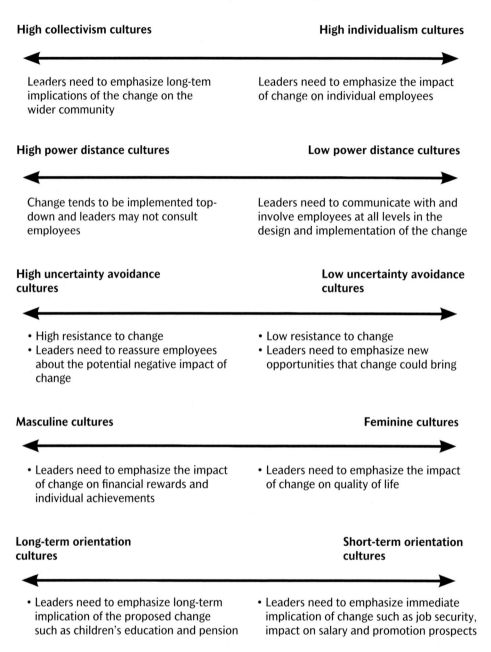

**High collectivism cultures**                                          **High individualism cultures**

Leaders need to emphasize long-tem
implications of the change on the
wider community

Leaders need to emphasize the impact
of change on individual employees

**High power distance cultures**                                      **Low power distance cultures**

Change tends to be implemented top-
down and leaders may not consult
employees

Leaders need to communicate with and
involve employees at all levels in the
design and implementation of the change

**High uncertainty avoidance
cultures**                                                                      **Low uncertainty avoidance
cultures**

• High resistance to change
• Leaders need to reassure employees
  about the potential negative impact of
  change

• Low resistance to change
• Leaders need to emphasize new
  opportunities that change could bring

**Masculine cultures**                                                          **Feminine cultures**

• Leaders need to emphasize the impact
  of change on financial rewards and
  individual achievements

• Leaders need to emphasize the impact
  of change on quality of life

**Long-term orientation
cultures**                                                                          **Short-term orientation
cultures**

• Leaders need to emphasize long-term
  implication of the proposed change
  such as children's education and pension

• Leaders need to emphasize immediate
  implication of change such as job security,
  impact on salary and promotion prospects

Individuals in cultures high on the collectivist dimension, such as Asian and Middle Eastern
countries, have the tendency to be concerned with the group's interest, goals, and needs. They
tend to put the duty to the group before their own needs and interests. This is best described by
the Japanese proverb, 'The nail that stands up gets pounded back down.' This is different from

reward for behaviour in individualistic cultures, where individual success is rewarded, as put by Freedman (2005): 'In China or Japan the nail that stands up gets hammered, while in Silicon Valley the nail that stands up drives a Ferrari and has stock options.' Interpersonal relationships between group members is highly emphasized and individuals try to avoid behaviour, such as open confrontation, that disrupts or destroys the harmony of the group. Individuals in collectivist cultures feel good about themselves when the group accomplish something. They tend to consider the repercussions of their actions on the wider group, and how their actions are reflected upon by their group members before they act. Therefore, in the management of change, leaders need to emphasize the long-term implications of the change on the wider community rather than the immediate impact on individual employees (see Exhibit 10.2).

**Power distance**  Power distance refers to the extent to which individuals in a society accept and expect an unequal distribution of power. Given that in all countries power is not shared equally, the power distance dimension ranks countries from high to low. In low power distance cultures, such as the Netherlands and the US, individuals are assumed to be relatively equal, and the social status between those who hold power and those who do not is small. People may refer to low power distance societies as egalitarian cultures. In these cultures, organizations tend to be flat and more decentralized, and subordinates expect to be consulted in the decision-making process. Also, subordinates feel comfortable to challenge their managers' directives. The ideal leader in a low power distance society is expected to be a 'resourceful democrat'. Resourceful democrats communicate and consult widely with, and show confidence and trust in, the people they work with. Therefore, during the change process, leaders need to communicate with and involve employees at all levels in the design and implementation of the change (see Exhibit 10.2).

In high power distance cultures, such as India and China, a high level of unequal distribution of power is accepted as legitimate and even expected. There is a high degree of inter-personal inequality between employees at different levels in the organizational hierarchy. Organizations in high power distance societies tend to have many layers of management. Also, people are status-conscious and, as a result, the chain of command within the organization is considered important. The ideal leader in high power distance culture is a benevolent autocrat. They are authoritarian but charismatic leaders. Benevolent autocrats act as superior father figures. They make all key decisions but tend to explain to their subordinates the need for such decisions. They tend to be controlling, less delegating, and difficult to approach. Leaders in high power distance do not feel comfortable with their employees challenging their directives, even if they believe that they are right. Upward criticism is unacceptable and, as a result, subordinates are often fearful of voicing their concerns or expressing disagreement with their line manager. Therefore, in high power distance cultures, change tends to be implemented top-down and employees may not be consulted in the process (see Exhibit 10.2).

**Uncertainty avoidance**  Uncertainty avoidance refers to the extent to which members of a society tolerate uncertainty. In high uncertainty avoidance societies, such as Japan, people prefer well-defined rules and structures and reject deviant ideas and behaviours. People in these societies are uncomfortable with the unknown and take steps to alleviate the unpredictability. Here, people tend to remain longer, and sometimes for life, within their organizations. However, while change might not be welcome in high uncertainty avoidance cultures, it is unavoidable (Zhou et al. 2006). Leaders in these societies are expected to be cautious and orderly. Change in these cultures tends to be highly resisted, and leaders must therefore spend a significant amount of time to manage the resistance (see Exhibit 10.2).

In contrast, in low uncertainty avoidance societies, such as Sweden and Australia, people are comfortable with uncertainty and ambiguity is tolerated and change to the status quo is often embraced. In these societies, people are not content with stable ways of doing things, and resent highly structured rules and procedures which are often seen as rigid red tape bureaucracy. The ideal leader in low uncertainty avoidance is a transformational leader, who tolerates risk and encourages more innovation. For example, a study of leadership styles in a multinational reported that, while Australian employees emphasized the ability to drive cultural change as a key leadership capability, Japanese and Korean employees believed that maintaining harmony was a key leadership capability (Yeung and Ready 1995). Change in low uncertainty avoidance cultures is resisted less than in cultures high in uncertainty avoidance (see Exhibit 10.2).

**Masculinity–femininity** This dimension bipolarizes societies into masculine and feminine cultures. It refers to the degree to which people in a society see themselves as assertive and interested in material things as opposite to being caring and more interested in equality and the well-being of their members. Hofstede (1980: 261) noted that:

> *masculinity is the opposite of femininity; together, they form one of the dimensions of national cultures. Masculinity stands for a society which social gender roles are dearly distinct: men are supposed to be more modest, tender, and concerned with the quality of life . . . femininity stands for a society where gender roles overlap: both men and women are supposed to be modest, tender and concerned with the quality of life.*

In high feminine societies such as Nordic countries, people tend not to show off their achievements—as individual achievements are often suspect—putting the quality of life, equality in society, and relationships with people in the group, particularly the weak, before material achievements (Hofstede 1983). In contrast, in high masculine societies such as the US, the 'public hero is the successful achiever, the superman' (Hofstede 1983: 83). Therefore, leaders need to put more emphasis on how change might impact on the quality of life in high feminine countries and more emphasis on how change might impact on financial rewards and individual achievements in high masculine countries (see Exhibit 10.2).

**Long-term orientation** This dimension looks at whether people in a society adopt a long- or short-term orientation in their social and business interactions. In long-term orientation societies, such as China, Japan, Korea, and Taiwan, in order to be thrifty, postpone short-term gains for long-term payoff, and approach business and social interactions with a long-term frame of mind. They aim to establish long-term business relationships rather than have short-term transactions. They may overlook short-term benefits for the sake of safeguarding ongoing long-term relationships. In short-term orientation societies, such as the US and UK, people put more emphasis on short-term transactions and immediate gain or loss from the interaction. Therefore, leaders need to put more emphasis on the long-term implications of the proposed change in long-term orientation countries and emphasize more short-term issues in short-term orientation cultures (see Exhibit 10.2).

## 10.3 **People involved in the change process**

There are likely to be several individuals or groups of individuals involved with any one change process—people who move in and out of important roles as the change progresses. Davenport (1993) has identified several players in the change process:

- The advocate, who proposes change.
- The sponsor, who legitimizes change.
- The targets, who are the people who undergo change.
- The change agents, who implement change.
- The process owner, who is typically the most senior member of the group targeted for change.

This chapter will mainly focus on change agents and targets. How change affects the people who undergo change will be considered in section 10.3.2.

### 10.3.1 **The change agent**

A change agent is the individual or group that has the specific role of implementing change in an organization. While one person is often the source of an idea or invention, a team is generally required to innovate, and thus the change agent very often leads a team. In many cases, the change agent (or agents) is an employee of the organization and is given special responsibilities. For example, the closing case study shows how Western managers at LG were asked to restructure several key functions and help LG reposition its brand globally. Often, however, external consultants may be recruited to effect change. In international operations, the change agent may often be an expatriate. Sometimes, the change agent is a consulting firm, such as the Canadian IT consultants, SolCorp, who offer specialist and change-management skills in corporate financial services, employing a group of North American and British specialists who operate worldwide.

If the change agent is the chief executive, some of the problems with strategic change management will disappear or be significantly reduced; for example, in many situations, there should be less difficulty in obtaining the resources required to bring about change. However, many chief executives do not have the time to be closely involved with any one specific change programme and some do not have the inclination; thus, they delegate the task to others. Change agents need not be a member of the top management team (the main board of directors at head office), but they are almost always managers. They have a particularly difficult task because (to paraphrase Machiavelli 1993) the innovator may face a lot of resistance from those who have done well under old conditions and little support from those

**Exhibit 10.3** The requirements of a change agent

**Relating to objectives**

1. Sensitivity to the way changes in senior personnel, management perceptions, and business conditions affect the goals of the change programme.
2. Clarity in defining objectives.
3. Flexibility in responding to changing conditions.

**Political awareness**

1. Being aware of potential coalitions and understanding their significance.
2. Continually ensuring that more senior management are backing the team. Continuing senior management commitment and involvement is of overriding importance.
3. Balancing conflicting goals and perceptions.
4. Being aware of the extent of their own power.

**Sensitivity**

1. Being able to empathize with people undergoing a change process.
2. Sensitivity to the organizational context in terms of where the forces for change and inhibiting forces might come from, and to the style of change process that will be acceptable.

**Communication and negotiation**

1. Networking skills to establish and maintain the appropriate contacts within and outside the organization.
2. Communication skills to inform team members, superiors, and networkers of progress and needs.
3. Ability to enrol others in plans and ideas.
4. Negotiating with key individuals within the organization for resources.

**Team-building and leadership**

1. Team-building abilities, to identify key potential team members, enrol them, and motivate them to ensure they work as a team.
2. Team management, to define team members' responsibilities and delegate authority accordingly.
3. Team leadership, to provide a vision for the future.

**Individual characteristics**

1. Enthusiasm for change.
2. Tolerance of ambiguity: being able to work effectively and efficiently in an uncertain environment.

*Source:* Adapted from D. Buchanan and D. Boddy (1992), *The Expertise of the Change Agent: Public Performance and Backstage Activity* (New York: Prentice Hall), 92–3. Reprinted with permission of Prentice Hall.

who may benefit under new conditions. The requirements of a change agent are set out in Exhibit 10.3.

## 10.3.2 The role of subordinate and subsidiary managers

Subordinate and subsidiary managers, particularly middle managers, play a very significant role in the management of change. Hampden-Turner and Trompenaars (1993) make the point that in the US, the top team specifies the strategy in a very precise way: top management knows, or thinks it knows, what is required. This way of operating is often carried over into the international sphere, with the US head office stipulating what is required for their foreign subsidiary managers to carry out. In such a situation the foreign, subordinate managers are the implementers of closely speci-fied change: their role is to make the resources available, make plans to implement the change, and control costs and resource usage. In such a situation, subordinate managers are likely to be seen as inhibitors of change, especially as the precise specification of the change developed by the top team has probably been made without the full knowledge of their subsidiary's situation and capabilities.

In contrast to US managers, Japanese senior management take a less precise approach to strategy. Hampden-Turner and Trompenaars (1993) illustrate this by contrasting the Japanese approach—where the senior managers would say to middle managers, 'We are going to make a microprocessor—what kind of microprocessor would you like the firm to make?'—with the US approach, in which senior managers would tell middle managers, 'This is the new micro-processor we want.'

Nonaka and Takeuchi (1995) describe the role of the middle manager in the more flexible Japanese situation. Such managers take the broad vision of top managers and combine it with the detailed, often tacit, knowledge of front-line employees, such as salespeople and factory operatives, to make the vision a reality. The middle managers thus have a creative, pivotal role in modern business—much more than the downsizers and lean-management gurus would have us believe. However, it is not apparent that this domestic way of operating can be trans-planted into production facilities in other countries.

One problem that middle managers have as the initiators of change is in gaining the ear of top management to obtain the resources they need to support the changes. Another problem is that technical people have difficulty in finding ways to translate their technical ideas into a form that allows senior management to evaluate the idea (Hampden-Turner and Trompenaars 1993: 98). This problem is particularly acute if expatriate specialists have to liaise with nationals in a language in which they are not fluent.

---

**KEY CONCEPT**

A change agent is the individual or group who has the specific role of implementing change in an organization. A change agent very often leads a team. Middle managers have a pivotal role in the change process. In Japanese companies, they take the broad vision of top managers and combine it with the detailed, often tacit, knowledge of front-line employees, to make the vision a reality. In many traditional Western firms, the middle manager is simply asked to implement detailed, centrally decided requirements.

---

## 10.4 **The change process**

### 10.4.1 **A model of the change process**

Change agents are concerned with initiating and implementing both incremental and transformational change. Both types of change process can be considered to involve three phases: unfreezing, adjustment, and refreezing (Schein 1947).

**Unfreezing**

The change process begins with a loosening up of the hold of established behaviour and/or beliefs, because there is a feeling that change is needed and feasible. Three ingredients must be present to some degree for unfreezing to take place:

- Serious discomfort, because there is evidence that does not support the current ways of thinking and/or doing. An example here is SVW's erosion of market share in the early 2000s.

- The connection of this discomforting information to important goals and ideals. An example is SVW's aim to regain the top spot in the Chinese auto market.

- Enough 'psychological safety' to support action. It is important that a group is able to see the possibility of resolving the issue without the group having to be disbanded or dismembered. An example is Volkswagen's actions to support the IJV to regain its market share.

If certain levels of profit and customer satisfaction are important organizational goals, two examples of discomforting information would be decreased profits and increased customer complaints. It is a common trick of politicians to invoke an external threat—real or not—to force changes in values and behaviours, and this device is available to managers. Nonaka and Takeuchi (1995) recount how senior Japanese managers put their middle managers under severe pressure by presenting them with very stiff challenges, in order to force change. A new leader with a new vision may be a catalyst for change, because he/she may see the major issues in a way that allows for their resolution: the new leader is providing the psychological safety net that the group will survive, keeping its integrity intact. However, without a period of prior discomfort, it may well be that the visionary leader will not be listened to: people are only ready to listen when they feel something is wrong and/or they could do better. An expatriate transplant into an ailing subsidiary has a greater chance of success than one joining a successfully led operation, since in the former case, the employees expect—and, indeed, may positively welcome—change.

**Adjustment**

Following unfreezing, adjustment can then take place. The deeper the cultural change being sought, the more difficult it is to bring about adjustment. However, the deeper the change, the more lasting and fundamental the adjustment is likely to be—and the more general are the consequences. If behavioural adjustment is coerced, the adjustment is unlikely to last when the coercion is removed, as shown by the inability of communism to survive the totalitarian regimes that coerced whole nations for decades.

As well as involving new types of behaviour by individuals, the adjustments made will generally include organizational changes, such as the implementation of new control systems and modifications to the way people are rewarded.

### Refreezing

Following adjustment, the new ways of thought and behaviour need to be locked into place in the process termed 'refreezing'. For refreezing to take place, confirmatory information needs to be provided to show that the new behaviours and/or beliefs more closely mirror the perceived reality. If such information is not forthcoming, then coping with the existing situation, together with a search for a new approach, will continue. The importance of confirmatory evidence means that the managers should ensure that it is provided. One way of doing this, is to ensure that the change programme includes some quick hits, so that some success comes early in the programme, rather than there being an extended period of uncertainty when success is unclear. Once sufficient confirmatory information has been gained, then the situation will stabilize, until further uncomfortable information triggers off the whole unfreezing–adjustment–refreezing process once more.

The unfreezing–adjustment–refreezing process can be observed in successful transformational change of various multinational firms. For instance, when Carlos Ghosn became the chief executive of Nissan in 1999, he purposely set out to unfreeze old practices. A key part of his approach was to use repeatedly the example of a recently failed Japanese bank to illustrate to Nissan's employees the dangers of not changing; he also made sure to communicate the difficult situation of the company to the employees in order to increase their willingness to change their behaviour. Adjustment took place thanks to using methods such as performance evaluations and a restructuring of the organization. Finally, refreezing was helped through Ghosn's relatively quick success in returning Nissan to profitability, which demonstrated to the employees the value of the changes made.

---

### KEY CONCEPT

Change management requires three phases: unfreezing, adjustment, and refreezing. The deeper the cultural change being sought, the more difficult it is to bring about adjustment. However, the deeper the change, the more lasting and fundamental the adjustment is likely to be.

---

### 10.4.2 People's reaction to change

When individuals have low psychological ownership in the proposed change, they typically resist its implementation and, as a result, may bring a well-thought-out strategy to its knees. Generally, almost everyone feels some sort of stress when facing and enacting change. An important requirement for the change agent is to be able to empathize with people who are undergoing change and to manage those individuals' self-esteem to reduce resistance to change. Esteem will suffer in many cases because skills will be devalued before other skills are fully learned. Part of the empathy is to understand the phases that affect

require different styles of change management. The appropriate style of change management depends on four factors:

- The magnitude of the change, and whether it is incremental or transformational.
- The fit of the organization to its environment.
- The time available for discussion.
- The support for change within the organization.

Depending on the above four factors, a firm may select a specific style of change management. Styles of change management differ considerably. Dunphy and Stace (1993: 905–20) have identified four such styles: participative evolution, forced evolution, charismatic transformation, and dictatorial transformation. These four styles are shown in Exhibit 10.5.

- **Participative evolution** is most appropriate for incremental change when an organization broadly matches its environment and only minor adjustments are required. It is also the appropriate response when there is a relatively poor strategic fit between the organization and its external business environment, but, when time is available for people to participate, and key individuals and groups favour change. The appropriate management style is collaborative or consultative. The **collaborative style** is one in which there is full input from all members of the group to the change required. A smaller level of participation occurs with the **consultative style**, where the people involved and affected by the proposed changes are asked for their views.

**Exhibit 10.5** Styles of change management

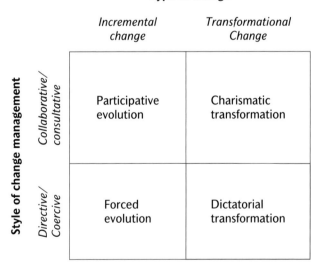

*Source:* Dunphy, D. D. and Stace, D. A. (1993), 'The strategic management of corporate change'. *Human Relations* 46(8): 905–18(p.908). Reprinted with permission of Sage Publications Ltd.

- **Forced evolution** is most appropriate for incremental change under similar conditions of organizational–environmental fit and time availability as for participative evolution. However, this is the appropriate approach when key interests oppose change. The appropriate management style is directive or coercive. A **directive style** is one whereby people are told what they are to do and they are reasonably happy with the changes, whilst a **coercive style** is one where people are not happy with the proposed changes and resist them.

- **Charismatic transformation** is most appropriate when there is a substantial mismatch between an organization and its environment, and when there is little time for extensive participation but there is support for radical change within the organization. The appropriate management style is collaborative or consultative.

- **Dictatorial transformation** is most appropriate when an organization does not match its environment, there is no time for extensive participation, and there is little or no support for radical change, but when radical change is vital for organizational well-being. When an organization is performing so badly that the chief executive is sacked, the new chief executive is often appointed to carry out a dictatorial transformation. The autocrat needs a clear vision of the organizational goals, but should let the people in the organization who know the operational details decide on the means of achieving it. The situation is like a ship in a storm: the captain knows the port they want to shelter in, but uses the expertise of the first mate to take the most appropriate course. The appropriate management style is directive or coercive.

---

**KEY CONCEPT**

Different styles of change management are likely to be appropriate at different times in an organization's existence, and the appropriate approach will not necessarily be the same for all parts of an organization.

---

## 10.6 Implementing change

Implementing change is never easy because of the inherent resistance to change within most organizations. But implementing change can be assisted through project teams and by moving people within the multinational firm.

### 10.6.1 Project teams

A project can be considered to be a set of processes aimed at achieving a firm objective within a specified timescale. Thus, the building of a new car production line would be a project; running that line would not. Project teams can play a key role in the management of change. For instance, project teams played a key role in Lufthansa's transformation from a state-owned airline on the verge of bankruptcy in 1992, to one of the most profitable airlines ten years later.

This transformation was made possible by the use of project teams, which reported directly to Lufthansa's chief executive and led the implementation of change strategies such as Programm 15 (to reduce the cost target for transporting one aircraft seat from 17.7 pfennig per kilometre to 15 pfennig between 1996–2001) and D-Check (another cost-cutting exercise from 2001).

The concern for rapid response has led to the demand for organizations to be flexible, able to cope with complexity, and be at ease with innovating and initiating change. Many years ago, Bennis (1969: 34) argued that one of the key descriptive terms for a flexible, organic organizational structure is that it is temporary. He claims that, 'these structures will be adaptive, rapidly-changing temporary systems. They will be project teams organized around problems to be solved by groups of relative strangers with diverse professional skills.' Very often, therefore, the project team will only exist for the duration of the project, being disbanded once the project is completed.

The use of project teams to tackle complex issues is widespread throughout business (Buchanan 1994; Bennis 1969: 34), so much so, that there is the view that management has become very much project-based management—at least for all managers when they are involved in change. This widespread use of project teams means that skill in project management has become one of the key requirements for managers.

One complication for project managers is the requirement to work with colleagues over whom they have no direct authority. This is particularly apparent when working internationally, when a project team is set up with people from several countries and/or involving several agencies. Another complication, as discussed earlier in this chapter, lies in the inclusion of individuals in the project team from units which have not empowered them to act on behalf of their unit and which require them to report back before anything can be agreed. This is a particular problem with some Asian cultures. There are individuals who expect to be fully consulted before others take action and introduce changes that will affect them (Anbari et al. 2004). The need for the project manager to be aware of the power they themselves have, and to use it appropriately, is crucial in these situations.

### 10.6.2 Moving people

One of the best ways of spreading ideas—and, by extension, best head office practice—is by moving people (Gupta and Govindarajan 2003). Moving people through the organization in a structured way is common in Germany and Japan, where an individual's career is framed by the firm rather than by professional qualifications (Lam 1998). When a person becomes a manager, they have a very wide knowledge of many aspects of the company and share a common mindset with other managers. Similarly, the composition of project teams can be designed so that the tacit knowledge generated and spread through team discussions will automatically be spread throughout the organization when the team members go back to their 'home' units and discuss what they have been doing.

Moving people can be a key part of a change strategy. For instance, Nissan's transformation from an unprofitable to a profitable multinational firm between 1999 and 2000 was greatly aided by moving people. One problem that Nissan faced in 1999, was that Japanese employees in functional departments failed to challenge existing work practices. So, Nissan set up nine cross-functional teams, each with line managers from different departments, to allow managers to see beyond functional responsibilities and to see how the success of their own department depended on cooperating with other departments. Learning about their business from a bird's-eye perspective allowed managers to be much more engaged in Nissan's change strategy.

### 10.6.3 **Expatriates**

One extreme variant of moving people is the use of expatriates—who will be defined here as professional or managerial personnel employed outside their home country on secondment to another part of the organization. This definition thus includes, not only the common relocation from a parent organization to one of its subsidiaries, but also the reverse move, and moves between subsidiaries. Thus, expatriates would include, for example, a French national seconded from the Paris head office to work in Vietnam, a Vietnamese seconded to Paris, and a Vietnamese sent to work in an affiliate in Algeria. Effective expatriates require an effective blend of good technical and good cross-cultural skills. There are many reasons for using expatriates in the implementation of change. The most obvious is that they are able to help implement new sophisticated technology or managerial practice at the subsidiary level. There is also the feeling of the parent that it will only be able to exercise appropriate control over its foreign subsidiaries if they are headed by someone whose first loyalty is to the firm, rather than to the host country and host nationals. In this respect, the expatriates are carriers of organizational culture. There is a considerable downside to the use of expatriates in the implementation of change. The cost of employing them can be considerable, especially if their transfer also means relocation of their family. Expatriates typically cost two or three times as much as the equivalent person in the parent country, and often very much more than a local person. The expatriate may be seen as simply a controller sent by the centre to keep an eye on the subsidiary, and resentment can build up. Being an expatriate is a difficult job, operating as they do at the interface between head office and the host organization. This requires them to be sensitive to other ways of working, and to be able to adapt to other social environments.

---

**KEY CONCEPT**

Implementing change can be assisted through project teams and through moving people within the multinational firm. A project team can be defined as a set of processes aimed at achieving a firm's objectives within a specified timescale.

---

## 10.7 **Communication issues**

### 10.7.1 **Difficulties in discussing issues linked to change**

It is generally important for the people who are affected by the change to discuss what the change means for them. The difficulty in discussing and debating change issues depends on the circumstances.

People are much readier to debate and discuss some things than others. This hinges on which ring of the cultural onion is being worked upon. Bowman (1995: 4–12) has described these as 'zones of debate'. People are reasonably happy discussing norms of behaviour but less so discussing values. Values may be discussed, but generally this would be outside formal meetings, as values often concern vested interests and personal reputations. But, to make major progress, there is a need to 'surface' the fundamental organizational beliefs and challenge them in order to build a shared vision (Senge 1990: 7–23). In general, however, the fundamental organizational beliefs are not discussed, often because they are never surfaced. The greater the feeling of crisis, however, the more people may feel that they must challenge some of the fundamental organizational beliefs, since these beliefs are failing them.

### 10.7.2 The role of language

The difficulties that people have in talking about change is made worse if individuals have different verbal fluency, and, obviously, this is particularly marked if one or more parties must use a language other than their mother tongue. Feely (2003: 206–35) describes the problems, from misunderstandings through to loss of face in group discussions and loss of power and authority. Neal (1998) interviewed 174 foreign managers working in the UK, and found that working with their UK colleagues in English was frustrating to them and that the language barrier made them feel like outsiders.

Although the number of active languages is shrinking rapidly, there are approximately 5,000 languages in the world (Hearn and Button 1994). Thus, an organization operating in many parts of the globe will have to accommodate many languages.

Whilst English is firmly established as the most popular language for business (some firms, such as the Swedish–Swiss engineering company, ABB, use it as their corporate language), its continuing ascendancy is not assured. Feely (2003: 206–35) takes the view that the dying out of many languages will benefit regional languages rather than English. He points out that the primacy of English in the second part of the twentieth century was due in large measure to technology: people needed to learn English to use computing and telecommunications and to enjoy TV and films. Technology has now advanced, so that low-cost translations are possible, and so people can use their own language and lose much less. He believes that the number of people learning English as a second language will peak within the next ten years and then start to fall.

Thus, in many parts of the world in future, English will no longer be the obvious language of business. Multinational managers may well have to be multilingual.

### 10.7.3 Business implications

The lack of fluency in one language has serious implications for conducting international business. It will make it harder to communicate between subsidiaries and the centre. This is likely to mean that head office centralizes decision-making, but with well-defined local autonomy.

As early as 1975, Johanson and Wiedersheim-Paul (1975: 411–32) found that firms preferred to establish their first foreign subsidiaries in countries that were 'linguistically close'. This finding is reflected in the fact that UK companies have established subsidiaries in countries such as Australia and New Zealand, physically located far from the mother country, rather than in the much nearer Continental Europe.

The mode of entry used to establish a subsidiary also varies with the 'linguistic closeness' of the two countries involved. Kogat and Singh (1988: 411–32) found that the entry mode into the US favoured by overseas companies differed, depending on this. UK and Canadian firms strongly preferred acquisition to joint ventures, as did the Netherlands and Germany, which both have a strong English-language orientation. In contrast, France and Japan, not noted for their English-language skills, preferred to enter through joint ventures.

### 10.7.4 **Overcoming language problems**

If an audit of an organization's language capability indicates a lack of competence, one obvious approach is to employ professional translators and interpreters. Whilst this can go some way to overcoming language problems, it can only go so far—it is really only of value in more formal situations, and tends to be expensive. More radical solutions are to establish customized training programmes for affected staff—as Volkswagen has done—but these involve a long-term commitment. An alternative is to adopt a single corporate language. The Swedish firm, Electrolux, the German firm, Siemens, the German–US firm, DaimlerChrysler, and the Italian firm, Olivetti, have all selected English as the language for formal communication. Nestlé has settled on two corporate languages—French and English. Using a corporate language does have the advantage of easing the maintenance of technical literature, helping with informal communications across national boundaries, and helping to diffuse a corporate ethos.

Even if a multinational firm chooses a single language in which to communicate, individuals within it typically bring with them their own sociocultural expectations to interpret and make sense of what is being said. Therefore, leaders need to be aware of their inherent ways of communicating and potential interpretations—or misinterpretations—by employees from different cultures. For instance, the differences between directness and indirectness in communicating may be interpreted differently in different countries. In some cultures, such as the Middle East, people prefer indirect ways of communicating and consider directness as rude and impolite. In contrast, in the US, people expect leaders to communicate using direct language and consider directness as evidence of clarity of thought.

Adopting a corporate language will do little to ease the language barriers with outside parties, however—with buyers, suppliers, and government agencies. Where such interaction is subtle and important, it may well be that managers with the appropriate language skills will be recruited. However, such personnel are in short supply, and therefore difficult to recruit. Those that are recruited are then special creatures—and become very powerful 'gatekeepers'. Staff will be tempted to bypass a formal chain of command if by doing so they can get access to the people they want to.

---

**KEY CONCEPT**

Fluency of language is an important aspect of successful communication between people, especially during stressful periods such as when change is being discussed and implemented. Language training and the adoption of a single corporate language are means of reducing the barrier that imperfect language skills can present to communication.

---

## 10.8 Negotiation with outside parties

A change strategy calls for considerable negotiation with people and groups within the organization, a very important area for negotiation is that with external bodies—customers, suppliers, and government agencies.

Management must pay attention to the fact that individuals from different cultures tend to adopt different conflict resolution strategies. Members of collectivist cultures, for instance, perceive and manage conflict differently from those in individualistic cultures. While people in collectivist cultures tend to avoid open conflict, people in individualistic countries tend to face it head-on. And when conflict does emerge after all efforts have been exhausted to avoid it, people in collectivist countries tend to resolve it in inner circles before it becomes serious enough to justify public involvement. Only when repeated efforts within the inner circle fail to resolve the conflict is the conflict likely to be resolved by top management in a top-down fashion (Ting-Toomey 1988).

Despite cultural differences, some negotiation frameworks are generic and can be used across cultures. One such framework that takes culture into consideration is Graham's (1985) five-step negotiation process.

1. Preparation. At this stage, the managers should learn as much as feasible about the people with whom they will be negotiating—their cultural background and what this means for negotiation, their negotiating style and what they wish to achieve at the end of the process.

2. 'Getting to know you.' This stage is where the parties learn about the personalities involved prior to getting down to the negotiation. It is relationship-building. The so-called 'low-context countries', such as those of northern Europe, the US, and Canada, tend to abbreviate this stage and proceed straight to stage 3—the real business. In 'high-context' cultures, such as most Asian, Latin American, and Arabic countries, it is considered very important to build up personal relationships and trust. It is no use people from low-context cultures trying to abbreviate this stage: people from high-context cultures are doing business with an individual rather than with an organization.

3. Task-related exchange of information. This is the stage where the parties concerned state their positions, providing the information to support their case. Negotiators from some

cultures—particularly Chinese, Russians, and Latin Americans—state an extreme initial position. North Americans tend to open negotiations with a position fairly close to what they will be happy with.

Negotiators from low-context cultures will see this stage as a free flow of information, asking questions and giving answers readily. The Chinese tend to ask a lot of very detailed and specific questions, but in a rather vague way. The Russians tend to be very well prepared in the technical details, and pose questions to elicit technical details. At the end of this stage, all parties should know the fundamentals of the proposition being put before them.

4.  Persuasion. At this stage, the fundamentals of the proposition are further explored, with the aim of changing initial positions. This stage has both formal and informal sides. The context is quite important, with each party deploying tactics to persuade the other parties to accede. Tactics that might be employed are calculated delays, expressions of time constraints, the presence of other partners in the proposal who could replace one of the parties, and so on. In such situations, body language provides important clues to the experienced negotiator.

5.  Agreement. At this stage, it is likely that both parties give ground somewhat. The American and North European style is to move incrementally towards an agreement, finalizing a portion of the proposal, and then moving on to the next piece. In contrast, Asians and Latin Americans are more holistic negotiators, going back and forth over the ground and only agreeing the full deal at the end of negotiations.

## 10.9 Summary

Change is a journey, not an event, and on this journey organizations face two types of strategic change—incremental and transformational. In general, incremental change is a managerial issue, while transformational change involves leadership. The general change process of unfreezing–adjustment–freezing is the same for both types of change, but the part of the culture that is changed is likely to differ. Three 'zones of debate' are recognized, each differing in the ease with which they are open to discussion.

People facing change often go through five phases as they discard the old and internalize the new: denial, defence, discarding, adaptation, and internalizing. It is important for the change agent to recognize the stages that an individual has reached and to empathize with the difficulties he or she may be having. The appropriate style of change management depends on four factors: the magnitude of the change; the fit of the organization to its environment; the time available for discussion; and the support for change within the organization.

The role of the change agent is a demanding one, with special emphasis on interpersonal and political skills. In particular, they must be adept at recognizing blocking tactics used by people who are resistant to change. Whilst it is possible within an organization to operate by diktat, negotiation is a fundamental part of any change process involving outside people and agencies. To understand the different ways in which people negotiate is thus vital for success. Communication between individuals and groups is vitally important in the change process, and in that process, language fluency is very significant.

## 📖 Key readings

- B. Senior (2005), *Organisational Change*, 3rd edn (London: Prentice Hall) is a good introductory book to key theories and concepts of organizational change.

- J. P. Kotter (1996), *Leading Change* (Cambridge, MA: Harvard Business School); and Buchanan and Boddy (1992) contain much useful material on the roles of leader-managers in change programmes. Kotter's book is written for managers and is practical rather than academic in emphasis.

- Chapters 4 and 5 of Nonaka and Takeuchi (1995) describe knowledge creation through project teams in Japanese companies.

- Carnall (2003) fully covers the way in which people react to the stresses and opportunities of change.

## 💬 Discussion questions

1. The strategic management environment may be characterized as chaotic, complex, dynamic, and turbulent—all generally increasing the level of uncertainty facing managers. How might changes in environmental characteristics affect the approach taken to global strategic change management?

2. How do you think the attributes of a change agent would differ across cultures?

3. One of the key challenges of strategic change across cultures is creating and managing global teams to design and manage teams. List and discuss the key attributes of a successful global team.

4. Multinational firms cannot use a 'one size fits all' approach when managing change in different countries. Discuss this statement.

## Closing case study LG global rebranding

LG, a 60-year-old producer of electronics and telecommunications products, is South Korea's second largest conglomerate and operates in over eighty countries. The company has recently embarked on an ambitious global repositioning strategy in order to compete with its South Korean rival, Samsung Electronics Co. The repositioning strategy started when Kim Ssang-Su took over as CEO in October 2003. Kim's strategy was simple: to turn LG from a white goods corporation that imitates others, into a digital trendsetter. His target was to make LG among the world's top three home electronics players by 2010. Soon after taking power, the new boss ordered LG's three main divisions—mobile phone, appliances, and digital display—to improve their productivity by 30%.

To make sure that all LG managers sang from the same hymn sheet, in 2004, LG gathered over 250 of its top management from around the world to a resort in the Korean city of Jaechon for a two-day strategy teamwork workshop. LG's management used the opportunity to hammer in its new global strategy of making LG a global brand. In 2004, LG commercialized the world's first 55-inch all-in-one LCD TV and 71-inch plasma TV. And by 2005, LG became the fourth largest supplier of the mobile handset market worldwide and developed a number of mobile phone applications and parts.

Nam Young joined LG in 2007 as CEO and chairman. He soon realized that the old ways of thinking were not changing fast enough to help it achieve its new strategy. LG needed to inject new blood and hired a number of Western managers to shake up its stodgy image.

*BusinessWeek* reported that Nam Yong and his Irish chief marketing officer, Dermot Boden, who worked for major corporations such as IBM, Hewlett-Packard (HP), Unilever, and Procter & Gamble, had several 'stormy strategy meetings', where tempers flared. Untypical of Korean managers, Nam realized the benefits of such heated debates and arguments and reportedly asked Boden, 'Why don't we argue more often?' Nam often commented that, 'It's usually through debate that great ideas arise.' In a country renowned for saving face, indirect communication, and dislike for open confrontation, it is reported that Western and Korean managers had heated arguments about how to implement the new LG strategy.

The diversification of the top management team was a critical part of LG's new vision. To become a global brand, LG had to have a globally mixed management team and embrace different management values. Soon after taking the top job at LG, Nam instructed headhunters to lure top talents from around the world to join the company. By 2008, foreign managers represented a quarter of LG's top management team.

In an interview with CNN, Yong reported that,

Just Korean talent itself is not sufficient enough, so I have to attract a best in class global talent into our organization, so that they can feel comfortable working in this environment. This means that English has to be a common language in our company going forward. So me speaking English is very, very important to encourage people to speak out with bad English instead of good Korean.

At the end of this recruitment programme, several key functions such as human resources, purchasing, and marketing were managed by foreign managers.

maturity stage of the life cycle, however, firms switch their attention from product innovation to process innovation.

## 11.2.2 Innovation and competitive advantage

In many industries, product innovation is a viable means of keeping one step ahead of your rivals and gaining a competitive advantage, albeit a temporary one. The life cycle model shows us that, in any particular product or service market, there is likely to be a relatively greater emphasis on product or process innovation at any one time. At the same time, since product innovation is a principal source of differentiation in many sectors and industries, the relative emphasis on product innovation in any particular market will further depend on the specific characteristics of the market concerned. Product innovation has assumed a top priority of US-based food manufacturer, Heinz, which has launched over 200 products since 2007. The company recognizes the importance of innovation in generating new sales, and currently approximately 11% of total company sales derive from new products introduced in the last three years, with this percentage expected to rise further. The company's global presence implies that product innovation opportunities also arise from adapting existing products to local needs in new geographic markets. For example, Heinz's success in Asian markets (particularly in Indonesia) with its ABC soy sauce brand, partly stems from the fact that the firm added a new pouring cap for the soy sauce bottle, including the introduction of lighter plastic pouches, acknowledging that the majority of Indonesians do not transport their groceries home in a car.

Product innovation often provides a valuable but temporary means of gaining competitive advantage, particularly where the barriers to imitation are low. From its origins as a low-cost manufacturer of bicycles for other leading brands such as America's Schwinn, Taiwan-based Giant is now one of the world's largest bicycle manufacturers, producing on average 460,000 units per month. The firm is also one of the few large-scale manufacturers able to invest in R&D and manufacture frames and forks out of technologically sophisticated alloys and carbon fibre. Product innovation, however, provides Giant only a limited time-based advantage, as there are effectively no barriers to entry in the industry and competition is intense since firms tend to purchase competitors' frames and forks as components for use in their own bikes. At the end of 2008, Giant revealed that it was about to distribute a new innovation, designed to appeal to urban commuters in particular—a frame containing built-in lightweight shock absorbers. The firm aimed to keep the design a secret prior to launch, being aware that such innovations are inevitably copied within a year.

Given the importance of innovation in gaining and maintaining competitive advantage, are some types of firms better at innovating than others? New firms are widely considered to be strong innovators. As our opening case study shows, Google, which was set up only in 1998, is already ranked second in the S&P/BusinessWeek Global Innovation Index which lists the top twenty five most innovative companies around the globe. Established firms, in contrast, are often less free to innovate in the way that they want to. Where innovation is 'disruptive' and does not build on existing technologies, established firms are less likely to devote the financial and human resources required to develop opportunities in relation to these new disruptive technologies. In fact, this has come to be known as the *innovator's dilemma*. In a study of the evolution of the disk drive industry, it was found that at each key stage of product innovation (and disruptive technological advancement), those firms which were least successful were the established firms which were concerned about the initial risk of lower margins and alienating existing customers (Christensen 1997).

Overall, whether new or established firms are better at innovating depends on the specific circumstances. Cross-industry research tends to show that product innovation at the time of new market entry tends to build on new knowledge rather than existing industry knowledge with new firms as the innovators and pioneers of the new market. Over time, however, innovation assumes a more incremental development trajectory. During the introduction and growth stages of the life cycle, therefore, most innovations are derived from new firms rather than established firms. In contrast, later in the life cycle, most innovations shift to information gained from experience in production by existing firms. New firms therefore, are not necessarily better at innovating than established firms, but research shows that different types of entrant are suited to specific types of innovation (Audretsch 1991).

Established firms are likely to have a relative advantage over new firms when technological innovation is continuous (and not disruptive) related to progress along a technological path (Dosi 1982). Similarly, established firms are likely to have a relative advantage when innovation is competence-enhancing, building on existing resources and capabilities.

In contrast, new firms are better placed to take advantage of technological innovations which are disruptive and other types of competence-destroying innovation, i.e., where existing capabilities do not retain value (Anderson and Tushman 1991). The origins of the US television industry show that the most successful firms entering this industry were existing radio producers, i.e., firms which benefited from both relevant experience and complementary capabilities (Klepper and Simons 2000). Similarly, the development of new online markets at the end of the 1990s showed that the relative success of new or established entrants related primarily to whether entrants had the relevant capabilities to compete and, thus, whether innovation was competence-enhancing or competence-destroying. For example, established firms are some of the most successful entrants in online grocery markets. Given that the Internet represents only a sales or order channel, existing resources and capabilities are complementary to the new business model since the goods being sold require physical delivery and leverage the firm's existing infrastructure and value chain activities. Conversely, many successful innovations have been pioneered by start-up firms such as Google, which developed an entirely new, faster, and more accurate way of searching on the World Wide Web with a new business model to match.

In some cases, however, the main barrier to innovation is not the lack of capabilities, but the inability of managers to conceive of the change required—what is otherwise known as *cognitive inertia*. Although film manufacture is essentially a chemicals business, both Kodak and Polaroid, US camera film manufacturers, were, nevertheless, able to develop the technological capabilities to enter and compete in the digital imaging market. Kodak spent nearly ten years before completing its transition to digital imaging before it announced towards the end of 2003 that the company would no longer invest in its film manufacture business and that it was going to invest US$3 billion in emerging digital technologies. The CEO, Daniel Carp, argued that the ongoing decline in traditional film markets left Kodak no choice but to cut the dividend by 72% and pour its resources into digital.

While Kodak was following a dual strategy for some time, the challenge of coming to terms with a digital future was more difficult for Polaroid. Polaroid's senior management struggled to come to terms with conceiving of a new business model which highlighted the revenue potential of hardware sales and overturned the underlying premise of their traditional model which focused on selling cameras at a reduced price to stimulate demand for film (Tripsas and Gavetti, 2000).

---

### Key Concept

Competence-enhancing innovation is where existing resources and capabilities retain value. Competence-destroying innovation is where the value of existing resources and capabilities is diminished. Established firms are likely to have a relative advantage over new start-ups in relation to innovation which is *competence-enhancing* rather than where innovation is *competence-destroying*.

---

## 11.3 Competing in technological markets

Innovation alone does not guarantee success. The importance of gaining an early lead in most technological markets suggests that there are competitive dynamics which are a characteristic of these types of markets. Specifically, the impact of network effects is particularly important.

Where network effects exist, the satisfaction that a user derives from consumption of a particular good increases with the number of other users consuming the same good (Katz and Shapiro 1985). Network effects can be produced directly, such as with physical networks like the telephone and the railways, or they can be produced indirectly, such as where the buyer of a personal computer is concerned with the amount of compatible software available. Expectations of success assume an importance, which helps to explain why markets subject to network effects are 'tippy', i.e., an early lead gained by a particular product or service is self-reinforcing. Imagine exerting force on an upright object—there comes a point at which the object's momentum cannot be stopped and the object falls or tips over.

---

### Key Concept

Network effects exist where the satisfaction that a user derives from consumption of a good increases with the number of other agents consuming the good.

---

Network effects also exist in markets subject to increasing returns, and the advantage gained from an early lead in the number of customers (or installed base) reaches a point where it is effectively self-reinforcing and 'unstoppable'. In most markets, even those subject to economies of scale, there will be a time at which further expansion of the product leads to rising costs per unit of output or diminishing returns to scale. Arthur (1996), however, realized that increasing returns to scale were a characteristic of those industries, particularly information-based goods such as computer software, where the position was reversed. In this case, most costs are incurred in producing the first unit of a good while the marginal costs of production tend towards zero (see Exhibit 11.3).

---

**Exhibit 11.3** Characteristics of industries subject to network effects

Network effects are strongest in hi-tech industries which tend to exhibit the following characteristics:

- R&D costs are large relative to unit production costs. For example, the first version of a software package could cost US$50 million to produce, while the second and subsequent copies could cost US$3 each.

- Many hi-tech products need to be compatible with a network of users. As with products subject to such 'network effects', the more the product gains prevalence, the more likely it will emerge as a standard.

- Hi-tech products are typically difficult to use and require customers to invest in training. Customers are, therefore, more likely to be 'locked-in' to future versions of the product.

*Source:* Adapted from B. Arthur (1996), 'Increasing returns and the new world of business', *Harvard Business Review* 74(4): 100–9.

---

Given that an early lead gained by one product can be self-reinforcing, the existence of network effects can produce a single standard, dominating the market. A classic case is that of VHS v. Betamax, where VHS, a small Japanese electronics firm, won the battle to establish the standard in video-recording technology, even though Sony-owned Betamax's technology was widely acknowledged to be superior. The continued dominance of the QWERTY keyboard, despite its inadequate design, illustrates the difficulties of displacing earlier dominant standards.

The most recent standards battle was that between the Japanese electronic giants, Toshiba and Sony. At the beginning of 2008, it was announced that Sony's Blu-ray technology was going to be the winner against Toshiba's HD-DVD format. However, it was not the launch of Sony's game console, PlayStation 3 (PS3) at the end of 2006 that led to Sony's dominance, but, rather, it was support from the movie industry. The two-year battle between the two companies was close throughout, as HD-DVD was backed by Hollywood studios Paramount and Universal Studios and Blu-ray was supported by Walt Disney, 20th Century Fox, and Metro-Goldwyn-Mayer. It was Warner Brothers, the largest player in the home video market, which finally cast its support for Blu-ray providing, an end to speculation on the final outcome. Shortly after the announcement, major retailers in the US, including Wal-Mart, Target, Best Buy, and Blockbuster, announced that they would sell only Blu-ray players. The losers in this battle included the 1 million or so customers who had bought HD-DVD compatible hardware and, of course, Toshiba, who had invested millions in developing the technology. Sony was set to profit, not only from sales of its Blu-ray players, but, more importantly, from the royalty payments from other manufacturers for use of the Blu-ray technology in their systems.

The ability to set standards is crucial in winning any standards battle. Shapiro and Varian (1999) argue that the winner is likely to be the one with the best strategy rather than the best technology. It depends on whether old technology is compatible with new technology, as well the compatibility of one firm's technology with that of its rivals. Sometimes, cooperation creates the best outcome, as in the case of Sony and Philips who cooperated in openly licensing their CD patents to establish CD technology. The seven key assets which are important in winning a standards battle are summarized in Exhibit 11.4. There is no simple formula that can be used to win a standards battle, since not all standards battles are alike. While a first-mover advantage is significant, it can ultimately be overcome by a superior technology if the performance advantage of the late entrant product is significant and if the users of the existing product can be persuaded to use (and, hence, learn how to use) another superior product. The history of the video games industry provides a clear example of this, as different firms from Atari to Nintendo to Sony have at separate times dominated the sales of games consoles.

From a resource-based perspective (see Chapter 5), valuable resources are typically those which are non-imitable or less easy for competitors to imitate. This is further compounded by the existence of *causal ambiguity*, which refers to the lack of certainty of whether and how certain resources and capabilities contribute to competitive advantage. Therefore, if the focus of innovation is a process or service, the existence of causal ambiguity may protect a firm and act as a knowledge barrier. Firms may also be protected by intellectual property rights (IPR) such as patents or copyrights. In fact, the granting of a patent is essentially the means through

---

**Exhibit 11.4** Seven key assets for winning standards wars

- **Control over the customer or users of the product.** Customers as well as technology suppliers can control key assets too, e.g., as in the recent case of high-definition technology and Warner's decisive impact on the standards battle, given its dominance of the home video market.

- **Intellectual property rights.** Firms with patents and copyrights controlling valuable new technology or interfaces are in a strong position.

- **An ability to innovate.** Beyond existing intellectual property, the ability to make proprietary extensions in the future provides a strong position today.

- **First mover advantages.** This can make all the difference, especially where network effects are in evidence.

- **Manufacturing capabilities.** Cost advantages can help you survive a standards war, or capture share when competing to sell a standardized product.

- **Complementary assets or skills.** Acceptance of the new technology will stimulate sales of the other products you produce.

- **Brand name and reputation.** Reputation and brand name are valuable in network markets, although expectations are pivotal since you have to convince consumers that you will win.

*Source:* C. Shapiro and H. R. Varian (1999), 'The art of standards wars', *California Management Review* 41(2): 8–32

> **Exhibit 11.5** Common types of intellectual property
>
> - **Patents.** These are exclusive rights to a new and useful product, process, substance or design. There is increasing standardization regarding the length of patents—twenty years from the time of filing the patent in many countries, including in the US and UK.
>
> - **Copyright.** Exclusive production, publication, or sales rights to the creators of artistic, literary, dramatic, or musical works.
>
> - **Trademarks**. These are words, symbols, or other marks used to distinguish the goods or services supplied by a firm. Trademarks provide the basis for brand identification.

which governments grant a reward for innovation and ensure that those who have incurred the costs of innovation are rewarded for their efforts. Intellectual property is typically protected through the use of patents, copyright, or trademarks (see Exhibit 11.5).

Firms may also license the use of their intellectual property (such as patents and trademarks) or their technology under specific conditions. The importance of patents is with respect to protecting the valuable knowledge assets of the firm, where the protection of an organization's intellectual capital is itself considered to form part of the organization's intangible assets. Survey research shows, however, that most inventions are not patented—on average, large European firms applied for patents on only 36% of product innovations and 25% of process innovations, although this rose to 79% in the case of pharmaceutical firms (Bessen and Meurer 2008). Patents are likely to assume greater importance in those industries and sectors where the costs of innovation are substantial, such as in the pharmaceutical industry. The Tufts Center for the Study of Drug Development, part of Tufts University in the US, reported that the average cost to develop and bring a new drug to market was US$801 million in 2001.

While patents are widely used in respect of products, a recent development has been the development of patents in respect of an organization's business methods or processes, such as the 'one-click' ordering process of US book e-tailer, Amazon. Similarly, online auction house, Priceline, has a patent on its Dutch auction methods of selling tickets online. In 2007 alone, nearly 12,000 business process patents were filed in the US. The US Patent and Trademark Office is said to want to cut down on these patents and even firms such as IBM and Microsoft, which have many of these patents, are also pressing for a reduction in 'pure methods' patents in favour of patents on inventions which use machines to produce tangible physical results.

Patents instead of copyright are also increasingly used to protect property rights in respect of software. The advantage of copyright is that it is an automatic law and is therefore not subject to any time delays. In contrast, software patents are often not publicly viewable until twelve or eighteen months after an application has been made, which can itself create a barrier to innovation. Nevertheless, the UK's Court of Appeal ruled in late 2008 that software should receive wider patent protection and, in particular, that complex software such as the programs designed to make mobile phones and computers work faster can be patented in the UK.

There is a paradox: as demands to own ideas or gain cheaper access to ideas increases, it is becoming harder to enforce their protection. Globalization has made it easier for intellectual property to spread to parts of the world where there is weaker protection for IPR (although this situation is beginning to change), while technological change has made it harder to protect ideas.

The difficulty of protecting intellectual property, given the development of new technologies, is exemplified by the music industry with challenges to existing business and revenue models. In the UK, for example, sales of traditional music CDs are in decline, there are fewer independent retailers, and, in 2007, the largest music retailer, HMV, posted a loss. This does not necessarily mean that there is an overall decline in the purchase of music. From the customer's perspective, there has never been more choice with broadband technologies facilitating music downloads over the Internet.

New technological innovations have created a new medium and distribution channel for music which is competence-destroying for traditional retailers. From an intellectual property perspective, the emergence of peer-to-peer (P2P) file-sharing technologies with the launch of Napster.com in 1999 was the first serious challenge to the industry, as users shared musical files with each other, directly infringing copyright laws. Following the closure of Napster in 2001 after a legal ruling, the firm was reborn in 2003 in the form of Napster 2.0, offering downloads in exchange for monthly user fees—similar to the pay per download models of other services, such as US computer firm Apple's iTunes.

While the traditional players in the music industry have been slow to react to the paradigm shift made by customers, they are slowly recognizing the need to adapt to survive and pre-empt firms like Apple from dominating online music sales. Cooperation is one strategy, as exemplified by the 2008 joint venture, MySpace Music, between three major music labels (Warner Music Group, Sony BMG, and Universal Music Group) and social networking site, MySpace. The website allows members of MySpace to listen to music and watch videos online for free. The joint venture aims to generate revenues from sales of merchandise, concert tickets, and sales of music downloads, and, of course, from advertising revenues.

In many industries, there are few or no property rights and yet innovation is an important source of competitive advantage. In the case of bicycle manufacturer, Giant, we saw how easy it was for competitors to copy its designs and reverse engineer its components. In the furniture industry, product design is typically an important determinant of a product's commercial success, with firms differentiating themselves through establishing reputations for innovative designs. In a study of furniture firms in Holland and Italy, Gemser and Wijnberg (2001) found that firms relied to a great extent on reputational sanctions to prevent other firms from copying the designs of their competitors and to aid value appropriation. In spite of the fact that Holland was an example of a strong IPR regime and Italy an example of a weak IPR regime, firms in both countries emphasized the importance of preserving a reputation for innovation which acted as a barrier to imitation.

The growing use of patents is, nevertheless, a significant global trend. According to the World Intellectual Property Organization (WIPO), the worldwide filings of patent applications have grown by nearly 5% annually since 1995, to more than 1.76 million applications in 2006. Between 2005 and 2006, the most significant growth in filings came from applicants in China, the Republic of Korea, and the US—growth rates of 32.1%, 6.6%, and 6.7%, respectively. To date, much of the work undertaken in emerging markets is by service companies, i.e., those selling software services rather than software products, who fear that filing their own patents would upset their clients. As we will show in the closing case study of this chapter, the attitude of emerging markets to patents is changing as they become more involved in research and development activities with international implications. While China is known for intellectual property infringement, the number of applications to China's patent office by Chinese inventors doubled between 2000 and 2003. Huawei Technologies, a Chinese communications equipment manufacturer, almost doubled its patent filings each year during the 1990s, to around 3,000 patents per year. Firms in emerging markets are realizing that, if they want to move up the technology ladder, they need to develop their own intellectual property rather than pay royalties for other firms' patents.

---

**Key Concept**

Patents are a public reward for innovation and a means of value appropriation.

---

To understand further the global management of innovation, it is important to understand the role of multinational firms and, in particular, to consider their role in knowledge transfer.

## 11.4 **Managing knowledge**

Most managers recognize the need to manage knowledge effectively. In Chapter 2, we recognized the importance of knowledge and intellectual capital in the new economy relative to the old economy. The importance of knowledge is embodied within the knowledge-based view of the firm which grew to prominence in the mid 1990s, in response to a period of time characterized by rapid technological change and uncertainty over the sustainability of competitive advantage. As Spender (1996) argued, since the origin of all tangible resources lies outside the firm, it follows that competitive advantage is more likely to arise from intangible, firm-specific knowledge which allows it to add value in a unique manner to other resources. Further, in Chapter 5, we identified the role of knowledge in underpinning the development of valuable organizational capabilities, while knowledge-based assets such as patents and other intellectual property are valuable intangible firm resources. A fundamental determinant of a firm's capability to innovate is therefore its ability to create as well as transfer knowledge within an organization. As Nonaka (1994) explained, innovation can be better understood as a process in which the organization creates and defines problems for which it develops new knowledge to solve them. An ongoing challenge for managers, therefore, is to create and manage knowledge effectively.

### 11.4.1 **Knowledge creation**

In developing his theory of knowledge creation, Nonaka (1994) emphasized that organizational knowledge is created through a 'continuous dialogue' or interplay between tacit and explicit knowledge. The distinction between tacit and explicit knowledge was made by Polanyi (1962), who argued that individuals tend to know more than what they can say or articulate. While explicit knowledge is that knowledge which is more easily codified, either in the form of written procedures and manuals or embodied in software, tacit knowledge is widely considered to be that knowledge which is more difficult to articulate. For example, while you might know how to ride a bicycle, you might find it difficult or even impossible to explain to someone else exactly what you are doing. Some individuals might also be better at articulating this knowledge than others and, hence, the degree of tacitness is relative to the individual concerned.

The importance of tacit knowledge is central to Nonaka and Takeuchi's (1995) view of how organizations create knowledge. They argue that knowledge creation is not a mechanistic process, since it depends on the more tacit or subjective insights and intuitions that employees gain through experience. Nonaka and Takeuchi (1995) showed that the process through which organizational knowledge is created is through a 'spiral of knowledge creation', which first starts with the knowledge of individuals (see Exhibit 11.6). There are four processes SECI through which knowledge is converted from one form to another:

- Socialization. This is the first stage in the knowledge spiral. It is the process by which tacit knowledge is exchanged through shared experience. It can be achieved in a variety of ways, for example, through an apprenticeship when an individual learns from a master or through a mentoring relationship. It can also take place through formal meetings or through more informal gatherings in a social setting.

- Externalization. This is the second stage in the knowledge spiral. It is the process through which tacit knowledge is converted to explicit knowledge, i.e., 'know-how' is converted to 'know-why'. Tacit knowledge can be synthesized and codified in a number of ways, from the use of analogy to developing new concepts, such as the outline of a new enhancement to a firm's offering as part of new service development.

- Combination. This is the third stage in the knowledge spiral. It is the process of converting explicit knowledge into other forms of explicit knowledge. It could include the development of new software to embody proposed changes to customer retention, for example. Alternatively, it could include the production of a report on a proposed new corporate venture or a review of existing customer registration procedures for an e-tailer.

- Internalization. This is the fourth stage in the knowledge spiral. It is the process through which explicit knowledge is embodied as tacit knowledge. Following the use or practice of explicit knowledge, individuals 'learn-by-doing' and acquire tacit knowledge through applying it in action. Reflection upon this experience is internalized and becomes embodied in an individual's tacit knowledge base.

**Exhibit 11.6** The knowledge spiral or SECI Process

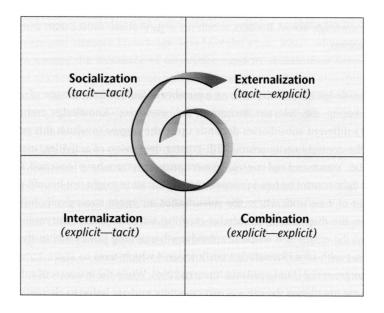

*Source:* Adapted from I. Nonaka and H. Takeuchi (1995), *The Knowledge-Creating Company* (Oxford: Oxford University Press), 62, 71. Reprinted with permission of Oxford University Press.

**Key Concept**

Explicit knowledge is that knowledge which is more easily codified, either in the form of written procedures and manuals or embodied in software. Tacit knowledge is widely considered to be that knowledge which is more difficult to articulate. Tacit knowledge (or know-how) is more difficult to articulate than explicit knowledge (or know-why).

A central challenge of knowledge management, therefore, is the challenge of transferring tacit as well as explicit knowledge.

## 11.4.2 Knowledge transfer within multinationals

Kogut and Zander (1993) originally showed that multinational firms are important mechanisms for the transfer of tacit knowledge across borders. The emerging conceptualization of the multinational firm as a knowledge-sharing network stems from the assumption that multinational firms exist because they can create, transfer, and deploy knowledge more effectively than could be achieved through market-based mechanisms (Foss 2006). From this perspective, the primary objective of the multinational firm is to maximize profits by building knowledge assets and deploying them. Multinational firms, therefore, face the particular challenge of operating effectively by generating knowledge across multiple boundaries, or what is called *distributive organizing* (Orlikowski 2002).

## Exhibit 12.1  Different views of Corporate Social Responsibility (CSR)

The World Business Council for Sustainable Development (WBCSD) asked businesspeople and non-businesspeople what they thought of the Corporate Social Responsibility (CSR) concept. This is what people in several countries had to say.

In Taiwan, it was suggested that the definition should address:

- Benefits for future generations.
- Environmental concerns (damage prevention and remediation).

In the United States, people commented:

- Include more emphasis on the role of the individual.
- Reflect the need for greater transparency.
- The term 'economic development' does not adequately capture the breadth of the economic role of business in society.

In Ghana, it was suggested that the definition should include the notion of:

- A global perspective which respects local culture.
- Building local capacity, leaving a positive legacy.
- Empowerment and ownership.
- Teaching employees skills and enabling communities to be self-sufficient.
- Filling in when government falls short.
- Giving access to information.
- Partnerships, because CSR does not develop in a vacuum.

In Thailand, people stated it should try to capture:

- The concept that the bigger the company, the greater the obligation.
- The importance of environmental mitigation and prevention.
- The need for transparency.
- The importance of consumer protection.
- Awareness of and change in people's attitudes towards the environment.
- The relevance of youth and gender issues.

*Source:* R. Holme and P. Watts (2000), *Corporate Social Responsibility: Making Good Business Sense* (Geneva: World Business Council for Sustainable Development, January): 8–9. Reprinted with permission of the World Business Council for Sustainable Development.

# 12.3 Corporate Social Responsibility (CSR) and stakeholders

The view that businesses should pursue certain social and ecological goals suggests that managers have broader responsibilities that extend beyond the company's owners and shareholders to include employees, customers, suppliers, and local communities. This view goes beyond corporate charitable donations, public relations exercises, or special employee benefits, all of which have been pursued by companies for a long time. It stresses that companies have responsibilities to their stakeholders (Pegg 2003).

## 12.3.1 Stakeholder view of the firm

Many scholars and managers now accept the idea that a firm has stakeholders (Chang and Ha 2001; Handy 1994). A stakeholder is typically defined as 'any group or individual who can affect or is affected by the achievement of the organization's objectives' (Freeman 1984: 46). Stakeholders include employees, customers, suppliers, stockholders, banks, pressure groups, governments, and other groups who can either help or damage the firm (see Exhibit 12.2). Freeman (1984) simply summarized the stakeholder approach as 'the principle of who or what really counts.'

**Exhibit 12.2** Generic stakeholder map of a multinational firm

The stakeholder approach, which was originally devised as just another tool for understanding organizations and analysing the business environment, is now mainly associated with CSR. Since managers usually paid enough attention to suppliers or governments in the past, the literature on CSR usually put emphasis on 'non-traditional' stakeholder groups such as pressure groups and local communities. It is those groups which put pressure on companies to accept social responsibilities and which traditionally have not been part of the firm's strategic analysis. The stakeholder view of the firm undermines the notion that a firm should only maximize profits for shareholders. Rather, the goal of any firm should be to satisfy the aspirations of all of the main stakeholders.

---

**Key Concept**

A stakeholder is any group or individual that can affect or is affected by the achievement of the organization's objectives. Stakeholders include employees, customers, suppliers, stockholders, banks, pressure groups, governments, and other groups that can either help or damage the firm. Freeman (1994: 411) summarized the stakeholder approach as 'the principle of who or what really counts'.

---

## 12.3.2 Stakeholder mapping

In order to design a strategy for dealing with social and environmental issues, a company must first identify who its stakeholders are and which stakeholders are the most important ones to talk to—this is called 'stakeholder mapping'.

Exhibit 12.2 shows a generic stakeholder map of a multinational firm. This can serve as a starting point for identifying the main stakeholders. 'Generic stakeholders' refers to categories of groups that can affect the firm or are affected by the firm, such as suppliers or government. While government is a category, it is the finance ministry, the environmental protection agency, or the country's parliament which can affect the achievement of strategic goals (Freeman 1984: 54).

However, the mapping of stakeholders is much more complicated than Exhibit 12.2 suggests, because a multinational firm faces different groups in different countries. Furthermore, stakeholders can be very different for different organizations. For example, environmental pressure groups may be crucial for a waste-treatment plant but may be of little importance to an online book retailer. Therefore, every firm must identify the specific stakeholders which are important to it, both globally and in each country of its operations.

Exhibit 12.3 shows a generic stakeholder map for the London-based Shell International. Under each of the headings, such as government or non-governmental organizations, there may be very different groups with different interests. Furthermore, Shell's subsidiaries in different parts of the world will have many other stakeholders. For instance, the stakeholders of Shell's Nigerian subsidiary will include contracting firms such as Willbros and Schlumberger, local host communities represented by village chiefs, youth leaders and women's groups, and different government agencies such as the Nigerian environment ministry and the Nigerian state-owned oil corporation. A failure to identify an important stakeholder may be costly to the firm. For instance, Shell in Nigeria failed to consider Ken Saro-Wiwa's MOSOP movement as a legitimate stakeholder and refused to talk to MOSOP, which was one of the key reasons for the company's poor relations with local communities in the country. This illustrates the importance of constructing precise stakeholder maps.

## Key Concept

A stakeholder map identifies a company's stakeholders and classifies them according to their importance.

**Exhibit 12.3** Stakeholders of Shell International

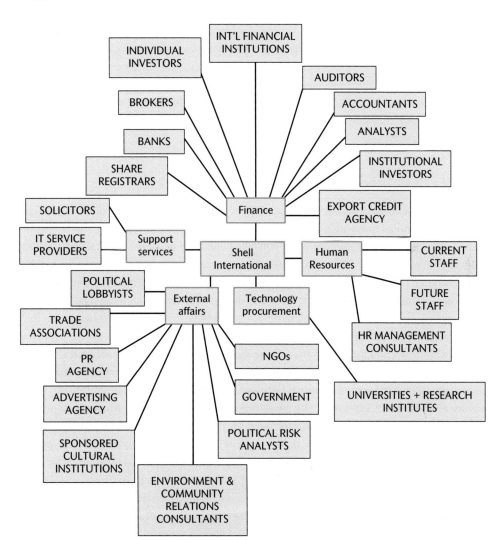

*Source:* Adapted from Platform website at http://www.carbonweb.org/. Reproduced with permission of Platform.

### 12.3.3 **Problems in stakeholder mapping**

Exhibit 12.3 shows that it is not easy to construct a stakeholder map. Freeman (1984: 58) pointed out that two issues must be considered when stakeholders are identified. First, the same group can have different stakeholder roles for the company. For instance, for Shell in Nigeria, the government is a stakeholder as a regulator, but it is also an owner (as joint-venture partner) and a financial institution (the Nigerian Central Bank). Multiple roles of the same stakeholder group can give rise to conflicting demands on the company. Second, stakeholder groups are interconnected and may influence each other. For Shell in Nigeria, the local communities (MOSOP) had an impact on environmental pressure groups; in turn, the media publicity generated by international pressure groups led a financial institution (the International Finance Corporation (IFC) of the World Bank) to withdraw from its participation in a Shell gas project.

A further complication in constructing a stakeholder map is that such a map is only useful at a particular point in time for a specific purpose. Managers should never forget that the relative importance of stakeholders may be different for different issues and projects. Therefore, stakeholders require different degrees and types of attention, depending on things such as their attributed possession of power or the urgency of issues, while levels of these attributes (and thereby the importance of a stakeholder) can vary from issue to issue and from time to time (Mitchell et al. 1997).

### 12.3.4 **Which stakeholders should the firm focus on?**

Firms cannot accommodate the interests of every stakeholder. There are just too many of them. A multinational firm which operates in many different countries has thousands of stakeholders with very different agendas and demands. Furthermore, stakeholders may have contradictory interests. One environmental pressure group may want the company to divest from a certain project, while another group may want the company to introduce anti-pollution measures but continue operating. But some stakeholders are just much more significant than others and it is important to identify who the main stakeholders are and how much power they have over the firm.

The firm may need to focus on different stakeholder groups, depending on several factors. One such factor is the firm's corporate nationality. Despite globalization, a firm's national origin can still account for many differences between multinational firms. Pauly and Reich (1997), mentioned in Chapter 2 (section 2.9.3), found that German and Japanese firms obtain most of their financing through banks, for instance, while US firms rely much more on capital markets. So, banks would be more important stakeholders to a Japanese or a German firm. With regards to CSR, US and Western European firms were more frequently targeted by the mainly Western-based pressure groups than firms from emerging economies such as China and Russia. So, Greenpeace will be of much greater importance to a British firm than to a Chinese firm.

As the needs of a firm change over time, the relative importance of stakeholders will change as it evolves. During the start-up stage, when the firm is most concerned about obtaining initial financing and entering the marketplace, the key stakeholders are likely to be shareholders, creditors, and customers. In contrast, during the maturity stage, firms are likely to act pro-actively towards most of their stakeholders including communities and pressure groups. On the one hand, firms are likely to be larger at the mature stage and will attract more scrutiny from stakeholders; on the other hand, firms will have more cash flow without particularly attractive investment opportunities (Jawahar and McLaughlin 2001).

The type of industry can also influence a firm's response to social demands by stakeholders. For instance, Greenpeace will be a key stakeholder for industries which cause major pollution, such as the oil industry; but, it will be of less relevance for garment manufacturers, which cause relatively little pollution. On the other hand, garment manufacturers must pay attention to pressure groups such as Clean Clothes Campaign, which targets garment production.

## 12.3.5 Critique of stakeholder mapping

Stakeholder mapping has been criticized because a stakeholder map is usually constructed by managers from within the company who have subjective views about stakeholders. One study found that top managers ascribed more relative importance to stakeholders who played a part in the traditional activities of the firm (owners, customers, and employees) than to the government or non-traditional stakeholder groups (Agle et al. 1999). Jawahar and McLaughlin (2001: 411) noted that:

> *functional managers, in order to increase their power, may exaggerate threats from their stakeholders, leading top managers to form an inaccurate picture of demands on the organization. Such acts of self-interest may cause the organization to be out of sync with the predictions of our stakeholder theory.*

Finally, stakeholder attributes are socially constructed, they are not objective reality. Managers may have different perceptions on issues such as stakeholder legitimacy compared with a stakeholder's own perception (Mitchell et al. 1997). As Freeman (1984: 64) reminded us, when the managers' 'perceptions are out of line with the perceptions of the stakeholders, all the brilliant strategic thinking in the world will not work'.

Ulrich Steger (2003) suggested that in today's fast-moving global business environment, managers often cannot be sure about either stakekolder groups or their demands. So, the use of stakeholder maps may be of limited value because key stakeholders may change or their demands may change. According to Steger, a focus on stakeholder analysis can only work if you have all the information: who all of your stakeholders are; what they want at a given moment (which could change); and how to rank the urgency of dealing with the most important stakeholder groups. But firms rarely have all the relevant information in today's global business environment. Managers may not know whether Greenpeace or another stakeholder is planning a campaign against the organization, but they might be aware of a public debate about a specific issue—e.g., about the proposed phasing out of a dangerous chemical or calls for better working conditions in a given industry or country.

Therefore, Steger (2003) suggested that managers should focus on issues which could become threats to the organization, rather than focus on stakeholders. He believes that, rather than preparing stakeholder maps, firms should have an 'early warning system' (EWS), which will scan the business environment for early signs of problems. Companies may already have some form of EWS, for example, consumer research aimed at detecting new desires, shifts in social attitudes, or incoming orders. But Steger believes that firms should also have an EWS for detecting external social pressures before they cause problems to the firm. This can be done with the help of systematic information gathering, dissemination of information within the organization, and simple management tools or checklists.

### 12.3.6 Issue analysis

One tool for issue analysis proposed by Steger (2003) is cross-impact analysis, which can be used by managers, for example, during brainstorming sessions (see Exhibit 12.4). By placing potential threats and opportunities in the business environment in relation to corporate objectives, managers can better understand how an issue could influence the organization. Steger recommends this tool for situations such as, for example, when ecological issues prompt

**Exhibit 12.4**   Example of cross-impact analysis

| | Potential environmental product-related developments | | | |
| | Potential for public criticism | Ability of consumers to switch to environmentally friendly substitutes | Stricter environmental regulations | Ability to innovate |
|---|---|---|---|---|
| Corporate issues | | | | |
| Safeguarding of competitiveness | – | – | – | + |
| Profit | 0 | – | – | ? |
| Qualified and motivated employees | – | – | ? | + |
| Quality level of products—user-friendly image | 0 | 0 | ?! | 0 |
| Diversification | + | + | + | ? |
| Globalization | 0 | 0 | – | +– |
| Distribution channels | ? | ?! | ? | 0 |

+ = positive influence
? = ambiguous/uncertain influence
– = negative influence
?! = unknown if it will have an influence or not and, if so, in which direction
0 = neutral

*Source:* U. Steger (2003), *Corporate Diplomacy—The Strategy for a Volatile, Fragmented Business Environment* (Chichester: Wiley). Reprinted with permission of John Wiley & Sons.

customers to direct criticism at a company because of its products and begin switching to environmentally friendly products. It could also be used in situations when a firm is confronted with stricter regulations on product quality, which could make innovation more feasible. This type of analysis might indicate that the ability of customers to switch to another firm's products is high or that the potential for innovation is higher than previously assumed.

One assumption underlying issue analysis is that most issues do not come entirely without warning. In most cases, managers could have detected the issue, as issues follow patterns or a set of criteria. In order to help managers decide how an issue might develop in future, Winter and Steger (1998) proposed a checklist which asks eight questions:

1. Are the arguments against the issue plausible?

2. Does the issue evoke emotion? Is it understandable—visual, touching—by the public?

3. Is the issue media friendly?

4. Are there connections to other issues involving the company or other companies?

5. How strong is the key activist group?

6. How isolated is the company?

7. How far have the dynamics of the crisis already evolved?

8. How easy is the solution?

The checklist can help to understand some of the dynamics of social and ecological issues. For example, the pharmaceutical industry has been frequently criticized for unethical practices but has rarely attracted major pressure-group campaigns in the same way as the oil or mining industries. The checklist makes clear to us that issues involving pharmaceuticals are usually very complex, difficult to understand, and not particularly media friendly. The side effects of a given medical drug may not be as easy to explain, not as easy to prove, and not as media friendly compared with, for instance, the direct effects of an oil spill on bird life. The activist pressure groups which focus on pharmaceuticals, are not as strong as activist pressure groups focused on oil-related or mining-related issues. However, major Western pharmaceutical firms have been targeted in campaigns related to AIDS drugs. Firms have been forced to cut prices for AIDS drugs sold in developing countries and to allow cheap imitations of drugs to be produced in those countries. The checklist could have helped pharmaceutical firms to forecast the rising importance of the AIDS issue. The issue evokes considerable emotion, the effects of high drug prices on poor HIV-infected Africans are easily understandable, and the issue is media friendly.

As with stakeholder analysis, one problem with issue analysis is that some information may not be known to the firm. A lack of understanding by managers might call for a deeper investigation of the issue in order to detect any changes in the business environment. As Steger (2003) pointed out, a precondition for the use of cross-impact analysis is that no predominating opinion should be allowed to prevail and that advocates of minority opinions are brought into the brainstorming sessions as well as outsiders with a wide background. As with stakeholder analysis, issue analysis relies on managers being open-minded to new trends and developments.

---

**Key Concept**

Cross-impact analysis is a tool for analysing the threats and opportunities arising from social and environmental issues in the external business environment. Potential threats and opportunities are analysed in relation to corporate objectives.

---

## 12.4 CSR strategies and innovation

Stakeholder maps and issue analysis are useful in providing a tool for an understanding of the changing external business environment. But identifying the key stakeholders and the key issues is only the first step for a company. A firm needs to develop CSR strategies to respond to social and environmental pressures in the business environment.

Strategic responses to social and environmental pressures differ widely between different companies, they differ between different industries, and they can also differ between competing firms in the same industry. But there are a number of generic CSR strategies for dealing with social and environmental pressures.

### 12.4.1 Generic strategies of social responsiveness

Carroll (1979) has identified four generic strategies of social responsiveness:

- Reaction. The firm denies responsibility for social issues, for instance, by blaming others or by pointing to the responsibility of government.

- Defence. The firm admits responsibility but tries to do the very least that is necessary; for instance, the firm may use CSR superficially to improve public relations without pursuing CSR seriously.

- Accommodation. The firm accepts responsibility and does whatever is demanded by the key stakeholders.

- Proaction. The firm seeks to exceed industry norms and anticipates future expectations by doing more than is expected.

A company's strategy can change over time. For instance, Shell's strategy in responding to social pressures changed from 'reaction' in the 1980s, towards 'defence' in the early 1990s, towards 'accommodation' in the late 1990s, and towards 'proaction' today.

'Reaction' strategies are unwise because the firm fails to deal effectively with the external pressures and it may suffer negative media publicity and further criticism as a result. 'Defence' and 'accommodation' strategies can help the firm to deflect external pressures by acting in a responsible manner, and most companies tend to choose one of these two strategies. However, all three strategies—reaction, defence, and accommodation—treat social and environmental issues as external threats. They allow the company to counteract external pressures to a varying extent, but do not allow for social and environmental issues to be seen as business opportunities. According to Michael Porter and Mark Kramer, only 'proaction' strategies are genuinely 'strategic', in the sense that they can help the firm to gain a competitive advantage from CSR (Porter and Kramer 2006). A 'proaction' strategy allows the firm to align social and environmental goals with its core business strategy.

---

**Key Concept**

Generic strategies of social responsiveness are basic strategies available to firms for addressing external social pressures. There are four generic strategies of social responsiveness: reaction, defence, accommodation, and proaction. Only proaction strategies allow firms to align social and environmental goals with their core business strategy.

---

## 12.4.2 Benefits of CSR strategies

CSR strategies can have many business benefits for a company. Detailed studies by the organization, SustainAbility (2001; 2002), suggest that the key business benefits are:

- Brand value and reputation (e.g., extending a trusting public image; building a distinctive image to achieve differentiation).

- Risk management (e.g., providing stakeholder views as early warning of possible problems; providing alternative viewpoints to reveal unrecognized assumptions).

- Human capital (e.g., increasing retention rates for employees; improving the employees' understanding of customer needs).

- Revenue (e.g., discovering new markets for existing products; developing new products and services).

However, it is often difficult to assign a monetary value to CSR strategies and many business benefits from CSR are intangible. When managers start engaging with non-traditional stakeholders, they do not necessarily know whether this will ever translate into higher revenues or better corporate reputation. Indeed, leading thinkers suggest that it would be wrong to see CSR as a return on investment because there are always better alternative investment opportunities that could yield a higher return than CSR. Parkinson (1999: 62) concluded that managers should accept that respect for social and environmental issues 'will sometimes require companies to make less than the maximum possible profits'.

Management thinkers such as Michael Porter argue that the main benefit of CSR strategies for firms is to discover future business opportunities and to confer a competitive advantage on selected firms. According to Porter and Kramer (2006), CSR strategies should be seen as 'a long-term investment in a company's future competitiveness'. By integrating CSR strategies into core business strategy, the main benefit of CSR strategies is in helping firms find new ways to grow and develop. According to Blowfield and Murray (2008: 152), CSR strategies should be treated as a 'critical link in innovation and learning'.

**Exhibit 12.6**  Key differences between levels of social innovation

|  | Strategic planning | Investment | Stakeholder involvement | Example |
|---|---|---|---|---|
| In-market innovation | Short term | Small- to medium-scale funding | Normally requires mainly internal processes, may involve external stakeholders | Petroleum company develops a low-emission fuel |
| New market creation | Medium term | Medium- to large-scale funding, may involve new resources and capabilities | Normally requires input from external stakeholders | Shell's investments in solar energy |
| Leadership | Long term | Large-scale funding, requires new resources and capabilities | Normally requires partnerships with external stakeholders | BP's initiative to combat climate change |

allows the firm to find new ways to do the things they do already, while new market creation enables the firm to do new things. Leadership refers to a firm's leadership in influencing policies and the formation of markets itself (Henriques 2005).

In-market innovation is the simplest and most common type of innovation. It involves the modification of existing products and services or the introduction of new products and services within existing markets. For instance, a manufacturer of appliances may add an eco-friendly cooker or fridge to its existing line of products; a petroleum company may develop a low-emission fuel; a bank may offer an ethical investment fund to existing clients.

New market creation can have a greater impact on the firm's strategy and can bring greater benefits to the firm. However, new market creation takes longer to materialize and is less common than in-market innovation. Examples include Citigroup's creation of microfinance services to poor creditors without a collateral, and Shell's investments in solar energy and other alternative energy sources.

Leadership is a complex time-consuming activity that can help to change the external business environment, thus only selected firms pursue such innovations. Leadership can encompass partnerships with other stakeholders aimed at changing business practices, lobbying the government in order to change regulations, or the creation of new CSR standards. One example of leadership was BP's initiative to combat climate change, which helped towards the adoption of a European-wide emissions trading system (see closing case study). Firms rarely succeed in creating new markets or in achieving leadership on their own. Typically, firms engage in new types of partnerships to achieve higher levels of innovation.

## Key Concept

Levels of social innovation are degrees to which innovation can impact a firm's business strategy. Innovation can occur at three levels: in-market innovation, new market creation, and leadership. In-market innovation is the simplest and most common type of innovation.

### 12.4.6 **Non-traditional partnerships and innovation**

Non-traditional partnerships can help firms to provide new perspectives, question existing practices, access new types of skills, and develop new integrated strategies. Partners can be other firms, government agencies, non-governmental organizations, academic institutions, and other stakeholders. For instance, the pharmaceutical company, Aventis, partnered with the World Health Organization (WHO) and the non-governmental organization, Médecins sans Frontières, to combat sleeping sickness, a tropical disease; while the auto manufacturer, DaimlerChrysler, partnered up with Shell Hydrogen (a Shell subsidiary), Norsk Hydro (a Norwegian energy firm), the government of Iceland, and academic institutions to test hydrogen vehicles and hydrogen refuelling infrastructure as well as to produce hydrogen from renewable resources (Holliday et al. 2002).

Non-traditional partnerships tend to provide firms with complementary resources. For instance, Aventis' partners provided the knowledge for working with patients in affected areas, the administration of drugs, and monitoring the impact of health initiatives, while Aventis provided the knowledge of drug manufacturing as well as research and development. Firms, government agencies, and non-governmental organizations can make different contributions in a partnership (see Exhibit 12.7).

There are obstacles to the success of non-traditional partnerships. Partners often do not share the same interests, there is often a lack of trust between partners, and partners often fail to share their core competencies with each other (Blowfield and Murray 2008: 268). However, a firm can maximize the value of partnerships by assessing each partnership at different stages: the exploration stage, building stage, and maintenance stage. Exhibit 12.8 provides simple principles for managing non-traditional partnerships. If managed successfully, partnerships can help firms towards better ways of doing business and entirely new ways of thinking about their business.

**Exhibit 12.7** Complementary contributions to partnerships

| Government contributions | Business contributions | NGO contributions |
|---|---|---|
| Strategic coordination through local development plans | Job creation | Broader perspectives on society and environment |
| Access to budgets for public services | Knowledge of procurement and supply chain management | Local knowledge |
| Regulatory provisions | Building local infrastructure | Mobilization of community participation |
| Brokering or capacity-building roles | Capital equipment, technical skills, and logistics | Independent monitoring |
| | Performance-led work ethic and access to international best practices | Local and international credibility |

*Source:* Adapted from M. Blowfield and A. Murray (2008), *Corporate Responsibility—A Critical Introduction* (Oxford: Oxford University Press), 262. Reprinted with permission of Oxford University Press.

**Exhibit 12.8** Principles for managing non-traditional partnerships

| Partnership exploration stage | |
|---|---|
| Find the most practicable strategy | Involve stakeholders in design |
| Be purpose-driven | Set realistic expectations |
| Be willing to negotiate | Be prepared to say 'no' |
| Consult | |
| **Partnership building stage** | |
| Appreciate the importance of perceptions | Accept that differences of interest will arise |
| Integrate cultural values and priorities | Encourage joint problem-solving |
| Build trust, confidence, and respect | Identify the important voices, rather than the loudest |
| Be willing to negotiate | |
| **Partnership maintenance stage** | |
| Recognize reciprocal obligations | Adapt to internal and external events |
| Have clear work plans | Measure added value |
| Maintain internal and external communications | Do not be a slave to business value |
| Be willing to negotiate | Instigate continual learning |

*Source:* Adapted from M. Blowfield and A. Murray (2008), *Corporate Responsibility—A Critical Introduction* (Oxford: Oxford University Press), 269. Reprinted with permission of Oxford University Press.

## 12.5 Summary

In the new global business environment, the public turns to business to perform social and environmental tasks. These new public pressures have given rise to Corporate Social Responsibility (CSR), which has been defined as 'a concept whereby companies integrate social and environmental concerns in their business operations and in their interactions with their stakeholders on a voluntary basis'.

There are two major objections to international firms assuming new social and environmental roles. First, it has been argued that businesses serve the sole purpose of making profit and they should not pursue any other objectives. Second, social responsibilities differ between countries and multinational firms face a dilemma as to which responsibilities to follow. But views are changing and many international businesspeople now accept that firms have a social responsibility to society. Indeed, CSR may provide various new business opportunities to international firms, particularly in terms of innovation.

CSR strategies, particularly, can lead to genuine business innovations in two key areas: environmental improvements and new products targeted at low-income customers in emerging economies. CSR strategies can lead to innovation at three levels: in-market innovation, new market creation, and leadership. The potential for innovation is greatest when firms leverage their core competencies and when firms enter into non-traditional partnerships with firms, government agencies, non-governmental organizations, academic institutions, and other stakeholders.

Our view is that firms will have increasingly to manage stakeholder issues in the same way as other strategic issues, as they are relevant to competing in a global market. Indeed, it is crucial that stakeholder concerns are not dealt with by a public relations or a stakeholder unit within the firm, but are incorporated into the formulation of strategic plans and financial budgets. To quote Michael Porter, 'Seeing strategy narrowly leads to missed opportunities and bad competitive choices.'

##  Key readings

- On CSR in general, see Blowfield and Murray (2008).
- On CSR strategies, see Porter and Kramer (2006).
- On social innovation, see Kanter (2008).

## Discussion questions

**1.** What are the key arguments against multinational firms promoting social and environmental objectives?

**2.** Why might socially and environmentally conscious firms be more profitable in the long-term than those firms which are not?

**3.** What problems do managers face in stakeholder mapping?

**4.** Take a company of your choice. Who are the company's main stakeholders?

**5.** What types of new products could be targeted at low-income customers in emerging economies?

**6.** Take one industry of your choice. Provide your own examples for each level of social innovation in that industry.

## Closing case study  BP tackles climate change and innovation

Like Shell in 1995, BP faced a crisis of reputation in 1996. BP was accused of complicity in human rights abuses in Colombia. It was revealed that the company had paid millions of dollars to the Colombian army, and had provided the army with photographs and other information about critics of oil operations, which allegedly led to intimidation, beatings, and disappearances of local people. The company's executives realized that BP needed to change how it managed its relationship with wider society.

The chief executive of BP, John Browne (CEO between 1995 and 2007), knew that corporate social responsibility could have many business benefits, especially by improving the company's reputation and motivating employees. He decided to focus on tackling the problem of climate change. In a speech to students at Stanford University in 1997, John Browne said:

> We must now focus on what can and what should be done, not because we can be certain climate change is happening, but because the possibility can't be ignored. If we are all to take responsibility for the future of our planet, then it falls to us to begin to take precautionary action now.

But even John Browne did not foresee how much BP would eventually benefit from social responsibility. BP's efforts to reduce greenhouse gas emissions (which contribute to global warming) exceeded all expectations and the company was able to save billions of dollars by being more energy efficient.

In 1997, BP set itself the target of reducing greenhouse gas emissions from its own facilities by 10% from 1990 levels by 2010. The company was able to attain this goal nine years early, at the end of 2001. The company then set itself a new target of ensuring that net emissions do not increase between 2001 to 2012. Since 2001, BP has made further progress. BP's greenhouse gas emissions declined by a further 22% between 2002 and 2006, at a time when the company's oil production increased in the same period by over 30% and its natural gas production almost doubled.

How did BP achieve these targets? The company's CEO, John Browne, believed that BP had to be creative in reducing greenhouse gas emissions. In 1997, he announced that BP would use internal emissions trading to achieve emissions reductions.

### BP's emissions trading system

Emissions trading is a technique for buying and selling the right to generate pollutants. Each BP business unit was assigned a target for the emission of greenhouse gases and a number of 'permits', each of which gave the business unit the right to emit one metric ton of carbon dioxide.

The company's business units were able to trade permits between each other. A business unit that was able to reduce greenhouse gas emissions was free to sell permits. A business unit that was unable to find economical methods of reducing emissions could buy permits. Therefore, the trading system introduced incentives for pursuing the most cost-effective methods for emissions reductions within the company as a whole.

A significant part of the emissions reduction was achieved through reductions in gas flaring. When a company produces petroleum, natural gas is often found in the same oil reservoir; if the gas cannot be used commercially, it is often burned or 'flared' at the site. As a result of emissions trading, BP estimated that the company was able to save US$650 million through decreased gas flaring, either by selling the gas or by increased energy efficiency.

The emissions trading system was operational from January 2000 until the end of 2001, by which time BP had achieved a 10% reduction in greenhouse gas emissions. BP's initiative also helped to change the external business environment. BP's experience in carbon trading earned the company an advisory role in developing both the UK's emissions trading system and the European Union's Emissions Trading Directive. While BP's emissions trading system did not lead directly to the development of European trading systems, BP was able to influence the selection of emissions trading as the preferred policy instrument for addressing emissions reductions within Europe.

## Awards for innovation

The emissions trading system demonstrated to BP managers that being socially responsible could help innovation and reduce costs. In 2001, BP started the Helios Awards scheme. The Awards are open to any BP employee and BP partner organization. They are intended to encourage entrepreneurial ideas from individual employees for projects that protect the environment and help towards better company performance. The awards helped to reduce greenhouse gas emissions still further.

One Helios Award was given to a project that used the chemical 'polybutene' to reduce the emission of smoke from motorbikes. BP decided not to keep the technology secret but to share the technology with others, so this innovation is now commonly used around the world. By sharing the technology, BP achieved a competitive advantage because the company had a leading position in the manufacture of polybutene.

In 2007, the 'green' award was given to a project that helped to reduce greenhouse gas emissions from BP's ships, which transport liquefied natural gas (LNG). LNG ships were powered by steam turbines; they had low energy efficiency and resulted in high fuel consumption. In partnership with the South Korean company, Hyundai Heavy Industries, BP developed a ship design incorporating a highly efficient dual fuel diesel electric (DFDE) propulsion system, together with a number of other pioneering environmentally efficient design features. Since BP ordered the first four vessels, the entire LNG shipping industry has embraced this technology. The DFDE system emits 25% less carbon dioxide and no sulphur dioxide emissions, which helps BP reduce greenhouse gas emissions and the financial costs of fuel consumption.

## New investment opportunities

BP's initiatives on climate change helped the company to discover new business opportunities outside the traditional oil and gas sector. In 2005, BP created a BP Alternative Energy business unit and the company has invested in renewable energy, including solar, wind, biofuels, and hydrogen. In 2008, alone, BP planned to invest US$1.5 billion in alternative and renewable energy technologies.

BP's solar energy business was already created in 1998 and has grown into one of the world's largest solar energy businesses, with manufacturing facilities in the United States, Spain, India, China, and Australia. The company's solar business unit became profitable in 2004 and higher profits are expected in the future. BP stated: 'The solar market is growing fast; and as one of the top solar manufacturers in the world, we are in an excellent position to benefit.'

In wind energy, BP planned to install 1,000MW of wind capacity by the end of 2008. In biofuels, BP has partnered up with the food and retail company, Associated British Foods, and the chemical company, DuPont, to build a US$400 million biofuel plant by 2010. In hydrogen, BP is planning to build a pioneering power generation plant in Abu Dhabi, which will use hydrogen gas to fuel gas turbines and generate 420MW of low-carbon electricity.

BP remains an oil and gas company and alternative-energy investments are only a small part of the company's business. But these new investments help BP improve its reputation and its long-term financial health, while helping the company discover new ways of doing things.

*Source:* M. Akhurst, J. Morgheim, and R. Lewis (2003), 'Greenhouse gas emissions trading in BP', *Energy Policy* 31(7): 657–63; D. G. Victor and J. C. House (2006), 'BP's emissions trading system', *Energy Policy* 34(15): 2100–12; C. Perceval (2003), 'Towards a process view of the business case for sustainable development: lessons from the experience at BP and Shell', *Journal of Corporate Citizenship* (9): 117–32; BP website at http://www.bp.com.

**Discussion questions**

1. What benefits did BP achieve as a result of the climate change initiative?
2. What 'levels of innovation' were involved in BP's initiatives?
3. To what extent can other companies imitate BP's climate change initiative?

# References

Agle, B. R., Mitchell, R. K., and Sonnenfeld, J. A. (1999). 'Who matters to CEOs? An investigation of stakeholder attributes and salience, corporate performance, and CEO values', *Academy of Management Journal* 42(5): 507–25.

Amaeshi, K. M., Adi, B. C., Ogbechie, C., and Amao, O. O. (2006). 'Corporate social responsibility in Nigeria: Western mimicry or indigenous influences?' *Journal of Corporate Citizenship* (24): 83–99.

Baskin, J. (2006). 'Corporate responsibility in emerging markets', *Journal of Corporate Citizenship* (24): 29–47.

Bhatnagar, S., and Cohen, M. A. (1997). 'The impact of environmental regulation on innovation: a panel data study' (Nashville, TN: Owen Graduate School of Management, Vanderbilt University).

Bielak, D., Bonini, S., and Oppenheim, J. (2007). 'CEOs on strategy and social issues' (McKinsey & Company).

Blowfield, M., and Murray, A. (2008). *Corporate Responsibility—A Critical Introduction* (Oxford: Oxford University Press).

Carroll, A. (1979). 'A three-dimensional model of corporate social performance', *Academy of Management Review* 4(3): 497–505.

Chang, S. J., and Ha, D. (2001). 'Corporate governance in the twenty-first century: new managerial concepts for supranational corporations', *American Business Review* 19: 32–44.

Freeman, R. E. (1984). *Strategic Management—A Stakeholder Approach* (Boston, MA: Pitman).

Freeman, R. E. (1994). 'The politics of stakeholder theory: some future directions', *Business Ethics Quarterly* 4(4): 409–21.

Friedman, M. (1963). *Capitalism and Freedom* (Chicago, IL: University of Chicago Press).

Frynas, J. G. (2009). *Beyond Corporate Social Responsibility—Oil Multinationals and Social Challenges* (Cambridge: Cambridge University Press).

Hamann, R., Agbazue, T., Kapelus, P., and Hein, A. (2005). 'Universalizing corporate social responsibility? South African challenges to the International Organization for Standardization's new social responsibility standard', *Business and Society Review* 110(1): 1–19.

Handy, C. (1994). *The Age of Paradox* (Cambridge, MA: Harvard Business School).

Henderson, D. (2001). *Misguided Virtue: False Notions of Corporate Social Responsibility* (London: Institute of Economic Affairs).

Henriques, A. (2005). 'Good decision—bad business', *International Journal of Management and Decision Making* 6(3/4): 273–83.

Holliday, C. O., Schmidheiny, S., and Watts, P. (2002). *Walking the Talk—The Business Case for Sustainable Development* (Sheffield: Greenleaf).

Jawahar, I., and McLaughlin, G. (2001). 'Toward a descriptive stakeholder theory: an organizational life cycle approach', *Academy of Management Review* 26(3): 397–414.

Kanter, R. M. (1999). 'From spare change to real change: the social sector as beta site for business innovation', *Harvard Business Review* 77(3): 122–32.

Kanter, R. M. (2008). 'Transforming giants', *Harvard Business Review* 86(1): 43–52.

KPMG (2005). *International Survey of Corporate Responsibility Reporting* (Amsterdam: University of Amsterdam and KPMG Global Sustainability Services).

Lanjouw, J. O., and Mody, A. (1996). 'Innovation and the international diffusion of environmentally responsive technology', *Research Policy* 25: 549–71.

McKinsey & Company (2007). *Assessing the Impact of Societal Issues: A McKinsey Global Survey* (McKinsey & Company).

Mitchell, R. K., Agle, B. R., and Wood, D. J. (1997). 'Toward a theory of stakeholder identification and salience: defining the principle of who or what really counts', *Academy of Management Review* 22(4): 853–86.

Ottaway, M. (2001). 'Reluctant missionaries', *Foreign Policy* (July/August): 44–54.

Parkinson, J. (1999). 'The socially responsible company', in M. K. Addo (ed.), *Human Rights Standards and the Responsibility of Transnational Corporations* (The Hague: Kluwer Law International), 49–62.

Pauly, L. W., and Reich, S. (1997). 'National structures and multinational corporate behaviour: enduring differences in the age of globalization', *International Organization* 51(1): 1–30.

Pegg, S. (2003). 'An emerging market for the new millennium: transnational corporations and human rights', in J. G. Frynas and Scott Pegg (eds), *Transnational Corporations and Human Rights* (London: Palgrave), 1–32.

Porter, M. E., and Kramer, M. R. (2006). 'Strategy and society—the link between competitive advantage and corporate social responsibility', *Harvard Business Review* 84(12): 78–92.

Porter, M. E., and Van Der Linde, C. (1995). 'Green and competitive: ending the stalemate', *Harvard Business Review* 73(5): 120–34.

Prahalad, C. K. (2005). *The Fortune at the Bottom of the Pyramid—Eradicating Poverty through Profits* (Upper Saddle River, NJ: Wharton School Publishing).

Prahalad, C. K., and Hammond, A. (2002). 'Serving the world's poor, profitably', *Harvard Business Review* 80(9): 48–57.

Sharma, S., and Vredenburg, H. (1998). 'Proactive corporate environmental strategy and the development of competitively valuable organizational capabilities', *Strategic Management Journal* 19: 729–53.

Steger, U. (2003). *Corporate Diplomacy—The Strategy for a Volatile, Fragmented Business Environment* (Chichester: Wiley).

SustainAbility (2001). *Buried Treasure: Uncovering the Business Case for Corporate Sustainability* (London: SustainAbility and United Nations Environment Programme).

SustainAbility (2002). *Developing Value: The Business Case for Sustainability in Emerging Markets* (London: SustainAbility, International Finance Corporation and Ethos).

Wilson, C., and Wilson, P. (2006). *Make Poverty Business: Increase Profits and Reduce Risks by Engaging with the Poor* (Sheffield: Greenleaf).

Winter, M., and Steger, U. (1998). *Managing Outside Pressure: Strategies for Preventing Corporate Disasters* (Chichester: Wiley).

World Business Council for Sustainable Development (WBCSD) (2000). 'Corporate social responsibility: making good business sense' (Geneva: WBCSD).

# Online resource centre

**online resource centre**

Please visit www.oxfordtextbooks.co.uk/orc/frynas_mellahi2e/ for further information.

# Index